Contemplating Dis/Ability in Schools and Society

Critical Issues in Disabilities and Education

Series Editor:

Eric Shyman, St. Joseph's College, New York

The social, legal, and political history of persons with disabilities in the United States and internationally has been significant, especially in the areas of social justice, civil rights, and cultural inclusion. This series will focus on various perspectives on issues involving the social, political, and cultural experiences of people with disabilities. Manuscripts in this series will address topics such as (1) legal developments at both the national and international level; (2) social and cultural models of disability and its outcome on the inclusion and/or exclusion of individuals with disabilities; (3) the benefits and challenges of the current educational system for children and adolescents with disabilities, including specific methodologies and categories of students (e.g., educational approaches for students with Autism Spectrum Disorder, inclusive education for students with disabilities); (4) philosophical perspectives of special education/education for students with disabilities; and (5) issues regarding transitional support services and approaches to community support for adults with disabilities.

Titles in Series

The Accidental Educator: A Life Contemplating Dis/Ability in Schools and Society, by David J. Connor

Reconceptualizing Disability in Education, by Luigi Iannacci

Contemplating Dis/Ability in Schools and Society

David J. Connor

LEXINGTON BOOKS
Lanham • Boulder • New York • London

Published by Lexington Books
An imprint of The Rowman & Littlefield Publishing Group, Inc.
4501 Forbes Boulevard, Suite 200, Lanham, Maryland 20706
www.rowman.com

Unit A, Whitacre Mews, 26-34 Stannary Street, London SE11 4AB

British Library Cataloguing in Publication Information Available

Library of Congress Cataloging-in-Publication Data Available

ISBN 978-1-4985-6821-0 (cloth : alk. paper)
ISBN 978-1-4985-6822-7 (electronic)

♾™ The paper used in this publication meets the minimum requirements of American National Standard for Information Sciences—Permanence of Paper for Printed Library Materials, ANSI/NISO Z39.48-1992.

Printed in the United States of America

To

Ms. Pat Loughran

My high school English teacher who always encouraged me to write

And

Uncle Freddie and Auntie Joyce

The first teachers in the family

Contents

Preface

From World's End to World's Center

I never wanted to go into teaching.

It struck me as too safe, too respectable. I held antiestablishment tendencies, or at least romanticized having them. As a teenager growing up in Northern England, I spray painted an anarchy sign on my bedroom ceiling, embraced punk rock music, dyed my hair every color, created art, and analyzed the world for both its joys and flaws. I was also a gay teenager without role models in the late 1970s, although the rumbles of liberation had reverberated from New York and San Francisco across the Atlantic and into my consciousness, creating hope for a different world. My spirit felt stifled in my hometown of Wallsend, known for being the place where Hadrian's Wall ended, a border built by Romans to keep out fierce Celts, signifying the Northern limits of an ancient empire. It was also the birthplace of the singer Sting. Like him, I grew up in the shadow of immense ships being built by half of the male workforce in town, the other half working down the local coalmines. Wallsend is part of a conurbation along the River Tyne where towns bleed into each other around the heart of Newcastle, the city in the seemingly archaic phrase, "Like bringing coals to Newcastle," meant to signify a pointless act. In the Broadway musical about our hometown *The Last Ship* (Sting, 2014), a character states, "Wallsend . . . ? More like World's End." On hearing this phrase, the sentiment resonated deeply within me. I have always struggled with having left home where my large family lives. When making a short speech at my surprise 50th birthday party there, I stated, "I may have left home, but home never left me." Wallsend was not the end of the world; but it did feel that way as a gay teenager.

In the late 1970s, the conservative government led by Margaret Thatcher created policies that wreaked havoc on the lives of many people. The industrial North of England, a bastion of the Labor Party, was brought to its knees.

Shipbuilding declined rapidly and eventually ceased to exist. Likewise, after centuries of production, coal mines closed. During this time, the strength of trade unions became severely diminished. Unemployment was at all times high, as was underemployment. This was my world. After high school, I attended the local art college but became disenchanted and left after one year only to find that I could not find a full-time job. This was followed by a year of receiving unemployment benefits of 20 pounds a week as a teenager. The future did not look promising. I therefore decided to return to university, only this time it would be in another part of England. Thankfully, I was accepted at the University of East Anglia (UEA), located on the outskirts of the market town of Norwich, close to Cambridge and the Norfolk Broads. My choice of subject was English and American Literature.

It was at UEA that I felt the world opened up for me. Coming from a working-class background in Northern England had not quite prepared me to engage with other students from across the country and around the world who were largely middle or upper-middle class. I actually felt a strange form of guilt in thinking of reading as a form of work while I knew other people of my age labored in factories or offices. After all, it was so pleasurable to be introduced to the rich history of English Literature in its entirety, as well as discover America's writers who had so forcefully shaped much of twentieth-century fiction, drama, and poetry. I kept a schedule, making sure I studied 40 hours a week, as that was the only framework I knew for what constituted acceptable time to labor. *Should I be here?* is a question that has followed me all of my life, including misgivings about fitting in at university. I often felt inhibited in contributing to seminars for fear I'd say something stupid. I recall once having to participate in a "round robin" wherein all students in a circle and had to read Shakespeare aloud and feeling an intense surge of anxiety that led me to blush, stumble, freeze, and ultimately ask the next person to prematurely continue. I had peers who admitted to scrutinizing my thick Northern accent, and although they claimed to like it, I felt like a novelty to them, as if *pigeonholed* (read: ranked) in some way. And yet, there was a mutuality of curiosity. I recall a new peer saying, "You're the first working class friend I've had," and me thinking (but hesitant to articulate lest I inadvertently offended), "You're the first Jewish friend I've had." There was a mix of honesty and implied patronization in such exchanges, yet there's also an openness that I could appreciate.

I share some of these personal issues of being working class in origin, gay, prone to occasional disabling bouts of anxiety, and being very curious about the world at large, as they have profoundly influenced my formative understandings of who I am and how that, in turn, continued to shape my perceptions of and relation to other people. Part of attending university means doors are opened in the form of opportunities. One such door for me was the summer exchange program that allowed students to work in other countries on temporary visas. I took a chance in coming to the United States in the summer of 1982. At that time, there was a cottage industry of cheap supply labor to privately run summer camps for urban (usually well heeled) kids spending the summer outside of big cities. By the time I'd applied, there were no children's counselor positions available, but there were jobs in the kitchen. After arriving at JFK and spending a night in the YMCA on Manhattan's 34th Street, an assorted bunch of Europeans were whisked in small groups to rural upstate New York where we worked six and half days a week. I prepared food, served it, and washed dirty dishes for three meals a day over 9 weeks and received US$100 cash at the end of it. Still, I had bed and board, my flight was paid, and liked the experience. Once finished, it enabled me to travel across the United States in a hippy-operated vegetarian bus to California, and briefly visit Canada and Mexico. Before this I knew international travel was definitely in my blood, but this summer took it to a new level.

This experience changed my life. I fell in love. Only it wasn't a person, it was a place. New York City. Having spent over a week there, I became enamored with the energy, the diversity of people, the pace, and seduced by the possibilities—real and imagined—of what could be. For the first time in my life, I saw HELP WANTED signs in windows that immediately triggered a plan to return as soon as possible. So, the next summer I entered the United States on a slightly different student visa that did not ship me off to the boonies as cheap labor, but allowed me to find a summer job and digs on my own in the Big Apple. Having an entire summer in New York City verified how much I loved it. I felt at home in the hustle and bustle, filled with excitement of being at the epicenter of the modern world. As the famous song says, I wanted to be a part of it. There was no doubt in my mind. So, I found a short-term apartment lease in Greenwich Village and a job in a vegetarian fast-food kosher restaurant on 42nd Street. I worked hard and played hard, knowing this was the place for me.

Fast-forward another year. As soon as I graduated from university with my bachelor's degree, I headed back to New York City, secured a Green Card, and worked in retail. The store was on Christopher Street in the Village, world famous for the 1969 Stonewall Riots, the birth of "gay liberation" and civil rights that changed the lives of so many people. Over the next couple of years, work life consisted of selling clothes and shoes, creating enticing window displays, managing a rotation of employees, and moving from minimum wage to a moderate management salary. I also wrote a novel based on that era, filled with thinly disguised portrayals of people I have come to know—artists and con artists, club kids and porn stars, drag queens and homeless people, musicians and neighborhood doyennes, bouncers and eccentrics, all part of the never-ending flow of people moving in both directions on

Christopher Street. The novel was rejected by over 50 publishers, with one expressing intense distaste that bordered on outrage for the parade of people described and the situations in which they'd been placed. I'd known it was a long shot all along, yet took some solace knowing at least I had the stamina to write. Like Sting's song, I was an Englishman in New York, and that's all that mattered.

But as time passed, I felt unfulfilled. There was a repetitive element to selling overpriced clothes. Days felt long (especially 12 hour shifts standing up on Fridays and Saturdays), and with two weeks holiday a year, I was seeing neither the world nor my family in the United Kingdom. I shared this sentiment with Jayson, a mature colleague who worked in the store on weekends. Through the week, he was a teacher and often sang the praises of his full-time employment. I had worked in blue-collar jobs all of my life—stacking shelves, tending bar, preparing food, selling clothes. At 25 years old, I reconsidered my reluctance in committing to any form of profession.

Why was I initially ambivalent about the possibility of teaching? I had two family members who were teachers. One was my mother's brother who taught woodwork, and the other was my mother's cousin who taught reading. They both seemed content in their choices, although in later years my uncle came to share that he often experienced a crisis of confidence in public speaking, something with which I could deeply empathize. At the same time, from my own perspective as a child, he acted quite authoritarian with my cousins, as if using his "teacher voice" all the time at home. My mother's cousin often corrected our speech and enunciation. In brief, I found the traits of being authoritarian or perpetually corrective of others to be unappealing. I wondered: Is that what teachers were supposed to be like? Would I have to learn to be that way?

I reasoned that despite teaching seeming an unglamorous—albeit respectable—job, I'd have the chance of engaging young people in reading and discussing great literature that I loved. Plus, teaching in New York City would mean I'd still be living the dream of a Wallsender in the Big Apple. Teaching here was bound to be different from doing the same job in the United Kingdom. If I didn't like it, I could always go back to retail or do something else. However, at that point in life, all roads seemed to have led me to the possibility of teaching. Despite my misgivings, I decided to position myself on neutral ground and give it a go. After all, how difficult could teaching be?

Thank You

To all family members and friends who are always supportive of my work.

To Eric Shyman, series editor, who has been a pleasure to collaborate with.

To Holly Buchanan, Assistant Acquisitions Editor, for her support and guidance.

To Cathy Maguire, Chris Leung, and Jen Samson for helping me multitask when running an academic department and completing my writing obligations.

To the reader, for taking a chance on this book.

Introduction

I write this, now in my 30th year of education. Thirty is a magic number because it allows retirement from the profession. Being at this juncture has given me a pause to look back, take stock, and understand what a life in education has meant and, conversely, what I have come to know about life through having a career in education. Despite my bumpy start, I came to thoroughly enjoy being a high school classroom teacher, coming to know how teaching and learning occurs, with a particular interest in students who struggle in learning and/or do not "fit the mold" of schooling. I was always interested in outsiders and underdogs, and felt the students I taught in segregated special education settings deserved more access to opportunities enjoyed by their nondisabled peers. From the very start, I became keenly aware of racial inequities within schools, teaching "self-contained" classes of "emotionally disturbed" students that were almost always filled with black and Latino males. Who gets included? Who gets excluded? How does that happen? These were questions I immediately began to ask myself. In the late 1980s, as one of the first round of teachers required to co-teach in New York City's initiative to promote more inclusive practices, I welcomed the chance to work alongside general educators with view to ameliorating what I thought to be an unnecessary divide.

After seven years of teaching, I took a position in an organization called Special Education Training and Resource Center (SETRC), a statewide network that placed professional development specialists throughout New York. My assignment was located within the Office of the Superintendent of Manhattan High Schools, a district that oversaw 33 schools, rising to 44 by the time I left. Moving felt right because I wanted to support and grow inclusive education practices in schools, believing that the existing special education system was a taken-for-granted form of disability apartheid (I know that word may be a tad strong for some readers, but it certainly felt that way at the time). During my nine years in this position, I came to better understand how schools, as organizations, functioned quite differently in their response to the federal, state, and city shifts toward increasing inclusive education. Also, I observed how a district's special education structures were coordinated, including the provision of mandated services such as speech and language, counseling, educational and psychological assessments, and so on, to thousands of students. In brief, I witnessed the operations of special education as a bureaucratic industry, noting how it appeared to benefit the professionals who were employed within it more than the students it ostensibly served. I also experienced a lot of push back about inclusive practices, oftentimes more so from special educators—both teachers and administrators—than from their general education counterparts, making me question why exclusive systems were preferred by so many professionals.

After accepting this position of professional developer, I also began to teach part time as an adjunct in a program coordinated by the United Federation of Teachers (UFT). I enjoyed teaching graduate level courses on special, inclusive, and multicultural education to in-service teachers who needed a master's degree for initial or permanent certification. Working directly with teachers was very satisfying as we could "talk shop" about best ways to teach and how to understand all students, but particularly those identified as disabled. After several years being a part-time professor and involved in developing programs for a network of schools, my interest in teaching adults in educational policy and practice grew. It was during this period that I sought to enter a doctoral program and applied to Teachers College, Columbia University. Much to my surprise, I was accepted. It changed my life.

Teachers College introduced me to a wide variety of ideas that rocked my world (largely in a good way, I hasten to add). While I had always been a critical special educator from my first year in the profession, I often felt at a loss for ways in which to express why many of our practices in the profession did not seem right. Coming to know differing philosophical groundings within various paradigms focusing on how we interpret and respond to human differences helped clarify my own beliefs. Moreover, being introduced to Disability Studies (DS) was earthshattering to me. It provided an alternative arena of thought I had always yearned for in response to the default position of anything to do with *disability and education* being automatically assumed as special education. Instead of being laden with deficit-based assumptions about disability, supported by pseudo-scientific claims, I found a far more satisfying and socially just way to express ideas about difference and disability than had ever been presented in a special education course. Even more exciting, DS was interdisciplinary, a fascinating field that drew upon a multitude of influences, including history, sociology, culture, media, and the arts.

And even more exciting than that, I encountered a small group of researchers and scholars from across the nation who sought to *apply* DS to education. It was then that I knew that had found my professional community.

In 2003, New York City Department of Education underwent a massive reorganization that had significant impact upon how special education was operationalized. I took advantage of this structural change, opting not to work at the newly configured district level, but rather return to working in schools, only this time as a literacy coach. I did this because my day would end at 3:30 p.m., allowing me time to buckle down and commit to my dissertation. For the next two years, I worked closely with many teachers in several schools, including the newly opened Harvey Milk High School for Lesbian, Gay, Bisexual, Transgender, and Queer (LGBTQ) students, focusing on the teaching and learning process for all kids. Simultaneously, my dissertation work continued, centering upon the knowledge and life experiences of black and Latino students with a learning disability (LD) who came from working-class or poor backgrounds. I chose this subject because I sought to return, in a way, to the kids I had taught in the first phase of my career. I wanted their voices to be present in educational research—because by then I had discovered deficit-based understandings of disability and racial inequalities were mirrored as they were elsewhere in society.

Graduating from Teachers College with a doctoral degree allowed me to apply for a full-time tenure-track position at Hunter College, City University of New York (CUNY). I have always had a soft spot for both Hunter and CUNY in general. Hunter, because I received my first master's degree in special education there, and CUNY because I'd earned my second master's in Creative Writing at City College. Both were good experiences. More importantly, I feel an affinity with Hunter students as the vast majority are working class, many being immigrants, and a large percentage being first in their family to obtain a master's degree. It is also a wonderfully multicultural institution with students from around the world filling the hallways, stairways, and cafeterias. I was happy when I got the job.

Since then, over 13 years ago, I have worked in the learning disabilities program in the Department of Special Education. As a department, we have grown exponentially over doubling our size from when I first began, largely due to funded programs such as Teaching Fellows, Teach for America, and Urban Teacher Residency. The heart of our program is called the Learning Lab, where every graduate student is supervised as they teach a child with an Individualized Education Program (IEP) twice a week for a year. Children come to campus, we come to know their families and we create a supportive atmosphere in which novice teachers grow and struggling learners learn. The Learning Lab exemplifies the best of what we do and prepares hundreds of teachers to enter New York City schools.

After coordinating the Learning Lab for some time, and despite all of my resolutions—never in a thousand years!—I became department chairperson. This involves overseeing over 1,000 graduate students, more than 20 faculty, and over 100 adjunct instructors and field supervisors. As an administrator, albeit a reluctant one, the position provided me with insights into how a large public university, schools of education, and a department of special education function.

During my time as a professor at Hunter, I have also endeavored to be a researcher and scholar, investigating a constellation of issues that I see as connected, including inclusive education, learning disabilities, the over-representation of minority children and youth in special education, teaching methods, and qualitative research methodologies. Currently, I teach in two doctoral programs within CUNY. The first is in Urban Education at the Graduate Center where I specialize in seminars on critiques of special education by using DS, and the second is at Hunter in Instructional Leadership where students explore all kinds of issues in schools pertaining to teaching and learning. In doctoral work, I enjoy participating in dissertations as a reader or chairperson, specializing in working with doctoral students researching issues of inequality. I have appreciated presenting on the topic of dis/ability, DS, and special education across the United States, and in other countries such as Argentina, Australia, Belgium, Brazil, Canada, England, New Zealand, and Scotland. Much of this work has taken shape within my seven written/cowritten or edited/coedited books, all related to how we can better understand disability in more expansive ways than has been portrayed in the field of traditional special education.

No one is more surprised than myself at how driven I became to write on the topic of dis/ability.

There is also great irony involved. From early in my career, I always wanted to get out of special education. It's not that I wanted to turn my back on children and youth who sometimes needed to be taught differently and well; but rather to make general education a place where these, and other struggling students, could succeed. This "wanting out" of special education has remained with me for the duration of my career. First, I studied for a second master's degree to become a certified English teacher to work in inclusive classrooms, but before that came to pass I was offered the job in SETRC at the regional superintendent's office. When accepted by Teachers College, it was third time lucky. I had previously tried for a doctorate in English offered by CUNY's Graduate Center, but was twice rejected. Determined to focus on general rather than special education, my resolve soon diminished when I encountered two progressive professors and their understanding of learning disabilities, Dr. D. Kim Reid and Dr. Beth Ferri. Both played a significant role in developing my research interests and being on my dissertation committee. When I sought a full-time university position, I wanted to work in a "progressive" department that supported inclusive education, yet knew Hunter's programs to be quite traditional, with a significant portion of professors holding a high degree of cynicism toward inclusive education. Nevertheless, I joined the faculty as I wanted to remain in New York City and had experienced firsthand, and benefited from, the quality of Hunter programs. No matter how much I positioned myself to exit special education, I somehow never did.

I share this succinct professional trajectory as, writing this in my 30th year, I am still trying to make sense of it all. When I came across the series *Critical Issues in Disabilities and Education* by Rowman and Littlefield, the use of "critical" within the title resonated with me, as did the fact that the discussion of disabilities and education did not automatically default to the phrase "special education." The book series is interested in the social, political and cultural experiences of persons with disabilities in the United States. Topics include, but are not limited to (1) legal developments at both the national and international levels; (2) social and cultural models of disability and its outcome on the inclusion and/or exclusion of individuals with disabilities; (3) the benefits and challenges of the current educational system for children and adolescents with disabilities, including specific methodologies and categories of students (e.g., educational approaches for students with Autism Spectrum Disorder, inclusive education for students with disabilities); (4) philosophical perspectives of special education/education for students with disabilities; and (5) issues regarding transitional support services and approaches to community support for adults with disabilities. When reviewing this information, I was struck by how these separately articulated yet interrelated topics have been the substance of my career. They say timing is everything. As I sought to reflect upon my career, and what it means, this series has provided an opportunity for me to examine critical issues related to disability and education.

WHY AN AUTOETHNOGRAPHIC MEMOIR?

Given the nature and scope of this book series, it struck me as a potentially interesting challenge to write an autoethnographic memoir of a career in (special) education, using my life experiences as a person, a teacher, and a researcher. I have long recognized the power of personal stories. All of my life, I have read autobiographies, biographies, and memoirs. As a professional interested in education, I have sometimes sampled autobiographies of administrators (Meier, 2002; Monroe, 1999), teachers (Ashton-Warner, 1986; Kohl, 1967/1988), and students (Mooney & Cole, 2000; Valente, 2011), autobiographical essays by students (Keefe, Moore, & Duff, 2006; Rodis, Garrod,

& Boscardin, 2001), and biographies of theorists used in education ranging from John Dewey (Martin, 2003) to Michel Foucault (Miller, 1994), Lev Vygotsky (Wertsch, 1988) to W. E. B. Dubois (Lewis, 1994).

While all of these sources provide insights into the knowledge of teaching and learning, it is the genre of memoir that particularly intrigues me due to the selective use of memory for effect, and the emotional intensity these memories often evoke. Two educational memoirs in particular stand out in my bookshelf. The first is Pulitzer Prize winner Frank McCourt's *Teacher Man* (2006) wherein he describes his career in New York City's schools, replete with student incidents and anecdotes, along with his contempt for the Board of Education. The second distinguished researcher Beth Harry's *Melanie, Bird with a Broken Wing: A Mother's Story* (2008), a memoir of loving and losing a daughter with severe disabilities. Both of these have "stayed with me" in a life full of books I've read. In addition, as an instructor in both inclusive education and DS courses I have often assigned students to read a memoir by people with disabilities from a provided list, asking them to contemplate the power of coming to know about disability from an individual—while contrasting that with "official" knowledge(s) (see Appendix A for a sample list).

Valuing Autoethnography

The use of autoethnography within education has grown considerably over the past two decades informed in large part, through the extensive work of autoethnographic researchers such as Bochner (1997), Ellis (2004), and Richardson (2000). A recent search within the Education Resources Information Center (ERIC) using the descriptors "education" and "autoethnography" yielded 226 results, with 109 pertaining to teachers, 24 to administrators, and 20 to professors, offering incredibly rich accounts of life experiences and their interpretation by an array of educators. In searching "autoethnography" and "disability," there are 12 hits, yielding a mixture of authors of people with disabilities and professionals who work with them. This small number of studies reveals an existing—if underdeveloped—interest in this area, also evidenced in the edited collection *Both Sides of the Table: Autoethnographies of Educators Learning and Teaching With/In (Dis)Ability* (Smith, 2013). I was drawn to creating an authoethnographic memoir for many reasons, including an exploration of blurring the personal and the professional domains. As described by Ellis, Adams, and Bochner (2010):

> Autoethnography is an approach to research and writing that seeks to describe and systematically analyze experience in order to understand cultural experience.

> This approach challenges canonical ways of doing research and representing others and treats research as a political, socially-just and socially-conscious act. A researcher uses tenets of autobiography and ethnography to do and write autoethnography. Thus, as a method, autoethnography is both process and product. (Para 1)

Attempting to create knowledge of the world by sharing experiences about a particular time and place, profession and culture intrigues me. This desire is undergirded by other reasons that I describe below:

Writing as a Methodology. Autoethnography largely relies upon writing as a source of generating data. Put differently, writing serves as a means for understanding. Richardson (2001) stresses the process of writing as a sense-making process. She notes, "Writing became my principal tool through which I learned about myself and the world" (p. 33). Through writing we select topics that are important to us, and explore why these topics are of importance. In the process of writing we get to choose, sort, organize, and describe—all with view to making sense for ourselves and other readers.

Self-Reflecting as a Form of Knowledge. The evolution of a personal narrative is an interactive process with the self, an internal conversation, replete with give and take. We must be able to critically reflect on our experiences and observations, bearing in mind our assumptions about how we make sense of the world. In the words of Brookfield (2009), self-reflection is "the conceptual glue that holds our perspectives, meaning schemes and habits of mind in place" (p. 294). It is interesting to consider that self-reflective writing about education arguably holds greater potential for shifting a reader's thinking than a research study about education. As Chawla notes, evoking figures such as Gloria Andaluza (1987), bell hooks (1994), and Audrey Lorde (1984), "I, for one, cannot name 'studies' that have shifted my world, but I can count on my fingers reflexively political writing that has caused some disruptions in the way that I encounter knowledge" (Chawla & Rodriguez, 2008, p. 19).

Self-Understanding in Relation to Others. Autoethnography can serve to help me understand myself in relation to the lived experiences of other people, along with the systems and structures in which we are all positioned. As a nondisabled researcher of life experiences of people with disabilities and an educator working in certification programs for teachers of students with disabilities, I seek to contemplate ways in which my own positionality creates and informs my interests and relationships with others in the larger community. Richardson's (2000) claim that "Autoethnographies are highly personalized, revealing texts in which authors tell stories about their own lived experiences, relating the personal to the cultural" (p. 931) resonates with me because I recognize the strong, mutually informative relationship between shaping the self and a community, within a particular culture.

Connecting to a Larger Community. In "looking inward," an autoethnographer uses him or herself as a tool at work to create knowledge that can be relevant to their community at large. By grounding knowledge claims in the personal experience yet relating it to the general population, the author holds potential to share information in an accessible manner with a large audience. As Ellis et al. (2010) note,

> The autoethnographer not only tries to make personal experience meaningful and cultural experience engaging, but also by producing accessible texts, she or he may be able to reach wider and more diverse mass audiences that traditional research usually disregards, a move that can make personal and social change possible for more people. (Para 14)

It is my hope that this text will reach an audience that includes educators and researchers who share interests in rethinking how dis/ability is conceptualized in educational theory, research, policy and practice.

Self-Participating in Data Generation. Autoethnography allows me to both participate in the generation of data in the form of personal stories and the subsequent analysis of that data. As Clandinin and Connelly (2000) point out, "The narrative researcher's experience is always a dual one, always the inquirer experiencing the experience and also being part of the experience itself" (p. 81). I believe that studying myself in the process of selecting and writing experiential episodes representative of my career will enhance my understanding of *what* specific ideas I consider important and *why* I consider them important.

Cultivating Personal Growth. An autoethnographic approach allows for personal growth and ongoing reflexivity in all aspects of my profession: teaching, researching, writing, and participating in community service. Crawford (1996) has highlighted the usefulness of autoethnography in this respect, elaborating,

> Autoethnography epitomizes the reflexive turn of fieldwork for human study by (re)positioning the researcher as an object of inquiry who depicts a site of interest in terms of personal awareness and experience; it utilizes the self-conscious or "pervasive nervousness" referred to by Geertz (1988) to reveal subjectively and imaginatively a particular social setting in the expressions of local and grounded impressions. (p. 167)

My desire for personal growth, I believe, is deeply rooted in being an educator, and by crafting "a life" in education, I seek to galvanize many parts that sometimes appear disparate.

Making Visible Subjectivity in Research. As Lincoln and Denzin (2000) urge researchers to "make ourselves visible in our texts" (p. 1053), an autoethnographic approach is in keeping with a postmodernist perspective. Put another way, autoethnography consciously violates accepted notions of objectivity within traditional social sciences. As Ellis et al. (2010) describe, "autoethnography is one of the approaches that acknowledges and accommodates subjectivity, emotionality, and the researcher's influence on research, rather than hiding from these matters or assuming they don't exist" (para 3). They continue, by being "self-consciously value-centered rather than pretending to be value free" (ibid), recognizing how an autoethnography can be purposefully aligned with a researcher's beliefs. It is therefore incumbent upon me to be honest and open in my assumptions and beliefs that are manifest in the episodes I selected to write and the analysis I brought to bear upon them.

Focusing on Educational Systems. Although autoethnography places the author's experiences at the center of the study, these are always inherently connected to the context in which that author writes. So, while Ellis et al. (2010) note that educators' personal stories are told by "authors who view themselves as the phenomenon and write evocative narratives specifically focused on their academic, research, and personal lives" (para 24), they also highlight the need for readers to relate to situations described. In brief, they note,

> Personal narratives propose to understand a self or some aspect of a life as it intersects with a cultural context . . . and invite readers to enter the author's world and to use what they learn there to reflect on, understand, and cope with their own lives. (Ibid)

By focusing on a career experience that encompasses many domains of education—classrooms, schools, districts, state networks, federal policies, university settings, national organizations, and international conferences—I reveal the connections among these components, along with attendant complexities about how educational systems are organized and ways in which people negotiate these systems.

Informing Others. Autoethnography can serve as a lens to inform others. As a critical special educator and DS scholar, I view this autoethography as having potential to inform and influence the actions of other educators and people concerned about education. This sentiment is echoed in Ellis and Bochner's (2000) belief that this methodology "provides an avenue for doing something meaningful for yourself and the world" (p. 761). In my particular case, I believe looking back on 30 years as an educator provides many talking points that raise opportunities to discuss issues at hand, how they evolved, and potential changes to propose with view to improving "how we do business." As Kelly-Jackson (2015) has pointed out, "Critical theorists suggest that education should be examined through a broad lens, taking into account the ways culture, politics, and power shape the lives of both educators and students" (p. 169).

RESEARCH QUESTIONS

Given my interest to write an autoethnographic memoir spanning three decades, the overarching questions I therefore posed in this book are

1. Throughout my career in (special) education what have I come to know about
   a. *teaching and learning in schools and universities?*
   b. *educational laws and their impact?*
   c. *specific models of disability and how they have influenced educators and educational researchers?*
   d. *educational structures and systems in relation to children, youth, and adults with disabilities?*
2. In what ways do answers to the above questions inform us about social, political, and cultural experiences of people with disabilities?

METHODOLOGY: THE PERSONAL IS THE PROFESSIONAL

In contemplating how to best approach the overarching first question and sub-questions, I am guided by the work of several autoethnographers who have helped shape this method. For example, in explaining her technique, Ellis (2009a) writes,

> As an autoethnographer, I am both the author and focus of the story, the one who tells, and the one who experiences, the observer and the observed, the creator and the created. I am the person at the intersection of the personal and the cultural, thinking and observing as an ethnographer and writing and describing as a storyteller. (p. 13)

As I have written elsewhere, it has often been difficult for me to separate the personal and the professional in terms of beliefs, values, and the desire to help shape a more equal and just world (Connor, 2005; Connor, 2008a; Connor, 2013; Connor, 2017; Valle & Connor, 2010). For me, the professional *is* personal. As with most educators I know, I have never conceived teaching and learning as an eight-hour day from which one can clock out, as if in a factory. I therefore view my experience over the last three decades as potential data from which I can mine.

Mining Memories

Our memories are not static or frozen in time. They are, rather, subject to a myriad of influences among which include the degree of desire to recall; the acuity of sensory perceptions; the ability to visualize; the reason for returning to the site of a memory; and the impact of knowledge developed and experiences accrued since the era or incident evoked. It is also safe to say that each time that the past is called upon, the narrative constructed is subject to change. Admittedly, it is not a simple endeavor to go back in time, to search through a seemingly infinite number of memories, each surrounded by a constellation of details. On one hand, it is common to believe episodes from an individual's life follow a linear trajectory through the passage of time. In other words, if we retrace our steps, we will find what we are looking for in the reverse order of when things actually happened. On the other hand—and more likely, at least in my own experience—memories also coexist within our fluid consciousness, a personal universe in which they collide, collapse, connect, and fuse at any moment, subject to internal and external triggers.

Writing Episodes

From this unpredictable, kaleidoscopic world of our consciousness, we can still create narratives that help give meaning to our experiences and offer insights into questions we raise. As Ellis (2009b) describes, "Storying one's experience offers the possibility of turning something chaotic into something intelligible and meaningful" (p. 280). A good story engages the reader beyond the surface of the text by triggering memories, creating connections, provoking novel thoughts, and generating new meanings. Indeed, when Bochner claims, "There's nothing more theoretical than a good story" (cited in Ellis, 2004, p. 23), he openly invites researchers and readers to analyze and reflect upon the ideas, ideologies, and paradigms that undergird the construction of narratives.

Narratives I sought to write consisted of both specific episodes and broader constellations of memories from each phase of my career. They included experiences I had as a teacher, a professional development specialist, a teacher coach, a teacher educator, a researcher and scholar, and as a department administrator. Specific episodes sometimes fit what Bochner and Ellis (1992) have described as "epiphanies," moments in which we experience that how we think about life has changed. In addition, I also sought to portray general eras or periods of time in which I had multiple experiences, many of which may be seen as "ordinary." Given the breadth of potential material, episodes predominantly featured the broadly defined areas featured in the research sub questions including teaching and learning in schools and universities; educational laws; various models of disability and how they influence educators and researchers; educational structures and systems; and experiences of children, youth, and adults with disabilities.

Analyzing Episodes

In analyzing written episodes, I sought to comment upon the major topics on which I focused, particularly in ways that they intersected with one another. The "slices of life" portrayed are therefore an opportunity to see how various domains of education come into play with each other in the real world. The relationships and influences among laws and legal provisions, teaching and learning in classrooms, professional beliefs and actions, educational systems and structures (at micro, meso, and macro levels), and the lived experiences of children, youth, and adults with disabilities. At the same time, in order to answer the second research question, I utilized a Disability Studies in Education (DSE) framework (Connor, Gabel, Gallagher, & Morton, 2008) to analyze the narrative with view to foregrounding the social, political, and cultural experiences of people with disabilities as they relate to larger issues of inequalities and social justice, including issues of race, ethnicity, social class, gender, sexual orientation, and dynamics of power.

In brief, the research questions I ask served to partly construct my framework for analysis, providing a degree of shape and consistency. Simultaneously, in valuing open-endedness, I sought to balance the analysis so that it was not overly inscribed, but rather a form of engaging with view to accepting a degree of "healthy uncertainty" (Forrest, Judd, & Davison, 2012, p. 710) in terms of knowledge claims. I remained mindful of how written recollections of experiences are reconstructed and analyzed by me as a different person "now," as it was when in the moment or era "then." At the same time, I was also aware of how analyzing narrative episodes from my career helped me understand the systems and structures that shape our culture, along with the actions and habits of the people who inhabit them, with view to contemplating what can be learned, as well as considering what can be changed for the better.

VALIDITY, TRUSTWORTHINESS, AND USEFULNESS

In thinking about how to best construct the shape and form of this text, I bore in mind the validity and trustworthiness of findings, and their usefulness. Regarding style and content, the overarching story within an autoethnography has to be coherent. The overall narrative should be engaging, accessible, and meaningful, constructed by the interfacing of narratives and the analysis they produce. In terms of validity, as Ellis et al. (2010) explain, "For autoethnographers, validity means that a work seeks verisimilitude; it evokes in readers a feeling that the experience described as lifelike, believable, and possible, a feeling that what has been represented could be true" (para 34). Aiming for plausibility in both narrative and analysis is crucial in establishing credibility. Walford (2009) agrees with this sentiment, further noting that a work of autoethnography should make readers *feel* as well as think, evoking a somatic, visceral reaction rather than a detached or dispassionate analysis. Other autothenographers such as Holman Jones (2005) "view research and writing as socially-just acts; rather than a preoccupation with accuracy, the goal is to produce analytical, accessible texts that change us and the world we live in for the better" (p. 764).

Calling to mind the "so what?" question, researchers have been taught when developing research, Bochner asks, "How useful is the story?" and "To what uses might the story be put?" (Ellis et al., 2010, para 34). In writing these episodes, I was able to reconstruct experiences, analyze my own perception, contemplate the significance of words I choose, and reflect upon how these stories ultimately help me to understand the lives of others, as well as my own, and the systems in which we all live, with greater depth and clarity. As Ellis et al. (2010) observe, an autoethnography can "be judged in terms of whether it helps readers communicate with others different from themselves or offer a way to improve the lives of participants and readers or the author's own" (para 34). The authors also share, "The questions most important to autoethnographers are: who reads our work, how are they affected by it, and how does it keep a conversation going?" (para 39). It is my hope that educators and those interested in education will read this book will engage with the issue raised, will keep conversations going, and, more than that, will take action to change our world toward making it a better one.

CAVEATS AND CONCLUSION

As I finished the first draft of this chapter before I actually began writing my autoethnographic memoir, I wondered (in mid-February 2017) about the months ahead when I endeavored to do what I have described above. Somewhere, deep down, I held a belief that this project was the right thing to do, the next step for me, documenting my career to date in (special) education. At the same time, I had some reservations. These included whether I could sufficiently utilize the act of writing and center myself as the object of study to be of value to readers. Additionally, while open-endedness and creativity involved in autoethnography beckoned me, I also recognized the risks of making myself vulnerable, and prone to critique. At the same time, as a critical special educator, it was only fair that I risk opening up about my experiences, the analysis I perform, and subsequent meanings I create, to the critique of others. I wondered, too, about charges of perceived egotism, narcissism, and "navel gazing"—all complaints by critics who mischaracterize autoethnography in general. Finally, I also recognized that I am subject to feelings of "impostorship" (Brookfield, 2005, p. 51), a phenomenon experienced when others perceive me as an expert of any kind. That has always made me feel uncomfortable, and yet, I do have a lot of experience that is the foundation of things I wish to share. All that said, I maintain a desire to improve our education systems for children, educators, and parents. It is my sincere hope that this book will help contribute to that goal.

THE STRUCTURE OF THE BOOK

The book follows my career trajectory. I consider each phase as distinct while recognizing they sometimes overlap. For the purpose of focus and clarity, I have treated phases separately as I believe each deserves its own story and analytic commentary.

In chapter 1, *Classroom Teaching*, I share memories from my years of teaching high school students labeled Learning Disabled and Behavior Disordered. I describe a rude awakening as an unprepared rookie teacher who struggled to make sense of the public school system, while trying to learn fast the art and science of pedagogy. It is here I began to grow highly conscious of how differences in race, social class, and ability enabled or disabled all students.

In chapter 2, *Staff Developer*, I focus on my time working as a professional development specialist in the Office of the Superintendent of Manhattan High Schools. In coordinating and providing "in-service" professional development to a network of administrators and teachers, I advocated for more responsible approaches to inclusive education, and describe how I became intrigued by levels of push and pull of support and resistance at city, state, and national levels.

In chapter 3, *Doctoral Student*, my focus shifts to what it's like for a working teacher/staff developer to take up the gauntlet of a doctoral program at an Ivy League school. Here, the instincts, wonderings, and nascent knowledge I held through informally studying education by "living it" every day emerged into a formal interest into educational research. With an increasingly critical eye toward special education, among the many theoretical groundings, I encountered the field of DS and felt a strong sense of kinship with the scholars I read, bringing their ideas into my practices.

In chapter 4, *Teacher Coach*, I share leaving the regional superintendent's office to work alongside teachers in public schools, helping them plan and assess their teaching on a weekly basis. I describe two of the schools in depth in an attempt to capture their unique cultures, including the students, teachers, and administrators. Both places were interesting for many reasons, including one being known as the first school established for LGBTQ youth, and the other for its high graduation rates of black and Latino males.

In chapter 5, *College Professor*, I narrate how the process of entering and navigating university life is filled with surprises—including both rewards and challenges—not unlike the first year of teaching. More importantly, I shift the focus onto the content of teacher education programs, including the perpetually ongoing process of defining and redefining content and skills on which they are assessed—and who gets to decide that. I also describe the tensions I felt as a critical special educator located within a traditional department, along with the politics of navigating tenure and promotion.

In chapter 6, *Scholar*, I share how the things I cared about in my various roles as classroom teacher, professional development specialist, and teacher coach could be brought into contemporary research. Most importantly, I chronicle ways in which—drawing from the work of scholars before me, and those alongside me—I sought to critique the limitations of special education while simultaneously advocating for the expansion of DSE. By describing the genesis of each book project and guest-edited special editions of journals, I reveal ways in which I strategized to maximize getting my interests, ideas, concerns, and suggestions into print, including collaborations with scholars such as Beth Ferri, Jan Valle, Susan Gabel, Scot Danforth, Wendy Cavendish, and Subini Annamma.

In chapter 7, *Doctoral Faculty*, I chronicle my interest in teaching DSE at the doctoral level, and how I developed several courses. This opportunity allowed me to unpack notions of (ab)normalcy, reframe dis/ability across contexts, and take a historical look at the paradoxes and problematics of special education in the interrelated areas of theory, policy, research, and practice. I share the joy and headaches of working on dissertations, and the pleasure of always being stretched when engaging with doctoral students. Finally, I discuss the work of beginning a brand new doctoral program, and the complexities involved.

In chapter 8, *Department Chairperson*, I explain the workings of a large Special Education Department, in a large School of Education, within a large public university. In my depiction, the day-to-day running of a department and all of its moving parts, sometimes seems like a huge teaching factory in which we produce a supply of educators for New York City. At the same time, I look for the humanity within our large, bureaucratic systems, wishing never to lose sight of the reality of teaching in public schools—seeking to help our students become good teachers.

In each of these eight chapters, after the main narrative, I include an analytical commentary. These commentaries allow me to analyze the featured issues in multiple ways, including selecting specific moments, general realizations, and memorable events for analysis. Sometimes, I extend an issue raised, provide additional examples, and include new information, all with view foregrounding observations to forge connections among the areas of teaching and learning in schools and universities; educational laws and their impact; educational structures and systems; different models of disability and their influence on educators and researchers; and the social, political, and cultural experiences of people with disabilities.

Finally, in the epilogue, I briefly share some thoughts as I look back on telling this story about my life in education that reflects the personal, professional, and political nature of teaching.

A Note from the Editor

The purpose of the *Critical Issues in Disabilities and Education* series published by Lexington Books is to provide a venue within which topics that fall outside of the mainstream research focus can be given voice to greater readership. While special education, the most common moniker for teaching students with various exceptionalities or dis/abilities, receives much attention in the popular empirical literature, there is considerably less attention paid to counter-narratives involving the social constructions of and social responses to the actually lived lives of individuals with disabilities. It is the goal of this series to provide the field with increased access to a collection of legitimate scholarly works exploring these issues from a depth and breadth not available elsewhere.

In *Contemplating Dis/Ability in Schools and Society: A Life in Education*, Dr. David Connor guides us through a journey that traces both his own history as a professional in the field of (special) education simultaneously with the development of Disabilities in Education, an ever-growing counter-field to special education of which he is a founding and continually influential member. This work provides the perspective that is so often missing from the dominant narrative, indeed, one that is even intentionally eliminated from the empirical discussions: the personal. While many "leaders" in the education field at large work tirelessly to address one of the most human-based jobs in existence from an ever "objective" standpoint, concerned with gathering evidence for therapeutic outcomes, the braver members of the field, like Dr. Connor, refused to accept that "teaching" should, or even could, be distilled into a set of data to be analyzed and reported in one chart or another.

It was within this context that he and a number of other scholars, now seen as the founders of Disability Studies in Education, worked tirelessly to establish a framework for studying the stories, struggles, social experiences, and actually lived lives of individuals with exceptionalities, or as Dr. Connor suggests, dis/abilities. This ever collecting body of work focuses on explorations of topics that are all but entirely ignored by the greater mainstream field, including sociopolitical perspectives of disability, social constructivist approaches to exceptionality, the intersection between human rights and ableism, among others. In this work, Dr. Connor uses his own journey as the juncture within which the development of the field of Disability Studies in Education took form, his role in it, and how he envisions the future of the field. It is at once an autoethnography, autobiography, historical critique, and guidebook for future dis/ability theorists who are interested in continuing the humanistic frameworks for study that he and his colleagues created.

Essentially, this work is somewhat of a compendium that can be used by a growing field to continue growing along the right path, from the wise perspective of someone who has not only seen it happen, but was essential in its happening to begin with. These stories will be essential to contextualize the history of this ever important field, and be of distinct use for its current and future scholars.

Eric Shyman, Ed.D.
Editor, Critical Issues in Disabilities and Education

Note to the Reader

I have purposefully used the term "kids" to refer to children and youth in schools throughout this book for several reasons. I believe this conveys a whole entity—rather than "students" that confines our conceptualizations of humans to one dimension. It also connotes affection, implying kids need care. I believe they do. On a practical note, it also helps separate kids from undergraduate, graduate, and doctoral students who are referred to at length throughout the book. Respectfully acknowledge that I also view students at all of these levels in their three-dimensional complexity and not in a reductive sense of only individuals who study.

Some names and physical descriptions of people have been changed to ensure anonymity.

Chapter 1

Classroom Teacher

My friend Jayson told me there was a possible vacancy or two at his school, that I should come and be interviewed, and he'd put in a good word for me based upon my general character, reliability, and work ethic.

"By the way," he added as if in an afterthought, "I work in special education."

"What's that?" I inquired.

"It's mainly classes for kids who need additional help," he responded.

"Okay, that sounds fine."

I had no clue as to what it meant or the implications it would have for how I would be expected to teach.

In the summer of 1987, at Jayson's suggestion, I informally visited the High School of Fashion Industries in Chelsea to find a ten-story building designed in art deco style that had opened in the early 1940s, looking less institutionalized than I had imagined. Wearing shorts due to 90-degree weather, I did not anticipate an interview, but when Jayson crossed paths with Charlie Bonnici, assistant principal of the English department, I ended up in his office for a chat.

The pleasant, round-faced man asked, "How might you teach *To Kill a Mocking Bird?* (Lee, 1961)"

"Um . . . the racism," I managed to articulate, taken unaware and feeling completely out of my depth. A few minutes later it was, "Thank you for your interest."

I vowed I'd be better prepared next time.

As it happened, soon afterwards, I was invited for an interview with Iris Davidow, assistant principal of the special education department. She was a short, thin, middle-aged woman with a wry sense of humor who sat behind a large desk and engaged me with a series of rapid-fire questions. We struck up a conversation that felt quite natural and based upon her impression together with Jayson's recommendation, she immediately offered me a teaching position in the special education department—pending the principal's approval. I shook her hand, turned around, and began walking toward the adjacent room to wait before we'd both go to meet the principal, when I heard her say,

"Wait a minute, wait a minute . . . come back."

"Yes?" I turned around.

"The pony tail has to go."

"Oh!"

"Yes, I can't take you up to meet the principal if you have a pony tail."

"Okay . . . I guess I can have it cut off," I volunteered.

"And the earrings," she said, squinting at my lobes, "They should go too."

I admit to being surprised but did not want to betray my response. In that instant, I realized that my fears of becoming a representative of the establishment were not unfounded. Apparently, to be a male with long hair and a couple of stud earrings—although in perfectly good-keeping with being then fashionable on the street—was not the right image for a teacher, even in a New York City school that focused on students majoring in fashion. As I stood on the threshold of entering public school, the institution struck me as neither progressive nor welcoming of diversity. In fairness to Iris, she was preparing me to pass muster with Mr. Bailey, a seasoned, conservative principal, variously described as "authoritarian," "old school," and "a dinosaur" (although more like all three simultaneously) who instilled fear into the entire faculty. And of course, almost everyone who has ever been through schooling had been taught to revere their principal.

I would return tomorrow for my meeting with Mr. Bailey, but first headed to a nearby barber's shop where my ponytail was unceremoniously snipped off like Audrey Hepburn's locks à la *The Nun's Story* (Blake & Zinnemann, 1959). In the film, the careful placement of snipped tresses on a silver platter provided a strong visual symbol of sacrificing one's individuality and personality to be part of the order. My own curly mess on the barbershop floor could hardly compare, but it did alert me to narrower expectations of how to look and act as I entered the institution of teaching under the principal's watchful eye.

Returning the next day, shorn and sporting no visible jewelry, I waited in the special education office for Iris. John, another teacher in the department who was also a friend of Jayson, instructed me, "Come this way a moment." He stepped into the adjacent empty office and before I knew it leaned forward, placed a kiss on my lips, and said, "Good luck." No sooner had he done this, John turned around and signaled me to return and wait for Iris.

I was still in mild shock, trying to make sense of the unexpected kiss, when I was shepherded into the principal's office by Iris to find a tall, stout, bespectacled older man wearing a well-tailored suit and a stern expression. Mr. Bailey began by asking a few bland questions about my background, and then inquired:

"What would you do if . . . you brought in a flask of tea every day, and you left it on the corner of your desk . . ."

"—Mr. Bailey, *please*—" Iris implored.

" . . . and when you came to drink it, you realized it was actually urine."

I sensed that he was either playing with me, testing me, or both, and my response to this question would weigh significantly in a potential hire.

"I think . . ." I began slowly to secure another few seconds of think time, ". . . the situation would not actually happen in the first place," continuing, "*If* I did drink tea from a flask, I'd never leave it out when I'm teaching."

Dourness made him unreadable, although the answer seemed acceptable.

"I asked," he explained, "as this happened to your predecessor . . ."

Iris gently shook her head from side to side in silence.

" . . . who then quit."

It seemed as if I'd passed the test. I was in, and made a mental note not to drink student urine.

The next step was to be processed by the Board of Education, usually ominously referred to as "the Board." My university transcripts from the United Kingdom needed evaluation. After being subjected to quick medical and psychological exams that seemed quite perfunctory, I was sent to a public health clinic to be tested for tuberculosis as per state law and found it shared premises, including a waiting room, with a clinic for sexually transmitted diseases. All along the way, I had to fill out what seemed like dozens of forms with the same basic information. At the Board I became frustrated when given the runaround by seemingly disinterested employees blowing softly on newly varnished nails and studiously avoiding eye contact. As it turned out, I discovered a labyrinth of teacher certifications, including a provisional version—which is what I needed. Apparently, teachers working in special education *first* needed 12 credits in general education before they could teach. However, due to such a shortage of special education teachers, waivers were being issued. With only a bachelor's degree in literature, the system allowed me to become a temporarily certified special educator. Without one credit in education—either general or special—and no teaching experience, without ever having set foot in an American classroom, without being familiar with the terms "learning disabled" (LD) and "emotionally disturbed" (ED), I was immediately employed to teach students with these labels. Completely untrained and unqualified, I was approved by the Board.

THE FIRST THREE WEEKS

I'd like to say that I hit the ground running, but I really just hit the ground. Hard. I immediately asked myself: What was I thinking in going into teaching? Not only did I want to quit each and every day, I wanted to quit each and every hour. I became physically sick and mentally stretched out of shape as the pit of my stomach sunk to new depths and my anxiety catapulted through the roof. I soon discovered there was so much simultaneously going in the act(s) of teaching and that I was responsible for it all. The buck stopped with me. I felt as if I was making multiple decisions every single minute (something I later became familiar with, and thankfully accustomed to, as part of what a teacher does), but at first it was exhausting. The "kids" as everyone referred to them, ranged in age between 14 and 21 years, were all African American, Caribbean, and/or Latino/a. Because it was a "magnet" school, meaning that entry was based on the interest in a potential professional area—in this case fashion—kids came from all five boroughs, some spending an hour and a half each way on crowded buses and subways.

I was designated a "homeroom" although I didn't quite know its purpose, soon finding out it was to take attendance, make announcements, distribute monthly transportation passes, and so on. A large blue Delaney Book with cards in slots on which I had to write students names and take attendance for each and every class that was placed into my hands. Physical classroom space was sometimes standard and at other times small, although there was always enough for a maximum of 12 students. The special education department took up the third and fourth floors, sharing the latter with the school cafeteria, making lots of noise and action in the hallway everyday.

My new colleagues appeared to be pleasant, but almost always running from point A to point B with furrowed brows and arms full of materials. Teachers did not have a base classroom and had to teach different classes in various rooms, so when the bell rang and doors flung open, hallways looked like a rush hour subway stations where students and teachers competed to get to their next assigned space. There were multiple bell schedules, depending upon whether there'd be short or long homeroom, school-wide meetings at the end of the day, and other reasons that made no sense to me. These schedules were all to the minute and never "rounded off," so they read like: 9:03–9:47 (two-minute change, then), 9:49–10:33, and so on. Despite always having one eye on my watch, I could never quite get it right. In addition, teacher and kids' schedules seemed to be always changing. I later came to learn that this was tied to many valid factors such as schools not knowing the actual intake of ninth grade students, unpredictable numbers of returning students, balancing numbers in needed classes, and hiring decisions subject to funding tied to fluctuating student numbers. This system sometimes meant just coming to know a class of students and then having to change to another group who already had two teachers before me. Plus, there seemed to be non-stop announcements piped into the room at all times about a variety of issues, be it messages from the principal, reminders about bringing in forms for free lunch, or meetings of various student social and academic clubs. In all of this non-stop, over-stimulating environment, filled with comings and goings of all sorts of students, teachers, support staff, and administrators, I also had to try to teach. *Try* being an accurate word choice.

As my friend Jayson had said to me the summer before starting, there's no feeing quite like the first day of classes when you're standing in front of the room and students are looking at you, watching to see what you'll do. I recall having an excessively dry throat, swallowing hard repeatedly, and praying it was indiscernible as I felt eyes burn into me, evenly divided between mild curiosity and pronounced indifference. One week before I had been shown a format for writing lessons:

Instructional Objective: Students will be able to (SWBAT)
Aim: In the form of a question, usually using "why" or "how"
(How does the narrator portray the hero?)
Do Now: A quick activity to help students focus
(List five qualities you associate with the word "hero")
Motivation: A "hook" that could be in the form of a question, visual, object
(Who do you consider to be a hero in your life? Why?)
Procedure: Series of steps to teach content information
(Let's read the next sections of the book about our hero)
Medial Summary: A repeated condensed version of the information
(Let's connect some of the main thoughts so far)
Key Questions: Check in for what's remembered so far
(Why do you think the hero responded the way that he did? What were some unforeseen consequences?)
Procedure: Continuation of teaching content
(Let's continue reading the next sections and discuss the actions and words of the hero)
Key Questions: Another check in for what was remembered
(What are some particular actions that, in your opinion, defined the hero's character?)
Summary: Wrap up of content. Can the student answer the "Aim" question?
(Write a paragraph about how the hero is portrayed that includes an example of at least one action and one thing the hero says that reveal who he is)
Homework: To be done by the following day
(Write a paragraph about the personal hero you identified, including an example of at least one action and one thing the hero says that reveals who he or she is).

I had never really considered the "behind the scenes" of teaching before now, imagining it rather as standing in front of students and sharing information with them hanging on every word, or at least pretending to. Now I was being asked to construct detailed plans in which I had to state desired outcomes and generate a host scaffolded questions. I had five classes a day that incorporated three preparations (in other words, I taught two sections twice, and one once). Every night at home on the kitchen table I drafted three plans that would sometimes take up to 90 minutes each, before grading homework. In the beginning, no matter the amount of time and energy spent, these plans had no guarantee of working well with students. They would laugh, refuse to do work, throw things, roll their eyes and say in Spanish "*Ayyy Diossss*!" (*Oh my God!*). On the train going home, I reflected upon what happened during the course of the day and invariably felt a great sense of failure.

The kids ran the range of desirous to be taught to flagrantly disregarding all of my efforts to teach. Some individuals could also switch these roles on a daily basis. I was shocked by students' behavior, language, and at times their over-familiarity. One day near the start of the semester, a particularly challenging student named Lucinda whose reputation preceded her swung open my classroom door, looked me up and down and yelled, "I don't know where the hell they got you from, but you better get your flat white ass back to where it belongs." I was taken aback that a student could address a teacher like that (and for a split second I wondered was my ass really that flat, or was she stereotyping me?), yet I realized it served a purpose. Lucinda did it for effect, and it worked. She had self-established as queen bee of homeroom and, as in many other cases, I had to learn to step back and rethink about how best to respond to students in situations such as this. Some girls were quite forward. One day I had to stop a pair from discussing out loud the type of underwear they thought I was wearing as I wrote on the chalkboard. In another instance, at the end of class, a 19-year-old female student pushed her telephone number into my hand and with a seasoned eye looking directly into mine told me to call her that weekend, adding, "You know what I mean."

Clearly, I was not being taken seriously, and it seemed as if I could not connect to students in the way they needed and I wanted. Woefully aware that I had bitten off more than I could chew, I wrestled with what to do, tending toward the highly preferable option of leaving. Sleepless nights preceded a dread of going into work. One day I felt so anxious that while walking down the block to school, tall buildings began to curve inwardly toward each other, as if I were an insect inside a Venus fly trap, watching a disappearing sky. At the end of the school day, as soon as my apartment door closed, I wept with sheer frustration. I had never had to struggle this much with anything before. My new daily challenges left me asking: Had I made a huge mistake and needed to quit? I called Jayson regularly whose pep talks had gradually lessened in intensity from mantras of "Give it a try" to a more doubtful "I don't know, David." He immediately told Iris and John, making me feel weak and even more vulnerable. But, instead of letting me off easy, they began to rally around, each separately pulling me aside.

"I know you," Jayson encouraged, "And I know you can do this. You have the qualities of a good teacher. Who knows, one day you might even end up teaching college."

"Come into my classes during your free period and watch me," John offered. "These kids have never met anyone from the UK before. Think of the things you can share with them."

"Just keep at it," Iris urged, "Take it one day at a time. I am willing to work with you one day at a time. Come check-in with me at the end of each day."

I am not sure which one of the three that said it, but one of them told me to go home every day and think of a single positive thing that occurred in my classes. It was such a simple thought, yet I clung to it like a shipwrecked sailor to a raft. I needed to see some light, a spark, even if it was fleeting. Sure enough, at home I recalled a student being happy when I showed her how to structure an essay, explained a topic, helped with a personal problem, or laughed at a joke I made. And, as the days passed, these sparks of small, singular instances that I first identified as outliers, as exceptions to the harsh blur of my daily experiences, multiplied significantly. Within a short period, I was surprised at the growing number of times where I saw "the light" in everyday situations. Surprisingly, my intense desire to leave began to ebb.

One seasoned teacher said, "If they like you, that's half the battle won." After a few weeks, I could tell that a number of students did. Many were intrigued by my Northern English accent that was invariably mistaken for Irish, close in intonation and cadence (in later years one group of students always referred to me as Mr. Leprechauner). The hard-boiled Irish American school secretary took a shine to me as I "served" an administrative period in her office organizing and filing student late attend slips of the day. When she found out I was working in the special education department, she'd shake her head and say, "The sins of the parents," as if that explained everything. My accent did not go unnoticed by faculty either, with one teacher permanently talking in a bad interpretation of a Liverpudlian accent (until one day, exasperated, I told him to stop), and another teacher whose age and experience commanded grand dame reverence within the school turned to me in line at the cafeteria and stated witheringly, "There was a time when they did not let accents like yours into the profession," and turned away. It was easy to feel out of place in such an environment, and I did get cautioned as Puerto Rican students of mine were now using phrases in other people's classes such as "Where's me book?"

Still, it was the kids that intrigued me from the very start. Each was unique and I wondered what their stories were. As a group, I found them loud and rambunctious, yet as individuals, they were interesting to talk to. One of the first that I came to know was Lana. She was a relatively shy girl who wrote creatively, and had a sly sense of humor. At the same time, I noticed something fragile about her, and came to find out that she had previously attempted suicide. I will never forget one day, out of the blue, she said, "I wish you were my father." Those unexpected words entered me so deeply that they impacted how I came to see myself as an educator. I thought, despite being different in terms of country of origin, culture, race, gender, and age, maybe I can connect to the kids after all? Maybe I do have things to offer. Maybe they see that I care, and that includes them. Other students liked English music and came to visit during lunchtimes to talk about Sade, George Michael, The Clash, or Queen. Damian one of the most emotionally unpredictable students in the department happened to be biracial with a white English father. He sought me out to chat about British culture and I was happy to oblige.

Lanon was considered another difficult student. Tall and lanky, with a quick temper, he was inclined to easily fly off the handle. One morning, when I asked him to complete an assignment, he responded by punching his fist through glass in the classroom door. It was at times like this that I thought nothing quite prepares an aspiring teacher for these circumstances. First of all, I was concerned Lanon had injured himself. Second of all, I realized that my simple request—typically expected of a teacher—had set him off. I was soon learning that kids who were volatile inside of school usually were so because of their lives outside of school and/or because what they were being asked to do in class wasn't a good fit for their state of mind that day or at a particular moment. Classroom management was of concern to all teachers, and I was no exception. Without a safe and organized space with expectations and rules, quality teaching and learning cannot occur. I quickly sought to "read the signs" if a student was having a bad day, and developed a policy of trying to "head things off at the pass" to preclude potentially troublesome situations, aiming to de-escalate rather than escalate.

Along with the encouragement of Jayson, Iris, and John, a teacher called Tom befriended me, too. Ex-military, former musician, faithful churchgoer, dean of the cafeteria, Tom was very straightforward, a no-nonsense man that students and faculty respected. Several times he sat me down to talk because, as he later shared, I looked like a deer in the headlights, walking down the hallway between classes with a permanently panicked look on my face. One time he noted, "It seems like it's crazy and chaotic now," he says, "Because it is." Tom's face was seasoned and kind. "However," he added, "after three weeks, it settles down." In that conversation, he assuaged some of my deepest fears. I could not imagine a year of teaching in these current conditions and I knew I was in, all things said, a relatively "good" public school. "If I can get to the end of September," I told myself, "Maybe, just maybe, I can actually turn this thing around and make a go of it . . . at least for the year."

THE FIRST FEW YEARS

As a teacher you soon learn that the world ends at your classroom door and stays within your four walls. At least that's how it feels. You're pretty much on your own. I had been given a schedule largely consisting of teaching English and math. As special education teachers, we were expected to obtain and analyze the general education curriculum, modify it, and hand it in to the department chairperson for approval. These modified courses were designed to help prepare students for Regents Competency Tests examinations (RCTs) needed to graduate from high school. With no courses in pedagogy, I defaulted into automatically imitating styles of teachers I had in high school. This meant a lot of lecturing and note taking. Although I was being faithful to the curriculum and teaching my little heart out, I was quick to learn that I was also missing the mark for many students who had difficulty in paying attention, organizing, self-monitoring, auditory processing, determining salient points, and scribing simultaneously. Students knew they had to be in school to learn, knew I was trying to teach them, and yet were disengaged and bored. In one English class, a student named Evie asked in front of the whole class, "Mr. Connor, why don't you teach more like Mr. Schwartz? He makes things fun, makes us role-play parts, have debates, does games."

I was stung hard. But Evie was right. That comment was one of the best things that ever happened to me as a beginning teacher. I'd assumed teaching to be "I talk, you listen; I have the information, you learn it." I recall some indescribably boring teachers in my own high school experience who simply wrote notes on the board and told students to copy them. That was the entire lesson (multiply by 180 days, and that was the school year). I'd also had other teachers who used question and answers in stimulating ways. Rarely had we been told to role-play or were given manipulatives to explore and learn. Around the same time, I was "officially observed" by Iris. Being observed was high stakes as it meant being formally assessed as satisfactory or unsatisfactory, with serious implications for continuous employment. By chance, it was my "worst" class, dominated by the notorious Chanté and Shawna, two ninth grade girls that reminded me of the gum-chewing-eye-rolling-hair-obsessed characters in classroom scenes of *Female Trouble* (Waters, 1974). Chanté would swing back and balance on the two rear legs of her chair, looking at me in the eye and spreading her legs before cackling with full knowledge of her inappropriateness. Shawna would try to physically push me away if I approached the desk to assist her. Iris was fully aware of how challenging they were as they simply tuned her out, disregarding anything she said, too. Her evaluation of the lesson was kind, as she wished to encourage me. However, Iris noted that teaching basic numeracy that day (addition, subtraction, multiplication, and division) was decidedly "dry." She advised me to use items students would be familiar with, such as buying rice and measuring soda.

I took both student and administrator feedback and shifted my thinking to be more around *engagement,* having students interact with me and each other, while linking the familiar (what they knew) with the new (what I was trying to teach them). One of the first successes experienced was creating a literal menu of foods that students knew and liked (burgers, hotdogs, fries, rice and beans, ice cream, cokes, etc.) and then creating a related problem for each student. For example, "If Shawna had a burger, fries, and a coke, (a) how much would she have to pay? (b) how much change would she receive from a ten-dollar note?" Or, "If Chanté bought two cokes and two ice-creams for her and a friend, (a) how much would she have to pay? (b) if she paid in quarters, how many would she need?" Along with a cartoon of a waitress and various types of food, I told each student to start with *their own* problem, and then try the others. I was amazed at the instantaneous shift in classroom culture. All students focused, started on their problem, and then—as they were already in motion—went onto others. It was a small but significant victory and one that I parlayed into many other activities, including having students make up their own menus as restaurant owners—all the time with an eye on practicing and developing math skills.

I also visited my peers when teaching, as many as my schedule permitted, to see the methods they used and how they generally worked with students. Tom was drill-major, with all desks lined up and facing forward, mainly lecturing, and asking students to think and demonstrate their knowledge clearly. There was always discussion, but with view to ensuring the answer was written down and filed in binders in a highly organized way. John was somewhat traditional, too, running a tight ship and excelling in connecting to students and making them feel special. When teaching Spanish, he used each of their names in complementary sentences such as *Virgil es muy guapo y inteligente* ("Virgil is very handsome and intelligent") and *Ana es linda y baila bien* ("Ana is pretty and dances well"). Jayson placed desks in a semicircle so he could circulate and attend to each student one-on-one. He was the first teacher I saw using a form of "the workshop model," coaching each student individually to achieve the next level of proficiency. Suzanne was a young, second year teacher with whom I became friendly. She, too, welcomed me into her classroom where she waved her arms around dramatically, laughed a lot, encouraged kids to write creative poetry and discuss the meaning of literature. It sounds ridiculous to say now, but I didn't know then that I could sit students in a semicircle, use a workshop model, or have them talk in pairs, so I began to integrate different teaching methodologies that also shaped classroom configurations, and student-teacher interactions.

Having classes of 12 students allowed me to get to know many of them fairly well. Although respecting the "boundaries" of teacher and pupil, I could not help but come to see them as young people with various life experiences to date, finding their way in the world. I noticed that the majority of students in special education classes were uncomfortable with this fact. They would often sit wedged against the wall so no peers from general education classes would see them as they passed by in the hallway. Special education struck me as "an open secret," the phrase used in queer theory to signify that everyone knows "it" but nobody talks about "it." I began to wonder if kids such as Chanté and Shawna acted in unacceptable ways because they had been placed in special education, or was it really vice versa, they were placed in special education for acting like they did? I knew kids were very sensitive, not wishing to be "outed" as being in special education under any circumstance. I recall once waiting with a group of my students in a room on the first floor before leaving for a trip. We were sharing the space with a group of students who were also about to go on a different trip and were being noisy. Their teacher then declared to her students in a loud voice for all to hear, "Settle down and be quiet. These students over here are in special education and they're not acting that way." To my student's credit, instead of responding to her publicly, they looked at me with restrained anger. One said in a low voice between gritted teeth, "You'd better tell her." Of course the student was right, and so I asked the teacher to step outside in the hallway (always being able to see the kids through the glass panel, knowing a good teacher never lets kids out of eyesight). When I explained why what she said made my students very uncomfortable, and respectfully asked her to think about her words carefully next time, she responded with a surprised "Oh." That she was allegedly the principal's girlfriend made me more than a little uneasy, but I felt a loyalty to my students, and a desire to protect them from unnecessary public humiliation.

Students from those years still stay with me in the form of permanent memories. It's a well-known phenomenon among teachers that most can name the kids they taught in their first year. For example, there was Joy, waltzing in late everyday with movie star glasses, ready to say and do anything to get out of reading. She talked about her handsome fiancé in the marines, showing his photograph to anyone who'd look, and couldn't wait to be married and freed from the drudgery of education. Joy was also one of the first severely dyslexic students I knew. There was Vito, a sweet, handsome kid who, when asked what he wanted to be, said “an archy-tet” (an architect). Willie, an introverted and quirky student, was an excellent artist with a schizophrenic mother (I later learned from reading his IEP) who snapped at me never to call their home. There were Damon and Chris, two gay students who got into a fight over Joanna, though faculty were not entirely sure why (although we assumed they weren’t ready to accept their sexuality in a world that was already hostile to them). There was Remmy, bitter and droll, 19 years of age with an old man’s face, putting down others at the drop of a hat, *schadenfreude* personified, reveling in everyone’s misfortunes. There was Kaylee, a pretty, taciturn girl with a few front teeth left—emanating a curious mixture of toughness and fragility. There was Laurence, a six-foot two Jamaican who spelled “tie” as “ty,” and proudly displayed a photograph of his girlfriend, always stating the obvious, “She’s white!” There was Maria who had 2 children by the age of 16, and had a difficult time focusing in class because she wanted to talk about them to anyone who’d listen. In sum, each kid was different. Each kid had a story. Each kid needed some form of academic, social, and emotional support, or more likely, a combination of the three.

While I came to know and like many students, while I was shakily finding my feet, and while my originally non-existent teaching skills began to grow—I made some split-second decisions that regretfully backfired. In one class, a girl named Claudette refused to sit down and instead ran around the room and climbed on desks making it impossible for me to teach. After various verbal requests, and moving closer to employ what my college textbook called “proximity control,” I lightly touched Claudette on the outside of her shoulder to steer her toward the empty seat. She exploded, directing a stream of obscenities at me. In that very moment, I wondered if she had been physically or sexually abused in some way. I had no proof, but her reaction to a slight touch was so extreme. This interaction certainly made for a drama-filled class, and Claudette was removed. Later that day, we were both required to sit down with Jayson, now unofficial dean of the special education department, to talk about what happened. As Claudette was castigated for unacceptable behavior both before and after the shoulder touch, I reflected on how, unwittingly, the slightest of physical contact could serve as a lightning rod.

In another instance, I am ashamed to recount, I recall working with Alysha, a girl who could not stop taking, incessantly interrupting the class, and cursing like a trooper. One day she came to class late as usual, entered talking loudly, interrupted the flow of the lesson, and ignored all directions from me. When I asked her to stop, get out her work, and join in, she replied,

“Go fuck yourself!”

Several other students in the room gasped audibly.

“Get out,” I responded in a firm voice.

"No, I am not getting out." Alysha challenged. "Make me."

I felt disrespected, angered, humiliated.

"We'll see about that," I said, quickly pulling her and the chair toward the door.

What I didn't count on was Alysha spreading her arms out horizontally, and grabbing onto the walls each side of the classroom door in a crucifixion pose. For a moment, it was push and pull with everyone watching. She'd made a move that created stalemate; no one could win. Realizing that the situation had escalated from bad to worse, I turned and walked to the special education office, requesting to that Alysha be removed immediately. She was, and I salvaged the lesson as best I could. However, the next day, as procedures dictated, both she and I had to appear before the dean of the entire school. I rightfully received a "you should know better" speech, and Alysha was read the riot act. While she had crossed the line, I had too. She could have been injured. The incident made me change how I responded to verbal insults in the classroom. Subsequently, beginning from a place of giving disruptive students the benefit of the doubt, after a matter-of-fact verbal reminder (or a few), I actively sought to de-escalate any potential conflicts. If I deemed a student could not transition into the lesson and was continuously disruptive to the education of others, I would ask the dean to remove the student—always with view to later speaking with the student outside of class about why he or she was choosing to behave in unacceptable ways (and sometimes, found out they had good reasons). It is never appropriate to explode when teaching, although it is indeed very human to do so. Witnessing numerous colleagues succumbing to "losing it" over the years, I worked hard on handling situations otherwise. There's no getting away from it, some days teaching was very stressful.

Inappropriate behavior of students was actually a norm in some classes. In another instance, I recall Charlie, a chubby student, always being reticent to start work, constantly engaging in back-and-forth as I encouraged him to write. One day he was doing it more than usual, distracting himself with some kind of object—a coin or a plastic toy—when I walked by and took the object, placing it in my pocket. "You can have it back at the end of class, Charlie," I said, "Right now, I need you to focus on your work." All of a sudden I felt his hand plunge in my pants pocket. I was mortified. "Gimme it back!" he kept repeating, "Gimme it back!" In return, I repeated, "Stop! You'll get it at the end of class." The other students looked on, some with amusement, and others with concern. After what seemed to be an inordinate amount of time, Charlie and I shuffled outside of the classroom like two rutting moose, and I asked a student to go fetch Jayson. As soon as Jayson arrived and demanded Charlie remove his hand from my pocket, he did, and then was escorted to the office to discuss what happened as, once again, I attempted to refocus a class. It was a strange incident, as I could have relented and gave Charlie the object back, but it would have set a precedent and felt more like a symbolic battle of wills. Something in me told me not to back down. After that, Charlie and I were wary of one another. I learned that simple actions that would have been taken by my own high school teachers did not necessarily apply here.

I also became very conscious of race. I was usually the only white person in the room, and kids often took the opportunity to remind me of the fact to see how I'd react. This came in various forms, from girls unexpectedly stroking the hair on my arms, saying they'd never seen any like that before, to the following exchange that occurred as I was in the middle of teaching an art class one day.

Me: "Any questions?"
Student: "Mr. Connor . . . ," a student began.
Me: "Yes?"
Student: "I have a question."
Me: "What is it?" (Assuming it would be about the task at hand.)
Student: "Why do black men have bigger dicks than white men?"

Of course the whole class broke out into laughter.

I wanted to say it wasn't always true, and managed to keep a straight (albeit red) face, mentioning the need to be appropriate at all times, but I was laughing to myself all the way home on the train. Kids would often approach the topic of race in a humorous way, telling jokes within art class, such as Eric's observation. "Did you know different races have different weapons of choice? Blacks have guns. Latinos have knives. And Whites . . ." he paused for effect, allowing students to look in my direction, " . . . have security."

Oftentimes, I too, would use humor to counter racial comments.

Student: "You're white."
Me: (Looking at my arms with an aghast expression) "Oh my God! You're right! How come I've never noticed before?"

This would usually invoke laughter and a comment of "Mr. Connor, you're crazy."

As long as the commentaries were not offensive, I could roll with the punches. However, on occasion, things could be tense. I recall in my second year, having a class who were generally difficult as a group. I had to instruct them in world history and when it came to teaching the slave trade for the first time, I did feel admittedly self-conscious. One of the students, Kofi, was very proud of his African heritage and used the situation to personalize "my ancestors" and "his ancestors," rousing the class into antiwhite diatribe, completely derailing the lesson. In the verbal melee, one student tried to stem the tide stating, "Not all whites are bad!" (I later found out that she was biracial with a white father). However, my attempts to teach were shouted down and I felt attacked, a little intimidated, and somewhat defeated. I sought advice from Tom and John, both African Americans, and they told me to change the content immediately—stop teaching about Africa and switch to the Middle East. In the meantime, Kofi's mother was summoned to the school. She was a beautiful, imposing young woman dressed in traditional African attire. Kofi was chastised for rabble-rousing and diverting lessons, and although his mother reinforced what the dean was saying, I suspected she was proud that her son had shared with the class many statistics of the middle passage that were not so graphically described in our textbook.

These experiences did not put me off teaching, but they alerted me to the sensitivity of race and how racial issues are presented in the official and unofficial curriculum. As students came to know me, I experienced a strange phenomenon in which they told me I "was not really white." This backhanded compliment indicated they liked and trusted me, to a degree. I was not like how they knew or imagined white people to be. However, being accepted and respected by students would never be automatic, it would always have to be earned. This was done, in large part, by how I engaged with students, supported them, managed them, and responded to their comments.

AS TIME WENT BY

Amid the daily challenges, I became genuinely interested in the phenomenon of teaching and learning. I didn't just want to be a teacher; I wanted to be a good teacher. Although I had taught math, it was not my area of expertise. Science, too, was not a good match for me, yet I do recall teaching sex education in Biology was the only time all students paid full attention for a lesson's duration. A colleague told me a student had one innocently remarked, "The only time I've ever seen a penis was in Mr. Connor's class." The mind boggles. I was surprised at students' questions that ranged from "Can you get pregnant if standing up?" to "Can you get injured from rough sex?" Ultimately, rather than the subjects of science and math, I asked to primarily teach English and Art because I believed students could be more creative in these classes.

What I came to note in English classes was the variety in students' abilities to read and write. It also became apparent that what students were "not good at," they did not like to do. It's a great irony that the only way to improve a skill is to practice it more. So many lessons had to shift students from the mindset of "I am not good at this" to working on things they were interested in and proud to share. While I could understand some amount of time on sentence combining and other rote routines (I do think there is a place for this type of work, if integrated well in a balanced way), the beauty of teaching writing lay in students sharing their thoughts and lives. Once I had been taught the steps of the writing process—Prewriting, Organization, Writing, Editing, Rewriting (POWER)—with view to publication for public consumption in some shape or form, I developed workshops for students. In each student's individualized writing folder, there were the POWER steps described, along with a list of student ideas, and always a piece of work in progress. Students produced poems, short stories, descriptions, and autobiographies that fascinated me. I made sure every one of them had a sample of creative writing and a piece of artwork on display in my classroom. On open school night, students would enter and immediately take their parents to their work on display, beaming with pride. I recall one student, Roberto, writing about how he accidentally set fire to and burned down his family's apartment causing them to go live in a homeless shelter. They never failed to surprise.

After taking a course on teaching playwriting, I developed a method to teach students writing three act plays in which the resolution could not involve a gun. This was a deliberate choice as many films, TV episodes, and even classic literature end with someone being shot. I was pleased when one quiet, somewhat aloof girl named Janine, labeled emotionally disturbed and often resistant to work, wrote over 20 pages. Yet, when I read them my heart slowed down. Her central character was a young black girl who went for a summer holiday to the Midwest and was gang raped by a group of white teenagers. The scenes were so vivid, the dialogue so crisp, I could not help but wonder if it had been her. Generally speaking, I noticed that writing seemed cathartic, helping students to connect with who they were, verifying they had something to offer, and validating their words in publication form.

In terms of literature, I found some of the classics, despite their obvious merits, to be unappealing to students. One example was Thornton Wilder's *Our Town* (Wilder, 1938). Although we had some fun with mock wedding ceremonies and graveyard scenes, it was not lost on me when students complained, "These are white people's stories." It was then I became more conscious of what was taught (and what was not taught) in the curriculum and the extent to which racial and ethnic diversity was missing. I began to include short stories by Alice Walker (1982), Toni Morrison's *Sula* (1982), Ntozake Shange's *For Colored Girls When the Rainbow Isn't Enough* (1975), selections from Piri Thomas's *Down These Mean Streets* (1967), and Zora Neale Hurston and Langston Hughes's *Mule Bone* (1930). Students were more likely to be engaged with the issues raised in these texts. At the same time, filled with intrigue and sexual tensions, "classics" such as Tennessee

Williams' *A Streetcar Named Desire* (1947) struck a still chord with students. I also decided to teach Shakespeare as students had never been introduced the Bard. I chose *Macbeth* (1992) because of its mystical atmosphere and battle-field action. Students enjoyed the challenge of the text, proudly carrying their books to school, letting the world know they were studying Shakespeare. Given that my high school students were usually reading anywhere between third and fifth grade levels, I had to find ways to break the work down. We had split text with the original Elizabethan English version one side, and a contemporary American-English version on the corresponding page. In addition, we had a comic strip adaptation. Some days we read selected passages from either side of the book and acted them out, other times we story-mapped, and other days I condensed and narrated the plot to move it along. I loved it when they "got" the text, although it was sometimes demonstrated in unorthodox comments such as, "Oooooooh, that Lady MacBeth, . . . she a B!" We even went to see a production for schools that was action-packed with sword fighting amid atmospheric dry ice.

In both English and Art classes, I applied from mini-grants from "the Board," and was pleased to receive them. These came in the form of visiting artists. One of them was Patrick Morelli, a talented sculptor whose bronze work of Kunta Kinte, the slave portrayed in Alex Hayley's historical fiction *Roots* (1974), raising up his new born child, stands outside the Martin Luther King Jr. Center in Atlanta. Morelli brought six-foot tall wooden figures that could interlock to be painted as part of a larger project he was coordinating to symbolize togetherness. Another visiting artist, Richard (last name escapes me), was a playwright and actor who came to work with a class consisting of all boys identified as emotionally disturbed. Richard had the kids do readings of David Mamet's *American Buffalo.* Given that the text consists of every other word being "fuck" or some other curse, kids were fighting for parts. I had to ask them to keep their voices down when performing. Although it was a contemporary classic, I didn't want their glee-filled renditions heard in the hallway. It was a notable shift from *Our Town.*

In Art, I set up life drawing classes with desks in a large circle. Kids held drawing boards that tilted in any direction that worked for them and drew still lifes or sketched figure drawings of peers. Occasionally I drew a portrait of a student during lunchtime, and once took home a denim jacket to finish a painting of LL Cool J for a girl called Sharlene who, a couple of years later, feigned a pregnancy for four months to gain attention. As a class, we entered art competitions and won some. Very Special Arts was an organization in Washington, DC, run by *The* Kennedy family that sponsored contests for students with disabilities (SWD). Our collective classwork was selected several times to be hung in prominent public places such as the windows of the Pan-Am building towering over Grand Central Station and at the South

Street Sea Port in lower Manhattan. One of my most challenging students, Harry, won a Manhattan wide art competition to celebrate the 100th birthday of W. E. B. DuBois. His design was a silhouette of many differently colored faces, symbolizing the color line described by DuBois. In the spirit of transparency, one of the main judges was Jayson, who had since moved to the superintendent's office as her personal assistant, helping oversee the operations of all high schools in Manhattan. Still, it was a good experience for Harry as winners were required to attend Carnegie Hall for a celebration of DuBois. The special guest speaker that night was Bill Cosby, then at peak popularity, who spoke out against rappers using demeaning language of "bitches" and "hos" when referring to women. When Harry's name was called out, he climbed the steps to receive his prize on stage, an autographed edition of David Levering Lewis's (1994) definitive twin volume biography of DuBois. Returning to his seat adjacent to mine, Harry rolled his eyes in disappointment, and handed me the volumes saying, "Here, you can have them." The book won a Pulitzer Prize, and the twin volumes still sit on my shelf at home.

Teaching was not all arts and academics at the High School of Fashion Industries. Our department also had a work-experience program called "Offsite." This consisted of a group of businesses in the nearby garment district that were willing to provide access to the workplace. Our students were assigned to be with a professional for approximately two hours a day. This work could take many forms ranging from assisting a designer to helping in the stockroom. The experience seemed to be worthwhile for some students, while not so much for others. Chaperoning students from Chelsea to and from nearby midtown Manhattan wasn't easy, and I always tried to keep them in a tight group. On the subway, unknown hormone-fueled males sometimes approached girls in the group, requiring me to make an unwelcome intervention (usually for both parties), indicating I was the teacher and we were actually on a school trip. At the sites, the philanthropic-minded adults who were paired with students sometimes expressed surprise at their lack of enthusiasm. Students, on the other hand, were under the impression that they deserved an unrealistic level of pay for their two hours. In my first year of working with the Offsites, my naïveté came to the surface again when asked by two black women why their currently assigned students appeared to be so unmotivated.

"They're from the ghetto," I responded before I knew it, as if that answer accounted for the student's lack of interest, knowledge, and exposure to the world at large.

"*We're* from the ghetto!" they replied, making a circular movement with their necks, as if to drive the message home. They were having none of my misplaced white-boy rationale. There were times like this when I knew I was a fish out of water with a lot to learn. Thankfully, I did have an open door in asking questions about race in America of my colleague John. A few weeks into my first semester, after the unexpected kiss, we began a relationship and soon after moved into an apartment. Our nightly dinner table became an open forum about anything, although much of it centered upon our experiences in life and education, including issues of race, class, sexual orientation, nationality—always topics of interest to me. Our partnership lasted for 27 years, and I credit it with being the crucible wherein invaluable conversations and problem-solving discussions occurred for most of my career.

John also worked with a group of students in the Offsites, allowing us to swap notes on a daily basis about the companies and kids assigned to them. While these placements for students were well intended, sometimes resulting in summer jobs, I also noticed some kids' lack of confidence masking itself as resistance or disinterest. One time I recall a student called Naya refusing to go into the workplace only to suddenly take off and run down the crowded street. My automatic response was to run after her (I was legally responsible for her, after all). What must we have looked like, a teenage Latina being chased by a white guy in a tie, yelling "Get back here!" bobbing through the jam-packed sidewalk outside of Macy's? When Naya's mother came to meet me at school to discuss this incident, she lowered her voice and literally disowned her daughter, stating bitterly and without further explanation, "She's not really mine. I have had to bring her up." Many years later, I bumped into Naya on a crowded subway train. At the same time we said, "Mr. Connor?" and "Naya?" "You remembered my name!" she smiled, and we had a cordial conversation in which she introduced me to her own daughter.

Bumping into former students happens every now and then. I once crossed paths with my first-year former-homeroom student Lucinda on Eighth Avenue.

"Weren't you my homeroom teacher?" she asked.

"Yes," I replied. "I remember that you once said to me, 'I don't where they found you but you better take that flat white ass back to wherever it came from.'"

"Did I say that?" her eyebrows raised before she started laughing. Lucinda then told me she worked for the post office.

I have always enjoyed bumping into former students and finding out how they've fared in life. Those I have encountered over the years have families and work as health aides, community artists, service providers to people with disabilities, messengers, cleaners, shop assistants, security guards, and so on. Others who I have never seen since they left school cross my mind from time to time, and I wonder if they managed to have a good life.

THE COLLEGE-WORK CONNECTION

There was no question that I would attend Hunter College to obtain my master's degree in special education. Both Jayson and John had graduated from there and told me it was the best program in the city's economically priced college system known as the City University of New York (CUNY). I had to start with obtaining 12 credits in general education as that's what was minimally needed before teaching kids identified as disabled, something that I was then doing. The system was already making little sense to me. My first classes were in educational foundations and teaching English. The former class was taught by a professor drier than a bone, with a midterm and final exam consisting of multiple-choice answers straight from a text the thickness of a telephone directory. The latter class's instructor was a dramatic professor dressed head-to-toe in black who made us practice teaching in front of each other. Analyzing the style of these two educators, I began to be more aware of how a teacher's choice of pedagogical methods made an impact upon student "performance." I received a grade of C when taking multiple-choice tests and an A for the creative exercises in lesson planning. These results confirmed a dislike of multiple-choice tests, as I rarely rose above a mediocre score. I note that although they're easier to construct and grade, in my opinion they serve as an inauthentic assessment of student's knowledge, particularly how that knowledge is applied. Plus, I believe creative thinkers can see *possibilities* in one or more answers within multiple-choice tests, as they can imagine alternatives. I was admittedly pissed off in getting a C, but moved onto the second semester, where I completed two other courses with grades of A, thereby completing my 12 credits in general education.

With one year of practice, I was quite eager to now formally learn about special education. I had been amateurishly figuring out the Board's procedures based on federal laws, the rights of students, and how special education worked in general. In brief, I was coming to understand special education as a world within a world, unlike the self-contained classrooms on the third and fourth floors of my school. Without wishing to overgeneralize, the formal study of special education allowed me to become familiar with theory, policy, and research that accompanied my own experiences of special education in practice. At first, the history of special education legislation seemed a million miles away from my daily interactions with José or Janelle, yet I began to connect some dots. In the *Introduction to Special Education* class, I recalled the professor show a video of a woman with severe and multiple disabilities talk frankly about her life, people's attitudes toward her, and limitations placed upon her world by society at large. Her eloquence moved me profoundly and, as we watched in the darkened room, I felt tears run down my cheeks. They were not borne of pity, but of something else. Although I could not imagine my life as her, I could feel a form of empathy, identification with the general human condition, of wanting to understand a different perspective and learn from someone else's experiences.

It struck me early on that the field of special education incorporated many diverse disabilities. Oftentimes, the specific specialty area of the graduate student speaking in class influenced the entire conversation. My own immediate interests, defined by the labels of kids I taught, were respectively the learning disabled, emotionally disturbed, and intellectually impaired. However, issues pertaining to blindness, deafness, autism, and severe and multiple disabilities were also addressed in classes. It was my first inkling of special education as a well-intended provision for citizens who needed different approaches to education. Great emphasis was placed on Public Law 94-142, The Education of All Handicapped Children Act, passed in 1975. I was shocked to discover that until then, school districts could legally reject children with disabilities. I also learned that the original law contained six major provisions: (1) a free and appropriate public education (FAPE); (2) in the least restrictive environment (LRE); with (3) guaranteed due process; (4) parental participation; (5) nondiscriminatory identification and evaluation; and (6) an IEP. This information helped me better understand the systems and structures that shaped the department I worked in.

One of the first things I had to do as a special educator was to write IEP goals and objectives for all of the students I taught. This obligation had resulted in several weekends of hand-written individualized statements in quintuplicate form. What bothered me from the start of this process was the pro-forma approach we tended to use. Teachers would write out 7–10 goals and simply mix them so each student would receive 3. All goals were formulaic, quantifiable, and generic, such as "Daisy will write a three paragraph essay with 80% accuracy" or "Lamoore will calculate ten word problems with 80% accuracy." Once the goals and objectives were written, we'd place them in the mailbox of the student's homeroom teacher who would then collate them into an IEP. Parents were not involved in the creation of objectives; they were informed of them. As teachers, we invited parents in to discuss the IEP for the semester, preferably on teacher-parent night. Otherwise we would do it over the phone and then mail the "agreed upon" documents home. After three failed attempts to be in contact by telephone, we could legally sign as department faculty and mail a copy to the parents. Iris was meticulous and so, either way, all IEPs were written, signed off, and placed in folders.

I began to experience a clash of reality between college classes and my daily work. In college, I was taught the noble nature of IEPs and their vital role in ensuring an individualized education. In contrast, at work, the majority of teachers saw IEPs as excessive and useless paperwork. Although we were reminded to read existing updated IEPs for students in our classes, very few teachers ever did. When I did read an IEP file, I often found the same type of goals year after year without anyone returning to check them off as completed. Browsing the psychological reports of students who I taught, I found them to be limited and trite, filled with clichés ("Yvan is a handsome, socially competent young man who expresses himself well."). Likewise, with social worker reports, I found the information somewhat invasive. Extensive family histories contained highly personal details of various members (miscarriages, incarceration, in-family adoptions, and so on). There was an air of genteel judgment that pervaded these formal assessments. That said, I did find the educational evaluations somewhat useful, although they reflected what I had often observed myself about a student. Despite being urged to read them at the start of the semester, I preferred to dip into the IEP folders part way through after I had gotten to know students myself. This way I could verify (or contrast) previous observations of others with my own. Given that many teachers saw IEPs as a necessary inconvenience (justifying classes of 12 students rather than 34), they were often completed in a rushed and disinterested way, frequently containing limited information and sometimes inaccuracies. On occasion, if I had a really challenging student, I would read the IEP folder much sooner in the semester. I recall doing such a thing for a student called Daniel who could not stop walking or talking in class, sometimes demonstrating aggressive tendencies while occasionally crying at other times. Over the first few weeks, Daniel had exasperated me, so I needed to know more about him. By reading his IEP, I discovered he had been abandoned at birth by an alcoholic, drug-addicted mother and had subsequently been raised by an aunt. Born dependent upon drugs, Daniel always had incredible difficulty in keeping still and concentrating. He also had a degenerative bone disorder, problems with vision, and a diagnosis of a short life span. When I closed that file, I realized that Daniel had so many problems on his plate that I shifted from a disposition of being frustrated with him to one of being primarily empathetic, with far more patience, now aware of his complicated biological and social history that had impacted his entire education to date.

Professors in my college classes clarified terms I was expected to use daily as a special educator such as "adaptations," "accommodations," and "modifications." Oftentimes throughout my career, I noticed that these terms were used interchangeably even by seasoned special educators. To clarify, accommodations and modifications were adaptations sometimes allowed when instructing or assessing SWD. Accommodations signaled external adaptations such as extended time when taking tests or an alternative location in which to take them. Modifications meant changes in the actual format, such as having questions read aloud or having answers recorded by a scribe rather than writing them. These were useful mechanisms to ensure SWD receive what they needed. That said, in my experience, schools tended to use the same modifications (extended time, alternative place) for all students with an IEP while minimizing modifications.

In college, we practiced writing IEP goals, and because of Iris and Jayson's modeling within the department, mine were accepted first time around while the majority of my peers had theirs returned to be more quantifiable and formulaic. What I came to notice at my school was the relationship between IEPs and compliance. External monitoring teams arrived to randomly pick through filing cabinets and pluck out a few samples to be analyzed. When this process occurred, Iris wanted every "t" crossed and "i" dotted to ensure that the department would pass with flying colors and therefore be left alone for a while. I cannot blame her for this, as tedious as it was to get all papers in order. Yet through this process, I began to see IEPs as symbolic representation of a child to the point of fetishization. The child may not have been to school for three weeks, but as long as the paperwork was in order and stored in the correct cabinet, the child was "present" for purposes of accounting.

I noticed early on in my career that parental-school relationships, despite being enshrined in law, were usually lopsided, strongly in favor of school, and often fragile. At parent-teacher conferences, it was more likely that parents of students who worked well in class showed up, as opposed to those with whom teachers wanted to have a conversation. I often saw a different side of students when their parents were present, and sought allies in their families, always being open to mutual contact. Following the leads of John and Jayson, I learned to begin a parent-teacher-child conversation by sharing two or three positive things about a student's work ethic and/or abilities ("She's organized, punctual, eager."), and then state the primary area of need that had to be worked upon ("And, she needs to really focus on her writing.").

One of the most interesting aspects of working with parents was to attend IEP meetings, usually the required "triennials" wherein full body of assessments had been given every three years to ascertain whether special education services were still needed. It was at these meetings—foregrounded within the law as places of communication—that I noticed blatant asymmetrical power relations at play. The parent was often a mother of color, surrounded by an "evaluation team" comprising of educational evaluator, school psychologist, social worker, and special education teacher, all of whom were usually white. Contrary to the intent of the law, all decisions had been previously decided about placement, type and frequency of service, before conversing with the parent. Each professional presented information before parent and student were asked to share thoughts or comment, and then all required forms were signed. I participated in dozens of these meetings, sometimes with a paraprofessional charged as being the Spanish interpreter. The meetings usually ran predictably smooth, unless the team had a heads up about a parent who wanted something specific for her child (e.g., a personal laptop, a one-on-one aide), a situation invariably characterized as "We're expecting a difficult mother."

At these meetings that I came to know the kids I was teaching through a different lens. While I understood kids primarily as learners in the classroom, this team viewed kids from what they called a "clinical evaluative" perspective. Parents were customarily told what intelligence quotient (IQ) their children possessed, oftentimes "low average" in the 1970s range of the bell curve. When I read the educational assessments based on batteries of tests administered to students pulled out of classes to complete them, I saw the results translated into approximate grade-level averages. Students who were 16 years of age, for example, may read on a third grade level and perform math on a fifth grade level. The likelihood as to why the discrepancy between age expectations and actual academic performance occurred could be cited from a range of reasons including auditory processing deficits, attention deficit disorders, minimal brain dysfunction, and so on. The overwhelming use of negative language—for example, deficit, disorder, and dysfunction—would lodge and linger in my ears. I knew these words were everyday language of professionals in schools, derived from the discipline of special education that I was studying at college. Yet, I also recall thinking how harsh these phrases seemed, signifying that a person was "less than," always primarily defined in deficit-based terms, emphasizing first what they did not have or could not do.

I had not even heard the term "learning disabilities" before I began teaching. In getting to know the kids I worked with, I came to see they had significant struggles in reading, writing, listening, speaking, calculation and conceptualization in math, attention, and general organization. Furthermore, they had any combination of strengths and weaknesses in these areas, but I wasn't quite sure as to *why*. Unofficial responses included "It's the sins of the fathers" (school secretary), "They have minimal brain damage" (Jayson), "They're really mildly retarded" (a colleague), "They're not retarded, they just have not been taught right yet" (a progressive colleague). At college, we learned the official definition of LD articulated in 1977 and stated within federal law:

> "Specific learning disability" means a disorder in one or more of the basic psychological processes involved in understanding or in using language, spoken or written, which may manifest itself in an imperfect ability to listen, speak, read, write, spell, or to do mathematical calculations. The term includes such conditions as perceptual handicaps, brain injury, minimal brain dysfunction, dyslexia, and developmental aphasia. The term does not include children who have learning disabilities which are primarily the result of visual, hearing, or motor handicaps, or mental retardation, or emotional disturbance, or of environmental, cultural, or economic disadvantage. (http://www.ldail.com)

The "imperfect ability" phrase always intrigued me, not knowing anyone with perfect abilities. Again, while well intended, the definition raised more questions than provided answers. I was struck by its attempt to sidestep the cultural contexts in which children are born and raised, particularly the effects of poverty. I also learned that *some* individuals who were once labeled mentally retarded (MR) now were located within the LD category. The establishment of LD category meant those so labeled fell within the "normal intelligence" range on the bell curve, that is, between quotients of 70 to 130. It appears that with the stroke of a legislative pen, mental retardation's upper parameter had been repositioned from 85 to 70, counting downward. To a novice special education teacher, all of this information seemed relatively contemporary and cutting edge. I'd been taught that LD had been "discovered" in the early 1960s, triggering a whole subset of evolving educational practices in response. We teachers of kids with LD, by far the largest growing group of SWD, were generally considered to be the next wave of specialists in the field.

And yet, I had difficulty in seeing a world separated into LD and non-LD people, or more broadly, the disabled and non-disabled. I was suspicious of such a notion that didn't make sense to me. That said, what I did appreciate about my education at Hunter College was its thoroughness in teaching methodologies for struggling students. Dr. Kate Garnett originated and built the LD program in which the components of reading, writing, and math were broken down into the most fundamental components to be analyzed that I immediately began to see where my student's current academic "breakdown" points were. Studying phonemic awareness, phonics, fluency, vocabulary, and comprehension revealed how complex the process of reading is, with each skill necessary to a large extent for success at the next level. Likewise, starting with the formation of letters, uniting and integrating visual, auditory, and kinesthetic elements of learning provided powerful insights into how some students need to be taught reading and writing in order to achieve academic success. Along with the technical aspects of writing—both script and cursive—more holistic ways were taught, too, such as "the writing process" that I then used immediately with my own kids. In addition, using game-like approaches to mathematics while providing manipulatives (blocks, paperclips, counters) and tools to learn such as partially blacked out multiplication tables allowed students to see patterns within mathematics and gain confidence in number sense. I grew to see that there was always a potential approach for every learner, and it was the responsibility of a special educator to find that correct approach. At the same time, many of the methods I was being taught struck me as simply good strategies for most kids—not just those labeled disabled.

Part of the LD program at Hunter was called the Learning Lab, a practitioner-based model involving actual children and youth with LD. Learning Lab was actually a seminar consisting of approximately 14 students who were all assigned tutee with LD. Twice a week, graduate students taught their tutees for a 75-minute session. On Thursdays, a professor supervised the teaching, pulling up alongside students on rolling stool while we all instructed our tutees. When the tutees left, our seminar was held, focusing upon what skills we were teaching and how. Over the course of a year, we came to know not only our own tutee in great depth, but also those of all seminar peers. The collective weekly dialogue concentrated on our own ongoing successes—both partial and full—and struggles in the process of teaching provided the foundations in customizing our instruction one-on-one while allowing us to have an ever-growing pedagogical toolkit. At age 23, my tutee, Eric, was the eldest in the group, with mild cerebral palsy and mild intellectual impairment. He was only a couple of years older than some young adults in my classes, as the law allowed SWD to stay in school until age 21. Eric was a good match as I was equally interested in teaching kids and adults. Some years later, when John was a principal, he hired Eric as a school aide, setting him on his path to a successful career. Eric and I are friends to this day; he is one of the nicest people I have ever known.

After five years of studying at Hunter, I had completed my master's program, and taken self-elected additional classes in Spanish to better understand my students, communicate with their families, and travel in the Americas. On graduating, I was given an award for academic excellence in special education. My mother and cousin Jacqueline flew over from the United Kingdom and by chance, when students were milling around before graduation, we three ended up chatting for a considerable time with college president Paul LeClerc (who went on to be Chief Executive Officer of New York Public Library). He shared with us that special education was one of his favorite programs.

I was very happy that day. The degree secured me permanent certification as a teacher of special education. That said, I immediately applied to another branch of CUNY, City College, located in Harlem, where I began a second masters in creative writing and literature. It was needed for me to become certified to teach English in high school, central to my plan of moving away from special education.

SOCIAL TIME

One of the most pleasurable things about being a teacher was spending social and/or conversational time with kids. I grew to incorporate interactive activities in my classes whenever possible as students usually proved active participants and I could better find out how they thought, expressed themselves, and generally made sense of the world. Once assigned work, students usually "got on with it," allowing me to visit each one and to assist each other if needed.

Having enjoyed school trips myself as a child, taking kids to places of interest appealed to me. The first school trip I ventured on was in conjunction with John when we took a group to see August Wilson's *Fences* (1986) on Broadway, starring James Earl Jones. When kids kept talking through the performance, I was initially horrified, and even further dismayed when constantly asking them to be quiet without the desired results. I had not realized this was their first ever trip to a theater, and learned they should have been better prepared by me in behavioral expectations along with some pre-teaching of the content they would see. The experience did not put me off and I discovered a great organization for kids to see live performances for a token $3 fee and regularly organized trips to see NYC's homegrown Alvin Ailey and The Dance Theater of Harlem along with various musical troupes from around the world. It was a cultural day out, kids were usually relaxed and well behaved, released from the bonds of school and being identified as "special education."

I found it amazing that the kids who lived in the five boroughs of New York City, even those in Manhattan, had not been to world-famous landmarks or renowned cultural institutions. We would enter the E subway line at 23rd Street and 8th Avenue, alight at 53rd Street to visit the Museum of Modern Art (MOMA), and students would ask, "Is this still Manhattan?" I thought, here we are in one of the world's major cities, the center of the art world, and kids don't know the treasures on their own doorstep because no one had yet introduced them. Some of my favorite memories involve trips to Radio City to see the Christmas Spectacular (no matter how tacky it was), The Museum of Natural History, The Metropolitan Museum, the Guggenheim, and the Frick Collection. At MOMA, I would bring them around Van Gogh's *Starry Night* and we'd discuss the colors and shapes. I'd tell them it was (then) worth about 50 million dollars and they'd fall over themselves laughing, telling me I was lying like crazy.

Sometimes, I'd justify a trip for a neighborhood walk, so we could see several sites at once such as the Museum of the American Indian, Battery Park, and the Statue of Liberty in lower Manhattan. When once assigned to teach a class by the whimsical name of "Visual Merchandising" (as the special education department's need to parallel teaching with general education offerings), I took the kids up and down 5th Avenue to look at displays in store windows while we also took in the Christmas Tree at Rockefeller Center and St. Patrick's Cathedral. During that trip, while observing the sumptuously decorated windows in the high-class department store Saks Fifth Avenue, on the spur of the moment I said, "Let's go inside and see how they do their displays." By then I wasn't as naïve as when I began my career, and told my eight or nine students to stick close by me at all times. As soon as we went through the door as a white man with a line of black and brown teenagers behind, security guards zeroed in on us. I smiled at them and began to point out to students various types of displays in a "teacherly" voice as we snaked through the store. At the time, I thought, *This is our right to be here*, despite signals otherwise from store staff. Later that night, I wondered if I had inadvertently made my students feel vulnerable and awkward, knowing they were unwanted in what I viewed as a public space.

An annual event in which all schools took part, The Circle of Champions, also provided an opportunity for a day out. It was hosted by George Washington High School at the northern part of Manhattan and served as an interschool sports competition for all students in special education departments in the borough. Every year, teachers and students alike put on shorts and a red and white T-shirt (sponsored by Colgate) before the long subway ride to the event. The host school was probably the only one in Manhattan with track, field, and bleachers, and the staff there put in an enormous amount of work to make the day a success. Students competed with each other in all types of events, and we all spent the day cheering on our team and sharing food. The first time I rolled up the sleeves on my T-shirt, students were surprised that I had a tattoo. One asked, "Mr. Connor, did you get that done in jail?" (It was long before the now-ubiquitous presence of tattoos, and revealed kids' associations with ink and incarceration.) One year, after the Circle of Champions had ended, staff and students were on the subway ride returning to school. The weather was hot, and the subway stuffy, full of people as we passed through Harlem, all standing, hanging onto straps. Staff had carried boxed lunches up for kids, along with drinks, and I was returning with the extras. Roberta, a challenging student with whom I had a fairly good relationship shouted irritably:

"Give me something to drink."

I handed her all I had left, a carton of milk.

"What else do you say?" I asked, prompting Roberta to be polite.

She pulled the carton, but I did not let go, slightly annoyed at her public display of bad manners. Instead of saying "please," she then yanked the carton so hard that it came apart, showering all nearby passengers with the contents.

I stood frozen, mouth hanging open, as I looked into black faces dripping with milk. For a moment it seemed like time was standing still. But it wasn't. I could see the drip-drip-drip of milk from a silent row of chins. After what seemed like a lifetime, my colleague Suzanne urged, "Say something! Do something!"

"I am so sorry," I heard myself say repeatedly, reaching for napkins and passing them out. Stony faced, the passengers wiped their faces. I saw Roberta from the corner of my eye slip away and open the door to the subway next car, leaving me to clean up the mess.

Although she was as regular as clockwork with attendance, Roberta did not come in for 3 days after this incident, deliberately steering clear of me. A truly tough cookie, she was often mean to students and insulting to teachers who dreaded having her in class. I had noticed Roberta only wore two nondescript sweatshirts, alternating them throughout the year, regardless of changes in the weather, suggesting that she washed one of them every night. Once, after a spate of acting out in my class and other teachers', I pulled her aside for a private conversation asking why she was behaving that way. It was then that this hard-boiled, street-smart kid broke down and told me her mother had cancer of the liver, and she was scared of her dying. Not long afterwards, Roberta left a note on my desk saying "God Bless you, Mr. Connor" and never came back to school.

THE SPECIAL EDUCATION DEPARTMENT

I may have just been lucky but I really liked working with almost all of my colleagues within the special education department. There existed a great deal of camaraderie, and I felt almost all of the teachers were very pro-child, truly wanting to help kids. A few exceptions existed, as special education tended to be a periodic repository into which Principal Bailey placed ineffective general education teachers and/or others with no other place to go. One such man originally taught how to be a furrier a million years ago, and now waited out the days until his pension, teaching in a perfunctory manner and referring to kids as "cucarachas." Mr. Bailey had told me to get out of special education while I could. He had always remained aloof and indifferent, never entering my class once, but periodically calling Iris to complain about my choice of clothes, such as a red shirt that looked insufficiently ironed. I didn't want to lose my job, so invested in some new white shirts and began sending them to be professionally laundered and pressed.

As mentioned earlier, the special education department was somewhat of a world unto itself. We had our own department meetings, events, middle and end of year celebrations. I noticed that general education and special education teachers tended to sit with their respective groups in the school cafeteria. It was here that I overheard jokes made frequently by general educators about special educators also *being* "special ed" (with special educators sometimes self-deprecatingly doing the same), implying slowness, stupidity, or general incompetence. Such times made me feel I was being *positioned* by the culture at large, somehow manifest in structures and systems, as inferior to general educators. Deep down, I knew I was as accomplished and as capable as they were, but the special education label stuck to teachers just as much as it did to students.

Truth be told, I knew little about general education. A few kids were mainstreamed, but the majority of 140 or so students in the special education department were our responsibility in a school of 2,200. Faculty cared for the kids, and the staff members were more diverse than in many other departments with a mix of African American, Caribbean, Latino/a, Chinese American, white, and gay faculty. I was fortunate enough to be able to discuss any issues about race that either arose spontaneously in classroom conversation, or was featured in the curriculum, with my partner John, or colleagues such as Tom, Jayson, and Suzanne. Yet there was an obvious social class divide in the world of schools that seemed to be taken for granted, with many educational professionals perceiving that kids came from deficit-based families and/or backgrounds. I wasn't sure how to best think this through, as I did not want to be prejudicial toward people because of their social background. At the same time, I had come to know America as a land of extremes when it came to wealth, with some of the countries' poorest districts being in New York City—parts of Harlem, Bedford Stuyvesant, and the South Bronx—where many of our kids lived.

Expectations for finishing school waned with each grade. When I taught a 12th grade class, it had half the number of students in a ninth grade class. Again, this pattern seemed to be recognized as part of the status quo. Over the years, my varying responsibilities in the department included being the Intake Coordinator for ninth graders and being the Transition Coordinator to help graduating students. Between 9th and 12th grade, I saw many students become disengaged, disenchanted, drop out, begin full-time work in minimum paying jobs, fall pregnant and go to a specialized facility, or move back to their zone school to cut down travel time. One of the largest groups to not complete high school were boys labeled ED. During one year, when the department had quite a few, and they were disrupting classes, boys labeled ED were programmed together only to be taught by male teachers. I had them for a double period of art every day. In all, 90 minutes with 15 boys identified as ED, and a paraprofessional to assist. It was one of the most challenging classes I have ever had. That hour and a half took so much energy that I was wiped out at the end of most classes. All it took was one kid to have a bad day and a domino effect would occur. The kids claimed to like their notoriety, enjoying being known as "*The* bad class" in the special education department. Although we taught and managed them for a year, ostensibly for the greater good of all teachers and classes to function, I felt that the arrangement never really addressed the learning and social issues of this group, and allowed them to revel in their label, ironically reinforcing it.

As a department, faculty always looked out for each other's safety as teachers were often put in precarious positions at any time. In regard to breaking up a fight, teachers were damned if they did and damned if they didn't. One colleague was removed in handcuffs after separating a fight between two girls, as one alleged that he touched her breast. He was cleared, but it seemed a humiliating example of a no-win situation. When two kids snapped and went for a full fight, faculty usually tried to separate them. If kids involved liked and trusted you, they were more inclined to engage with you in attempts to defuse the situation. Conversely, if the kids involved were unknown, they would be far less likely to care about any efforts to stop them. I had my share of breaking up fights, dreading it, but intervening anyway as the alternative of standing by was intolerable. The best option, I learned, was to develop a honed sense and head off any potential friction between students by using a variety of methods (talking them "down," physically separating them, sending one out of the room, etc.). John, then an assistant principal of special education in another school, separated a fight only to have his back injured. Subsequently, the painful and unexpected twist to his spine resulted in wearing a surgical corset for six months, inhibiting some travel plans, and managing a lifetime of periodic physical therapy. After witnessing the consequences of his well-meaning intervention, I no longer broke up fights, and sought school safety officers (amid taunts from students, "Look at the teacher! He's too scared to jump in!'). As I said, you're damned if you do, and you're damned if you don't. All I knew was I had one back and did not want to risk it anymore.

Once a student set fire to the notice board in the hallway (it was not Robert who had torched his family's apartment). As the flames leaped up the wall, Tom ran along the hallway knocking on everyone's door, urging them to evacuate immediately. Instead, calmness descended upon me and I walked to the fire extinguisher on a nearby wall, removed the pin, pointed at the fire, and sprayed as if I did it every day of my life. The blaze was under control in seconds with kids laughing and yelling, "Look at Fireman Connor!" Thankfully, the annual mandated hour-long fire drill training that made faculty yawn had finally come in useful.

Around the same time, five years into teaching, Iris had nominated me for an award as an outstanding special educator, jointly sponsored by the local branch of the Council for Exceptional Children (CEC) and the NYC Board of Education. I was both humbled and honored by this gesture, attending a ceremony at the Board's headquarters where I was presented, along with approximately 30 other people from around the city, with a certificate and had my photograph taken with the local CEC chapter leader (whispering under her breath, "How nice it is to have the Irish represented"). By chance, not long afterwards, Joanna Coles, an old college friend from the United

Kingdom who was a reporter for *The Guardian* newspaper told me she was heading a team coming to New York for a series of feature stories about life here. Along with profiling the allegedly hottest nightclub at the time (Tabu) and chronicling an undercover night spent in a homeless shelter, she wanted to do a piece on public education. Could I help her out by arranging a visit to the school where I worked? I was given the blessing of the new principal Charlie Bonnici (the pleasant, round-faced man who once asked me questions about how I'd teach *To Kill a Mockingbird*), and received clearance from the superintendent's office. Joanna came with a photographer, shadowing me for half-a-day, talking to kids, teachers, and the principal.

The article came out a few weeks later on *The Guardian's* front page called "A tough place downtown: Joanna Coles spends a day with Manhattan's Teacher of the Year." It had a photograph of me engaging with a student called Ronald (who sometimes came to school wearing stiletto heels) as he drew a severed head. The text itself praised me highly but painted the school in a less favorable manner, emphasizing the poverty of kids' backgrounds and selectively citing a bitingly sarcastic poem on my wall by Samantha, one of my students, called "Ain't it Great to be Black?" I had conflicting feelings. It was a thrill to have 15 seconds of fame (seriously, how many teachers do?), but I truly felt my local CEC award had been grossly exaggerated and I knew I was nowhere near the best teacher in Manhattan. Moreover, I agreed with the principal's assessment when he told me I looked good and the school looked bad. In a strange way, I felt as if I'd unwittingly betrayed the school. As a result, I didn't share the article with many people, and it wasn't circulated to peers. My family was nonetheless proud that I was featured in a newspaper, Joanna eventually went on to become star of the TV series *Project Runway* and editor of *Cosmopolitan*, and I became wary of the press.

Meanwhile, I was happy to represent the special education department within the school and also within the district at the Office of the Superintendent of Manhattan High Schools. At our school, my colleague Luke and I would occasionally present methods and strategies for SWD to general education faculty although, again, I simply viewed much of what we shared as good teaching. I joined the school-wide Human Immunodeficiency Virus (HIV) Awareness Committee as I thought little was being done to educate teenagers. Although it was a committee mandated by the superintendent, the school appointed administrator actually seemed embarrassed that we had to do this and, in my opinion, did not treat it seriously. Subsequently, I self-nominated as secretary, recording the minutes, formalizing the process, and urging an action plan that included awareness of all faculty members.

Over the years, I had been sent to the Office of the Superintendent to represent the department on a number of district-wide committees and professional development projects. Engaged in this work, I had come to know some of the superintendent's special education unit staff quite well (plus, it was always good to see Jayson in his new role). Based upon my own desire to keep learning, my interest in education had now encompassed "in-service" professional development within special and general education. I was concerned with questions of how do teachers keep themselves fresh, up to date with changes, interested in what they do? What opportunities do they have for professional growth? And, who is responsible for providing it?

THE BEGINNINGS OF INCLUSIVE EDUCATION

If there ever was (and arguably still is) a case for the continued professional growth of all teachers, it is inclusive education. By the late 1980s, the federal government had grown concerned about high costs and low outcomes of special education, particularly for high incidence or "mild disabilities"—such as learning disability, emotional disturbance, intellectual disability, and speech and language. My high school was one of the first to be selected by the Board of Education to do this. Luke and I were both assigned two general educators teaching English as a Second Language (ESL) to students for one period a day. Told that I was purposefully assigned to one veteran teacher because he had recently been rated as unsatisfactory, part of my placement was to help get him back on his feet to a satisfactory level. To state the obvious, the man was not happy to share his class. The second teacher I had been assigned was a larger than life woman, in possession of booming voice, who bellowed a wholehearted welcome with an I-am-open-to-learning-what-we-can-from-each-other attitude. There was no preparation, no training, except to say it was a new initiative from the Board and we had to do it.

At first, I was highly anxious. I'd never been in an American general education classroom before and was used to teaching kids who struggled academically. The special education stigma, as previously noted, applied to teachers, too. Would I be good enough? Would my co-teacher see me as an equal? Would the general education kids be able to tell what I didn't know? The myths and fears that initially hung over me like a heavy cloud soon evaporated and, as it turned out, from the very start I enjoyed working in general education classes. Surprisingly, in my experience I found there were no major differences between students categorized as general or special, and oftentimes, there were none. Left to ourselves, having no formal guidance and four other classes to plan for and teach daily, all teachers involved agreed to simply share the instruction by alternating weeks, and equally dividing all work needing to be graded. In addition, we set aside time for a weekly meeting to review kids' progress, discuss ideas how best to teach the curriculum, and develop appropriate materials.

"Your handwriting is *soooooooo muuuuuuch* neater than mine," boomed the larger than life teacher from the back of the room when I stood at the chalkboard. I sensed a potential subliminal rivalry of which I made a mental note, including how to best convey reassurances that I didn't envision team teaching as a competition. The other (unsatisfactorily rated) colleague struck me as there-but-not-there when he taught, without much presence and with little effort. As he spoke, kids would ignore him and talk to each other, leaving me conflicted on the sidelines. I was pained to see this but also annoyed because when it came my turn to teach it always felt an uphill task trying to engage tuned-out and resentful students, who became borderline hostile when instructed to work. Subsequently, more than usual I resorted to raising my voice and reading the riot act, yet it all seemed strained and lopsided when little or no effort was coming from my colleague. Still, he was heartened to have his load lessened and to see "what worked" in my classrooms so he could utilize them in his other sections. Not ideal arrangements, but we all made them work the best we could.

The following semester, Luke and I were assigned two different colleagues, still working with teachers of ESL students. Of my two, the first was initially hard to read, as if she were suspicious of intentions behind the Board's initiative and the perceived intrusion of special education. The second was a highly personable Indian woman possessing a great rapport with students, who was very much open to working with me. Knowing no other way to collaborate, we continued the alternative week teaching plan that at least helped with a 50-50 presence at the front of the room. Having equal status and credibility with my colleague and all students was important to me. Not long into our partnership, I was facilitating a whole class discussion and the topic of NYC police came up. Students had differing perspectives, and as I was summarily comparing and contrasting them, my suspicious colleague jumped in with urgency and said, "You can't tell them to go to the police if they need help!" Now less naïve than when I started teaching, I realized this, and was not unquestioning of how some police officers treated the poor, people of color, and immigrants. While initially taken aback in the moment, this comment endeared me to my colleague, and I assured her I knew full well her concern. In our subsequent conversations, I found out she was a socialist in disposition and active in immigrant workers' rights, which made me like her even more.

At the year's end, our special education department hosted a Thank You Breakfast for all general educators who taught "our" students. The team teachers came, as did those mainstreamed students. Early in my career, once I realized what mainstreaming was, I advocated on behalf of many students to go into general education classes for part of their instruction. It was a bittersweet phenomenon as I hated "losing" those students from my own classes but knew they would be happier and benefit more from being with non-disabled peers and the general education curriculum in a content area they loved. Part of me always felt I was pushing them out of a comfortable nest. Some needed persuading (read: encouragement and confidence building) whereas others were raring to go and took flight in ways they never would have had they stayed in special education classes.

In regard to general and special education teaching collaborations that had been thrust upon us, I thought we did "okay." At the same time, team teaching was an opportunity we did not exploit enough. Our good faith attempts were made without much vision. We reacted to being told we had to do it without sufficiently knowing why or how. One day, with little notice, team teachers were informed we were all going to a citywide meeting. Taken by chartered mini-bus across town to another high school, we were shepherded into an auditorium filled with teachers from other schools across the city. Much to our horror, we were directed on stage to chairs that faced the audience. Several higher uppers from the Board shared information about the "LRE initiative" and then those of us on stage were all asked to say some words about our experience. No warning. No preparation. No organization. Despite a rush of anxiety, I managed to get through the task, noting that faces in the audience ranged from looking bored or indifferent to impatient and angry. After the event, on the way back to school, I asked myself "What was *that*?" with distinct aftertaste in my mouth of somehow feeling used.

It seemed as if team teaching and the integration of SWD into general education classes was a red hot potato. I began to notice feature articles in the United Federation of Teachers (UFT) newspaper that strove to be neutral, yet subtly signaled a sense of "beware" in case students were denied services and/or teachers prevented from the provision of full and contractually guaranteed programs. Mainstream newspaper articles about inclusive education varied in focus such as citing the cost of special education or controversial test cases of disabled children whose parents sought their inclusion in general education as preferable to a special education placement:

"This could be the end of special ed.," said Iris.

"At least as we know it," observed a colleague.

"That'll never happen. There will always be a special ed.," replied another.

"That's right," said yet another, "Who's going to put up with all of the stuff that we do? General ed. teachers aren't. They have enough to do."

"Without special ed., general ed. can't function," a fourth teacher chimed in.

Although I am paraphrasing responses heard on several occasions, I found myself not sharing the general reticence, a sense of doom-and-gloom, felt by a large proportion of special educators. Instead, I wondered, why the resistance toward including "our" kids? Whenever I talked to students in the department, the majority wanted to be in general education classes.

So much of what I saw in special education was not specialized at all; it was simply teaching the same thing to smaller classes. Only a few teachers in the department customized instruction as was assumed by the profession and superficially reflected in the institutional IEP. In all of this, I saw kids labeled disabled getting the short end of the stick in terms of academics and social opportunities with peers. Additionally, I was deeply aware of the racial fault lines of special education. I could tell that although it was ostensibly benevolent, special education served to separate and contain a portion of society based upon their "disability" as if that, in and of itself, were a justifiable reason.

So, while I was studying for my second master's degree that was needed for certification to be a general educator (one who would be welcoming of SWD in class), an opportunity presented itself. For some time, I had been participating in a district-wide committee designing and providing professional development for special educators throughout Manhattan high schools, when a district-office position became available as a full-time staff developer. Given that I had been trying to make sense of special and inclusive education for several years now, I decided I would take this job if I could provide an emphasis on helping teachers, administrators, and parents better understand and create inclusive classrooms. I knew I would really miss the kids. At the same time, I thought if I could impact more educators' thinking in clarifying *why* to be more inclusive along with *how* to do it, I would have the potential for helping shape changes in education that I sought to see.

After seven years of high school teaching, I left the school where I began, becoming assigned to the Office of the Superintendent of Manhattan High Schools. It seemed like déjà vu as once again I was filled with perpetually shifting amounts of eagerness and anxiety, unsure of what the future would hold.

COMMENTARY

Teaching and Learning in Schools and Universities

In looking back to the first years of my career in special education and contemplating what I came to know about teachers and learning in school and universities, I am reminded of how painful it was to enter the profession. I can count on my fingers how many times in life I have wept from "sheer frustration," and most of them occurred during the first three weeks of teaching. I found the experience to be very destabilizing and somewhat traumatizing, leading me, no doubt to look, as Tom described, the proverbial "deer caught in the deadlights." I have often wondered, had I not been "trying out" the profession of teaching, had I instead been a sure-fire educator from the get go who had studied education for years before entering the profession, completing a robust program that included student teaching with a seasoned mentor, how different might things have been? The question is pertinent to teacher education because teacher shortages in special education led to my being a novice who was "rubber stamped" and expedited to teach, contingent upon achieving the required minimum number of 12 college credits.

Just as there was a shortage of special educators in 1987, there is a scarcity *now*. For over three decades, the numbers of new teachers leaving the public school system within the first five years has remained steady at approximately 50 percent (Ingersol & Smith, 2003), with twice as many special than general educators exiting, in part due to "long hours, [and] crushing paperwork" (Hale, 2015, para 1). These shocking statistics merit an honest look as to why a profession functions with half of its ranks in a revolving door, leaving those invested for more than five years to determine how best to manage schools, factoring in the predictable exit rate of the peers they welcome into their schools. Being a teacher can be overwhelming. There's so many things to learn and do, so many rules and regulations, so many students, and so many distractions from the very act of teaching. To compound feelings of overwhelmedness, the discovery of schools being both spatially and racially divided by dis/ability made me question how much schools both mirror and shape society, that is, to what degree does it reinforce the status quo or strive to grow in progressive ways? After all, it is schools that have been the litmus test of institutions when society responded to calls for both racial integration in the 1950s and the inclusion of citizens with disabilities in the 1980s.

In returning to the topic of how to best prepare teachers, my own case—not untypical at the time—was very much a matter of sink or swim. While I agree that nothing prepares us for a task more than experience itself, the situation felt like an extreme (even desperate measure) to get teachers in front of classes. The in-joke was that the Board would hire you if you had a pulse. It pains me to think that the United States, symbolized by New York State, did not systematically invest in and sustain its teaching force, along with risking the loss of those teachers it initially attracted. How much has that changed since then? The answer is "somewhat," although it is still far from enough. The legislation of No Child Left Behind (2001) strove to ensure that all teachers are "highly qualified," although that phrase is defined by each state. In addition, organizations such as Teach for America (TFA) and The Teaching Fellows (TF) initiative of New York City were conceived in response to the ongoing dilemma of teacher shortages, including in special education. These organizations recruit people who have one summer's training consisting of two college classes, some access to kids in summer school, and professional development by the Department of Education (having changed the name from "the Board," in restructuring more than a decade ago). With two months' preparation, these people commit to becoming teachers for a minimum of two years.

Having now managed these programs at the university level for over a decade, I can see their use, and still prepare college instructors for when "the rubber meets the road" in those notorious first three weeks where many graduate students enter classes swollen-eyed from crying. Some are in disbelief at what they're seeing or what they've been told to do, and despite our strong assurances that "It gets better," several quit around this time. I will take up the pros and cons of these programs later in this book, but for now, I only wish to call attention the local education authority's response to getting underprepared people into classes with some of the most vulnerable *and* challenging students in the neediest of districts. Surely, incentivizing, preparing teachers for the long run, and supporting them throughout their careers is a better way to invest?

I was well aware of being on the cusp of failing throughout my first three weeks in teaching, and would undoubtedly have done so were it not for the help of Jayson, John, Tom, and Iris. That they "saved me," indicated a level of genuine care they felt for, and responsibility toward, their shared profession. Indeed, seasoned teachers and administrators were the reason why many of us stayed in the profession. Initially surprised to see, there were no formal mentoring models, I was pleased when the UFT developed one six months after I began. Jayson became appointed to discuss "the business" of teaching and learning for 40 minutes a day. By then I was feeling much more at ease in learning the ropes, and could tap into the camaraderie that was a feature of the special education department, somewhat of an anomaly in a school of over 2,000 students and multiple departments.

What I imagined teaching to be and what teaching was actually like, were two entirely different things. I assumed students would be naturally interested in whatever I taught, but learned immediately that I had to work to gain and maintain their attention. There seemed an awful lot of "behind the scenes" thinking that had to be done first without any guarantee that it would work. The format of the lesson plan provided a helpful framework with which to begin, yet the plan also seemed restrictive if the lesson took on life organically. It was always a dilemma whether to go with the flow of genuine interest, partly shaped and led by students, or redirect conversation back to the original lesson's script. With time, it became easier to make that judgment call, balancing the formally identified knowledge with the interests and contributions of kids.

Although it was years before I would be introduced to the ideas of Paolo Freire (1970), ironically by a student I taught a graduate class, when I did they became associated with what I always refer to as "Evie's comment." In my first semester of teaching, a 16-year-old girl who witnessed me trying hard also saw I wasn't hitting the mark, and offered advice in a way that invited me to consider changing how I taught. Evie's request that I teach more like Mr. Schwartz, an educator adept at integrating all kinds of interactive activities that centered students in the process of learning, resonated with me. In later years, I came to know what I was originally doing as a novice teacher—utilizing what Freire termed "the banking model." This meant I believed that the teacher held the currency of knowledge and had that responsibility to place it within students, imagined to be somewhat empty containers waiting to be filled. However, Evie and her peers' preferred mode of learning that proved more effective in terms of interest, engagement, and assessment was far more participatory and counted on students entering the dialogue to share connections they made and interpretations about what they were learning. It wasn't until my doctoral studies that I became familiar with the framework of Cultural-Historical Activity theory (Stetsenko, 2002) and its focus upon analyzing what people think and feel when engaged in a specific activity. By then, I had come to understand learning to be an engagement between teacher and student based upon what the teacher had elected to teach while relating it to what the student already knew and/or wanted to know. Whereas the banking system of education assumed a level of detachment viewed as human transactions, the critical pedagogy of Freire sought interactions to connect with who students actually were, their thoughts about the world and their place within in, and how to be critical with view to creating change. While admittedly quite a large theoretical leap, Evie's comment helped me take my first step to create a critical consciousness about what it meant to teach. Teaching meant connecting with students, through respecting and integrating their knowledge and interests into the content of teaching.

One of the many areas in which I did not feel prepared to teach was reading. I had a lot of teenage students who read on third to fifth grade levels. They disliked reading in general, and I learned quickly never to require students to read out loud because it was painful and publicly humiliating. There was no direct reading support, no one-on-one, and exacerbated by years of resistance, it saddened me that many underdeveloped readers exhibited no desire to practice although I understood it as part of human nature to not wish to constantly do what we're bad at.

As mentioned, a few years into teaching and into the LD content of my master's program, I was introduced to *Recipe for Reading* by Nina Traub (1977) a program that narrowed down how to form letters, say them individually, and combine them in consonant-vowel-consonant combinations and build skills from there. When I returned years later to Hunter and taught as an adjunct, the program had by then also introduced Wilson Reading System (Wilson, 1996) which meticulously broke language down to patterns and levels, leaving no stone unturned in the teaching of language. While variously perceived of as tedious, arduous, thorough, time-consuming, or a combination of all, the Wilson approach methodically dissects, teaches, and builds knowledge on practice of the English language. This meticulous approach works for many struggling children, teenagers, and adults. I have seen its use grow in schools to help kids with dyslexia, but it is not used widely enough. This focus on the sounds of letters and structures of words was missing from the curriculum in my formative years as an educator and, in retrospect, I wish I had of known about these approaches from the beginning.

In terms of the bigger picture of high school knowledge, the whole notion of a parallel curriculum adapted from general education intrigued me. Once secured, we pared the general education curriculum down to specified knowledge and identified skills that kids were expected to demonstrate. Paralleling curriculum was a strange idea, and felt as if the general education was being diluted and slowed down, although it was taboo to use those terms. Instead, a certain expectation was being placed upon special educators to use their expertise and create customized versions of curricula for their classes. (Getting general education teachers and administrators to share their texts was often a chore, feeling as if we were trying to pilfer someone else's store). The parallel curriculum was such a commonplace phenomenon that I became employed by the Board to do overtime in developing and editing parallel courses that were eventually distributed citywide.

A concept that I also became aware of early in my career was the official and hidden curriculum (Glossary of Education, 2014). The official curriculum was given to us in terms of topics and areas to study, set texts, and other sources, designed to teach certain knowledge and certain skills and tacitly uphold a certain reality. In contrast, the hidden curriculum included knowledge, skills, and expectations of what was not explicitly taught but rather tacitly conveyed and reinforced in multiple instances. This implicit knowledge pertained to one's "position" in society in regard to social class, race, ethnicity, nationality, sexual orientation, gender, and so on. I linked the unofficial curriculum to my initial fears of becoming "part of the institution," a heightened anxiety (part punk, part hippy in origin) about inadvertently reinforcing unequal power dynamics that reinforced hierarchies. The incident with Kofi in my Global Studies class had shaken me. I felt as if the problem of historical racism had been brushed under the carpet in the interest of maintaining classroom control, yet ironically it created an interest in *not* excluding and ignoring race, although that seemed the easiest, safest, and overall preferred way to go. Years later, as a teacher coach, I observed an experienced white educator teach slavery to a classroom largely of teenagers of color. Her emphasis was on an economic system, presented as a matter-of-fact way. She did a nice job with the facts, names and numbers that could possibly come up on state tests, but I left wondering about what was not said—the unofficial curriculum—including the emotional impact, available visceral images unused, the devastating phenomenon of commonplace inhuman cruelty, and slavery's impact upon contemporary society. I have often struggled to think through what it means to be a white teacher to kids of color in terms of explicitly acknowledging that it's still very much "a white world," as John would say, another concept within the hidden curriculum.

College learning was also complicit in maintaining an unofficial curriculum. In almost all examples of SWD presented to me in special education classes (case studies, research cited, video clips, etc.), all were white. This jarred with my daily reality, and would eventually lead me to the topic of my dissertation, life at the intersection of learning disability, race, and social class for urban students of color. There was also a clash of realities between some professors and students. In an educational foundations class during my second semester, I became frustrated and irritated when a longtime professor was not—in my assessment—teaching us properly. The class was completely devoid of meaningful, substantial content, with the professor requiring 25 of us to sit in a circle and bring up work-related topics we wanted to talk about. However, when we did, he would dismiss them and change the subject to anything *he* wanted to talk about. Enduring weeks of this behavior with other rookie teachers who had travelled to take this mandated class after a long and arduous day at work, learning neither content nor technique, I was fed up. The final straw came when a first-year peer who was earnestly struggling in class behavior asked what he should do when kids began throwing chairs across the room, and the professor told him surely he was exaggerating. Like clockwork the professor then switched to talk about Cher's dress at the recent Academy Awards. Disgruntled and in disbelief, I began to whisper in conversation with a peer, sitting part way across the room. The professor then stopped the class and said to me:

"Can you stop having a conversation? It's a distraction."

I replied, to this day not knowing fully why, with:

"We're not. You're just being paranoid."

Immediately angered and flushing bright red, he stood up and marched wordlessly out of the room, despite being in mid-class.

I realized what I had said served as an unexpected attack of sorts. I was angry. I had no respect for the professor due to his unwillingness to engage first-year teachers whose current and sometimes harsh realities he summarily discarded and steered the conversation to self-indulgent pablum (admittedly, were we not in an education class, I would have been happy to chat about Cher's Bob Mackie creation at the Oscars). The class was temporarily in shock, too, myself included. Some peers came up to me and shared they were glad I said what I did because it was "a bullshit class" and "a waste of time." Others were annoyed and told me I'd been rude to the professor. I hadn't meant to openly insult him, close the class down, and appear (what I hoped was uncharacteristically) mean in public. But it was an emotionally charged year and I thought: *Here we are, trying to be teachers and get through each day. This is a class we're required to take and pay for with our hard earned money. The professor is getting paid a good salary and is teaching us nothing. He is not doing his job and we deserve better than this.* My only regret was the reason for my discontent had not been explicitly and constructively stated. In brief, the professor did return to class the following week and acted as if nothing had happened. Classes took on somewhat of a more focused turn, although he never addressed me directly again.

I share this story that newly emerged during my analysis of the official and the unofficial curriculum because I found, roughly estimating, that only about half of my graduate classes were relevant to my daily job of teaching. The courses seemed to have so much arbitrary "stuffing" that detracted from a coherent program. Above all, I valued learning methods that would work with children who had specific learning challenges. I also valued learning about the types of disabilities, theories about why they existed, and what could be done to support kids and their families. Educational Foundations was the department in which the offending professor was housed. As an academic institution, I would come to find out in later years, that educational foundations programs were charged with either dominating teacher education programs or weighing in with unequal influence within the degree's curricula (Steiner & Rozen, 2004). My interest in teacher education's curriculum, where it comes from, which knowledge and skills "get in" and emphasized, and which knowledge and skills are omitted and discounted, and the degree of practitioner-based focused started, in part, with the neglectful professor incident.

Educational Laws and Their Impact

I underestimated knowing about special education laws when I began as a teacher, finding them somewhat interesting but not necessarily directly connected to my daily practices. I did, however, find them frequently invoked at IEP meetings. Taken together, the six elements of Public Law 94-142 manifested themselves this way: (1) A Free and Appropriate Public Education (FAPE)—all kids with disabilities had a right to enter school and an assured place; (2) The LRE usually meant special education, once in, it was never out; (3) guaranteed Due Process meant there was a lot of paperwork, timelines, and stress to ensure compliance was achieved; (4) parental participation was sought pro-forma, and signatures were needed, without much, if any, authentic parental input; (5) nondiscriminatory identification and evaluation was implemented, although value-free assessments seemed impossible; (6) an IEP existed for each student and was revisited every semester to update. The professionals coordinating at the center of all proceedings were employed due to the law. Because they were expected to evaluate, document, and manage kids with disabilities, these professionals seemed to be perpetually entrenched within the limited discourse of special education as a field of study (derived from science, medicine, psychology), legal phraseology within federal law, and local educational policies.

Special education was often perceived as a huge and constantly growing bureaucracy by general educators and special educators alike, yet with that image came the heft of the law on its side. Things had to be "done right" or there could be legal implications for noncompliance or "wrong" decisions. Yet, as I have written elsewhere (Connor, 2012b) core concepts within the law were open to interpretation, including whether a student met the criteria for a disability, the placement of the student in the right environment, the degree to which parents were consulted with and listened to, the identification tools used, and the accuracy of how all elements within the IEP were integrated and implemented. All of the personnel, placements, and procedures played a significant role in special education being perceived as a separate entity that materialized in its own separate place from general education. It seemed to me that inadvertently, the end to exclusion from education now clearly stated in law had resulted in children and youth with disabilities getting in the door of the school, but only so far to designated spaces in the building. Special education departments, floors, and rooms were notoriously placed as an afterthought in the least desirable places such as basements, top floors, and distant hallways (I saw this repeatedly as I began to visit more schools over time).

There was definitely a stigma associated with special education. As Goffman theorized in his landmark work *Stigma: Notes on the Management of Spoiled Identity* (1963), disabled people were historically recognized as a cause of fear and anxiety in non-disabled members of the population. Although fashion industries had not tucked the special education department away like a mad woman in the attic, it was, in part, on an undesirable floor shared with the student cafeteria. The department had not existed for long and it was openly spoken of that Mr. Bailey would rather special education not be there, typical of principals during its establishment within each school and subsequent expansion. Interestingly, special education faculty almost always kept company with other special education faculty even when eating, a sign of insularity that reminded me of Beverly Tatum's (1993) best-seller on racial politics, *Why Are All of the Black Kids* [or apparently, special educators] *Sitting Together in the Cafeteria?* I assumed it was a feeling of safety and comfort sought within outsider status.

That the kids definitely felt stigmatized about having a disability label and "being special education" was never talked about among professionals as a distinct topic. This may possibly be due to the fact that by then, the institution of Special Education had evolved into becoming highly clinicalized (Skrtic, 1991), suggesting that the reality of students and the professionals who served them were quite disparate. The special education system continued to often not make sense to me. For example, accommodations and modifications that were meant to be individualized had actually became standardized (time, place, etc.). The unofficial interpretation of special education believed by many people, including educators, was that despite claiming to be a beneficial provision of services for SWD, it was rather a dumping ground for all kids who did not fit the mold (Brantlinger, 2004; Lipsky & Gartner, 1997). Indeed, such notions seemed to reflect, in part, the comments of special educators as they voiced their opposing thoughts about inclusion, "There will always be a special ed.," and "Who's going to put up with the stuff that we do?"

Models of Disability and their Influence on Educators and Researchers

It has been documented that children and youth placed in special education have identified as "rejects" from general education, often feeling anger and the desire to "act out," self-inscribing into labels that have been placed upon them in schools (Connor, 2008b; Mooney, 2008; Piziali, 2001). Before I entered the field of special education, my primary associations with disability were physical and sensory. In my job, these associations came to be "cognitive" and "emotional," as the largest groups of students labeled with disabilities in schools were those identified as speech and language impaired, learning disabled, emotionally disturbed, and cognitively impaired (formerly known as, and still referred to by some, as mental retardation). These categories, in contrast to, say, being paraplegic (physical) or blind (sensory), seemed much harder to pin down and fully understand. The battery of assessments used to determine these high incidence categories were based, in large part, upon subjective interpretations of academic performance and social behavior. As such, high incidence categories have been labeled as "soft" disabilities (Harry & Klingner, 2006; Karagiannis, 2000), seeming to be quite fluid with the potential to bleed into each other. For example, the field of special education has historically claimed that 40 percent of LD students also had significant characteristics found in the category of emotional disturbance (Silver, 1981).

Even though I did not then have the language to critique challenge these categories, I wondered about how labels became the defining terminology associated with the education of a child. I also witnessed firsthand how many students rejected the label of disability, refusing to go to the governmental agency designed to help them transition from school to employment. The kids did not consider themselves disabled when they were with their family, peer group, or love interest, and these observations raised questions for me such as, can an individual reject a label if they don't feel it is part of their actual identity but rather an unwelcome imposition? Is a label left at the school-door and forcibly worn again upon return? I know now that these were nascent ponderings about who gets to define difference in schools, who takes liberties by giving labels, and conversely, how being labeled psychologically impacts a person, making their difference "real" although it is invisible. While I knew many students did need additional help, I reflected upon the inadvertent effects of labeling, especially negative associations (Smith, 1986; Tomlinson, 1982), imagining if we could have schools where kids received what they needed without the excessive bureaucratization of difference. At the same time, I knew rights had to be guaranteed by law and, without laws, kids would possibly not get the additional support needed. Labels were tied to numbers and numbers were tied to funding and funding was tied to employment. It reminded me of the absurd connections throughout the strange but popular children's song, "I know an old woman who swallowed a fly."

I noticed that professional organizations featured in our college classes had different definitions of disability, varying slightly, never radically, from the federal script. At that point in my career, I confess to not paying much attention to educational research. John had bought me several volumes of a behavior disorders book for Christmas, but I thought the format of simple listing of research suggestions about what to do if a child does "X" (fill in the blank) was overly simplistic and wouldn't work with most of the kids that I knew. After trying to be more interested in what research claimed, I eventually dropped all subscriptions except *Teaching Exceptional Children* because it was teacher-focused in terms of sharing practical strategies. Engaging with research in the field would wait until my doctoral program. However, when I later transitioned into higher education, it eventually became of concern for me that the teachers do not tend to read research and many (special) educational researchers do not know the daily lives of teachers. Why we accept this as another part of the status quo in education amazes me, and if forced to choose—I'd come down on the side of teachers who are trying every day to make a difference in the lives of children. Unlike the usually scientifically structured research methods that seek to measure the effectiveness of a particular method of instruction, the contextual nature of teaching and learning is always within a highly complex culture, something that is now being recognized (Artiles, 2015; Arzubiaga, Artiles, King, & Harris-Murri, 2008; Trainor & Bal, 2014; Bal & Trainor, 2016) although, troublingly, it has been historically dismissed in securing federal grants that are weighed heavily in tenure and promotion evaluations (Artiles, King Thorius, Bal, Neal, Waitoller, & Hernandez-Saca, 2011).

Educational Structures and Systems in Relation to People with Disabilities

Trying to make sense of special education, as "an outsider"—someone who didn't know it existed, was unfamiliar with American schools, teaching practices, and organization—in relation to general education, was always a work in progress from the start. At first, in an attempt to expand background knowledge I read "classics" such as Herbert Kohl's *36 Children* (1968) that reflected some of my own tentative observations on teaching, along with more contemporary works of Jonathan Kozol such as *Savage Inequalities: Children in America's Schools* (1991) and *Amazing Grace: The Lives of Children and the Conscience of a Nation* (1995). These authors had a large impact upon me as I could see how racial divisions intersected with economic disparities, creating a permanent social underclass that Derek Bell described as at "The Bottom of the Well" (1992). It was easy to see the lives of many kids as being "without" things (a safe neighborhood, sufficient money, one or two parents, enough clothes, school supplies, and so on), and default to thinking of them having deficit-experiences. But it was also many kids' "normal," and they had a form of resilience that served them well. At first, by invoking my own high school experiences as the default template of how I taught, I unconsciously imposed upon kids certain cultural expectations, values, interactions, and knowledge that was rooted in being white, British, and working class. I always viewed the teaching profession as a bridge to lower middle-class life, so was somewhat aware that schools are generally patterned on middle-class norms and expectations. Where did my students and I fit into this picture? Here I was, white, British, and now lower-middle class by profession, teaching Americans, working-class and poor students of color. Whose values were being taught? Who was expected to change and be molded via the curriculum? There were thousands of teachers across the city in similar or equivalent situations; mine was only one case. I contemplated how much a teacher's work is to cross cultural divides, and the faith needed to do that. All of these thoughts percolated in my consciousness, along with another important consideration—the students that I taught were also identified as disabled.

Students in the special education department had the additional challenge of negotiating their placement in special education. To them, it signaled official conference by the education system of inferiority, someone who literally can't make the grade. Faculty in my department often spoke of "our kids" who "couldn't function" in general education classes. The "us" and "them" mentality ran so deep that many professionals could not see beyond the two structures of special and general that barely overlapped in terms of mainstreamed kids and students receiving resource room services. Having a separate department raised the questions of who belongs where and why do we have these structural arrangements? From the very start, I felt for kids who were placed in a separate subsystem, wondering why it was culturally acceptable to have part of an organization only for SWD? I also noticed that students labeled LD and ED (and sometimes MR) were habitually mixed together while their needs could be quite distinct. The justification put forth was they had similar needs for a smaller, more-structured environment, and therefore could be combined. It seemed that the system was speaking from both sides of its mouth—these categories need special educational approaches, but the approaches could be given in the same place, at the same time, by the same person. Expecting all special educators to possibly individualize instruction for each student in each class struck me more as an idealized myth. To cynics, it was sometimes easy to see special education being equivalent to an unofficial dumping ground (Lipsky & Gartner, 1997; Sailor, 1991; Skrtic, 1991). After all, this was how people with disabilities had been treated throughout history—separated, contained, and diminished from full status, oftentimes characterized as animals (Stiker, 1999). It was not a long stretch to see parallels in the special education department in which students referred to as "cucarachas" by a senior teacher biding his time to retire.

The rigidity of the two systems, and the presumed inferiority of all things special education (students, curriculum, and sometimes by association, faculty) impacted how I thought about myself a teacher. When initially required to co-teach in general education, I experienced feelings of inferiority and unworthiness, terrified of making a mistake in public as if it would somehow reveal me as not a "real" teacher. This is what systems can do to professionals as well as children, make them internalize an institutional title such as *special education* that is constantly reinforced through local and national culture, as if it were a fact, thereby creating two types of students and two types of teachers. For years I had imagined teaching in general education to be significantly different from special education, but in my own experience of co-teaching, I was shocked it was not.

One pattern I noticed early in my own teaching, and that of my peers in special education classes, was the emphasis on remediation. Some teachers saw this as their primary function, while others viewed it as part of their mission along with teaching content parallel with general education. Kids would often complain about the task, asking "again?" when they looked in disappointment at the learning menu of the day. Such impressions of special education were adroitly portrayed in an episode of the cartoon television show *The Simpsons* when Bart is placed into special education after his family moves to a new neighborhood. To paraphrase, Bart is subjected to writing the letter "a" over and over on a circle of paper (lest he cut himself), and participate in musical chairs where no one loses because "everyone's a winner," spoofing perpetual remediation, safety concerns, and the promotion of self-esteem above all. He asks his teacher belligerently, "Let's get this straight . . . I'm supposed to be catching up, and you're giving me the same work again and again?" Bart's misplacement aside, the issue of remediation is central to teaching all students as it raises questions about what to focus upon as priority, with special education portrayed as relentless in this realm. The repetition of instructional experience, repeated failure at mastery, "being held back," and other related student experiences are not adequately addressed in educational research. It was not until later years that I began to tie many of my nascent concerns of this era to what we conceive of—in society and in education—as "the normal" child, defined by milestones and grade-level expectations, all culturally determined and prone to shifts over time in relation to societal expectations or demands, depending upon how viewed (Baglieri, Bejoian, Broderick, Connor, & Valle, 2011). Demonstrated knowledge and skills once expected in first grade are now expected in kindergarten, some even in Pre-K. For the students who can't academically perform "on time," the label of disability waits in the wings. These expectations are directly linked to America's world standing in terms of a student's average performance not only in reading (National Center for Education Statistics, 2016), but increasingly in the quartet of science, technology, engineering, and mathematics (STEM), anxiously associated with predictions of jobs and a prosperous economy (Alper, 2016).

In such a competitive society and world, a high school diploma serves as an entry point into adulthood and work. It was therefore alarming to see half of the students in the department not achieve this sanctioned entry point and be labeled with the term "high school drop out," surely intensifying their own sense of failure. That students were kids of color conveyed a sense of social reproduction, of being at the bottom of the barrel with a lot less hope of a financially secure future than other citizens. These patterns, I could see, reinforced racial hierarchies that surfaced in so many ways within schools. I recall one Latina in my homeroom looking at an Asian American student, the only one in the entire special education department, asking seriously, "What's she doing here? I thought those people were supposed to be smart." I also remember having a conversation with a Puerto Rican paraprofessional who literally said, "White people are smarter." These types of incidental comments reveal the larger belief in a racial hierarchy of intelligence, a powerful vestige of scientific thinking in the nineteenth century that reverberates throughout the twentieth century (Gould, 1996), and on to this day. In indirect ways, such a hierarchy appeared to exist in the educational system, with most school administrators being white males, and in comparison, most paraprofessionals (or educational assistants) being people of color. Originally, paraprofessionals were introduced to public schools to breach the cultural divide between teachers and the communities they served. However, in the eyes of kids and some paraprofessionals themselves, it was easy to see how school structures mirrored a racial hierarchy.

Returning to the notion of "belonging," I found the word to be crucial in thinking about the concept of inclusive education. "Our kids don't belong in general education," could be heard from some special educators while, "These kids don't belong in general education," could be heard from some general educators. Much of these thoughts hinged upon, "They'll never be able to do the work" without actually contemplating the rights of students to have work adapted or modified within general education. This topic of "the work" and its ability to be changed by teachers for students who needed it became raised as a general bone of contention, and would be one I explored in more depth as a staff developer. Meanwhile, the topic of academic, social, and emotional belonging would come to be reflected in teacher-friendly educational literature such as Paley's *You Can't Say You Can't Play* (1993), Shapiro's *Everybody Belongs: Changing Negative Attitudes toward Classmates with Disabilities* (1999), and Sapon-Shevin's *Widening the Circle: The Power of Inclusive Classrooms* (2007).

The Social, Political, and Cultural Experiences of People with Disabilities

In characterizing the start of career in special education, I entered a system that was officially separated by disability but also unofficially separated by race. While the latter was unjustifiable given the history of the United States, the former was seemingly justified by the educational system and the professional discipline of special education. Special education served as "an open secret," basically "outing" all SWD who had to negotiate their position as labeled students, hiding their status from general education peers (Connor, 2008b). In a nutshell, disability signified diminished social capital.

In regard to political experiences, here defined in terms of power relations, SWD felt disempowered within schools, a great irony given PL 94-142 that was designed to provide access and support. That 50 percent or more of SWD did not graduate attests to their discomfort in schools, and that many refused to go to the governmental agency designed to help them indicated the rejection of their label. These patterns conveyed a sense of shame in relation to disability, with a rejection of most things related to special education.

While over 50 percent of all disabled students at that time were classified as LD, I noticed little or no representation in the media, realizing that they did not see their reality "mirrored." There was an occasional mainstream movie about an adult who could not read and a woman who helped him, such as *Stanley & Iris* (Sellers, Winitsky, & Ritt, 1990), sensitively portrayed by Robert De Niro and Jane Fonda. Another was *Love, Mary* (Cohen & Day, 1985) a TV film based on the true story of Mary Groda-Lewis who struggled with dyslexia and became a doctor, that I showed to my students to discuss. There was also *The Cosby Show* (Corsey, Werner, Kukoff, & Leahy, 1984–1992) featuring a dyslexic son, Theo Huxtable, based on Cosby's experience real life child, Ennis, in what is now considered a moment in television history wherein the then most popular black family openly grappled with the implications for their child's LD. Yet, there seemed little out there for my students to see themselves in a positive light. While these few portrayals were sympathetic, much of what I saw portrayed in the media about people with disabilities was overwhelmingly negative—sad, pitiable, unlovable, burdensome, and suicidal. This reminded me of my own realization as a teenager about portrayals of LGBTQ people that were also overwhelmingly negative—sad, pitiable, unlovable, burdensome, and suicidal. Just as I refused to believe the latter about LGBTQ people, I also began to question the portrayals of people with disabilities. Just as homosexuality had been pathologized as a disorder until the late 1960s, I began to see tentative connections with how people with disabilities were understood. I sensed a great disparity between the definers of a label and those people defined with that label. I would later come upon a book called *No Pity: People with Disabilities Forging a New Civil Rights Movement* by Joseph Shapiro (1993), whose opening sentence was, "Non-disabled Americans do not understand the disabled" (p. 1). This simple thought carried a great deal of weight in how I began to shift my thinking about understanding disability, special education, and inclusion.

Chapter 2

Staff Developer

I have always found it ironic that the term "professional development" (PD) tends to elicit negative reactions in a considerable number of educators. For many, at best, PD evokes inciting boredom and wasting time. I was privy to a conversation in which one teacher shared that if he had to die, he wished it would be during PD as the transition would be so subtle the shift would be imperceptible. At worst, PD equates with hostility, active in the form of simmering anger, or passive in the form of yawning noncompliance (as in "I'll skim the newspaper" or "Let me get my knitting out"). Of course the vast majority of educators were not like this in my experience, but I was originally surprised that those who were (and could empathize, to some degree, with their frustration). For myself, as a learner, as someone who sought to grow practices and improve skills, I enjoyed attending PD, particularly by other classroom teachers. I began attending sessions coordinated by the superintendent's staff developer for special education, Linda, and realized that the litmus test of a good PD session was to placing ideas, and preferably materials, in the hands of teachers to give them the option of incorporating them next day into their classrooms. These ideas and materials did not have to be fancy, but appropriate for kids in their classes. At the same time, I noticed a level of genuine collegiality when teachers came together from different schools, and discussed our daily challenges—particularly emphasizing "what works" when it came to instruction. At the High School of Fashion Industries, Principal Bonnici had shifted the atmosphere of fear and isolation cultivated by Principal Bailey by bringing faculty together in meetings to share different pedagogical approaches. For example, a seasoned general educator taught us how to manage a classroom of students in cooperative learning tasks. Although I had used group work before, cooperative learning was so much better. Instead of expecting students to "figure it out" and assume (or rather hope) they'd work in harmony, tasks were shared by students who all played different roles yet were interdependent upon each other, influencing motivation and a healthy dose of peer-pressure to get the job done. Time was structured in such a way that all students were engaged, making contributions and having their voice heard, ultimately sharing a grade.

I recall admiring the woman who guided us through the process of learning by first immersing us in the task, and then after completion, facilitating us analyze the process as learners, thinking, "A teacher of teachers . . . Wow!" Something in me wanted to be as good a teacher as she was. At the same time, a curious sense of ambivalence possessed me. On one hand, I knew I had the drive to be a good teacher. On the other hand, there existed a nagging feeling of unworthiness ("Who am I to think I can teach other teachers?"). The answer to this question would come sooner than I thought. The principal had placed my colleague Luke and I onto a "menu of PD options" during our monthly mandated faculty meeting. He'd even provided the title, something along the lines of "Tips for Teaching Special Education Students." I felt simultaneously horrified and flattered, emotions strangely incompatible as oil-and-vinegar. The session was to be 45 minutes long at the end of a Monday. Sunday nights *always* meant a bad sleep, after a late afternoon and evening spent prepping classes for the week, grading all students' work, and organizing as much as possible. High anxiety meant no deep sleep, but rather tossing and turning, ceaselessly going over things I had to do, willing the night away in a semi-comatose state so I could just go to work and get on with the inevitable. This time, on the eve of presenting to colleagues, only intensified the usual pattern and I lay repeating, "Just think, at this time tomorrow, it will be over . . . Just think, at this time tomorrow, it will be over."

I'd secretly hoped general education faculty would pick another option, but instead we proved to be a very popular choice. All seats were filled, leaving standing room only. Looking out across a full room of my colleagues' expectant faces, a familiar pain took hold in the pit of my stomach. Déjà vu. It was exactly the same as my first day of teaching kids. Nonetheless, we dove into action, demonstrating some quick "warm up" activities to get attention of learners by providing fun (and meaningful) things to do within reach while harnessing enthusiasm to general class participation and specifically the task at hand. In addition, we facilitated an open discussion about working with kids who may not fit the proverbial mold. At the end of the session, feedback was positive, and along with a sense of unbelievable relief, I felt satisfied that—despite considerable misgivings—I'd risen to the occasion. It was times like this that I noticed teaching involves a degree of pushing oneself out of a comfort zone, of trying new things in order to grow. I became aware of the need to harness personal fear, have professional faith, and be open to the dynamics of what may organically occur in any given situation. Those

45 minutes also made it clear to me that general educators had a genuine desire to know more about kids with IEPs and how to support them. We had provided, thanks to the principal's insight and push, a forum in which we could all discuss how to potentially expand our teaching repertoire by sharing with one another—and it felt powerful. In retrospect, I do not think we did an excellent job, but given the circumstances and parameters, a fair one. Iris told me some people had thought the substance was not sufficiently deep, and I was open to this comment, as nervousness can be masked in many ways, including "let me whiz through this" rather than create deeper engagement. In future, I aimed to focus on substance over speed, although there would always be times—depending upon highly variable contexts of presenting—when I just wanted to whiz through it.

Having found a little more confidence in working with teachers, Linda at the superintendent's office invited me to provide some workshops for other special educators from Manhattan high schools. I pushed myself and agreed to do them. But when I began to speak at the first session, I sweated profusely, so much so that two enormous circular stains radiated from my armpits, almost stretching down to my waist. Painfully aware, I could only think to say "Meet Victoria and Niagara . . . they tend to appear when I present." The audience laughed, and once that occurred, I became very much at ease, relating to the group of adults as I would my kids. With these opportunities, I came to find out that I enjoyed teaching adults, and when a new full-time position was added at the superintendent's office Linda encouraged me to apply for the job.

MOVING OUT, MOVING IN

I had feelings of guilt about leaving the kids I had been teaching. Due to the size of the department's small classes, it was common for special education teachers to get to know their students very well—sometimes teaching them from 9th to 12th grade. Kids' faces and stories would linger on the surface of my consciousness for years to come, and I was heartened by the thought of possibly returning should the new job prove not to be a good fit. At the same time, I had been becoming a little bored with the repetition of teaching some classes (as much as I admired Steinbeck, I winced at the thought of teaching *The Pearl* one more time), experiencing the sensation of treading professional water, staying comfortably afloat but remaining in the same place. There was some time to go before finishing my master's degree in creative writing at City College, so I could not yet become a general education English teacher. The opportunity of working at the superintendent's office actually intrigued me. I'd get to see, and participate in, how 33 high schools were led and supported. I realized I could take what I had learned as a teacher, collaborate with other educators, and focus on the quality of instruction for students with disabilities (SWD), while advocating for more inclusive environments.

The superintendent herself was a dynamic woman named Mrs. Black, a proud daughter of working-class Irish immigrants. Her working-class sensibilities contributed to a no-nonsense attitude that was accompanied by a healthy sense of humor. I admired her from a distance, a little intimidated (as I often felt) by people in positions of power. What must it be like to be responsible for hundreds of administrators, teachers, service providers, and over 20,000 or 30,000 kids, I wondered? Jayson had become her friend, confidante, and personal assistant. Mrs. Black relied on his smarts for managing part of her work, and he served her capably. While Jayson and I did not socialize as regularly as we once did, I always felt indebted for his encouragement to enter the teaching profession. This was our third job in the same place, and we knew we could rely upon one another.

The superintendent's office was located within Martin Luther King Jr. High School (MLK) behind Lincoln Center on the Upper West Side. The building itself was square and squat, five floors including a basement where the special education department was located. The mid-1970s architecture, in the guise of being creative, placed glass-enclosed hallways around the school's perimeter leaving all classrooms without any direct daylight. MLK did not have a "good" reputation, contrasting with LaGuardia High School for the Performing Arts (on which the film *Fame* was based) located literally across the street. Again, I saw the racial divide in New York City as mainly black and Latino students attended MLK, while white and Asian American students dominated LaGuardia's population.

Located on a hallway of the third floor, the superintendent's office was a nondescript series of interconnected rooms. Linda's office was big enough for two desks, so I moved in and we became professional roommates. As the space itself was half of an actual classroom, one side still had a floor to ceiling blackboard. So, the first thing I did was use colored chalk to create a long series of faux windows overlooking the view of a little wood cabin, complete with smoking chimney, at the edge of a lake and flanked by a forest under a setting sun. Little did I know then that this trompe l'oeil would stave off claustrophobia and remain intact for the duration of my nine years there.

WORKING IN THE SPECIAL EDUCATION UNIT

The position of staff developer in special education was an interesting one to think through. It took me a little time to acclimatize in terms of where I was located within a network of bureaucracy. Technically, the position was funded via New York State through a renewable federal grant it received to support special education mandates and initiatives. New York State's network—Special Education Training and Resource Centers—consisted of approximately 160 people, with about a quarter of them located in New York City, each of the 32 districts having 1, along with each of the 6 high school divisions (1 per borough plus 1 for Alternative High Schools spread across the city). I was placed in the district of Manhattan high schools. Given that the state paid my salary, I was of "no cost" to the Superintendent's Office, and provided to assist with professional development in special education initiatives. The job was a two-pronged task, as I was expected to "train" people in state mandated regulations and their ongoing changes, as well as develop and provide locally needed PD identified by the superintendent or her designee.

The "designee" was my new immediate boss called Dom Capone, a quadrilingual Sicilian American who loved to utilize uncommon words. Dom's assistant Ted Fletcher worked in the office part time and served as a special education supervisor for the balance of the week. He was English-born, but raised in New Jersey, and we hit if off straight away, starting a professional affiliation that exists until this day. As part of my job, I was expected to work with anybody related to special education, including principals, general and special administrators and teachers, paraprofessionals, parents, and service providers such as educational evaluators, school psychologists, and counselors. I would be in charge of coordinating the locally defined needs of special educators, administrators and other faculty. Additionally, "the Board" could pull on us to provide citywide trainings or centrally based initiatives they were spearheading. In sum, the job's parameters were wide, the constituents varied, and the time demands challenging—as many PD events occurred after school hours and on weekends when teachers were free.

As anticipated, during the first semester my anxiety was through the roof. One task meant periodically presenting to all assistant principals of special education, including my former boss, Iris. I recall thinking how difficult and challenging their jobs were, the importance of their positions, and who the hell was I to take up their valuable time with information New York State wanted them to know but they often did not want to hear? The first time I had to stand up and address this group I froze part way through my short impromptu speech, resurrecting the feeling of being a deer caught in the headlamps of their eyes, imagining them thinking *How did he get here*? I felt Linda gently tug at my sleeve and whisper, "Sit down," which I did, red faced, ashamed of being immobilized by my own anxiety. I resolved to work on this problem, deciding that whenever I would address them or other groups "higher" than me in the hierarchy of educational structures (assistant principals, principals, superintendents and their cabinet members, officials from the central Board), I would be ready to begin with a thought, question, or statement designed to challenge the audience in a respectful way.

(DIS)FUNCTIONAL SYSTEMS?

By working as a staff developer (and technically still employed on a "teacher line"), what I began to see emerge was the structure of interconnected organizations. Federal laws, polices, and initiatives pertaining to SWD were charged to states who, in turn, had to guide local education authorities (LEAs). The NYC Board of Education was my "umbrella" LEA, and it, in turn, had to ensure that federal laws, policies, and initiatives were implemented. The Board, in turn, informed the 40 or so local districts who in turn made sure that all principals knew what was expected. However, when anything special education related was directly provided to principals, they usually forwarded it unread to assistant principals or supervisors of special education. These administrators became the point people for "all things special ed.," and expected to lead, supervise, and evaluate teachers in their department. The assumption that information "from the top" would cascade down to actual teachers, students, and parents "on the ground" was sometimes challenged at one or more levels. When I had to provide PD mandated trainings for, say, changes in the format of IEPs due to reauthorizations of IDEA that emphasized more involvement by general educators, there was always considerable pushback, with predictable comments such as,

"What will they think of next?"

"What do we have to do now?"

"The State [Education Department] is crazy."

"Have they ever been in a school?"

"I'll believe it when I see it."

Being part of a statewide network required attending three one-week long sessions per year in the state capital of Albany, two and a half hours north on New York City. These meetings were a mixture of NYS information that we needed to know, sometimes giving us a "heads up" as to what LEAs would be expected to do, and PD provided to us, to help maintain our interest and creativity in supporting children, youth, and adults with disabilities. The state also had several projects, including the "LRE Initiative," in my early years and "Systems Change" in my later years. The former initiative meant presenting to all administrators and selected schools on rethinking what constituted the LRE for SWD, and advocating for more placements within general education with supports. The latter initiative was an earnest attempt by NYS to look at how and where kids with different labels were taught system-wide throughout the state, and ask how could we change to a more inclusive culture?

Linked to these initiatives were conversations about what "outcomes" for SWD were the result of special education, and did they justify expenditures? Increasingly, the federal and therefore state governments were monitoring funds and noticing the disjuncture between what was invested in the current system versus what it produced. One measure was the number of SWD who graduated high school with a local or Regents diploma. In comparison with nondisabled peers, the rate was abysmal. As indeed were employment rates, levels of employment, and integration into the larger community in general. On the other hand, many parents were savvy enough to threaten or actually sue the local LEA for not providing "an appropriate" public education for their child. In extreme cases, some students were being flown weekly from one end of the state to another, attending specialized boarding schools and returning home on weekends. It was at state meetings that I observed how special education supported many people, but not equally or fairly, with middle- and upper-middle class LEAs providing different experiences for children with disabilities that influenced degrees of inclusiveness or restrictive placements.

On the lighter side, as staff developers we shared all kinds of activities and methods of engaging audiences around issues we had in common. Some of these made me groan inwardly. For a period of time, we were all told to identify as agents of change and provided with buttons reading, "Change Agent." At one of our trainings, as an opening activity, we had to find a partner we did not know, stand face-to-face and study the person, then turn around to change three things about our appearance, before resuming a face-to-face position. We then had to each figure out what the changes were (such as earrings taken off, a brooch removed, or a tie loosened). After doing this physical activity, we had to engage in a philosophical discussion about what change meant, and how—in many cases—people perceive change as a form of loss. This activity was used many times with varying degrees of success in future trainings, but struck me as a superficial way to begin a deep conversation.

THE UNTHINKABLE

It was at the beginning of a statewide meeting in Albany that my colleagues and I first heard about a plane crashing into the World Trade Center. Shocked and confused, we rushed to our hotel rooms to watch the television, and looked on in horror as another plane ploughed into the second tower. Then the unthinkable happened. These two pillars that defined New York's celebrated skyline, symbols of confidence, wealth, and America's standing in the world, imploded and fell to the ground, leaving massive piles of debris and billowing smoke that darkened the sky. It was surely a bizarre optical illusion, a bad joke, a clip from a disaster movie? While my eyes were seeing it happen, my brain was telling me it could not be happening. Immediately I thought of two schools where I sometimes worked, located on the adjacent block to the towers, wondering how teachers and kids were evacuating from high floors. I worried about John, now working at the Board's Brooklyn offices at a training institute for new principals. His morning subway ride took him past the World Trade Center. All phone lines were down. Sitting on the edge of the bed, we watched chaos unfurl in familiar streets. It was the day when all New Yorkers were traumatized. My friend Michael, a dean at the nearby Borough of Manhattan Community College, later told me he watched people jump frantically from the World Trade Center and with flailing limbs plunge to their inevitable death below. In the two schools I knew, staff managed to get all kids and colleagues out of their buildings and away to escape from the collapse. Before leaving her school to safety, one principal was in contact with her sister, trapped on a high floor of the burning World Trade Center across the street. Her sibling didn't survive.

Being in Albany somehow made the event even more surreal. The day after found me traveling back into Manhattan. Thankfully, John had been in contact and let me know he was safe. We lived a few blocks south of Penn Station and as I walked out of the building, scorched air filled my nostrils. Everything smelled burned. Fighter jets were flying low over the city as a precaution to prevent any other potential attacks. I looked south where I'd usually view the World Trade Center, only to see what I thought seemed a hole in the sky where the towers once stood. From my apartment window I watched smoke rise from ground zero, three miles away. Reporters on TV were then estimating 10,000 people had died. That's what I was looking at from my living room, dust containing the particles of thousands of New Yorkers. It was an unbelievable sight to try and make sense of. When the final figures declined to less than 3,000, it was like feeling a guilty pleasure because 7,000 lives had somehow been miraculously restored. The office of the superintendent was responsible for relocating several schools short term into shared space with others, and we all pitched in for days in emergency arrangements as New York, still stunned, began to pick itself up from the floor.

LOCAL SPECIAL EDUCATION INITIATIVES

While we could never go back to "normal" again, there was some satisfaction—and even a welcome distraction—in buckling down and getting on with work. As the chairperson of the District Advisory Committee on PD in special education, I oversaw a grant that allowed decisions to be made about what was needed at the local level. A committee of teachers, administrators, and paraprofessionals, we surveyed our constituents and provided different forms of PD in response to requests. Some of these options included borough-wide conferences, after-school workshop series, provision of arts-based residences (like ones I once had), and specialized training in reading programs such as "Starting Over," for students identified as cognitively impaired. Regina Zacker, Deputy Director of Special Education in the Division of High Schools, administered the grant and was in many ways a visionary in terms of professional development, and someone from whom I learned a lot.

It was these "home grown" projects, organic in nature that I enjoyed the most. They often involved working *with* professionals, exploring issues toward solving problems, rather than being a conveyor of information when sharing changes in state or city policies. I also came to visit many different schools and special education departments from around the borough, stretching from George Washington HS in the north to HS of Leadership and Public Service by the World Trade Center, from Richard R Green HS on the Upper East Side to Park West HS in Hell's Kitchen. The schools ranged from drab, prison-like constructions with metal frames on windows and airport-type security for anyone who entered, to old (as in turn-of-the-twentieth-century) but cheerful and cozy edifices, to brand new sparkling modern buildings, to refurbished commercial loft spaces. Principals, too, varied as much as the buildings that housed them. I was somewhat in awe of most of them, although I soon found out they were largely ordinary people who had started as teachers, worked hard, and had a great sense of responsibility toward their students and faculty. Some had reputations for being "tyrants" or "bitches"—indicating the same thing, albeit differentiated by tellingly gendered language—as if the former denoted strength in the form of a feared but respected leader, and the latter simply implying a hostile female. I developed some favorites, and it was not coincidental that they were either former special educators or teachers of English Language Learners and were inclusionists at heart. One always referred to the local education authority as "The NYC Board of Dread" and the field as "special dread," as if no further explanations were needed.

All schools had equal opportunity to call upon me to present on issues in special education, and sometimes I felt as if I were summoned to do "the dirty work," that is be the messenger of changes in state and city regulations. I was known for a while (sometimes with more than a hint of sarcasm) as "Mr. LRE" because one of the first things I had to do was call attention to reinterpreting LRE to mean less restrictive than it was currently conceived. It was challenging presenting to faculty in mandated meeting times as they were understandably tired and frequently unreceptive to what I had to share. Likewise, on designated professional development days wherein I shared

NYS regulations on one hand and ways to implement them on the other, they could be downright ornery, telling me they did not want to hear what I'd be talking about or attempting to ridicule my credentials. On one occasion, it did not help that the principal had slipped away, signifying she did not want to be with her own faculty. In retrospect, the year of teaching the boys labeled ED helped prepare me, as I would never lose sight of my presentation's objective and always bring the conversation back to it. I'd also inform the audience that although I worked at the superintendent's office, I was also a teacher who shared the same union, interested in figuring out better ways to support kids with disabilities and their teachers. It was useful to open a presentation with something self-deprecating about me, something respectful about them, an acknowledgment of how hard their job was, and a question or comment to engage them. While prone to the usual bouts of anxiety, I was cautiously confident in these situations, believing I was doing the right thing for kids. While I never became oblivious to comments of "people like you," public knitters, or newspaper readers, I tended to put them in perspective, thinking that many teachers were oftentimes isolated, inadequately informed and supported, and constantly functioned close to the borderline of overwhelmedness. That said, it pained me that teacher dissatisfaction and anger was not channeled in more positive ways. If educators were closed down, romantic notions of "change agent" (I did not delude myself) counted for naught, no matter the shiny buttons distributed by NYS Education Department. To this day, I don't think there's much difference in teaching teachers or kids, and when I bring this up to a graduate class who are current teachers many are initially offended, until we explore issues that include interest, motivation, and relevance. As always, having a sense of humor helped. On one occasion I recalled working with many teacher teams to make school plans for the increased inclusion of kids with disabilities. Tensions were high as the superintendent's office was being asked to document how we were assisting schools in changing their culture in this regard, and we were asking people to consider real changes that could be sustained versus lip-service or superficial options. One angry teacher stood up and pointed his finger at me in front of all those gathered working in groups, and began,

"What YOU need to do—"

"I don't have to do anything—," I cut him off, "Except get through this day." And then, touching my forehead, chest, and shoulders, I made the sign of the cross.

Everybody laughed and the man sat down. By invoking religion (I am a lapsed Catholic, but vestiges surface periodically) and conveying that palpable tension in the room was also felt by me, I was desperate to hold my ground. A thought that always helped me: *Yes, this can be difficult work, but there's a reason behind it, and it involves creating equitable opportunities for kids who have been marginalized.*

One of the most difficult groups to work with was service providers in special education—school psychologists, educational evaluators, counselors, and speech and language providers—the latter sub-group being the best of the bunch as they provided direct educational support to students. The administrator of the speech and language group was hardworking and thought in innovative ways to provide kids with support, encouraging flexible service delivery in both pullout and push-in models. In contrast, the other supervisors often clashed among themselves as "their people" in the schools sometimes did not get along in managing caseloads requiring the collaboration of an educational evaluator, counselor or social worker, and school psychologists. There was definitely a pecking order, with psychologists self-appointed at the top, invested in the instruments they used that brought great heft to the proceedings in IEP meetings, which of course—unfortunately—they often did. Educational evaluators had the twin responsibilities of administering a battery of assessments and coordinating new referrals, any requested changes, and triennials, along with keeping an eye on how teachers coordinated annual IEP updates, upon which they relied. Counselors and social workers, like providers of speech and language services, were also very child centered.

The supervisors oversaw their people in terms of managing "clinical services" at all schools, as well as operating a district level Committee on Special Education (CSE). The operation had a relentless emphasis on compliance, and each professional's annual performance evaluation tied to meeting projected numbers. At the superintendent's office, there was a sense of "this is required by law, so let them get on with it." Yet it was also looked on as a side effect of special education legislation, rights, and regulations. I always had the sense that being an educational evaluator as a tedious job, although far easier than teaching. In fact, all educational evaluators were former teachers and maintained their status being on a "teacher line" in terms of salary and benefits. They could go home at 3:15 p.m. without worrying about lesson plans or grading papers (or have the option of overtime, as most did, because there were always so many kids being processed). Most had been in the system for years, and thought of themselves as survivors who had seen regimes come and go. I was responsible for coordinating and sometimes directly providing PD to these educational evaluators. In my first year there, one walked up to me and said, "I'm just giving you the head's up that I know you're a nice guy and have to share this information but I really don't give a fuck about what you say." At least I knew where I stood. That's part of the charm of New York City.

I viewed this group as problematic for many reasons. Despite being seen as a necessary inconvenience at schools, these professionals managed all IEP meetings. While this was their daily work, it was easy to see the importance of these events being the nexus of power that determined kids' labels, placements, parental input, and influenced a kid's identity and future options. They were at least 90 percent white overseeing the fate of over 90 percent kids of color, and seemed to "rubber stamp" cases at the end of set procedures, essentially unquestioning of the system in which they worked that was beneficial for them. When I presented to service providers on issues of LRE and increased inclusive practices they often pushed back hard. On one hand, I understood that they feared in case kids with IEPs would not survive and flourish in general education. On the other hand, they were largely unprepared to fight for any changes that would lead to an improved system. Despite including the topic of kids of color in special education, they did not make any connections between the processes they managed and the current state of affairs. To bring it up was "unfair," and I recall reading my evaluations from that session (I always distributed sheets for feedback) that included an African American counselor writing, "If you dare to mention my race," before a critique of the issues. I learned there was no easy way to approach important issues such as historical and current structural practices that upheld segregation—as the topic often shut down and/or angered people for different reasons.

In brief, I found "the clinical office" within the special education unit to be a production line without much nuanced thought, manufacturing batches of students to be processed for fear of external monitoring by the State Education Department. Except for speech and language, administrators were largely uninterested in providing PD to their staff with regard to making changes. It struck me that special education was more industrial than scientific, filled with workers who assembled papers and managed procedures that resulted in maintaining the status quo. Occasionally I was asked to sign IEPs at the office for students I did not know because "a teacher's signature was needed by law." As much as I wanted to help my colleagues, I declined, as the IEP is a legal document that I could be held accountable for, and truth be told, the child's actual teacher should have been at the meeting, contributed, and signed. The request simply verified my feeling that the clinical conceptualization of special education has helped make it into a factory.

EMPHASIZING INCLUSIVE EDUCATION

In contrast to the challenge of coordinating and providing PD to clinical professionals, I enjoyed building relationships with specific schools and teachers and administrators within them. Several new schools started at the time of my arrival, and others had begun continued to develop over the years, making the district number rise to 44. One of my favorites was the Richard R. Green High School of Teaching located in an old building on the Upper East Side. The principal included all kids from its inception, normalizing that structure for all staff. Special educators there were particularly caring and very proactive in team teaching, figuring out logistics of adapting activities and exams, and advocating for their students while teaching them self-advocacy skills. My colleague Ted Fletcher from the superintendent's office was also the special education administrator, responsible for this and other schools, and we worked closely in bringing faculty together to share what they did with other schools trying to become more inclusive.

In the mid-1990s, New York State's emphasis on LRE meant we could foreground our efforts on this area, which is what interested me the most, and I pondered: How do we actually do this? How do we go forward and change things, given where we are now? Ted and I began a district-wide focus by creating a day of PD for educators from the newer schools who had been charged with figuring out inclusive models and how to best make them work. The event took place in the student cafeteria at the High School of Environmental Studies in Hell's Kitchen, sitting at long tables with built-in benches. (Interestingly, the school building had once been Metro Golden Mayer studio headquarters, with Darryl Zanuck's office now being that of the principal). The school cafeteria was humble beginnings but participants appreciated sharing their daily work and learning from others via networking with peers. We capitalized upon this small group and subsequently created opportunities for teachers to come together regularly, as well as visiting many schools to see for ourselves what was going on, and what was needed.

The assistant principals of special education, for whom I grew to develop their monthly meeting, were quite divided on inclusive education. Debates were heated, and attempts to expand the number of special educators involved in team teaching were resisted by many. The origin of resistance by special education administrators was of interest to me, as I could see the possibilities in inclusive education, and was puzzled why they couldn't. Reasons included: some administrators did not want to persuade their special education staff or engage with their general education counterparts; others did not want to further complicate programming; some worried about how to evaluate a teacher who was team teaching; others believed kids "on both sides" would simply fail. I was willing to engage with these concerns directly otherwise they'd continue to provide roadblocks to movement. Subsequently, I made presentations (with colleagues, as we deemed appropriate) to assistant principals of all high school content areas about why schools were moving this way, and how to do it. Issues of budgeting and programming were looked at with view to options for assigning teachers to general education classes. Extensive and ongoing PD was provided every semester to special and general educators programmed to team teach; and we opened the larger discussion of changing expectations in general education. By this, we stressed the point that not only could work be modified for kids with disabilities, it should be the norm. It was the job of the special educator to work with the general educator to ensure any needed changes would be made.

Over time, when special educator school-based leaders realized that increased inclusion of kids with disabilities was not going away, they did begin to shift. When I took a group to visit an inclusive high school in Brooklyn wherein the assistant principal of special education had done an excellent job—far more so than any in Manhattan. Some of our assistant principals were affronted that we had to go to Brooklyn to see a version of inclusive education in action, but that was the point—it was being done, and done well, so why not learn from it? Some staunch naysayers seemed to delight in reasons why not to even try—and this, I think, is problematic for those charged with doing PD in large systems.

New York State and the NYC Board were steadfast in stating that a move toward more inclusive education was a priority within official policy. An increased emphasis was placed upon co-teaching, yet a lot of misinterpretation still ensued, so I decided to write a booklet to clarify basic ideas, calling it *Team Teaching: A Brief Guide to Sharing the Classroom.* The text was deliberately short and to the point, as I knew teachers had very little time. The brightly colored cover featured two teachers working together, as I wanted it to attract attention. In general, the book explained the *whys* and *hows* of team teaching, incorporating perspectives from general and special education teachers, kids, and administrators, as well as sampling some of the literature that supported collaborative practices, particularly emphasizing the work of Friend and Cook's six models of co-teaching (1996). I applied for a grant to have the text professionally reproduced, and hundreds of spiral-bound copies went out from our office to all Manhattan High Schools, as well as sample copies to all school districts across the city. It turned out to be a popular resource, and when requests for additional copies were made I told colleagues from around the city to simply xerox and distribute as needed. I knew that in the future I wanted to write a "real" book, and this was my trial run.

In deciding how to move the superintendent's office forward with PD, the special education unit sought a university partner who would collaborate and help us think through ways to expand and improve our efforts. As a result, we formed a close alliance with Bank Street School of Education, long known for its progressive approaches to teaching and learning. Professor Claire Wurtzel was the point person and we began a partnership that helped us take a look at how the district was structured in terms of each school's customized needs in terms of PD, with view to providing it. This project ran for two years and involved monthly PD on Fridays at the headquarters of the UFT, and support at the school level by superintendency staff and Bank Street consultants. It was important to me to have PD at the teacher's union as it symbolized their approval. We asked for at least two representatives (one special and one general educator, preferably working together) from each school and budgeted money to pay substitute teachers for that day. For our main shared focus, we hired experts who had been certified in methods developed in the Strategic Instructional Model (SIM) by the Center for Research on Learning located at the University of Kansas—the number one school for special education in the country (https://kucrl.ku.edu/sim).

Developed by Don Deschler and colleagues and developed into popular texts (Deschler, Schumaker, Harris, & Graham, 1999), SIM was a specific approach to learning in which teachers explicitly taught students, step-by-step, how to become, and remain, organized. This involved sharing units and lessons with students, along with commonplace teaching procedures such as comparing and contrasting two concepts, and content-related vocabulary. Each procedure came with an interactive graphic organizer and an acronym to help recall the steps. These strategies were modeled, taught, and explored by teachers at our PD, with the view of them having something new and helpful to use in their classrooms on Monday. We also provided, and referenced, the book *Teaching Every Adolescent Every Day* (Deschler et al., 1999), bringing legitimacy of research-based education to what we were doing.

By and large, I saw the value of highly structured and organized approaches, as long as they could be flexible when needed. I didn't feel like we were "selling a bill of goods," but rather working with teachers for them to see the value of principles underpinning the attempts by Kansas University and encourage them to use the devices as is or modify them. Interestingly, some teachers grasped the SIM ideas and used them in their classes, while others did them half-heartedly, and yet others avoided them—not changing their instruction for kids with disabilities who had been placed in their classes. In working with approximately 60 teachers per session, I experienced the range of educators, including those who were open and willing to try any reasonable idea, to those appearing indifferent (yet possibly open) to attempts of changing the system, to those who were cynical and sometimes hostile. I was happiest working with the first group, as they were "easiest to teach," healthily tested by the middle group, fully knowing my desire to make them invested in change; and the final group . . . I did my best, and challenged them respectfully about their views (allowing them to do the same to me). However, I was always still taken aback by the anger and bitterness in some teachers. While I could understand it to a point—feelings of being "let down" by an educational system that could appear uncaring, unsupportive, and grinding in terms of routine and responsibilities—I also thought: *We're being paid, as professionals, to figure out how to improve a system that we agree needs improving. Why not contribute?*

Another project I valued enormously as a staff developer was increasing the focus of teachers upon student work. My alliance with the UFT led them to invite me to collaborate in developing school-based PD in which teachers analyzed and discussed their student's work with view to reflecting upon, and consider changes in, their own teaching practices. This was my introduction to "protocols" in which a set of steps are taken along these lines: (1) teacher presents situation including a written version of assignment given to students; (2) peers ask "clarifying" questions, to help establish teacher's intent and teacher responds; (3) then peers ask "probing" questions to get at teacher beliefs about the work, and teacher responds; (4) teacher presents three levels of student work samples to be analyzed; (5) peers analyze and provide "warm" feedback, emphasizing evidence of student understanding of task; (6) peers provide "cool" feedback with evidence of student's partial or non-understanding of work; (7) finally, teacher responds to all feedback (McDonald, Mohr, Dichter & McDonald, 2003). Using this approach as the basis of PD in schools proved effective in engaging teachers about their daily work as it foregrounded student learning in terms of evidence—and related that evidence to teacher directions and expectations.

In working closely with Bank Street College, one of the most interesting projects I became involved in was *All Kinds of Minds* (Levine, 1993; Levine, 2002), a comprehensive way of thinking about differences among children that presented learning as a complex phenomenon involving simultaneous processes such as attention, higher order cognition (complex thinking), language, memory, neuro-motor functions (movement), social cognition (making and maintaining friends), visual-spatial abilities, and temporal sequential ordering. Claire Wurtzel led this initiative in which we focused deeply on each construct with groups of teachers, one day a month over the course of a year. Each teacher chose an actual student to work with, administered a learning profile assessment, and developed instructional approaches that supported the student. One of the features of Dr. Levine's work was a process he developed to talk with kids about their disability; it was called "demystification" (Levine, 2002, p. 278). The process intrigued me as it provided a framework through which teachers could talk with kids about their learning differences while emphasizing their strengths first and having them take ownership of areas they needed to practice and work on. I'd always had difficulty in special education's general practice—at least in my own experience—of not directly explaining and discussing a kid's learning problems with the child. I had attempted a similarly intended process myself when a teacher, albeit clumsily, as I wanted kids to recognize their strengths, not be primarily defined by their needs yet be aware of and work on them, as part of their own agency.

All of these initiatives were tied to our district's efforts to support inclusive education. I was quite moved when one year my then superintendent, Granger Ward, agreed to co-present with me in Albany at a statewide conference sponsored by the New York State Education Department. Special Education had felt somewhat of a "PS" to much of what goes on at a district level, so to have the direct participation of my superintendent was professionally satisfying.

During these years, I still missed working with kids, so decided to develop a project under the auspices of transition services, which were also being emphasized at this time. There was a transition linkage coordinator (TLC) by the name of Marilyn Scher who guided teachers appointed as the TLC to each school in ways to help prepare students to graduate and secure post-school opportunities. The project was to provide and support high school kids with IEPs to "sample" college by taking a class while still at high school. It involved me teaching on Saturday mornings to "test prep" for the student entry exam, take them on a campus visit to LaGuardia Community College in Queens, and have personal interviews with the coordinator of disability support services there, Matthew Joffe. Once the admissions test was passed, students could take one course from a menu of options. These ranged from creative choices (such as photography) to remedial classes to strengthen reading. Matthew was multiply disabled, with Möbius syndrome, partial blindness, cerebral palsy, and motor impairments. He was also very active in disability theater, had been featured on television, and willing to present on life as a person with a disability to schools and organizations, using his personal experiences and perceptions to challenge many myths and stereotypes (Richardson, 2001). We became friends and enjoyed the student college experience collaboration for years until CUNY changed its admissions requirements and made the entrance exam harder and along removed remedial classes.

CHANGING TIMES

During the nine years working at the superintendent's office of Manhattan High Schools I came to know the structures and systems of special education in ways that I did not see as a teacher, including the emphasis on compliance, case management, and clinicalization of the field. I also became interested in educators (teachers, administrators at all levels—from local to state) who sought change, those who appeared indifferent, and those who resisted change. Each "type" merited engagement in different ways. I'd come to understand that the most effective PD was job-embedded and participatory. Inclusive educational practices had grown, and even the most reticent of people had begun to take them seriously. On a personal note, the premature death of two influential colleagues in their early 50s brought home the message of how important it is to spend our time in worthwhile ways. Jayson, special assistant to the superintendent, and the man who persuaded me to try teaching as a profession, died from AIDS complications. Dom, the executive assistant to the superintendent for special education, passed way from cancer. To this day, usually when in a challenging professional situation, I channel both of them, asking myself, "What would Jayson do?" or "What would Dom say?" Jayson's smarts and Dom's kindness have guided me both during and after their lives as educators.

There were other changes, too, that were quite sobering. One day, when returning from visiting a school, I tried to enter the Martin Luther King building to get to my office, when I noticed people fleeing to exit. The school's reputation had declined, becoming subject to media coverage of gang-related activities. For some time, metal detectors had been installed for everyone to pass through, conveying a prison-like atmosphere more than a place for learning. There'd been several incidents that caused concern, including the sexual assault of a girl by multiple male students in a boys' bathroom, along with an increase in weapons possession. However, on this particular day, shots had been fired by a student on the floor where I worked and the building was on lockdown. I waited outside the building next to Lia Galeano, the superintendent's secretary, but police told us all to move on. We were shaken enough to visit a nearby restaurant and order a potent margarita. The incident got to me—kids trying to shoot kids when in school—on the floor where I worked. Endangering themselves and others. It was like having a bucket of ice water thrown over me. I was shocked and sickened to be living in violence-drenched society, with guns easily available, and cold disregard for human life. Instantaneously and profoundly depressed, I downed five more margaritas and barely remembered getting home, except for holding on to a fence by the side of my building, legs buckling, and thinking: *I hope my neighbors don't see me like this.* On finally making it to the apartment, my head was immediately in the toilet bowl to catch the contents of a heaving stomach.

At times like this, when momentary despair has entered the picture I've asked, "Where do we go from here?" feeling temporarily fixed in powerlessness, and ineffective in the face of interlocking oppressive systems. Of course, like most things in life, the answer is not to give up but recognize that something had to change. The Board was aware of the school's problems and, as is often the case with "troubled" schools, decided to phase it out and replace it with several smaller one with a specialty focus.

In addition, there were many changes around this time with the Board of Education transitioning into a radical reorganization of its own structure. Michael Bloomberg, mayor of New York City, stated:

> The need for comprehensive reform of the special education system in our public schools is manifest—for too long, the system has failed shamefully to help our children learn and raise their levels of expectation and achievement both in the classroom and in life. We will no longer tolerate a largely segregated and largely failing system that unmercifully ravages the lives and future of our children. (Friedman, 2014, p. 32)

The schools' chancellor, Joel Klein, appointed by Mayor Bloomberg, explained the new reforms:

> We are focusing our energy and resources on significantly improving classroom instruction by providing proven professional development for our teachers so that they can most effectively meet a wide range of learning needs in each classroom. . . . At the same time, we will still hold schools and principals accountable for ensuring that as many students as possible are able to be educated in general education classrooms. (Campanile, 2003, p. 27)

The Children First initiative, starting in 2003, was the city's response to pressure from the federal government to raise academic standards, as expected in the legislation of No Child Left Behind. The premise of Children First was to shift from a poorly performing school system to one in which the institutionalization of evidence-based practices would increase equitable outcomes for all students. With an initial focus upon establishing coherence, stability, and rigor throughout the system, its three pillars for systems change and improvements were empowerment, leadership, and accountability. In other words, local schools were empowered via principals and designees to more effectively promote student academic success, along with the institution of an accountability system based upon improved assessment, data use, incentives, and reporting mechanisms. With 1.2 million children in 1,500 schools, and approximately 135,000 of kids having IEPs, changes, though much needed, would also send reverberations of shock and panic throughout the system (O'Day, Bitter, & Gomez, 2011).

The Board announced that the community school districts and high school superintendencies would be reconfigured into 10 new regions across the city, and required to implement common approaches to math and literacy for students in general and special education. This news was like a tsunami alert for people working in the superintendent's office, signaling the dismantling of our current reality and professional positions. Funded by the state, I was guaranteed a position and told I'd be reassigned to one of the new 10 mega-districts. However, I knew I was in need of a change again, unable to think how I'd conduct research and manage writing my dissertation if I continued to work long days and most weekends. I needed two years to finish my doctoral degree, and decided it would do me good to go back into schools full time. So, given the emphasis on new ways of looking at literacy, I applied to be a literacy coach.

COMMENTARY

Teaching and Learning in Schools and Universities

Because their profession requires a constant focus on learning, teachers are faced with the ongoing challenge of making decisions pertaining to how they cultivate learning within their students. At the same time, like everyone else, teachers are learners and, by the nature of our profession, no one can ever be "done." In other words, it's assumed that teachers will be lifelong learners, open to whatever will improve their professional abilities. As a professional development specialist, I experienced that most teachers *are* interested in engaging about teaching and learning, and usually far less interested in any presentations around laws, regulations, and polices. In my role, I had to work with these two broad scenarios that inspired different reactions.

What I came to know is the phrase *mandated staff development* is a kiss of death, and that's understandable in some ways, after all, who likes to learn in "forced" conditions? In contrast, electing to be in a learning situation by choosing something of interest pertaining to teaching and learning evokes a different disposition for learning altogether. The challenge is that teachers and administrators are expected to do both mandated and self-elected PD, and in a world where high demands are placed upon them, including constant shifts in knowledge of policies and practices. Indeed, because so much changes in our field, in an effort to keep teachers up to date with methods and research, New York State required all certified teachers to document 175 hours of self-elected PD every 5 years (http://www.highered.nysed.gov/tcert/resteachers/175.html).

My preferred choice of coordinating or providing PD was/is either full or partial peer-to-peer involvement. The experience of having a good teacher teach other teachers—such as when I participated in cooperative learning workshop early in my career—leaves a deep and lasting impression. It is said that Bette Davis wanted her tombstone to simply read, "She was a good actress." There's something solid about aspiring to be good, and this thought drove me when I began my career—I wanted to be good at what I did. I'd also venture to say that in my experience most teachers want to be good at what they do and are usually open to whatever may help them become more effective in their profession. "Good" teachers also paradoxically know they can never be "good enough," because professional growth—like personal growth—should never stop; by nature, it's always a work in progress. In returning to the topic of peer-to-peer professional development, it is most powerful when it is job-embedded and ongoing. This arrangement contrasts with most mandated PD events that tend to be "one off," informational, often presented by personnel external to the organization and not always focused on student outcomes (Guskey, 2002). I noted that if district/school partnered with a university, if both parties collaborate to develop projects that were site based, and matched to teacher interest and motivation, and existed over time, then they were the most satisfying and successful to teachers.

In this chapter, I remarked that "teaching involves a degree of pushing oneself out of a comfort zone, or trying new things in order to grow." Regardless of whether you're teaching kids or teachers, the audience needs convinced that what you're attempting to engage them in is worth their attention by being useful and/or interesting. Some of the most successful engagement of teachers in an audience was because a topic spoke to them directly about their daily practices and relationships with kids. There is no magical one way of doing anything that will be successful with all kids. The best we could do was to offer models that had been somewhat successful such as the Strategic Instructional Model that made the teaching and learning process explicit to students (Deschler et al., 1999), ways to engage in looking at student work (Bluthe, Allen, & Powell, 2015), and insights into all types of learners in classrooms (Levine, 2002). This way, some of the "highly structured and organized approaches [worked] . . . as long they could be flexible when needed."

In closing this section, I want to acknowledge that it's not only the formal way of learning that occurs in educational institutions, but informal, often personal ways of learning, also exists in equally powerful ways (Smaller, 2005). My invocation of colleagues Jayson and Dom as educators is to convey how much I learned simply by being with them, watching them in action when teaching and presenting, connecting with all people in the room, responding to challenging situations, and leading the way. It's a misnomer to say I "absorbed" them, but I can say with certitude that part of who they were as educators became internalized in my ongoing desire to be a good educator.

Educational Laws and their Impact

The laws pertaining to special education have been seen by some as a double-edge sword in that provisions for rights made therein have given rise to an enormous bureaucracy that provide and monitor an unfettered sprawl of services with guarantees that cannot possibly be met (Lipsky & Gartner, 1997; Skrtic, 1991; Thomas & Loxley, 2007). What's on (legal) paper and what's in (actual) practice can vary enormously. One sticking point is the idea of an IEP. Can genuine individualization actually take place for all students with IEPs? This is a contentious topic because legally the answer is "yes." In fact, special education is predicated upon this principle of customization to give kids what they need. Yet, while well intended, this notion can become problematic if schools and teachers can say (and prove) that they don't have the ability, personnel, or financial resources for provisions stipulated in the IEP. Such situations have led to push-and-pull of who belongs where, with some cases reaching the State Court levels such as *Oberti v. Board of Education* (1993), and Supreme Court levels such as *Board of Education v. Mary Rowley* (1982).

Individualization symbolized in IEPs can be viewed as a civil rights law that evaluates the degree of need on a one-by-one basis, thereby placing the onus on families to secure what's needed to provide an opportunity for their child to have a successful education (Keyes & Owen-Johnson, 2003). Unfortunately, it can be argued that making a case for accessibility can often feel like a significant struggle or even a fight for families (Valle, 2009), with this phenomenon of petitioning for access appearing antithetical to universal design for learning wherein the beginning assumption is how everyone is to be included (Wehmeyer, 2010). When LRE was foregrounded and arguably reinterpreted to be more liberal during the Regular Education Initiative started by Madeline Will (1986), then for the Office of Special Education and Rehabilitative Services (under the US Department of Education), and emphasized in federal and state policies, I was able to trace a line from central government's decree all the way to a general education classroom level and teachers' thinking. When one misguided PD colleague would talk to a group of administrators and teachers about mandated changes, they would soon experience at their school, stating definitively with gravitas, "*It's the law*," I'd wince, as being law did not necessarily make it "right" in the eyes of teachers who had learned to think about kids with disabilities belonging to—and needing—a separate place (after all, that had been the interpretation of the law for many years). As much as the state wanted "systems change" there was a mismatch with the daily lives of teachers and their beliefs. I therefore found it imperative to engage with teachers in their current thoughts, beliefs, and knowledge, while discussing the state's proposed changes. For many teachers, it was perceived of as untenable to include more kids with disabilities, and the last straw in terms of increasing expectations placed upon educators (Gal, Shreur, & Engel-Yeger, 2010). Some teachers truly feared moving toward greater inclusion would have insufficient or no support altogether, based on past initiatives (Fuchs & Fuchs, 1994).

It was during my period as a staff developer, NYS began to include SWD in their data collection. When I entered the profession of teaching, SWD were required to take state mandated examinations. However, their scores were disaggregated, literally signifying *they were not counted.* This system had allowed any "lower functioning" kids to be labeled by schools as disabled so they would not be factored into the overall results. The state now made a point of including kids with disabilities in reporting data from all tests, including new and more challenging Regents exams, in an annual booklet. And while a raise in standards did show a modest rise in SWD passing exams, this policy may have also been responsible for increasing the number of drop outs, as happens when standards are raised abruptly without corresponding support (Jacob, 2001).

It was during my position as a staff developer that the entrenched separatism of special education within every level (federal, state, regional, and local) became apparent. I understood that it was necessary to have special education within educational organizations, but was alarmed at the degree of separateness. While the foundational knowledge base of special education was firmly entrenched in the medical model, "It struck me that special education was more industrial than scientific, filled with workers who assembled papers and managed procedures that resulted in maintaining the status quo." The committee on special education where I worked, mirrored on a smaller scale in schools, was a production line with workers who barely lifted their heads from their desks. I wondered to what degree inclusion could make headway in this system?

Models of Disability and their Influence on Educators and Educational Researchers

In keeping where I left off in the previous section, "I came to know the structures and systems of special education in ways that I did not see as a teacher, including the emphasis on compliance, case management, and clinicalization of the field." In brief, special education was seen primarily as a rights-based model, but clinically framed, in large part by actual definitions in IDEA rooted in predominantly medicalized understandings of disability, a combination that creates tensions in conceptualizing human differences. Few people will argue with the civil rights aspects of having a disability and protections under the law. However, it is the nature of those protections being predicated upon deficit-based understandings of disability that are problematic, even contradictory from a genuinely "rights" based perspective (Connor & Ferri, 2007).

Again, while composed of well-intended people, the teams that evaluated kids to determine whether they had disabilities served as a sorting and labeling process that lead to placement, usually in pre-existing segregated environments. Educational evaluators, all former special education teachers, saw themselves in some degree as protectors of kids and providers of services to them. The mass scale of initial referrals and, in turn, triennial evaluations, created an industry into which professionals self-inscribed, unquestioning of the status quo. School psychologists in particular have always been invested with great power to make official determinations as published in the DSM-V. In general, evaluation teams have historically been viewed as functional cogs in the system that uphold the status quo, inhibiting progressive growth (Valle, 2016; Valle & Aponte, 2002; Weatherly & Lipsky, 1977). In my experience, these ranks are filled by lower-middle-class whites who seem to rubber stamp mostly children of color with labels they are less likely to give to white kids. Serving as small cogs in the machine, there's a disincentive to question the hand that feeds, and they do not query their role in maintaining inequities they'd seem to accept as inevitable, saying it's "unfair" to broach these issues, a sentiment echoing findings in the research of critical special educators (Brantlinger, 2003; Tomlinson, 2017).

It has been claimed that field of psychology holds too much influence in the field of special education, making those many DS wary of its intentions (Olkin & Pledger, 2003). Special education has a fascination with what constitutes an ever expanding field of abnormality as reflected in DSM-V's quadrupling in length over the last 50 years, prompting one critic to ask if abnormal is the new normal and, "Why will half of the U.S. population have a diagnosable metal disorder?" (Rosenberg, 2013). There is also concern about how it conducts field trials (Jones, 2012), and a continued use of IQ tests despite their value being fundamentally discredited (Gundersun & Siegel, 2001; Offit, 2017). When educational research on disability draws heavily on psychology, it can be argued—as it has been done by disability activists—that research benefits the researchers themselves and people in disability-related professions far more than the people they ostensibly study yet exerting a powerful influence about disability-related knowledge (Oliver, 1996).

Educational Structures and Systems in Relation to People with Disabilities

In 2003, Mayor Bloomberg and Chancellor Klein's joint statement about the need for comprehensive reform of the special education system in public schools stated, "We will no longer tolerate a largely segregated and largely failing system that unmercifully ravages the lives and future of our children" (Friedman, 2014, p. 32). Part of their plan included a renewed focus that included PD for teachers, increased resources, and a shift in expectations of who is responsible for kids with disabilities. Klein additionally stated, "we will still hold schools and principals accountable for ensuring that as many students as possible are able to be educated in general education classrooms"

(Campanile, 2003). The separateness of special education was expected to change, as principals became *directly* responsible for kids with IEPs in their schools, overseeing services provided, and tracking academic and graduation success rates via state exams.

Indeed, the previous system had seen spending on kids with IEPs to be three times more than nondisabled students (Hehir et al., 2005), all things pertaining to special education overseen by certified supervisors, and poor academic results and graduation rates in an age of growing accountability. I recall the superintendent's office special education staff constituting approximately 33 percent of all personnel, whereas the percentage of students served with IEPs was around 12 percent. These local statistics symbolize the unease at federal and state levels about how special education was organized and administered. Charges of cutting costs being the primary motivation for changes inevitably followed, and there was justified concern in that some principals, among other things, may (1) see students with IEPs more as a liability for overall statistics rather than a priority; (2) designate responsibility to an already over worked teacher; (3) use earmarked funding for special education toward different projects; and (4) even deny students access to their schools (Connor, 2012a).

Most principals, along with teachers "had been in the system for years, and thought of themselves as survivors who had seen regimes come and go," and so adapted to these special education reforms that placed more students in general education. A main thrust of the reforms was a significant increase in collaborative teaching classrooms. As "inclusion" or "inclusive education" is never mentioned in federal law, it was never used in any of the district's educational discourse, including on IEPs—apparently too loaded a word. Although there was a degree of pushback including administrative fear of the need to "persuade their special education staff or engage with their general education counterparts, . . . to further complicate programming, . . . to evaluate a teacher who was team teaching . . . [or fear that] kids on both sides would simply fail," more classes were planned and programmed at every school. It was by then 15 years after I'd been involved in the pilot program of the collaborative model at the High School of Fashion Industries.

The writing had been on the wall about increased inclusion before Bloomberg-Klein's reform of special education, as throughout the 1990s there was a slow but sure emphasis toward inclusive education that snowballed by the end of the decade (Lipsky & Gardner, 1997; Skrtic, Sailor, & Gee, 1996; Villa, Thousand, & Chappie, 1996). Assistant principals and supervisors of special education were now in the maelstrom of how to best cultivate more inclusive classrooms at their schools, feeling pressure, and some working through conflicting beliefs of their own as the system that had taught them almost everything to do with disability was separate from general education now expected them to change their paradigm and help dissolve—or at least redraw—the line. One of my biggest breakthroughs in working with special education administrators as a group was emphasizing that inclusive education wasn't about kids suddenly fitting into a general education mold and being indiscernible from all others in the room. Rather than saying of students "they can't do the work," teachers could and should change that work—as needed. This simple point served as a revelation to many teachers and administrators and conveys the rigid notions associated with what is allowed in general education classrooms.

The Social, Political, and Cultural Experiences of People with Disabilities

The slow shift to inclusive education intended to diminish the number of segregated classrooms in schools. Students who experienced segregation largely preferred having access to general education classrooms (Keefe, Moore, & Duff, 2006), although a minority missed the specificity of having the support of a "go to" person in and out of class (Vaughn & Klinger, 1998). Detractors of inclusive practices tended to emphasize that being included physically into general education classes did not guarantee social and emotional integration (Pavri & Luftig, 2010). Indeed, consciously building classroom communities so "everybody belongs" (Shapiro, 1999) and kids know "you can't say you won't play" (Paley, 1993) were topics developed in practice-based literature, along with "widening the circle" to encompass more people (Sapon-Shevin, 2007). That said, the experiences of SWD being socially reintegrated into general education classes ran the gamut, from success stories (Danforth, 2014; Keefe et al., 2006) to perceiving diminished status compared to nondisabled peers in the eyes of teachers and peers (Ruijs & Peetsma, 2009). What is evident in reviewing this literature is the paucity of actual voices of SWD, and the need for "how discussions of school inclusion might be expanded to reflect disability voices" (Biklen, 2010, p. 337).

In switching focus again to my professional colleagues, I became further aware of social experiences with Matthew and Jayson. Matthew often described to me the limited options he had for transportation, entertainment, and recreation due to his impairments. As his physical features are asymmetrical, his walk is an uneven gait, and he talks without moving his lips, people usually stared when we walked down the street, sometimes addressing me to speak on Matthew's behalf, verifying much of what DS scholar writes of being made a public spectacle (Garland Thompson, 2009) and perpetually infantilized (Fries, 1997). When Jayson's health declined due to AIDS, he left the superintendent's office never to return.

In his prolonged dehabilitation that lasted over two years of hospital care, not one of his family members came to see him. Such was the stigma of AIDS.

The political experiences of SWD included how school systems were shifting toward increasing their time with nondisabled peers. Inclusion remained a hot potato and for some educators—both general and special—serving as a "tipping point" in job responsibilities, with many not necessarily thinking it to be in the best interest of all kids, including the president of the Teacher's Union (Shanker, 1994). On the other hand, many general educators welcomed SWD into their classroom, seeing it as a positive shift in policy, if done responsibly (Vaughn & Schumm, 1996). When inclusive classes were *not* developed responsibly, it proved to be a disservice to kids and teachers, becoming well documented in special education literature (Kauffman & Hallahan, 1995).

In contemplating Matthew, by directing the Office of Support Services for Students with Disabilities at a large community college, he was able to advocate for and support the student body. Additionally, by being "out there" in the larger community as a member of a disabled theater group performing live events and featured in a documentary, he "claimed" (Linton, 1998) his disability, utilizing it to reach others and educate them about disability issues.

While the disability rights movement had grown after other minority groups politicized, organized, and embraced what had once been viewed by the majority as an inferior identity—African Americans, women, gays and lesbians—claiming disability with pride as an identity did not resonate with most school kids who sought to escape their culturally determined disability labels. Indeed, it always struck me that school-based support teams appeared to be taking liberties by giving labels. That said, the demystification of disability with students proved to be a powerful tool in shifting their own understanding about who they were as people what their disability meant in the context of their own lives (Levine, 2002). This is something I have seen practiced successfully in private schools as part of their culture, but it remains lacking, by comparison, in public schools.

Meanwhile, support groups and networks were forming all over the country for people with disabilities and parents of kids with disabilities. Matthew once described to me the wonder, awe, and sense of belonging he felt when first attending the conference for people with Möbius syndrome. Attention to the condition had been gained through the movie *Mask* (Starger & Bogdanovich, 1985), a story about a high school student with facial and bodily anomalies, starring Eric Stoltz in the main role, and Cher as his feisty mother. In the documentary featuring Matthew, I was interested in the thoughts and feelings of people with facial differences, noticing how powerfully they expressed themselves when talking directly into the camera. Screened segments in my graduate classes really packed a punch, impacting students in ways typical textbook readings did not. It became clear that people with disabilities talking about their own experiences was a very powerful tool for educators, and something I have attempted to always feature in classes. As disability activist James Charlton urges in the title of his book *Nothing about Us without Us* (2000).

Chapter 3

Doctoral Student

I suppose everyone creates their own mountains to climb. This was one of mine. The idea of starting a doctoral degree appealed to me, but not in special education. I therefore applied to CUNY's Graduate Center to study for a PhD in English literature, as by then I'd finished a master's degree in creative writing and literature. I did my "homework" and took a doctoral course at the Graduate Center as a non-matriculated student, attended GRE test-prep courses on Saturdays, and sought reliable reference writers. But—alas!—my application was unsuccessful for two years in a row. After meeting with the director of the program to ask ways in which I could improve my chances, I came away more discouraged, now privy to the numbers of applicants versus actual seats and a snarky comment about my GRE scores not being sufficiently high.

It seemed like a doctorate in English was not my destiny, so I began to consider one in education, as long as it would not be in special education. For the third year in a row, and now with diminished confidence, I sent off my application. Only this time the doctoral program was at Columbia University within the Department of Curriculum and Teaching at Teachers College (TC). The institution was Ivy League and highly competitive, so I knew it was a long shot. Although tending not to be superstitious, the night the application was mailed, I dreamed I was sitting at a bus stop in a darkened street when my Nana (mother's mother, who had died years earlier) walked by me and said, "It will be alright." When I received my acceptance letter, all I could do was think of that dream. I didn't know if it was wishful thinking combined with anxiety, yet I recalled John's phrase, "When the dead visit us in dreams it is to bring us a message."

I wasn't quite sure why studying for a doctorate meant so much to me. All I can say was it felt right. I had a lot of energy and drive, and wanted to channel them in a meaningful, productive way that would keep me growing as a learner, and contribute to problem-solving ways to improve the educational system, particularly for kids identified as disabled.

The Department of Curriculum and Teaching at TC was in the process of redesigning its doctoral program and I would be part of the initial cohort entering in the fall of 1999. The redesign was, we later found out, due to allegedly high rates of unfinished dissertations. A total of 64 people entered in that cohort, and by the end of the year it had dropped to half. The introductory doctoral seminar was a four-hour class on Thursday nights, co-taught by four faculty members: James Borland, Nancy Lesko, Michelle Knight, and D. Kim Reid. Over the first few sessions, I became aware of the breadth of experiences my peers had as general and special educators, counselors, administrators, and consultants. Immediately, we were on a treadmill of weekly readings and writing obligations. Timelines were strict, and points were easily lost. I recall having a paper returned because it was five lines over the assigned length. The reason given was, "When you publish, you can't go over the specified amount." I thought this response was overly rigid and—as I later found out when actually publishing—not entirely true. When I emailed the professor to point out how much time I had spent getting the assignment "right" that it had taken me into the middle of night on work day, and the page limits were not "over" to an egregious extent, I received the response, "Please feel free not to contact me again." I considered sharing the email with the college president, along with a note about how I was paying thousands of dollars from my life savings to take this degree, and had found clear directions and common courtesy to be lacking in a leader. However, I figured that action may result in me becoming persona non grata in the program, so I bit my tongue and simply lost respect for the person.

I had usual feelings of being unworthy to be in the group, wondering when the professors would find out they'd made a mistake in my acceptance. At first, I was reticent to speak in class but, as the weeks went by, became more comfortable. One of the first people I met was Jan Valle when we were grouped together because of our interest in learning disabilities. She was smart, funny, charismatic, and accomplished—already working as an adjunct in the master's program there. We hit it off straight away. Years later when I confessed to her that she was my role model of how to act and talk in a doctoral seminar, so poised and at ease, inspiring me to think "I want to be just like Jan Valle," she almost fell off her seat laughing.

I am not sure if it was because I wanted my money's worth or simply fear of failure, but I sank my teeth into learning like I never had before. Ploughing through set texts, reading and rereading assigned articles, and completing self-selected additional readings became the norm. Studying the genre of academic writing, analyzing the conventions of how researchers structured their articles, pondering the meanings of epistemology, ontology, and methodology absorbed me. I had never really thought of knowledge as a concept before: What constitutes knowledge? Who decides? What is truth? Who decides? What is knowledge's relation to truth? What are ways that we can find out new knowledge? What is scientific knowledge applied to social sciences? Can it be as infallible as it claims to be? Or, is scientific knowledge a form of social knowledge, an invention of humans, and only one of many ways of looking at the world? What is the nature of knowledge and truth when studying teaching and learning? These questions fascinated me because of their open-endedness and their ability to stir educational researchers in so many different ways.

Unexpectedly, despite a resolve to remove myself from the world of special education, I found myself thinking about learning disabilities again. This was largely due to coming to know D. Kim Reid, a veteran of the field, who had shifted from positivist conceptualizations of LD to post-positivist interpretations of it as a social construct, that is, LD as a phenomenon created by society for students who did not meet cultural expectations of literacy. This type of thinking was radical to me, and refreshing. While Kim Reid acknowledged some biological differences within the human brain, the scientific reasoning of LD did not hold water for her. Rather, learning differences were part of human variation, and as a society, we had created LD. In our seminar, she introduced us all to the work of Christine Sleeter a former special education teacher who narrated the history of LD in an alternative way to official renderings. Reading *Why Is There Learning Disabilities? A Critical Analysis of the Birth of the Field in its Social Context* (1987) stopped me in my tracks. Sleeter's version described the creation of a LD label because the United States had abruptly raised standards after Russia had sent Sputnik into space, and subsequently, an unexpectedly large number of middle-class white children began to fail school. The category was invented, Sleeter claimed, to keep these students apart from other disability categories and common labels prevalent at the time such as mentally retarded, slow learner, emotionally disturbed, and culturally deprived. In contrast, LD was primarily used for white, middle-class students, who were "normal" except for an expected level of academic performance. In brief, Kim Reid's openness in considering multiple versions of what LD meant served to draw me back toward the field I had viewed as insular and limited.

As the end of the first semester drew to a close and the final high stakes literature review was to be coauthored by four peers, I was in the same group as Jan and two other students. We chose contemporary research in LD, first meeting in my apartment to discuss a plan and divide sections and responsibilities, and then went our separate ways to complete individual tasks. When it came to merge our components, we decided to do so as a group, in Jan's small studio apartment near campus. On a Saturday morning in December, we began our work, cowriting each sentence, checking in for agreement. Food was delivered several times, and much later, Jan's husband, Paul, came home, removed his hearing aids, and went to bed across the room, leaving us to work until the early hours of Sunday morning. That day (and night) symbolized whatever it took to get the job done, we'd do it.

In the second semester, doctoral students continued to explore different research paradigms with view to where we currently positioned ourselves. Reading various versions of educational histories, we began to understand how much the politics of public schooling was inextricably tied to a nation's identity and aspirations, both national and international. The "curriculum wars," that is, what gets taught and emphasized, and what does not get taught and is de-emphasized in the content of education was fascinating, encapsulating battlefields wherein words and ideas were used to assert, attack, defend, and rebuff—always with view to being victorious in staking claims in the terrain of knowledge. Race, social class, gender, and nationality were foci in classes, and mixed with policy, politics, and civil rights. These topics were duly analyzed within educational research, and linked to different theoretical frameworks, researcher dispositions, choice of methodologies, types of analysis, and results or findings. Sometimes, highly venerated faculty such as Maxine Greene presented to us, along with other distinguished professors and advanced doctoral students.

They say a good doctoral program should destabilize the worldview with which you entered it, and that was certainly the case at TC. The breadth and density of ideas, the plurality of perspectives, the diversity of thinkers among faculty and peers proved to be an incredibly stimulating environment. Along with intellectual growth came growing pains. Being introduced to so many ideas meant making sense of them individually, and in relation to each other. The more we engaged with philosophers and their theories, the more strain I felt within daily practices of coordinating district and school level PD. Yes, the ideas we studied were fascinating, but how might they be relevant to a teacher who feels overwhelmed or an administrator seeking change and was receiving pushback from reluctant staff? I would find that learning to navigate dissonance is par for the course when entering a doctoral program. It's like being invited to a party where everyone is a stranger and, as the night rolls on, anxiety grows about whether the right alliances are being made in terms of ideas being introduced rapid fire, and you're wondering if you really fit at all? I kept returning to the question of what was being indisputably claimed in the name of science, and observed how the social class and racial structures in society appeared to be repeating themselves. It seemed that the privileging of some knowledge (science, medicine, psychology) over others (cultural, social, historical) was linked to upholding the status quo of inequalities in society. As a culminating activity, we wrote our first research proposals, and it began to sink in: I had made it through the first year, and the ideas to which I had been introduced would not let me look at the world or life in the same way again.

RETHINKING DISABILITY

The concept of LD had changed for me. For years I'd sought different ways to think about kids other than the available scripts that were primarily deficit-based. Now I was seeing that the demands placed upon bodies in society were constantly shifting and that now, in the twenty-first century developed Western world, literacy and mathematical skills were privileged over all others. If students could not reach the set standard expected for everyone, they were now considered disabled. However, this line of thinking rested on many unquestioned assumptions, including culturally determined norms based on the desires of governments. Reading and writing were recently developed processes in the evolution of the human brain, and exacting literacy standards for the masses were very recent, with compulsory school laws in the United States coming into effect less than 100 years ago. It seemed only natural that not everyone's brain could respond to these specific demands. Did that make them dysfunctional? Or, was it a more accurate to think of such folks as casualties in a society that disabled them through structures, systems, beliefs, and attitudes? Having worked with kids for years, I could see how damaging the label of LD was, akin to psychologically wearing Hester Prynne's scarlet letter signifying her alleged sin (Hawthorne, 1850).

By taking us out of the field of special education literature as a starting point, Reid's seminars became a place to engage with the ideas of Mikhail Bakhtin, Lev Vygotsky, and Michel Foucault in relation to learning disabilities. We explored how power works in terms of knowledge, how ideas become reified and solidified so they appear as "reality" to people. Bakhtin's work was useful in analyzing power exchanges through dialogue in which meanings of LD were negotiated and renegotiated (1986); Vygotsky's zone of proximal development (ZPD) was crucial to thinking of ways to teach students with LD reach their next level (1987); and Foucault's use of archaeology and genealogy to explain the human invention of any construct and its structural impact on society, including LD, proved invaluable (1972, 1977, 1994, 1995). Along with James Gee's (1999) meticulous work on discourse analysis that showed how power worked within micro levels of professional and personal conversations, these thinkers provided a means to expand limited notions of LD in particular and special education in general. I recall a class assignment in which I had to audio record a conversation about LD and examine power dynamics. Because the superintendent's office contained the district level committee on special education, I asked if I could observe and record an initial IEP meeting. As it happened, the family was white and middle class. Their daughter had been assessed and, although the learning profile seemed to me to fit the category of LD, parents requested the label be speech and language impaired. They also wanted to start filing to have their daughter attend a private school at public expense, although that was premature in terms of procedures. Still, they were granted their wishes and the ball was set in motion. In my micro analysis of the conversation, utilizing tools supplied by Gee (1999), I was able to render the subtle dynamics of who steered and controlled the dialogue. The well-heeled parents knew what to say, when to say it, and did so in such deft ways that the conversation seemed relaxed and natural. Contrasting this with many IEP meetings I had participated in as a teacher, I recalled how parents were usually viewed as someone to sign off on decisions already made.

This critical line of inquiry into LD continued with Beth Ferri who joined the TC faculty during my second year of study. Building upon work done on various competing discourses, Beth led a doctoral student research group that sought to explore the lived experiences of teachers with LD. Four of us—Jan Valle, Santiago Solis, Donna Volpitta and I—each had the responsibility of interviewing a teacher three times, transcribing conversations, and analyzing them with view to the sources of knowledge about LD (official/institutional and cultural/media), that informed the teacher, along with instances of self-knowledge based upon personal experiences and from teaching students with LD. My participant, Patrick, was serious and earnest, sharing, "My experience of being a struggling learner, I think, is invaluable to the classroom" (Ferri, Connor, Solis, Valle, & Volpitta, 2005, p. 70). I found the process of doing research to be both fascinating and labor-intensive. When we merged all of our data and collaboratively wrote the piece, there was a true sense of community based in large part upon our interdependency. Each one of us had to "come up with the goods" and in doing so were growing academically, finding our feet as educational researchers. Deciding to go for broke, we submitted our manuscript to the *Journal of Learning Disabilities*. Peer reviews came back mixed although veering toward the positive, and it was a good experience to revise the manuscript. The piece came to be published with the title *Teachers with LD: Ongoing Negotiations with Discourses of Disability* (Ferri et al., 2005). Interestingly, what additionally emerged across all four narratives was whether participants should self-disclose their LD to students and colleagues at their school, and how much they often agonized over this issue. Recognizing the topic of self-disclosure to be of interest, we returned to the data and excerpted different elements, writing a second article titled *The Disability Closet: Teachers with Learning Disabilities Evaluate the Risks and Benefits of "Coming Out."* After presenting this topic at a TC conference, we visited a room full of journal representatives, and the editor of *Equity & Excellence in Education* expressed interest in our work, leading to its publication (Valle, Solis, Volpitta, & Connor, 2004).

I was loving the experience of my doctoral program until required to take *Statistics I*. Signing up with two peers for support, Sally and Kenny, I optimistically thought they may know more than me, but came to find out that we were all in the same boat. Statistics was neither our interest nor our strength, and the instructor was straightforward and somewhat sympathetic, watching us over the top of his glasses struggle through the class. We *just* made it, and then braced ourselves for *Statistics II*. Mercifully, Jan's husband Paul had helped tutor us through parts of our first class, but we needed to find a professional tutor for our second. The class instructor himself was sweet and empathetic, trying to dissuade us from taking a "P" (pass) option, rather than a letter grade. But we were way out of our depth, and, after first bombing and then re-taking the midterm, in desperation discovered a professor who would help us for a mere US$300 cash fee per a session. In these sessions, clinging to tentative understandings and occasional light bulb moments, we (sort of) "got it" enough to regurgitate or apply the "it" to a very similar example. But our grasp was always tenuous, easily forgotten, and we lost both sleep and money in trying to keep up. Two graduate level Greek women in the same class kindly volunteered to help us, too. Kenny, Sally and I are forever indebted to them for helping us scrape through. Despite all of the growth experienced since joining the program, I suddenly felt like an impostor again, even a bit resentful that we had to go through such an ordeal, ashamed to share the experience—as we all felt so stupid.

Other classes continued to be interesting. Nancy Lesko's curriculum class allowed us to see recent developments in fields such as critical race theory, queer theory, feminist theory, and disability studies, all of which interested me. Bronwyn Davies, a well-established scholar visiting from Australia taught a three-week summer class on collective memory work (CMW), a feminist method of inquiry that she had helped refine and develop (1994, 2000a, 2000b). Students were required to participate in CMW, and in a group with three peers, we began exploring our memories with view to a research question we posed: *How are our bodies constituted as schooled beings?* By this we meant, how did we become students in relation to teachers, including ways we self-inscribed into the available scripts, or resisted and transgressed them. Part of our memory sharing, a collective interest revolved around the first time we remembered being "disciplined' by a teacher, what that looked and felt like, and what we learned about ourselves as people, as students, and how the world worked. We decided to write our accounts of first being disciplined in the form of poetry, doing an individual and cross analysis of all four poems, searching for how boundaries and regulations are constructed, along with consequences for not adhering to them. I thought this form of qualitative methodology was highly creative as well as informative. Davies liked our final paper, describing it as a "good start" in engaging with this type of work, encouraged some revisions, and suggested submission to a journal. Following her advice, we submitted "Tales of Body/Space Invasions in School" to *The Journal of Qualitative Inquiry*, receiving a tentative acceptance—condition of major rewrites—by editor Norman Denzin, a pioneer and megastar of qualitative research. His advice was sage, and contained the old adage of "less is more," so we pared down the commentary and foregrounded the poems, leading to its eventual acceptance (Connor, Newton, Penisi, & Quarshie, 2004).

By now, I had become very interested in the interdisciplinary field of disability studies. Beth decided to teach a course dedicated to DS for students concentrating in LD. The readings were wide-ranging, reflecting many fields of study, and I found DS encouraged expansive ways to conceptualize and theorize human differences. What came out of this seminar was our increased confidence to challenge the existing limitations of LD (and other disabilities) in the field of special education. One of main texts was *Claiming Disability* (1998a) by Simi Linton, a powerful treatise that included her assertions that special education *is* not the answer but actually part of the problem. As wheelchair user, and former professor of education, Linton culled from her own history, experiences with children and teachers in schools, various forms of media, histories, sociological, anthropological, and medical studies, weaving disparate yet connected sources to make powerful points about the oppression felt by the disabled population as a result of imposed limitations—all in a coherent volume that advocated disability to be "claimed" with pride, as were other markers of identity related to race, gender, and sexuality. Appearing at TC to introduce the film *Leibe Perla* (Kowarsky & Rozen, 1999), a documentary about little people in both contemporary times and Nazi Germany, I found her perspective on disabilities moved me as her ideas resonated with my personal and professional experiences. As a young gay man, I was an activist with view to educating straight people of how "normal" being gay was, and it was their misinformation, fear, and stereotypes that had to be addressed, not me. Likewise, I knew there had to be different ways for society to conceptualize people with disabilities as equals to nondisabled people, but it seemed like I'd been searching for the words since I entered special education, perhaps even before that. Disability Studies helped give me the words I'd previously searched for in vain.

PRESENTING: RESEARCH AT CONFERENCES, PRACTICE IN SCHOOLS

While DS was interdisciplinary, there was a great irony in that educational researchers who were interested were viewed as outliers (Bogdan & Biklen, 1977; Gallagher, 1998; Heshusius, 1989; Skrtic, 1995). After all, many professionals within the field of DS had a history of unpleasant experiences in schools, many of them segregated. That said, a small group of scholars from National Louis University in Chicago decided to host a conference on the idea of disability studies in education. Given our research on teachers with LD and their unique contributions of knowledge based upon their own experiences as a student and a teacher, along with their personal mediation of cultural messages, Beth thought it would be a good idea to present. So off we flew to the Windy City, not quite sure what to expect. To our surprise, the conference was very small, with only about 30 people in attendance. The organizers, Valerie Owen, Terry Jo Smith, and Paula Neville, had created a weekend of scheduled presentations punctuated by breaks that allowed conversations among participants. A seasoned scholar named Bill Rhodes was celebrated, given an award by Scot Danforth, recognizing his critical work on ways in which special education labels pathologized children. In Rhodes's speech, attendees came to know he had been blackballed within the field of special education for daring to critique its ideologies, including those that were once his own that he now ought to revise (Rhodes, 1995). This was a pattern, I would also come to find out, that had happened to other special educators who sought to question school systems, classroom structures, disability labels, and research methodologies (Gallagher, Heshusius, Iona, & Skrtic, 2003).

The most nerve-wracking part of the conference was to present our own research. When that morning came, we took our four seats behind the presenters' table, and added a fifth as Robert, one of our participants, had come with us. As the clock ticked, we only had one person in the audience. It was Paul, Jan's husband. Our hearts sank. We'd came all this way to Chicago and had no one to hear our presentation. It was then Beth sprang up, walked out and, after a few minutes, came back with Ellen Brantlinger in tow. Ellen was pretty much a megastar in some circles, as she had published a rigorous analysis and scathing critique of the limitations of special education research that had been published—once rejected by special education publications—in the top-tier *Review of Educational Research* under the title "Using Ideologies: Cases of Non-Recognition of the Politics of Research and Practice in Special Education" (Brantlinger, 1997). Many scholars in the field of special education were outraged at her sharp analysis that rendered them hypocritical, self-serving, and self-positioned to be immune from critique. Several high-profile scholars responded in what appeared as foot stamping and insult-hurling rather than a constructive dialogue. For example, Kauffmann (1999) referred to Ellen variously as "self-loathing" (p. 245), "among scam artists" (p. 249) and "charlatans" (p. 250) responsible for "scurrilous reviews of special education" (p. 245). This imagined "giant" who dared to speak back to the established order did not look Amazonian as might be expected, but rather took the form of a bespectacled, Jesus-sandal wearing grandmother. With Ellen and Paul (bless him) as our audience, we were nervous and happy in equal measure, and proceeded to present. Afterwards, Ellen's questions were insightful, gently probing, and conveyed an earnest interest in our work, strongly encouraging Robert, our research participant, to "come out" at work as LD. That was our introduction to presenting research at a national conference.

The rest of the conference was interesting, too, as what united us as educators was the desire to assert alternative conceptualizations of disability within educational research and practice. In addition to Scot Danforth, I also met Susan Gabel, Linda Ware, Deb Gallagher, and Phil Smith, all of whom I would come to work with in some shape or form. But at that moment, I had no idea this would come to pass. During the last session called Town Hall, we pulled our chairs into a circle and had a semi-structured conversation about our dissatisfactions with special education, and our desire to enrich and expand thinking around disability and education without everything being placed into the default box of special education. The culmination of the conference was a strange mix of being happy to have found some fairly like-minded people, but recognizing that the work ahead seemed formidable at best, impossible at worst. Still, the groundwork has been set. Previously, Linda Ware had hosted an international conference at Rochester University funded by Spenser Grant in which disability and exclusion was looked at across several educational contexts. A few months later, Scot Danforth had also created the Coalition for Open Inquiry in Special Education (COISE), coordinating a panel presentation at the national conference of The Association for Severely Handicapped (TASH), titled "Ways of Constructing Lives and Disabilities: The Case for Open Inquiry." In wondering about what to call the group at our conference, Susan Gabel shared that she'd already applied for permission with The American Educational Research Association (AERA) to have a Special Interest Group called Disabilities Studies in Education (DSE). We agreed to utilize the name for our loosely assembled group, and that point became the galvanization of our collective desire to change how disability is understood within education.

Presenting at AERA for the first time felt harrowing, although in retrospect, it's par for the course of any aspiring doctoral student. Being on a panel with established scholars made it feel worse, although I took some solace that they, too, once upon a time had started with baby steps. On top of that, I wasn't quite ready to present our collective study, assuming that Beth would take the lead. While preparing in the conference room, she decided to step back and have a doctoral student speak for us all. My name was next in the lineup, so I was charged with speaking after Mara Sapon-Shevin, whose books and articles I loved (Sapon-Shevin, 1996, 2007a, 2007b). After her strong presentation that oozed with confidence, I trembled a bit and delivered mine in a shaking voice. But I got through it, proving to myself that it could be done. The best part of the experience was being in the host city of New Orleans, and we all needed no excuse to go out onto Bourbon Street and soak up the seemingly perpetual festivities.

And so DSE began to evolve, nurtured between the gigantic event of AERA with over 15,000 attendees presenting their research on the conservative and predictable to the radical and unpredictable, and the annual DSE conference with 50 people or less coming together to share our current thinking and research projects. Having DSE made into a special interest group automatically established legitimacy, and our business meeting attracted folks who would then come to know about our DSE conference. Titles of the first four DSE conferences spoke volumes about our interests and concerns: *Disability Studies in Education: Critical Reflections on the Themes of Policy, Practice, and Theory* (2001); *Education, Social Action, and The Politics of Disability* (2002); *Traversing the Chasm between Disability Studies and Special Education* (2003); and *Reforming, Restructuring, Resisting in Special Education* (2004). We decided to host the fifth conference at TC with a more generalized theme, *The 30th Anniversary of the Individuals with Disabilities Education Act and Its Impact on American Society* (2005), and organized selected papers into special edition of *Disability Studies Quarterly* (Valle, Connor, & Reid, 2006).

I feel I have been truly fortunate in crossing paths with a small constellation of colleagues from across the country, which steadily grew larger and included international scholars, who all sought to develop an alternative framework to special education for conceptualizing and responding to the paired issues of education and disability. The establishment and growth of DSE has grounded me, kept me hopeful, motivated, informed, and challenged in trying to think of ways to best help educators educate children with diverse abilities and impairments. We have used DSE to push and expand the existing boundaries of research, theory, practice, and policy, offering an alternative paradigm to the master narrative of special education. Scholars such as Douglas Biklen, Ellen Brantlinger, Diane and Phil Ferguson, Lous Heshusius, Tom Skrtic, and Steve Taylor were engaged in this type of work "before Disability Studies had a name" (Taylor, 2006, p. xii). In their wake came the scholarly work of Scot Danforth, Nirmala Erevelles, Kathleen

Collins, Beth Ferri, Susan Gabel, Chris Kleiwer, Susan Peters, Phil Smith, Terry Jo Smith, and Linda Ware—all who sought to actively challenge the status quo. Doctoral students interested in DSE made a conscious decision to position their work within its growing cannon, including Sue Baglieri, Gregg Beratan, Alicia Broderick, Kala Narian, Joe Valente, Jan Valle, and myself. In turn, other waves of recently minted doctorates with a DSE focus including Subini Annamma, Christy Ashby, Jessica Bacon, Meghan Cosier, Danielle Cowley, Brent Elder, Elizabeth Grace, Chris Hale, Kate McLaughlin, Diamanke Michell, Emily Nusbaum, Fernanda Orsati, Priya Lalvani, Katherine Vroman, and Julia White are among those who have helped to grow the field. International colleagues such as Missy Morton from New Zealand, Roger Slee from Australia, Julie Allan from Scotland, Geert Van Hove from Belgium, and Tanya Titchkosky from Canada, along with their peers and doctoral students, have helped nurture and grow DSE in ways that have informed us all. Suffice to say that much of my doctoral experience was being part of this group that sought to create shifts in educational thinking about disability.

One of the reasons I was drawn to DSE was its compatibility with inclusive education. In many ways, it allowed me to use new ways of thinking about disability, citizenship, and rights that I could utilize in PD. There was always a balance I sought when doing PD around inclusive education to meet participants where they were in terms of thinking, then respectfully challenge them about the source of their current beliefs, who provided them with the sources of knowledge, and what did they know about education according to people with disabilities themselves? I also gently pushed audiences as to why they justified exclusion. These approaches usually served me well as I sought to link their personal and professional beliefs to shifting educational policies and politics.

A particular PD session that stands out is one where I was asked to present to all principals how to expand inclusive classrooms through co-teaching. Once a year, their monthly meeting was dedicated to special education issues. The thought of standing in front of 40 principals and the superintendent was nerve wracking. In preplanning the event with the deputy superintendent and her principals' advisory committee, I bargained. In order to teach them more about co-teaching arrangements (the *how* of responding to inclusive classrooms), I needed to spend the first half of our time together focusing on *why* it is important. Simply stated, I wanted time to engage them around their beliefs about disability, and the place of disabled students in schools and society. I would do this by actively using DSE as a lens through which I wanted them to see the issues, likely in a very different light. To my surprise, they agreed, and I crafted a two-part session called "Students with Dis/abilities: Team Teaching as an Option in The New Continuum of Services," deliberately omitting the term of special education as it signified a separate place rather than a service.

In a nutshell, the first half consisted of taking the audience through a series of related topics that included (1) me gathering what they perceived to be popular notions of special education, in addition to their own; (2) requesting that they be open to reconsider disability as both private citizens and public employees; (3) describing why I'd be using the lens of DSE for the session; (4) using the "minority model" of disability to clarify certain issues; (5) listening to voices of "the disabled"; (6) asking them to consider what it means to be "abled"; (7) exploring "What is meant by 'disability?'"; (8) foregrounding able-bodied privilege; (9) challenging the status quo of how education has evolved; (10) contemplating the politics of exclusion, and seeing certain parallels between Brown v. Board of Education (1954) and the Reauthorization of the Individuals with Disabilities Education Act; (11) relating topics we've been talking about the issues of access and integration into schools. After the break, we looked at Friend and Cook's (2006) models of co-teaching, and problem solved around logistical issues such as programming joint planning time and formal observations. At the end of the session, I felt I'd done my best in balancing audience members' personal and professional thoughts about disability, where disabled students belong, who is responsible for their education, and how we all had a role in creating the shift to more inclusive classrooms being symbolic of a more inclusive world. I had been so anxious about this presentation, worried whether I could use DSE in meaningful, relevant, and practical ways, and was enormously relieved when it was over. Principal evaluations were good, and my superintendent was pleased. DS scholar Linda Ware had previously asked, "Dare we do disability studies?" (2001) and documented how it could be used in high school classrooms. I was glad I'd dared, and could see how DSE provided leverage in presenting issues about inclusion in a more pressing, socially just light than mere changes in policy. Interested in engaging with others about how to incorporate DSE in their professional work, I decided to write about the experience as a form of narrative autoethnography called "Infusing Disability Studies into 'Mainstream' Educational Thought: One Person's Story," and submit it to a brand new journal called the *Review of Disability Studies*. It became my first published article, and I took heart in knowing there was a place for personal experience within educational research (Connor, 2004).

Presenting one's work in the form of completed research, works-in-progress, and position papers was expected as a doctoral student. Occasionally, in addition to AERA and DSE conferences, other venues included the Society for Disability Studies (SDS) and the Council for Exceptional Children (CEC). Shuffling between the SDS and CEC were like living in two different realities in regard to how disability is conceptualized and what each organization's priorities are—broadly speaking, respectively equal access to all aspects of society or—remediation. My disposition was far more with SDS, yet at the same time, because I worked in teacher preparation, I wanted to always make instruction (without defaulting to remediation) remain on my radar.

One of the most interesting events I attended was the First International Queerness and Disability Conference, held at San Francisco State University. It was the first time in my own awareness that an intersectional lens was used between queerness and disability. As a result, there was much excitement. When a call for proposals to present was circulated, it stated "Artists, Activists, and Academics" would be coming together to explore the dual concepts simultaneously. Given that we had just finished our paper on teachers with LD and the "disability closet" we thought this may be an interesting venue to present our work at a conference. So, Jan Valle, Santiago Solis, and I flew out West.

The conference organizers stated it would be a gender neutral and chemical-free environment. That meant the dorms, bathrooms, toilets, and showers were "co-ed" and inter-gender friendly. I recall arriving in the communal shower area and finding only one new bar of soap and, after using it, slipping it into my toiletry bag, imagining how it would otherwise travel to different body parts of other participants. Later that morning, at the opening ceremony, as Jan, Santiago, and I sat next to each other, one of the first announcements made by a conference organizer at the podium was, "Will the person who took the soap from the bathroom please return it?" I slid down my seat a little, and slipped out during the break to do just that.

As the invitations to submit a proposal had stressed artists, activists, and academics, we had assumed those presenting and attending would be roughly a third of each. How wrong we were. It was approximately 85 percent activists, 10 percent artists, and 5 percent academics. People had come from all over the country to be with other queer and disabled people and the diversity of dis/ability and queerness was simply stunning. Sexuality and disability pride was palpable, reflected in the program in such sessions as *Fucking Sexy Gimps* and *Ethical Slut, Devotee, and/or Monogamously Coupled*, I had always liked being challenged to think "out of the box," was comfortable with other queer and disabled people, yet here felt an unambiguous tension in the air. There was so much going on and everyone was "doing their thing" whether they were performance artists or not. In one session, Jan told us she'd seen a performance artist stand up from her wheelchair, unbutton her pants, reach into her vagina and pull out an object shaped like a heart. In another session I attended with Santiago, a white Muslim lesbian stood up in the middle of someone else's presentation, and shouted that she was feeling a lot of "honkeyism" (whiteness) in the room. This brought the proceedings to a temporary halt, with everyone waiting respectfully to see what would happen next. After a long period of time, the woman then stated, "I've just had a seizure . . . can someone tell me what I just said?" To be honest, we didn't quite know how to respond to the situation, or the conference in general for that matter, feeling an odd and uncertain mix of excitement, curiosity, and unease. So much was going on that challenged us.

The venerable DS scholar Paul Longmore had opened the conference, suggesting a sense of typicality to the proceedings. Yet the keynote speakers, like most presenters, reveled in their atypicality. One called Vicky D'Aoust was a deaf, wheelchair user who rolled to the front of the room wearing a neon orange bra on her upper torso, clothes pegs on her nipples, and a silver tinsel wig. Her presentation blended quotes from Foucault with accounts of personal sexual experiences with her partner and invited third members, describing how they used sign language to communicate during intimate sexual acts. There were also less "showy" presenters, and I recall watching deaf writer and activist Raymond Luczak describe his creative process and works, along with explaining how when persons use sign language, depending on their own personal style, it can be sexy. A panel of gay and disabled male fiction authors spoke of their drive to write, including erotica involving the disabled body. Conversations were openly had about differences for disabled queers to have partners who were gay or disabled. Another panel discussed and debated fatness as disability, and the pros and cons of belonging to a support/empowerment group. While attending one panel, an audience member stood up and yelled, "I'm crazy! Are there any other crazy people here? I came all the way from the East Coast, and I want to meet other crazy people." Some hands were raised and a meeting was arranged.

When it came to our turn to present, we shared a panel with queer stutterers. By then we'd ascertained our presentation would not primarily be to academics but largely queer and/or disabled activists and could be interrupted at any moment, and so tried to temper the language to make it more accessible. Mid-presentation, the self-described "crazy" woman raised her hand, complaining about the academic language used, and not long after stood up to shout a stream of words indicating her displeasure at the presentation, and the conference in general. We made it through, and then the queer stutterers shared their particularities of discrimination experienced, including mockery by the GLBTQ community. At the end of the day in the Town Hall session, announcements were made, often about the logistics of the conference—including changes made to accommodate requests, as well as evolving ad hoc meetings for newly formed groups such as queer disabled people of color, and queer people with psychiatric disabilities. One added item, read from the podium with the announcements listed above was "for those who are interested, tonight there will be a lesbian orgy held in Room 900 of the dorms, starting at 10:00 PM." That night, speaking on the phone with John about the conference, repeating the events of the day, he responded in his classic understated way, "That doesn't sound very professional." It was, indeed, a far cry from a CEC gathering.

The edginess I'd felt throughout the conference became manifest in the final Town Hall meeting where keynote speakers and conference organizers were subjected to a coup by the two newly formed groups—queer disabled people of color and queer "mad" people. Each took the microphone and shared a manifesto, critiquing the lack of racial diversity at the conference, and the disrespect experienced by "mad" attendees hearing stereotypic slurs such as "insane," "nuts," and "crazy" being liberally used within presentations and attendee conversations. After accepting the shift in the final proceedings, any attendees were encouraged to use the microphones to share their thoughts. One person critiqued the organizers for not mentioning the land on which the conference being held was originally Native American. Many folks spoke or signed about their personal needs, and dissatisfactions with society at large, and some aspects of the conference.

What became apparent was how the needs of one self-identified group were often perceived to be at odds with the other. For example, blind attendees wanted chair arrangements reorganized, while wheelchair users preferred the wider aisles as originally configured. Folks who wanted and received a "quiet room" (to get away from the fast pace and stress of the conference) complained that it was located next to the noisy main auditorium. Service dogs that were essential to some attendees caused allergies in others. Some wanted "trigger warnings" in the program about the potential dangers involved in the topic presented. I was not quite sure what to make of how the conference ended. Was it a revolution within a revolution? Did what started out as a radical idea self-implode? Or was what occurred largely a good thing, raising awareness about race and madness within the queer disability community? Regardless, I felt for the conference organizers who had went out on a limb to create a new space for community, *and* valued the experience of coming to know the complexities involved in balancing the needs of everyone in fair ways.

CONTEMPLATING EXCLUSION AND INCLUSION

My interest in including everyone in social spaces and educational systems continued to deepen. Beth Ferri, now my adviser, invited me to collaborate on research she had already begun. The project was looking at the concept of "exclusion" in education, as it was portrayed in media, with two main—and interconnected—areas of race and disability. As the 50th anniversary of *Brown v. Board of Education* (1954) was approaching, and as the 30th anniversary of PL-94-142 (1975) (now Individuals with Disabilities Education Act) was a year later, looking at the nexus of race and ability seemed timely. Beth's idea was to dig deep into why some people want other people to be segregated for their educational experiences. We would do this by examining public discourses, particularly in newspapers where op-eds, letters to the editor, and political cartoons provided evidence of the dynamic public interchanges. Together we located and analyzed over 1,000 pieces of data from the period of the *Brown* ruling that mandated desegregation of schools and, to a much lesser extent, the 1975 law that assured a free and appropriate public education to students with disabilities. We looked at *why* segregation and exclusion from "the mainstream" is defended, and ways in which established educational systems resisted "progressive" changes. Working on this large project brought home ways in which racial segregation was still widespread, and achieved in significant part by the special education system.

As we gathered the data, and patterns began to emerge, Beth and I wrote on the topic of special education and racial segregation, publishing articles in a variety of venues. This process taught me how to look for angles in writing about the same topic, so that new points could be made, and a wider variety of people would read it because of where it appeared. Our work included "Special Education and the Subverting of Brown" in *The Journal of Gender, Race & Justice* (2004); "Tools of Exclusion: Race, Disability, and (Re)Segregated Education" in *Teachers College Record* (2005a); "In the Shadow of Brown: Special Education and Overrepresentation of Students of Color" in *Remedial and Special Education* (2005b); and, "Integration and Inclusion – A Troubling Nexus: Race, Disability, and Special Education" in *The Journal of African-American History* (2005). Our book was also published by Peter Lang around the same time as these articles, the first in their series of DSE edited by Susan Gabel and Scot Danforth, titled *Reading Resistance: Discourses of Exclusion in Desegregation and Inclusion Debates* (2006).

I had found working closely with an adviser sometimes presented unexpected opportunities to publish. When Beth left TC to work at Syracuse University, Kim Reid became my adviser and dissertation chairperson. As mentioned previously, Kim's thinking about learning disabilities had changed over a long career, and now she wanted to share her thoughts on what she believed learning disabilities were. Although Kim had gained a reputation for being controversial in the field of LD, some peers had an interest in her ideas, leading to an invitation to create a special edition of the *Journal of Learning Disabilities*. As a result, she cowrote a touchstone article with Jan Valle titled "The Discursive Construction of Learning Dis/ability: Implications for the Classroom, Parents, and Research" (Reid & Valle, 2004) and invited a variety of scholars to respond. Essays from 10 well-established LD/special education scholars were coordinated, including Ellen Brantlinger, Carol Ann

Tomlinson, Troy Mariage, Virginia Berninger, Beth Harry, Alfredo Artiles, and Curt Dudley-Marling, among others. Each author's contribution wove their own work, interests, and beliefs about LD into their response, variously challenging, critiquing, and extending Kim and Jan's arguments. Due to a miscommunication, one of the featured authors had submitted a response, rather than waiting to do an analysis of all responses in relation to their touchstone article. Kim needed someone to step in fast, and asked me. I thought it too good an opportunity to pass up, so agreed. What I didn't count on was the degree to which I struggled to provide a coherent analysis of all responses. In addition, due to time constraints, I had to take them all in my suitcase with me on Christmas vacation in Trinidad and Tobago. Each morning I'd get up early, leaving John sleeping, and sit on the hotel terrace rereading and scrutinizing each manuscript for the points made by established scholars. I also saw a chance in my closing article to introduce ideas from DS to a wider audience. The project had now grown into a double special edition, and I titled the article, "Studying Disability and Disability Studies: Shifting Paradigms of LD—A Synthesis of Responses to Reid and Valle" (Connor, 2004). I wondered about issues of impartiality, but figured I was arguably no less, or no more, impartial in my beliefs than traditional special educators.

Dissertations are always the most formidable part of a doctoral program, where students conduct research themselves in an attempt to contribute to the existing body of scholarly literature by bringing new knowledge into the world. I had entered the program with the goal of researching ways to make collaborative teaching more effective. However, as with most doctoral students, after being exposed to so many rich sources of theory, history, research, methodologies, and so on, I changed my focus. Instead, I wanted to concentrate on the lived experiences of the kind of kids I used to teach, documenting their perspectives, providing evidence of their knowledge, and comparing it to existing forms of knowledge about LD in particular and special education in general. As I had rarely seen urban kids of color with LD prioritized in the field's literature, I wanted to make sure they were represented. So, I began to develop my research plans to study urban kids at the interstices of learning disability, race, and social class.

One thing I have come to learn about proposed research is how difficult it can be to get access to the population with whom one seeks to work. From the outset, I wanted the kids involved to be participants, actively involved in researching themselves and understanding the three issues in which I was simultaneously interested (disability, race, and social class). I recall the Institutional Review Board (IRB) requiring that I call them "subjects," which speaks to some of the problems within limited conceptualizations of educational research. I obliged by changing the word to receive approval, and reverted to my original choice when writing up my actual dissertation. Also, I was fortunate to have professional contacts working in institutions that served the population sought. I surmised that working with young people who had graduated from high school a year or two previously would allow us to discuss their experiences throughout the whole arc of kindergarten to 12th grade. Bearing that in mind, Beverly Marcus, a teacher at the Richard R. Green High School coordinated a yearlong program for students who graduated and wanted to become certified classroom paraprofessionals, serving children with disabilities. Once I had been approved by the IRBs of TC, the New York City Department of Education, I first sought approval by the district's deputy superintendent, and then the principal of the school, I made a presentation to a class of 15 young women in the paraprofessional training program. Each had been labeled LD in their school years, and all were either African American or Latina. I took the first five applicants, and had several waiting in the wings, should one of their peers withdraw. In addition, my colleague Matthew Joffe who coordinated the support center for students with disabilities at LaGuardia Community College distributed my flyer seeking research participants, and chatted with students to see if they may be interested. In both cases, it was highly personalized professional connections that permitted access to the group I sought to work with.

Culling from previous courses, assignments, and papers, I began to develop different components of the dissertation. For example, I used Foucault's (1972) work in a critical analysis of the special education system, and how disabled bodies were constituted by society. I utilized critical race theory (Haney Lopes, 1996; Ladson-Billings & Tate, 1995) and DS (Davis, 2006; Linton, 1998) to look at intersectional experiences of participants (Crenshaw, 1995; Collins, 1990). As one of my methods, I used individual and collective memory work, based on the work of Bronwyn Davies (2000a). I also continued including autoethnographic accounts of my own experiences, having seen the usefulness of method in the previously described PD for principals (Connor, 2004). Most importantly, I sought to present the data in narrative form as portraits because they conveyed real people, and humanized the methods process.

To work with the young women, I travelled to their school once a week for almost a semester where we had focus group discussions and individual interviews, wrote memories, drew representations, and explored together what their lived experiences were by first individually centering LD, race, and social class, and then considering them all simultaneously. All the while, I was developing a portrait of each one, sharing the work as it grew, welcoming their feedback and requests for changes. I transcribed all audio and videotapes myself as I wanted to take the time, slow down, and consider every piece of information shared. When working with the young men in their first year of college, I had to meet with them separately, as their schedules were so jam-packed we could not coordinate a group meeting. In lieu of group meetings, we agreed to add additional interviews for us to explore the issues of disability, race, and social class separately and then simultaneously.

I had never worked on such a big project single-handedly, and although there were only nine participants (including myself), there was a substantial amount of data to organize, analyze, and manage. Veering on the side of not wanting to throw out what they said (unless it was repetitive), I strove to incorporate as many of their words as possible, deciding that they all deserved their own chapter, as well as me doing an additional cross-chapter/participant analysis. Subsequently, my dissertation grew to be almost 600 pages in length. To this day, I have vivid memories of coming to know each of the participants: Channel's desire to hide being in the special education department from her peers; Precious' quiet ways, and sense of isolation; Vanessa's hilariously irreverent sense of humor; Michelle's fatalistic take of her position in society; W. G.'s resentment of overprotective parents; Michael's vivid depictions of being frequently stopped by police; Jared's optimism and delight in learning; and Santiago's earnestness in discussing all topics. After feeling like it took forever to write, I defended my dissertation in April 2005 to a committee consisting of Kim Reid, Beth Ferri, Michelle Knight, and Janet Miller. It was titled "Labeled 'Learning Disabled': Life In and Out of School for Urban Black and/or Latino(a) Youth From Working Class Backgrounds" (2005). It was a strange feeling to step back and accept that it was complete.

Around the same time, TC had decided to host the 5th DSE conference within a week of graduation. Ellen Brantlinger was chosen to receive the Senior Scholar Award in DSE and I had been selected to receive the Junior Scholar Award in DSE. In the program, we had to introduce each other before presentations were made, and it was one of the proudest moments in my career. Ellen was a superhero, someone who had been able to analyze the flaws within special education research, and call out the hypocrisy of anti-inclusionist scholars whose ideologies were not explicitly stated in their own work, while they harshly critiqued pro-inclusionist scholars. Ellen had done this at a national level, much to the chagrin of the field, with several outraged high-profile scholars lashing out in highly personalized and demeaning diatribes against her (Kauffmann, 1999; Kauffman & Sasso, 2006).

Jan Valle had also completed her dissertation on mothers of children with LD across a 50-year time span. Together, along with several others in our cohort, we walked in two ceremonies. The first was for all of Columbia's graduating students, and we sat in the giant square on sunny day, with proud parents and family members in the audience. August Wilson, chronicler of African American experiences in the United States throughout the twentieth century and one of my favorite playwrights, was given an honorary doctoral degree in the ceremony (sadly, he died a few months later). After that and a quick buffet lunch in the Department of Curriculum and Teaching at TC, we walked to the Riverside Church, and a smaller ceremony in which graduates of TC were individually hooded.

Jan and I were so grateful to family and friends for all of the support during the doctoral years that we wanted to say thanks. So on the night of graduation, we threw a celebration party, inviting 150 people to Moran's, a big Irish American restaurant in Chelsea. We danced, drank, and laughed—so happy to be with everyone. It was our moment to feel on top of the world, and indeed that night we did.

COMMENTARY

Teaching and Learning in Schools and Universities

My first response to engaging in assigned course readings was: Why wait until a doctoral program to learn such important information? For example, until that point I had never heard of disability studies or the social construction of disability. When I then began to immediately introduce these concepts to graduate level inclusion classes I was teaching as an adjunct, students were quite taken by the discipline, ideas put forth, and writings of scholars such as Charlton (2000), Davis (1997a), and Linton (1998), and asked a similar question: Why haven't we heard about DS in our other special education courses? This phenomenon of knowing or not knowing made me think of knowledge as a commodity, something to be accrued, stored, exchanged, advocated for, and used as a tool to help create the most persuasive arguments about what's important to a listener of reader. The interrelated questions I pondered—"What constitutes knowledge, and who decides? What is truth, and who decides? and, What is knowledge's relation to truth?"—all undermine the fixity and stability of knowledge, convincing me that it was highly contextual, and always partial by nature, as so many influences and considerations made it shift and be in flux. This conceptualization of knowledge varies significantly from scientific knowledge that is taught to be the highest form and the most valid (Towne & Shavelson, 2002). However, when applied to the social sciences of studying people in contexts, such as teachers and students as they are engaged in the teaching-learning process, scientific laws cannot be applied in the same way as they can to, say, measuring the physical universe and interactions among, say heat, soil, water, and plants. Although various variables can be employed and I saw them as tools to tell "the story" of what's being investigated, I could not help but remain skeptical of claims that results—in essence boiling down the complexities of human experience to numbers—are a "pure" and accurate representation of knowledge. I don't wish to dismiss quantitative research in general, and can see its value in many ways. However, what bothers me is its largely unquestioned dominance in the field of education, particularly special education, for mathematizing and dehumanizing the lived realities of people with disabilities, including kids in schools. In contrast, considering the social context, which admittedly lends itself to a more sociological lens, is where I think it most useful for educators to start thinking about interests and "problems." In sum, scientific knowledge is a form of social knowledge, an invention of humans, and only one of many ways of looking at the world, a point I'd come back to time and time again in my teaching and my writing.

As mentioned, "pondering the meanings of epistemology, ontology, and methodology absorbed me." In other words, thinking about the knowledge base and methods researchers use to discover or construct what is "truth" in the form of a new knowledge claim fascinated me. When I first read Deborah Gallagher's "*Do we know what we think we know?*" (1998) that openly questioned the field of special education, I admired her straightforward honesty in questioning established knowledge, with the subtext of "How can we be so sure?" Similar to Rhodes's experience for when critiquing the concept of behavior disorders, Gallagher was unofficially blacklisted in mainstream special education journals for years. Her reasonable questioning of the field's certainty based upon it's paradigms and methodologies served to silence important ideas pertaining to how educators conceive of, and respond to, human differences.

The triumvirate of epistemology, ontology, and methodology, I came to learn, could be explicitly addressed in a researcher's theoretical framework. When constructing one, the researcher explicitly shares his/her beliefs and positionality. Of course, in most quantitative studies, by virtue of it being a dominant model, scientific thinking is *assumed* and therefore no justification is necessary for a theoretical framework. This state of affairs, however, centers quantitative designs as the default position, a normed center, that sees no need for researchers to justify their premise, ideology, or knowledge claims. As the scales are significantly tipped in this direction, the world of research is definitely skewed to the point of being elitist in some journals about qualitative or mixed investigations. In a review of *Learning Disability Quarterly* over the course of a year, for example, the journal published 0 percent qualitative studies and 14 percent mixed methods (Connor, Gallagher, & Ferri, 2011). Discovering the narrowness of the field of special education research, and equally the subfield of LD, was disturbing as I could not relate to them as a career special educator, even albeit a reluctant one. I then recalled how much of the research shared in university courses, including my master's degree, was of this nature—and realized special education seemed to deliberately avoid diverse ways of thinking.

Educational Laws and their Impact

The fifth DSE conference was held at TC and titled *IDEA at 30: Looking Back, Facing Forward—A Disability Studies Perspective*. Jan Valle, Kim Reid, and I thought it apt to bring a DS lens to the law. While IDEA was a cause for celebration in many ways, in others it was a cause for concern, and definitely worth discussing a public forum, so we proposed a special edition of *Disability Studies Quarterly* on this theme. Selected conference participants shared related scholarship about media coverage of inclusive education creating fear about unruly students and anger over financial costs to the general public (Rice, 2006); the institutionalization of racism and ableism within IDEA (Beratan, 2006); the complexities and contradictions of integrating d/deaf students into hearing classes (Rosen, 2006); and the problems of using disability metaphors and subliminal stereotyping (Ben-Moishe, 2006). What these and other contributors shared was their need to problematize the major disability education law and view disability as primarily political, having very real material consequences on the quality of school and life. In addition, most authors noted that the medicalized language of legal definitions of disability reinforced stereotypic notions of illness, incomplete status as humans, and the need to be fixed or cured (Valle, Connor, & Reid, 2005). Smith's (2005) contribution interrogated the concept of individualism that undergirds IDEA, so integral to American culture, reinforced within its title. At the same time, she suggested the reality of interdependence over dependence throughout society, and the exacerbation of inequalities due to the well-intended but misguided law *No Child Left Behind* (2002).

In regard to better understanding disability, DS scholar Simi Linton claimed special education was part of the problem (1998a). This phrase has always stayed with me as I hear echoes of Malcolm X's famous line, "We didn't land on Plymouth Rock. Plymouth Rock landed on us" (X, 1964). What both phrases have in common is the disconnect in perception of reality between the disabled and nondisabled, black and white. In retelling the commonplace historical narrative from the minority point of view (be it the origins and evolution of the United States, or the ostensibly benevolent structures of special education) the tellers both (1) galvanize citizens negatively impacted by the world's current configuration of advantaged and disadvantaged groups, and (2) risk "closing down" the advantaged citizens as knowledge of an alternative story to their world view is too hard to bear. But that does not make the reality of minority speakers any less valid.

While it is interesting in drawing parallels between race and disability to make a point, it is even more interesting to contemplate them as they intersect with each other, and social class. Without a doubt, it is the white middle class who benefits the most from IDEA (Blanchett, 2010; Ong Dean, 2009), even when disadvantaged in comparison to their racial and social class group (Hale, 2012). When parents are college educated, aware of their rights, comfortable using language of the law, and in particular—can afford a lawyer to attend school meetings—they are far more likely to secure what they want for their child (Valle, 2009). This can be in the form of a specific label, a predetermined school placement, accommodations and modifications, and specialized equipment. For example, I was once called in to work with an almost all-white school of gifted students as so many parents were pushing for a classification of ADD to ensure that their child could have extended time on high stakes tests such as Standard Achievement Tests (SATs). Likewise, I witnessed the phenomenon of parents steering the conversation so the student under discussion would be given a private school placement at public expense. As stated, "The well-heeled parents knew what to say, when to say it, and did so in such deft ways that the conversation seemed relaxed and natural." In contrast, in "the many IEP meetings I had participated in as a teacher, I recalled how parents were usually viewed as someone to sign off on decisions already made." In addition, different disability labels for the same learning profile of students are common and have historically been influenced by race and culture (Harry, Allen, & McLaughlin, 1995; Zhang, Hsu, Kwok, Benz, & Bowman-Perrott, 2001). For example, the girl in the meeting I discuss in this chapter was identified as "speech and language impaired," a label that sounds relatively benign in comparison to a learning disability. In sum, variation in education, social class, race, and language made for very different outcomes for students, including overrepresentation of kids of color in "soft" disability categories and restrictive placements (Blanchett, 2006; Karagiannis, 2000).

Models of Disability and their Influence Educators and Educational Researchers

Coming to know the social model of disability was a breakthrough for me. Its premise of disability being a natural part of human diversity, focusing on the person complete "as is," and the need to advocate for access to all aspects of society were areas I'd believed in. Moreover, writings within DS provided new and powerful evidence to engage the fields of general and special education, and advocate for inclusive education. Linton's words were very thought provoking, particularly her critiques of academia, including "the enormous energy society expends on keeping people with disabilities sequestered in subordinate positions is matched by the academy's effort to justify that isolation and oppression" (1998, p. 3). When contrasting the lived experiences of people with disabilities oftentimes in memoirs and autobiographies, their justified critiques of schools, media representation, limited protection by law, and access to all aspects of society with the clinically framed, inaccessible research and saturated deficit-based language of special education literature, I could see the rightful anger and frustration of people with disabilities. Being defined, and spoken for, by other people who were not disabled—was neither just nor accurate.

Simple changes in presenting disability, without first relating it to special education, created opportunities for challenging existing ways of thinking. The very idea of demonstrating, particularly to educators, that anything mentioning disability *and* education becomes automatically placed in the box of special education, was illuminating to most. It also provided me with the chance to introduce DS, its "grass roots" origins of people with disabilities claiming their right to self-describe and self-define, and rectify damaging, misleading, and limited ways of thinking that permeated our culture. As Linton then describes,

> Disability studies has arisen in the past twenty years to focus an organized critique on the constricted, inadequate, and inaccurate conceptualizations of disability that have dominated academic inquiry. Above all, the critique includes a challenge to the notion that disability is primarily a medical category. (1998, p. 2)

Other DS scholars have critiqued the field for denouncing medical aspects of disability in one fail swoop such as Shakespeare and Watson's (2002) well-placed comments about conditions like chronic back pain, and degenerative disabilities such as Tay-Sachs and anencephaly that merit attention. That said, when it comes to education and the plethora of "soft" disability categories that are culturally determined versus organic, such as speech and language, learning disability, behavioral disorders, and intellectual impairment that together constitute approximately 85 percent of all school-based disability categories, I can clearly see Linton's point. Other educators interested in DS did too, hence Ware's 1999 international conference exploring in/exclusion and Danforth's pushing the envelope that year by forming the Coalition for Open Inquiry in Special Education (COISE). It is safe to say that the burgeoning writings within the growing interdisciplinary field of DS and special education's noticeable resistance to inclusion—as revealed in Brantlinger's (1997) article—politicized and motivated a small number of critical special educators to develop a different way of conceptualizing disability and education. As Heshusius (2004) explained:

> Millions of hours of measuring and ranking people in the history of special education inquiry has been informed largely by the self's (and thus also by society's) need to rank, predict, and control. There are ways of assessing students' learning in deeply contextualized, meaningful, and life-oriented settings, where self-organization holistic principles, and voice are honored. But that has rarely

been the way in which mainstream special education has done its epistemological and methodological business. (p. 216)

It became clear that an alternative model had to materialize.

Educational Structures and Systems in Relation People with Disabilities

In working on the two big projects within my doctoral studies—the book *Reading Resistance* (Ferri & Connor, 2006) and my dissertation that eventually became *Urban Narratives* (Connor, 2008a)—my interests gravitated to the intersection of disability and race. The first project revealed ways in which kids of color were identified as disabled in greater numbers, and this was used to maintain racial segregation after the *Brown* ruling. Using a variety of approaches such as increasing tracking, the rapid rise of intelligence tests, and acknowledging perceived discrepancies among black and white students by white teachers (many black teachers having lost their jobs), inequities continued. Newspapers at the time portrayed marked academic differences, symbolized in one teacher's commentary, "The Negroes in her room were slower in almost all subjects than Whites. They seemed to have poor work habits and a tendency to inattention. The result, she felt, was to lower the academic achievement of the whole class" ("Study made," 1956, p. 12). Education systems across the country became racially tiered, with special education at the bottom, filled with a disproportionate number of kids of color and in segregated settings. In reflecting on these civil rights years, Williams (1987) notes, "Nobody needs to explain to a Negro the difference between the law in books and the law in action" (p. 35). That these systems developed and reproduced across the decades is a sad fact, chronicled by Losen and Orfield's now classic edited book *Racial Inequalities in Special Education* (2002).

The New York City system was not much different from other large cities such as Chicago and Los Angeles in their provision of education for kids with disabilities (Hehir et al., 2005). Teaching in a segregated high school special education department had led me to notice how such systems held racial structures in place, and I returned to the roots of my own experience for my dissertation. I wanted to explore and understand special education from the inside, to listen to kids, their perceptions and words, so that would convey the difference between what Williams called "the law in books and the law in action" (1987, p. 35), a phrase easily translated into the theory and practice of education. In contemplating how kids understood societal structures in relation to their disability label, the organization of special education, their positionality as disabled/raced/classed, their everyday relations, and social interactions, I came to find that school, and particularly special education, was one of the many social structures that *contained* disabled students, shaping their sense of self and confidence in negotiating the world at large. In brief, they came to know their *place* in society.

Interestingly, the research conducted with educators labeled LD revealed how school systems were not receptive to teachers with LD. Several of them feared disclosing their LD in case their perceived status would be diminished in the eyes of colleagues. One participant expressed how revealing his status would risk being "scorned, burned at the stake . . . . I don't think I'd have as much credibility . . . I should have more credibility" (Valle, Solis, Volpitta, & Connor, 2004, p. 8). Another self-described, "I was once a self-hating learning disabled person" (p. 11). A third noted, "I think, God, there's such a stigma for someone who has a learning disability," although he was quick to add, "I don't think that's true for myself" (p. 8). "People look at you differently" (p. 10), explained a fourth participant. Without wishing to oversimplify quite complex narratives, our findings revealed how schools are not conducive to disabled educators being themselves, although several stated that they did let certain students with IEPs know their status in order to counter deficit perceptions.

Social, Political, and Cultural Experiences of People with Disabilities

The social experiences of kids with disabilities are impacted by the peers with whom they are educated. More restrictive settings limits access to social opportunities with a typical range of kids (Sapon-Shevin, 2007a). Participants in my dissertation study shared stories of how they hid their status as disabled from friends and romantic partners, negotiating how to play their cards when they were "busted" by a family member or another student. Several describe complex ways they dodged questions and awkward situations. Like the teachers with LD, they feared humiliation, yet at the same time learned ways to manage to whom they disclose, strategizing to share who they were with sympathetic people who they hoped would not pass judgment. Being in a disability minority creates individuals who keep their antennae up in order to negotiate a variety of contexts, yet can also be draining for some. In contrast, when the majority in a context is disabled, such as in the Disability and Queerness conference, and participants "claim" disability, there is a sense of pride that swells the air bordering on euphoria. Yet, in this venue, the expectations were perhaps too high, too Utopian, if such a paradoxical concept exists. In the desire for equality, everyone receiving everything they needed and/or wanted, some inequalities remained—prompting, unfortunately, some dissatisfaction and disarray. Nevertheless, there was still an earnest sense by most participants to try and understand what occurred during unexpected shifts in the program and tenor of the conference.

I became much more aware of the political experiences of disabled people during the doctoral program. Rereading history with view to studying disability revealed ways in which people deemed different—physically, cognitively, emotionally, sensorially—have been perceived and respond to by societies over time (Stiker, 1999). One of the most memorable instances included the study of eugenics, the scientific rationale for eradicating people with disabilities on both side of the Atlantic manifest in sterilization laws in the United States (Lombardo, 2010) and the rise of the Nazi Party in Germany (Kuhl, 2002). In *Leibe Perla* (Kowarsky & Rozen, 1999), screened by Professor Ferri, the title character weeps as she remembers being subjected to human experiments in the early 1940s by Josef Mengele, a Nazi doctor obsessed by experimenting upon dwarves and twins, while the director compares her own life as a little person half a century later. Such histories are what gave rise to the disability civil rights, captured by two New York sisters in their book, *From Charity to Confrontation: The Disability Rights Movement* (Fleischer & Zames, 2011). Three of four educators with LD in our study were born after the civil rights movements and revealed different degrees and ways in which they became politicized—including the rejection of limited cultural scripts and the inventions of their own—to self-advocate and ensure, in their way, they support kids with disabilities.

The cultural experiences of people with disabilities became evident throughout DS, especially the arts. I discovered the plays, poems, and anthologies of Raymond Luczak (1993), Lynn Manning's *Weights* (2005), Riva Lehrer's fine art renditions of people with disabilities (2004), Jim Ferris's poetry (2004), Rosemarie Garland Thomson's analyses of literature (1997), and many more creative pieces that provided provocative insight into the same questions that intrigued me: "What constitutes knowledge, and who decides? What is truth, and who decides? What is knowledge's relation to truth? and What are the ways that we can find out new knowledge?" Renditions of living with a disability and the different formats and genres these representations took helped inform, and expanded, my own thinking. Bringing these artifacts into special education and pedagogy-focused graduate classes helped students see the broader picture of disability as diversity, and to be active in countering limited scripts and stereotypes (Connor & Bejoian, 2006), while exploring alternative ways to incorporate disability into teaching (Connor & Bejoian, 2007).

Chapter 4

Teacher Coach

When the NYC Board of Education changed its official name to the NYC Department of Education, it signaled a symbolic reinvention that placed the chancellor under control of the mayor. As news of impending radical administrative changes reached the superintendent's office where I worked, it was perceived as disastrous—the end of a world as we'd known it. The office would close and everyone would need to find new positions either within or outside of the newly defined 10 school mega regions across the city. Now nine years with SETRC, I was in a more fortunate position than others as my job was guaranteed via state funding. However, rather than work in the new regional office I decided to take a chance and go back into schools as a teacher coach, one of the new citywide positions created within the new order. Several factors influenced my decision. The main one was to create sufficient time to conduct research and write my dissertation. Being privy to statistics on folks who had either dropped out of doctoral programs or completed all courses but then were unsuccessful in completing their dissertation made me wary as it had happened to some close friends, as well as some peers within the program. I did not want it happening to me, and knew the next two years would be crucial in executing the actual work and then writing it up. The second factor was I thought it would be both interesting and good for me to be closer to the daily realities of teachers and children, after having experienced the educational machinery outside of schools. In sum, this reentry was a strategic move that I hoped to be win-win, that is completion of the doctoral program and refresher/expansion of school-based knowledge.

The application process was online, a sign of the times in 2003, purposefully designed to weed out employees who had not yet developed and maintained their technology skills. Despite the calculated decision, I also had some mixed feelings about going back full time into schools. Would I be worth my salt? Did I still have "it" in terms of teaching kids and being part of a school-based team? The job posting itself was that of a literacy coach, someone who would assist principals in implementing central DoE initiatives, including their new program called Balanced Literacy. The job description indicated that the literacy coach would be positioned to work with two teachers in two schools to provide in-depth, job-embedded, professional development that would have a direct impact upon student learning. As I enjoyed teaching English and working collaboratively with colleagues, it seemed if this position would be a good fit for the two years needed, I'd projected to complete my research.

As it turned out, the description didn't quite match the actual job. Because of my previous experience in professional development and background in both special education and literacy, I was made a "lead coach" and given a different schedule. Like all other coaches, I was assigned two schools to work with. In addition, I was given two brand new literacy coaches to mentor, involving weekly visits to their schools. Also, I would be part of a small group of PD specialists working with—and advising—four assistants to the superintendent who oversaw all coaches for the region. The job seemed more layered and sprawling than I initially imagined, but I saw that everyone was in the same boat, trying to figure out their place in a newly configured system, prioritized by a determined Mayor Bloomberg and his appointee Chancellor Klein eager to do the mayor's bidding.

The first few months as coach involved patience and a steep learning curve. Principals of two schools where I was placed (who I will write about in more depth later in this chapter) did not want me assigned to two teachers as per the original job advertisement, but rather work with *all* of their faculty, particularly those in language arts and history. This meant nine faculty members at one site, and six at another, as well conduct school-wide PD that was in tune with the principal's vision. I also visited two schools where new literacy coaches had been assigned to provide support in the way of mentoring the coach. Additionally, Fridays were reserved for the new region to work with their small cluster of lead coaches to help them plan PD for all coaches and then provide it. In brief, I found the position to be more complex than originally anticipated involving numerous personalities on the continuum of advocating for (usually at the district level) or resisting (usually at the school level) these centralized changes.

My two mentees experienced both successes and challenges in working with teachers they were assigned. I observed one, Robbi, actively working with a seasoned teacher who embraced the changes and used set texts of Ramp Up to Literacy in classes where I saw students actively participating and learning occurring. At the same time, I had to assist him with an aggressive union representative who kept trying to sabotage Robbi's attempts at working with new teachers. We were, I assured the representative, all part of the same union, and collectively working toward improving student learning, not—as he was asserting—interfering with and manipulating new teachers. Elizabeth, my second mentee, worried about her effectiveness, not seeing changes sought within the time originally expected. She worked with one teacher who refused to consider repositioning desks to promote a more interactive class. I recall Elizabeth asking for help in presenting to a small group of ELA teachers what the DoE's new initiative was and how it related to children and their classroom practices. Due to limitations of coordinating daily schedules and some teachers being unable or unwilling to stay after 3:15 p.m., we were reduced to present in a 40-minute lunch period, providing sandwiches, and endeared to engage them with what the district was trying to implement. While our makeshift posters were falling off the walls in the tiny room, and my mentee was shooting glances at me seeking reassurances and support, I thought, *There has to be better ways to do this work.*

And yet, like most people working in a massive public education system, we were doing our best with limited time, space, and resources to try and educate. Both of my mentees' schools were a mixed bag, with some faculty who "came onboard" working with new coaches and attempting a new framework for teaching literacy with their support. Other faculty members were seemingly indifferent, noncommittal, somewhere in the middle, waiting to see if new approaches would gain traction or would eventually fade away like so many other initiatives had. There was also the resistant group, perceiving any proposed changes via school administration as equivalent to sleeping with the enemy. These were the three broad groups I had seen in audiences throughout my years in PD at the superintendent's office, and now working alongside them in their own school context, actually intrigued me as they reflected the intricacies of human elements within formal educational structures.

HARVEY MILK HIGH SCHOOL

The most rewarding part of this professional period was coming to work in depth with two assigned schools. The first was Manhattan Village Academy (MVA), which surprised me, as it had a reputation of being a well-run school with high academic standards, and I wondered if it was as needy for a coach as others were. However, before sharing my experiences there, I will focus on the other school unexpectedly given to me within weeks of this new job, after some rearrangements by the superintendent. Harvey Milk High School had just opened and it was news around the world. Why? It was the first openly established high school for LGBTQ youth. It had already been a small program in the "alternative schools" district for many years, associated with the Hetrick-Martin Institute, located in the East Village. Now it had conferred status as an actual school. Of course, the LGBTQ community was largely elated, and I had watched the hoopla of Harvey Milk's opening on TV with throngs of crowds in the street and visits by celebrities such as Rosie O'Donnell.

But the first few months had not gone well and the Department of Education was aware of the situation, that, in turn, leaned on the superintendent of my region wherein the school was located. Apparently, the kids were ruling the roost. Many of them were very street wise, had bad experiences in previous schools, with most kids struggling academically, and a larger than usual number with IEPs. Given that many of these kids had traumatic experiences including being bullied in and out of school, abused (physically, sexually, emotionally), coupled with difficult home lives, and had rarely felt safe in public place—their new school had become a sanctuary where they wanted to meet, greet, and be who they were. In sum, their temple of learning had morphed into a social gathering beyond their wildest dreams. After paying a visit and seeing the poor level of organization in the school and instruction in classrooms, the superintendent was unexpectedly in the hot seat holding a politically hot potato. He brought me in for a conversation and explained the situation. After hearing him out, I asked, "So, what will be your strategy?" He leaned forward over his desk and said, "*You* are my strategy."

At that moment, I felt a surge of so many conflicting feelings. Pressure. Honor. Anxiety. Flattery. Intrigue. Curiosity. Caution. Self-doubt. Each seemed to vie for top position in my consciousness, only to be summarily pulled down and replaced by another, without ever stopping. Bottom line, I realized it would be a fascinating challenge, yet knew I could not single-handedly change a school culture, and rather sought to contribute one of many team players.

What I soon came to know was that while it had long been in the works, permission had been granted during summertime for Harvey Milk to open, meaning principal, teachers, and other school personnel had to be quickly assembled. And while all of the ingredients had been speedily placed into the pot, they were not blending, but were actually at odds with one another. The principal chosen was a nice man, and well meaning, but inexperienced. A couple of teachers had quite a bit of experience, but the majority did not, and several were brand new and without adequate preparation. On my initial visit, I saw classes where the instruction was largely low-level, disconnected from kids, and with a high rate of student absences and latenesses. A couple of teachers stood out for their classroom presence and the higher level of instruction they sought. To be fair to the teachers, I saw a wide discrepancy of student levels and abilities, something I was sure that they and the principal had not anticipated, or even had been prepared for. About one in three students had IEPs and about another third could be classified as "struggling learners," a phrase I preferred over "at risk" which permeated professional discourse at the time.

I also made a professional blunder on my first day there. After we visited all classes together, the principal invited me into his office to ask for my initial impressions about the teachers and their teaching. Part of this job, I had learned, was to walk the tightrope between teachers and principals, supporting both in the school's shared mission to teach all students, without betraying confidences. I shared my opinions of all teachers, always first emphasizing what effective things I had seen and heard. Except for one named Adelaide. I had previous multiple professional experiences with Adelaide and none of them were good. The first time was when she was a student in my graduate class where she aggressively challenged me as to why I'd not given her an A in a paper that was littered with grammatical and spelling errors. I'd found the conversation odd, given that the paper was in front of us with all errors corrected, and grammar and spelling were part of the grading criteria. The last time I'd seen Adelaide was when I had to give PD at her high school for the day, and she said something dismissive before standing at the back of the room and slipping out soon after I started. I was surprised to see her teaching at Harvey Milk and in her class observed that day, I assessed the instruction as far too basic. The principal shared he was not satisfied with Adelaide and planned to let her go as soon as he could, probably within days. Uncharacteristically, I agreed with him, sharing that I had found her to be unwilling to receive constructive feedback and uncooperative in previous encounters. What I did not notice was the secretary in the corner of the room. By the end of my meeting, the principal and I had selected the two days a week I'd work there and the people with whom I'd work.

But Adelaide was not let go within days. The principal was. When I showed up to Harvey Milk, assumedly informed by the secretary, Adelaide knew my assessment and was quick to pounce, verbally berating me for "not being a real teacher," and refusing to collaborate. Taken aback by the unexpected level of hostility, and conscious of my need to hold ground, my automatic rejoinder was, "You need to learn how to teach." This seemed neutral enough. Before long the new principal, Danny, arrived. He met the body of students as a group, was very down to earth, openly shared his history and life as Puerto Rican gay man, conveying the impression that he was a good "fit" for the context of the job.

Although the dust had not yet settled from the school's grand opening, Danny provided a consistent, balanced presence, and he had previous experience in promoting a whole school culture of learning. He adopted a policy called "Learning to Learn" with seven components that both teachers and students reflected upon daily. These were posted in all classes, illustrated with cartoons I created—emphasizing with gentle humor the value of students taking increased ownership for managing their own learning, while helping others to do the same. The place started to settle down quite a bit.

In comparison, I remember the first few visits to Harvey Milk. It was a small school with about 90 kids on register, of whom approximately 60 regularly attended, resulting in classes ranging from 4 to 16 kids, give or take. Because it was a safe space and accepting of how students wanted to present themselves, several dressed as the other gender. Given the history of rejection and scorn, these kids were now in a place where they could be themselves. Yet, as with many teenagers, dressing was the primary focus of some, and schoolwork became minimized in favor of appearance and socialization. In some learning situations, it was a constant battle for teachers to gain and maintain attention. In several classes, because students were so emotionally fraught, there were as many adults in the room as kids, ready for when fights broke out. Unfortunately, not all students were supportive of one another, and teasing was rife.

I recall observing one class and noticing a student called Candy, born male and identified as female. She was African American, tall, skinny, and wore a medium length teased-out wig, short skirt, and high heels. Candy had great difficulty in completing basic mathematical operations. While sitting working patiently at her table one lesson, another student teased her a little too much and without any warning signs she jumped up and started swinging at him like a prizefighter. It took four of us adults to break up the situation, with one—a very experienced educator who'd worked in many places—saying she had truly felt scared. In sum, the school was an unpredictable place. Within one minute, a student who would be rejected and mocked in any other school setting was sitting with dignity, doing her best to complete the work, had snapped and become totally "street" with no-rules fighting and a torrent of verbal abuse. It seemed that the stereotypic teenage practice of aligning within factions, becoming embroiled in simmering rivalries, and widespread disrespecting ("dissing") were ironically exacerbated in this setting. Some students were homeless, living in shelters, others were in group homes, rejected by their families or vice versa. One time a group made the evening news being arrested for allegedly turning tricks by the notorious Christopher Street piers. To state the obvious, kids there were both challenging and vulnerable at the same time.

As both a gay man and an inclusive educator, I felt ambivalent about the school. On one hand, I could see how Harvey Milk was a sanctuary for kids who had been subjected to all kinds of abuse in their previous educational experiences, justifying its existence. On the other hand, just like issues of disability in schools, I wanted to see all public institutions providing a supportive and welcoming culture for LGBTQ kids. As the school was developing its own culture and identity, unique situations presented themselves. For example, students were prohibited in going to the bathroom at the same time—as it could be a place to have sex. After incidents involving students being excused from a lesson to go to the bathroom and then returning dressed as another gender, a rule was introduced that required all students to remain consistent in the gender they adopted when arriving to school in the morning. This type of approach seemed fair to me because it (1) honored student's choice of identity first, and (2) sought to minimize distractions from schoolwork in classes. Of course, we knew this was new territory within education that would perhaps horrify many US citizens who'd see this as a contemporary Sodom and Gomorrah rather than as accepting human diversity as is. Indeed, there were always factions who actively sought to shut down the school, including a powerful Christian-identified group based in Florida that charged Harvey Milk HS was discriminating against straight kids and therefore illegal. As there were actually a few heterosexual kids within the school who supported their LGBTQ peers, the place did not close, despite drawn-out, tedious attempts to derail it, and actually inspired public and private schools to open in other parts of the United States and around the world.

I wasn't quite sure how to interpret a comment that was said to me in the superintendent's office: "Treat Harvey Milk as if it is one big special ed. school." I did recognize that the majority of kids were similar to those I taught at the start of my career in terms of needing structure, routines, accommodations, modifications, and creative ways to engage with the curriculum. They certainly weren't shy. The first time I sat next to a group of kids in a classroom they asked, "Are you gay?" I said "Yes," and they smiled, leaving me unsure if they'd be different should I have declined to answer or say no. I wondered if they perceived the newfound school to be a social experiment in a fish tank. After all it was featured in both national and international news—a spectacle viewed by some students as glamorous with a hint of notoriety, while religious detractors saw it as an abomination tantamount to a media freak show. Music Television (MTV) had allegedly sought a reality-show type documentary without success, unsurprising after such a wobbly school start and a then yet-to-be proven-success story.

The kids were mostly fun to be with. They held vogueing competitions after school in which they endeavored to outdance each other, "throwing shade" in the process. There was Jackson, a quiet, wiry kid with an afro who blended with any group he sat with; Jahira, a big figured young woman, who loved poetry; Miguel, a forever-smiling musician and one of the nominal straight kids; Nahia, a charismatic girl who constantly provoked teachers into power struggles to make them lose face; Mauricio, with Bolivian and Korean parents who eventually graduated and came to Hunter College; Bryan, whose mother openly derided him for not being a proper man during a parent-teacher conference; Jackie, a street-smart self-described "bull dyke" with anger management problems; Dino, an obese and bitter trans kid who came to see his friends every day and resisted working with ferocity; Leon, a supersmart wisp of a guy whose academic performance allowed him a choice of good colleges; and Terrance, a dark-skinned handsome young man who I saw years later dressed as a woman walking through my neighborhood . . . . The list could go on and on, for the school was filled with interesting kids that had not fit the proverbial mold and so made their own in order to be themselves and survive.

Except for one, the teachers were pleasant to work with. As the staff numbers were small, I was asked to work with those in ELA, history, special education, and science. I became friendly with Errol, an older African American teacher who had been an actor and loved to teach drama. I enjoyed working in his classes, as I did Brian's, a fairly inexperienced and highly motivated teacher with a creative approach to working with kids. My method was to have them send their plan the night before so I could study it. Depending upon mutually agreed upon arrangements with the teacher, I could make suggestions before the class, although it was usually after. I asked them to identify a particular lens through which I could view the lesson, such as levels of student engagement, balancing of activities, levels and types of questions, and so on—and/or general feedback based on what transpired in class. My rule was to meet them as soon as possible after the lesson, preferably during their first available free period, lunchtime, or immediately after school. Our work was to be primarily in conversation form, talking about what happened in terms of teaching and learning, especially evidence of learning via student work, and ways we could use what we observed to "feed forward" into their next lesson. In addition, I always documented the meeting in the form of a personal email as soon as possible. This way, I developed relationships that were part of teacher's weekly expectations and routines. My commitment to individualized, targeted, helpful feedback always guided me and helped achieve largely trusting relationships with educators who knew I was an ally and a resource.

I recall soon after the new principal arrived, he asked if I would coordinate a full day PD session at the school for all faculty members. In conjunction with his vision, I mapped out an interactive day in which all faculty participated, focusing on a mission, vision, and framework of expectations for the school. On a professional note, as a participant in these occasions, I always saw them as an opportunity to self-reflect, identify what was working, what needed improvement, and contribute with colleagues with view to making the organization work better. That said, some educators avoid these sessions like the plague, as they do involve personalizing one's professionalism in public. On this particular day, most of the faculty and staff at Harvey Milk were quite open about their first two months not being what they thought it would be. Many openly wept, I assumed from deep frustration and unexpected disappointment. They had tried so hard, and were dissatisfied with the beginning of what had been heralded radical and hyped as revolutionary. Staff had experienced a school largely full of academically needy kids with difficult histories. The middle-class norms for behaviors and expectations on which many educational assumptions rested were in sharp contrast with the kids who walked through the door every day. On that occasion it was very touching to bear witness to so much vulnerability in the room, with teachers knowing they had to figure out a better way to support the actual population rather than an idealized one they had imagined they'd serve.

That Harvey Milk started out as a difficult school was not a surprise. It originated as a program housed in Alternative High Schools, a New York citywide district for schools that had special missions. Although a handful of schools were high performing and creative, with students assessed by portfolios rather than Regents exams, the majority were for kids who had experienced failure in traditional settings—those with attendance problems, school phobia, who preferred work-focused curricula, and so on. In some ways, the original incarnation within alternative schools had expanded, and the alternative students had now been mainstreamed in the public eye.

Two of the teachers were Teaching Fellows (TFs), the first ones I'd known. This meant they were part of the DoE program akin to a homegrown version of Teach for America. In brief, TFs were employed as teachers and part of their tuition paid to receive a master's degree and guaranteed employment for two years. I saw them do their best every day I was there and, at the same time, could not help but wonder what a challenging introduction to teaching they'd experienced. At Harvey Milk HS, the majority of students were kids of color, labeled disabled or "at risk," often with an uneven educational history, and at various stages of comfort levels of being LGBTQ. I asked myself why hadn't the DoE selected more seasoned teachers. It was painful for me to sit through one new teacher's class as students were verbally abusive, ignoring directions, and basically doing what they felt like. I questioned my own use in such circumstances. It would be futile to take over a lesson, undermine the teacher, and work uphill to get attention and get kids to do work in a subject I was not qualified to teach. So I circulated, redirected their attention one at a time, and helped them engage with the information. It was such a mismatch all around, although the teacher and I did focus on structures, routines, and management in our sessions. One day I experienced a level of surrealism in this classroom that was recognized by a student. I was being observed for the day by my supervisor, so had brought her into that particular class. The student looked at me and said, "The teacher's watching us, you're watching the teacher, and she's watching you. That's fucked up." I could not help but smile inwardly. It did seem like Foucault-on-steroids in the form of hyper surveillance, without any clearly defined results.

In the meantime, Adelaide refused to work with me and I informed the principal that it was probably for the better. He was not happy, having observed her class, and I suspected he was a little intimidated. Adelaide had made racial innuendoes to other staff who noticed her self-imposed absolution from the requirement of coaching in the form of job-embedded professional development. This actually saddened me. However, because we worked in close proximity and I was part of the Harvey Milk community actively working with kids and all other faculty, we adopted a professional attitude. I made a token peace offering of an educator's pass I had that allowed free entrance into a major museum for the summer. In sum, a truce was made, though we both knew trust would never happen. I told myself there had to be lessons to be learned from this disturbing situation.

By working at Harvey Milk High School for almost two years, I was happy to be connected to the larger gay community in New York. In some respect, it was a partial connection, but nevertheless a meaningful one. I appreciated sitting at the graduation ceremonies held in a small, intimate Off-Off-Broadway theater, and see the kids beam with pride and a sense of accomplishment. Thanks to Danny the principal, and the ongoing support from the superintendent, but largely from the commitment of teachers and support staff in their daily work, the school shifted from being a place with borderline dysfunction and chaos to one of relative stability.

MANHATTAN VILLAGE ACADEMY

The other school I'd been assigned was MVA located within a commercial loft building, formerly an ice-cream factory, in the heart of Chelsea. As previously mentioned, I was surprised as it had a good reputation. Mary Butts, partner of educational historian Diane Ravitch, started the school in 1993. Part of its mission was to create a more student-centered educational experience and its staff worked closely in preparing students to create portfolios that were completed for purposes of graduation in lieu of state examinations.

The principal, Hector, was a tough and caring Dominican-American who could flip between English and Spanish with great ease. By coincidence, he was also a friend of my partner John. After working in the Principal's Leadership Institute at the Department of Education, John left to become a principal again—a few blocks from MVA—at Ballet Tech, a collaboration with noted dancer Elliot Feld who had his own company. As big as it is, New York sometimes seems small in terms of who knows who. In addition to knowing Hector, I happened to know Chris, the lead teacher of MVA, as I'd taught him in a class on *Inclusion* at Teachers College. We'd had a good rapport in class, and Chris's ideas and written work was excellent. So, in some ways, I had an entrée into MVA, as the principal and lead teacher knew me before starting, and their trust helped me quickly gain some footing with other faculty there.

It was also a time of transition for MVA. While it was originally one of the leaders of the pack in alternative schools who graduated students based on their portfolios, times were now different and the politics of change entered in the form of mandated Regents exams. This decree from Albany meant that the schools' creative and innovative culture had to shift to accommodate state requirements. Hector guided staff ably, but changes did not sit well with some members, and others left. The question became how not to throw the baby out with the bathwater. In other words, how could a school still provide a creative and innovative education for students AND prepare them well for the exams that served gatekeepers to graduating with a diploma and entering college.

With less than 400 students, it was a place where all teachers came to know all students. There were four areas in the school—one for each grade—that contained ELA, science, math, and social studies classrooms, as well as common area outside. It was a clean arrangement, with additional space for a nice cafeteria, exercise hall, library, computer room, along with additional classes for Latin, Spanish, art, and resource room. All students with IEPs were fully included. I was impressed by the organization and culture of the school. I saw firsthand how regularly scheduled meetings among faculty allowed everyone to contribute to policies, develop curriculum, problem solve logistics, and conference about specific students. Each teacher belonged to two teams. The first team was by grade level—9th, 10th, 11th, or 12th. This arrangement was particularly effective for ensuring all student progress was shared. The second team was by content, allowing the ELA, math, science, and social studies staff to meet from 9th through 12th grades to make sure each one knew the curriculum of the other, and how targeted skills and identified knowledge was built upon in each content area. Every Tuesday included an after-school meeting for the faculty where issues were discussed and new initiatives introduced and developed. I was responsible for coordinating the latter, and attended the meetings of ELA and social studies where possible, as well as sampling those from each grade. All in all, I found the faculty to be very hardworking and dedicated to their jobs. It was implicit in the atmosphere that nobody liked a slacker as it would mean additional work for others. Each link in the chain played an important role in how everything worked.

I enjoyed working with MVA's teachers, and set up a routine of visiting eight of them over the course of two days a week. This permitted experiencing the 9th–12th curriculum in ELA and social studies, and observing ways in which teachers taught knowledge and skills—usually in highly creative ways—that were designed to accumulate in preparation for the Regents exams. As with the Harvey Milk faculty, my method of support involved analyzing their pre-lesson (helping, if requested), actual observation, oral feedback via a discussion later that day, and then a follow-up in writing in the form of a template I developed. Maintaining a file for each teacher prevented me getting crossed wires. In some ways, I set up my own treadmill to keep me focused, on my toes, and in a rhythm. It was important to show that I supported each teacher in both the philosophy of the school and its expectations, as well as recognize their individualized needs and interests as educators. Again, it was sometimes a tightrope walk as, in order to be effective, I had to gain and maintain their trust, and they had to know I could interface with their principal without betraying confidences.

Thankfully, I developed professional bonds with several staff members, including two first-year ELA teachers, Fran in 9th grade and Sarah in 11th. I was taken aback how well they taught in their first year. Both were easy going yet had good classroom management skills, as well as being highly organized, widely read, and most impressive of all—conveyed their own interests to students in consistently engaging ways. It was a good experience to see them teach weekly, how they experimented, took risks, learned and improved by doing . . . so much so that I really believed they had no idea how good they were (of course I was subliminally comparing them to my own fumbling attempts to initially teach). Some time after, as result of our work together, I asked Fran and Sarah to collaborate with view to publishing in teacher-friendly venues so others could benefit from their work. We eventually came to work on three projects. The first documented ways in which teachers can utilize classic literature, taught creatively, to help build essay skills (Connor, Bickens, & Bittman, 2009). The second chronicled the use of multi-genre autobiography to develop academic skills for students transitioning into 9th grade (Bickens, Bittman, & Connor, 2013). The third focused on urban high school classrooms in which students identified as LD and ADD were successful (Bittman, Bickens, & Connor, 2014). Likewise, I enjoyed visiting Chris's class. He was an excellent teacher, very much present—think "loud," in a good way—always making sure his students were aware of themselves as learners, helping them set their own goals, with view to self-improvement. In all of these, classrooms were debates and role-plays, puzzles and challenges, choices and support. Kids quickly recognized the energy and effort these teachers placed in their work. Chris and I also would come to collaborate on writing a couple of articles. The first was my desire to chronicle the methods he featured in his daily classes that ultimately served for over 90 percent of his students to pass the social studies Regents exam first time around (Connor & Lagares, 2007). The second article featured ways in which Chris embedded exam preparation throughout his curriculum, so it was genuinely infused rather than being taught separately, thereby helping students become strategic thinkers, planners, and problem solvers around the challenge of performing well in exams (Lagares & Connor, 2009).

It was not always smooth sailing at MVA and like anywhere else, as much as I tried to be deft at side stepping internal politics, I was occasionally drawn in to them. A teacher flat out resented me being in her room and one day snapped and told me so in front of several colleagues. It was a little awkward, but I tried to understand "being on the other side" and having a visitor every week who sought collaboration around constantly analyzing the practice of teaching and learning in regard to the curriculum. I did not take the outburst personally, and viewed the situation as a challenge. Soon afterwards, we engaged in professional conversation regularly and I delved into her lessons in ways I thought would be most helpful—always checking and verifying—so I could provide materials, activities, questions, varying perspectives, and so on. I joined collaborative working groups of kids, and often sat closer to a one I could see needed help and was open to receiving it. In another instance, I sensed a teacher did not trust me, despite getting along, and occasionally co-teaching. I put it down to the reality of school politics, and accepted the limitations of my locus of control. All in all, I appreciated their efforts to welcome me into their rooms and work together, discussing the bread and butter issues of teaching and learning.

On a related note, I did get mileage in teachers' good graces by joining them for a drink on Friday nights at a local bar called *No Idea* (somewhat problematic when a cab driver asks where you're heading to). I found the ritual similar to when I was a teacher, a communal form of relief grounded in satisfaction that the week was over and there was some time to relax and/or do other things. It was times like that when I really felt nostalgic about being a classroom teacher, working in a tight and communally supportive atmosphere. I could envision myself back in the saddle in MVA alongside highly motivated, bright, committed colleagues teaching ELA in inclusive classes. Likewise, I could easily imagine working in the special education position at Harvey Milk, providing support to kids who needed it the most. After all, those were my roots. At the same time, and with a backward glance, I never quite knew if I was romanticizing the daily reality from which I once sought change.

I did enjoy being closer to kids again, yet they weren't quite sure how to interpret me or my role. I sometimes volunteered that I was there to work with teachers, supporting them in how they taught so we could help all students learn. Over the course of two years, I was variously presumed to be an experienced administrator, an administrator in training, a student teacher, a teacher's assistant, and a school psychologist. I had originally hoped to team teach on a regular basis—as the original job posting had indicated—but working with approximately 16 teachers in their classrooms over 4 days made it unrealistic in terms of planning and commitment. Still, when asked, I "special guested" such as in teaching the Industrial Revolution in Northern England, creating a poetry slam for students, or occasionally filled-in if the teacher had to step out of the room. When covering or "minding" a class when the teacher stepped out, it was like going back to square one—a fight to gain and maintain attention. I could never be a substitute teacher. Without daily interactions, coming to know students' personalities, abilities, expectations, along with the formal ties of teaching and assessing learning. These situations verified what I already knew; effective teaching is rooted in a bond with those we consistently teach.

I came to know some students, particularly ninth graders through their autobiographies developed during their first fall semester. Each one shared family histories and defining moments, realizations that had shaped who they were, family joys and pain, proud and sad moments. I recall a girl called Tanya writing about losing her grandmother in an American Airlines flight, not long after 9/11, headed to the Dominican Republic. She captured the moments when she arrived home, unknowing of the situation, and the neighbors crowded into her apartment, all looking at her with pity but unable to bring themselves to tell her. There was a nice-natured boy of Arabic descent called Omar who was slower than most of his peers. I noticed that his friends looked out for him when they did group work. Omar was eager to learn, and I took him to visit LaGuardia Community College to meet my friend Matthew Joffe there, have a walk around, and show him what could be the next steps in his educational trajectory. Years later I bumped into Omar on the street and he enthusiastically showed me his T-shirt logo representing his idea that there's strength in people who think differently. He'd become a self-advocating disability activist of sorts.

While I liked the overwhelming majority of people I worked with in schools, the kids, and the administrators who oversaw coaches from the superintendent's office, and although I appreciated coming to know two distinctive school cultures in great depth, I did not get the same degree of satisfaction compared to teaching and coordinating large initiatives. Coaching meant I was gypsy-like, roaming from classroom to classroom, eking out quiet spots for post-lesson conferences, without my own base. I was touched at the end of each year when at MVA's faculty award ceremonies they gave me a plaque from my service to the school. Perhaps my ambivalence toward this job was influenced by a desire to push ahead with my dissertation work. After all, I juggled coaching with collecting data at a community college and another high school. It was a long and demanding process, transcribing audio and videotapes, keeping track of participants and their contributions. Yet it was also a labor of love. I felt it a privilege and an honor when the research participants shared their histories, thoughts, and feelings. On the other hand, in some ways, making progress with the research helped fuel me to focus on coaching work. It seemed a win-win situation as seeing teachers in action every day, noticing what worked and what didn't, speculating why, provided me with many ideas that I could then share with other educators in day job presentations and in night job graduate classes.

As mentioned in the previous chapter, during this period special education was changing across the city, something I believed worth documenting to show the political shifts (Connor, 2012a). As the license of special education supervisors was abolished, itinerant administrators disappeared, leaving only assistant principals of special education in large schools. In middle and small size schools, principals were now expected to have a much stronger handle on special education issues. In reality, they often designated the highly bureaucratic responsibility to a special education teacher. In terms of instruction, as more kids with IEPs were now being included in general education, the fear was there were few or no accommodations and support structures.

In the new regime, superintendents appeared to have far less power, although they did still rate principals' job performance. It seemed incredulous to me that several superintendents shared a suite of offices and a single secretary, without any staff of their own, and could not enter a school unless the principal invited them in. One of the superintendents invited me to make several presentations to principals on differentiated instruction as a way to support teachers supporting all kids in inclusive classrooms. I always wondered: If I were a principal, how would I receive this information? To what degree is it doable? Of course I did believe it was doable, yet knew the idea would vary in how it would be received and acted upon at each site. Such factors included the disposition of the principal, the school culture's understanding disability as diversity, teachers' sense of responsibility to all students, time for planning, allocated resources, and so on.

When I left this position, I missed the teachers I had worked with on a weekly basis. MVA went from strength to strength, and is one of the most sought-after schools to get into. Its graduation rate of African American and Latino males is very high, and has been a focus of study by a prominent university in New York. Harvey Milk remains a small school that serves as a safe space to a vulnerable population. Thankfully, many more schools now take seriously the human rights of LGBTQ students, and incidents of physical and verbal abuse have declined as straight-gay alliances have flourished. For two years, I had juggled being a coach and carried out my dissertation study. With my doctoral degree I could now apply to teach full time at a university.

COMMENTARY

Teaching and Learning in Schools and Universities

It was a fascinating experience to return to public schools full time for two years. Above all, I was surprised at the degree of nostalgia I felt—to be back among a community of teachers who had at heart what's best for kids. They worked hard, and some played hard, as witnessed during Friday nights when faculty met in a local bar. Steam was let off, pressure lowered, and professional skins were shed in the shared pursuit of relaxation. The Friday night ritual had been part of my existence when I was a teacher, and I suspect will continue as long as teachers exist. Spending down time with teachers reminded me of deep respect I have for those who do the work year after year, somehow finding a balance, their motivation serving as a form of resistance to the unfortunately familiar phenomenon of burn out (Sklaalvik & Sklaalvik, 2007).

That both principals reinterpreted the intent of the job application—in the sense of originally working with a couple of teachers—did not phase me. After all, the principals knew what they wanted for their faculty and attempted parity of support among teachers in English language arts and social studies. Oftentimes, between the two schools, I saw 16 teachers apply their trade on a weekly basis. I witnessed all kinds of teaching and learning in action, and was kept on my toes when required to provide meaningful feedback that would help in one or more of three broad and interrelated areas: planning, teaching, and assessing (Richards & Renanya, 2002). By informally dialoging with teachers about these three elements, I offered suggestions and explored possibilities for the lesson's architecture, motivation, pedagogical choices, content taught, and forms of formative and summative assessment (Robb, 2003). Being anchored in a deep, empathic respect for teachers, based upon having been one, helped in creating and sustaining professional relationships based in the context of their work (West, 2002). At the same time, I always grounded myself by asking *What am I giving them in terms of defining, improving, extending their practices?* For my own purposes, I informally categorized teaching "in motion" in the following categories: (1) outstanding; (2) very good; (3) good to middling; (4) somewhat struggling; and (5) really struggling. While I would never overtly rank teachers, believing that each of us is a work in progress and can move in either direction on this holistic continuum, the needs, interests, and current abilities of each educator could be customized akin to principles reflected within differentiated instruction (Tomlinson, 1999). Each school had a particular focus every year, so honoring that focus while also paying attention to what the teacher self-identified as his or her interest at that particular moment of their professional growth became our common ground. Regardless of being anywhere from outstanding to really struggling, the basics of teaching—constructing a lesson, determining objectives, student motivation, questioning techniques, engagement, formative and summative assessments, resources and materials, and connection to students—were the "bread and butter" that sustained our conversations.

As previously mentioned, I was surprised a teacher coach was assigned to MVA because the school was high performing. Working with a master teacher such as Chris Lagares served to reinvigorate me, too. His dedication, drive, and thoughtfulness of teaching students social studies was evident in that Chris always started from a place of Universal Design for Learning (UDL) without consciously recognizing that. By this I mean all levels of questions, in-class activities, and projects were designed to provide access to a variety of students that exemplified thoughtful planning and teacher creativity, always with an eye on the desired end results (Tomlinson & McTighe, 2006). Integral to Chris's work with students was his cultivation of their metacognition or "thinking about thinking" that made them more comfortable, confident, and strategic in completing classroom activities, knowing their own strengths and areas of need as learners (Connor & Lagares, 2007). Chris also helped students transition into thinking of themselves able to exert a great deal of influence over their own learning, particularly through studying independently and preparing for examinations (Lagares & Connor, 2009). Students were able to carry these skills to other classes and use them to succeed in them, too.

One of the many strengths I observed at MVA was a structure that permitted all grade-level teachers to know all 100 or so grade-level students and share their impressions, observations, and concerns at routinely scheduled meetings. Sitting in these gatherings, I saw the power of teachers collaboratively working together, sharing as an expectation, with the students always being in the center, the heart of the conversation (Thousand, Villa, & Nevin, 2006). Likewise, although Harvey Milk struggled as a school in terms of being grounded in teaching and curriculum, once the principal had introduced a framework for learning that unified the teachers, and tapped into students' self-reflection about their individualized learning process, a shift for the better took place.

Educational Laws and their Impact

When assigned to MVA and Harvey Milk, although technically a literacy coach for the whole school, I was naturally curious as to the type and quality experiences of kids with IEPs. Overall, both schools were quite inclusive of kids with high incidence/"soft" disabilities. At MVA, there were two teachers who provided special education teacher support services (SETSS). They held small classes in what was named The Resource Center or something similarly benign so as not to use the phrase "special education" and invoke the stigma attached. I visited these teachers—Jenny and Cyndi—periodically as I was interested in how they supported students, and witnessed the close relationships they had with them. A strong teacher-student connection in this arrangement is not surprising, as the teacher supports students through instruction and coordination of information with their content area teachers, a lynchpin also serving as an advocate. Students are included sometimes still like the opportunity to have a teacher who they can go to on a regularly programmed or as needed basis, and this arrangement is also favored by special and general educators (Idol, 2006). Cindy and Jenny were flexible enough to utilize a "push-in" model wherein they entered certain classes and made themselves available to all students, but with a particular eye toward those with IEPs. This arrangement allowed them to know teachers' pedagogical styles and course content, and they'd have a better understanding of how to work with students they shared. The only aspect of this model that gave me pause to think was that during community service where students went outside of the building, students with IEPs remained in school to work with their SETSS teachers. On one hand, it could be argued that they lost out on social experiences connected to the real world. On the other hand, the additional individualized time to focus on academics served them well in keeping them abreast of their peers every week. Ultimately, given the concerted efforts of the school to graduate all students to be well prepared for college, it seemed a reasonable decision, even if it was understandably unpopular with some students (Connor & Cavendish, in revision).

At Harvey Milk, the supportive arrangement was similar, including one special education teacher with his own room where students received Special Education Teacher Support Services (SETSS) support daily in small groups. However, a mismatch existed between the abilities of a relatively new teacher and the high needs of his students, making unproductive learning situations commonplace. Observing this occur, I reflected upon variation among teacher preparation programs around the city, and how some institutions graduate teachers with much stronger knowledge bases and skills sets than others. Although prominent scholars of education have defended our profession (Berliner, 2000), critics of teacher preparation programs has been their lack of practical knowledge and general teacher readiness (Steiner & Rozen, 2004). At times, I saw firsthand how disadvantaged and vulnerable kids needing additional academic support received untrained or undertrained teachers (Laczko-Kerr & Berliner, 2002), prompting flashbacks to my own first year.

The school system itself had changed, shifting from self-contained classes for students with disabilities to providing support through SETSS. The changes had occurred in part, I believe, by the growing number of small schools unable to sustain a parallel system that exited in many larger buildings. While working in the superintendent's office I had seen these schools grow, and they began by incorporating kids with IEPs into general education classrooms, providing various types and levels of support. As these changes occurred, I always viewed SETSS/resource room as a valuable service, a mechanism through which kids could receive individualized support without that being the defining principle of their school experience. General education teachers in smaller schools such as MVA and Harvey Milk now saw kids with IEPs as their shared responsibility with special educators (McLeod, 2001). And, to state the obvious, a system is only as good as the teachers within it.

Models of Disability and their Influence on Educators and Researchers

"Treat Harvey Milk as if it is one big special ed. school," the superintendent said to me as he leaned across his desk. I wasn't quite sure what to make of the analogy. If he was thinking from a traditional viewpoint, was I to view HM as disordered, dysfunctional, deficit-based and in need of an intervention? That seemed such a loaded thing to say. Or perhaps, knowing my background, was he trying to make me feel at ease by tapping into an assumed special education disposition? Regardless, I knew the school needed to rethink their direction. For the kids with IEPs, who were largely kids of color from working-class or poor background, their identities were positioned at the same interstices of disability, race, and class as the students I was currently studying in my dissertation (Connor, 2005). Their location on the nondominant side of multiple binaries, that is, disabled versus able-bodied, of color versus white, working or poor versus middle class, *in addition to LGBTQ versus heterosexual*, meant their lived experiences, perceptions of the world—and their place in it—were unique, and quite complex. Yet, I am not sure how many teacher education programs prepared professionals who are able to understand and effectively teach such kids if issues of ableism, racism, classism, homophobia, and transphobia were not taught. Their markers of identity shared a form of perceived inferiority in comparison to the "norm" signified on the other, more valued, side of the binary. It is precisely because of the complexities of kids' lived realities—wherein one or more markers of identity is considered in relation to the other(s)—that more intersectional understandings should be recognized, forging intradisciplinary research in fields such as special education (Erevelles & Minear, 2010: Ferri, Gallagher, & Connor, 2011) and interdisciplinary research featuring education (Annamma, 2017; Hankivsky, 2012; Taylor, Hines, & Casey, 2011).

What I did notice in my conversations with relatively new-minted teachers working in my two designated schools was their teacher education programs had featured a focus on inclusive education. Several of them had student teaching placements in inclusive classrooms. Even more surprising was, a few even had been introduced to disability studies, with its premise of seeing disability as a natural part of human variation and view of inclusive education from a rights-based perspective (Fleisher & Zames, 2011; Shapiro, 1993). Coming to know this information gave me hope in the changes that I desired to see as an educator. Still, I knew teacher education programs varied enormously, and was curious how they prepared both general and special educators for inclusive work, and what body of literature they used. Special education as a field had recognized a divide between researchers, broadly defining them as traditionalists and reconceptualists (Andrews et al., 2000). The schism ran deep, relating to conceptualizations of disability, the purpose of schools, the nature of learning, the role of the teacher, the types of instruction, and the origin of failure being either individual or societal. It appeared that special education as a field was experiencing an identity crisis, and judging by lamentations and outraged traditionalists, the time span of their criticisms suggests it is actually a permanent one (Kauffman, 1995; Kauffman & Sasso, 2006; Kauffman, Anastasiou, & Maag, 2017).

Educational Structures and Systems in Relation to People with Disabilities

Perhaps because I was working full time with a variety of faculty members from two schools, as well collaborating with coaching leader Andrea Lowenkopf on district-wide projects, I thought more than ever about teacher dispositions toward all students. In particular, I was interested in how models of disability actually shaped existing educational structures and systems in relation to people with disabilities. Here, I believe it is worth briefly examining the two main contrasting models of disability—the medical and the social—as I have done elsewhere (Connor, 2013a) in order to contemplate their implications for structures and systems.

1. *Concepts of Disability.* If teachers view kids' disabilities via a medicalized lens, their primary understanding is a deficit that exists within an individual, a phenomenon that is something to "cure, accommodate, or endure" (Andrews et al., 2000, p. 258). Such a disability is permanent, fixed, and "owned" by the person. In contrast, if teachers view kids' disabilities through a sociocultural lens, what we consider disability lies in the interaction between student characteristics and the context, something that's relative to the dynamics being enacted.
2. *The Purpose of Schools.* Using a medicalized lens, teachers believe schooling is about mastering skills and strategies to improve skills, predominantly in literacy and numeracy. Literacy is often viewed narrowly, as in deciphering a text. However, if a sociocultural lens is used then the understanding of

literacy is broadened, to mean the acquisition of discourses including talking and acting associated with classrooms, and nonhome ways of talking and interacting, strategizing, knowing about knowing, and an awareness of how to do school "right" and academics successfully. In other words, literacy is about deciphering, and participating in social practices.

3. *The Nature of Learning*. When teachers use a medicalized lens, they think of learning on an individualized process, one-to-one or in small groups. In essence, learning is viewed as atomistic, with an emphasis placed on discrete parts; additive; classroom specific; best done with others on the same level; acquired knowledge from the teacher. In contrast, a sociocultural lens views learning as an inherently social activity. By working with others, students become socialized into strategies and practices that become internalized largely through dialogic interactions. Learning is viewed as holistic, recognizing discrete parts; recursive, nonlinear; grounded in culture and history (with kids achieving higher order thinking through the use of social and cultural tools that have historic significance); best occurring in heterogeneous groups, so kids can "grow into" behaviors; an exchange of knowledge, acquired through reciprocal relationships between teacher and learner, both of whom have agency and ability to change the discourse.
4. *The Role of the Teacher*. When teachers adhere to a medicalized model that is grounded in positivist research, it is teacher directed, often rote style, teaching skills in isolation, and seeing development through reinforcement. In comparison, a sociocultural lens is grounded in constructivist research, in which instruction is student-centered with view to authentic learning occurring within a specific context. Teaching leads to development, with students and teacher constantly negotiating toward the next level or zone of proximal development (Vygotsky, 1987).
5. *Instruction*. In using a medicalized lens, teachers conceive instruction as explanation and practice. As such, instruction is often in the form of a highly plotted lesson, sometimes "packaged," with an emphasis on avoiding errors. In using a sociocultural lens, on the other hand, teachers conceive of instruction as an interpersonal process, teacher-guided, with view to a gradual release of responsibility. Thus, a transfer of knowledge and skills occurs through the acquisition of the discourse. Instruction is contingent upon teacher observation, evaluation, and then redirection in the form of scaffolding. Errors are insights to understanding, and necessary for teachers to observe in helping students work toward the next zone of proximal development.
6. *Failure*. In the medicalized understanding of disability, failure is the inability to perform skills and strategies in schools—and is therefore located within the child. In the sociocultural understanding of disability,

> failure is related to (lack of) access to school-based discourses. In other words, the learning environment provided determines the degree of student success or failure.

I have described these two ways of thinking about disability in detail as I saw evidence of both approaches being used, although teachers would likely not identify the theoretical categories. It struck me that the smaller schools of MVA and Harvey Milk veered toward more sociocultural approaches in general education classrooms, of course, depending upon each teachers' style. The SETSS/resource setting was more inclined to be direct instruction, usually individualized, and highly specific in terms of expected outcomes. In other words, I witnessed a blend of approaches to teaching, possibly influenced by educators who enjoyed being creative, yet also narrowed their focus once students were engaged with the content, in order to provide test-taking strategies designed to support them passing all required state exams.

Interestingly, although New York City's Department of Education policies had changed and included a more conscious integration of kids with IEPs, well-intended reorganizations were being primarily viewed as money saving with fears that general traction gained to date for kids with IEPs would be eroded (Alvarez, 2011). Consumer groups such as Advocates for Children became vociferous in their complaints that transitioning from a largely segregated special education system partially resulted in neglecting to provide legally mandated services to some of the most vulnerable kids (Sweet, 2006). Such complaints have echoed down to the present, citing discontent with a bureaucracy that outsources responsibilities in the form of voucher systems of remuneration that do not materialize (Chapman, 2017).

Social, Political, and Cultural Experiences of People with Disabilities

One of my main recollections from this time was observing how students at MVA helped each other in classrooms. In particular, Omar's friends always made sure he was focused and supported in the task at hand. Although slower than many of his peers, Omar expressed a genuine desire to know the task and complete the work, and his enthusiasm served him well. There were a couple of other kids who looked out for each other when in groups, and in talking with them, I came to find out that several had known one another since elementary school. Having moved through the public school system together, it was second nature for them to check in and make sure that those in their peer group "got it," whatever the task was. Teachers cultivated an atmosphere of assisting one another, and group work was a large part of the norms there.

Kids at Harvey Milk became politicized about their sexuality through attending the school. As a safe haven, it foregrounded LGBTQ histories, concerns, and perspectives in the curriculum and everyday lessons, when deemed relevant by teachers and students alike. Affiliated with the Hetrick-Martin Institute, the school deliberately cultivated a sense of pride in students, seeking to undo much of the shame that can be associated with queerness. Life at the intersections galvanized students in a greater general awareness of social inequalities, and these were openly discussed in any classroom. It was around this time that I became a voracious reader of memoirs, autobiographies, biographies, and other writings of people with disabilities. I wanted to know—and compare—their knowledge about disability with renditions in teacher education texts. In one such volume, I came across Audre Lorde's powerful words that merged the multiple discourses in which she found herself:

> As a Black lesbian feminist comfortable with the many different ingredients of my identity, and a woman committed to racial and sexual freedom from oppression, I find I am constantly being encouraged to pluck out some one aspect of myself and present this as the meaningful whole, eclipsing or denying the other parts of self. But this is a destructive and fragmenting way to live. My fullest concentration of energy is available to me only when I integrate all parts of who I am, openly, allowing power from particular sources of my living to flow back and forth freely through all my different selves, without the restrictions of externally imposed definition. Only then can I bring myself and my energies as a whole to the services of those struggles which I embrace as part of my living. (1998, pp. 192–3)

Lorde's words penetrated my thoughts and convinced me that intersectional analyses of lived experiences are necessary to better understand other people's realities. Most importantly, I thought educational researchers benefit from understanding kids' realities, to better understand them, and figure into pedagogical choices.

In terms of cultural experiences, kids at Harvey Milk vogued at lunchtime and after school in the student cafeteria in the manner of what used to be called "The Faggot's Ball," featured in *Paris Is Burning* (Livingston, 1990). It was a legacy passed down from outsiders who reappropriated the ideals of beauty paraded on catwalks in Paris and Milan and, unlike those exclusionary and exclusive arenas, creating a space that was inclusive and accessible to all. Meanwhile, at MVA, kids came to know disability representations in classics such as *To Kill a Mockingbird* (Lee, 1961), *Of Mice and Men* (Steinbeck, 1937), and *Fences* (Wilson, 1986). Each of these texts features an intellectually impaired character in the shape of Boo Radley, Lennie, and Gabriel Maxson (the latter associated with Traumatic Brain Injury). Each character is tragic in their own way—a recluse, a gentle giant with a violent temper, and a disoriented war veteran. What some DS scholars have pointed out is that the majority of disability representations served as plot devices rather than realistic, well-rounded characters (2000). In other words, when imagining disability, writers tend to present limited and/or inaccurate versions of life with disability, that tend to reinforce reductive stereotypes as they play an integral role in a narrative's progression. The same phenomenon can be seen in modern and classic cinema. Realizing this, I became interested in helping teachers develop ways that films can be analyzed in high school classrooms with view to unpacking representations with a critical eye, and balancing nondisabled people's representations of the disabled with documentaries in which they speak for themselves (Connor, 2017b).

Chapter 5

College Professor

Becoming a tenure-track college professor in New York City is highly competitive. There's a huge surplus of applicants for any position. I was encouraged to submit applications elsewhere, but I could only ever imagine living in NYC. Besides, John and I had a cozy apartment in Chelsea and he would not move anywhere else either. Hunter was my first choice because I'd graduated from a strong teacher training program there, believed in it as an institution, and had subsequently worked there for five years as an adjunct professor. Professor Kate Garnett was my adviser, and the first person to suggest I consider entering a doctoral program. She was eager to have me apply for a temporary one-year position as a full-time substitute while a tenure-track line opened up. The usual mix of contradictory feelings washed over me when I temporarily joined the faculty in the Department of Special Education. I was still on a natural high after completing my dissertation and finishing my doctoral degree, yet realized I'd slain one dragon only to find myself looking in the jaws of another in the form of obtaining, and then successfully securing, a tenure-track line.

As much as I felt drawn to Hunter, I did have some misgivings. The Department of Special Education was quite traditional, and within a range of disability-specific programs, several were not particularly inclusion friendly. I recall one colleague disparaging Dorothy Lipsky and Alan Gartner, both pro-inclusion educators who taught within CUNY and authors of a book that influenced my own thinking in terms of hope—*Inclusion and School Reform: Transforming America's Classrooms* (1997), something I documented in later years (Connor, 2015a). These respected scholars were referred to as "those two," followed by a dialogue about "the damage they have done." In fact, their book had a major influence on me, providing an epiphanic moment. How? It was the first volume I read that was openly critical about the exclusionary nature of schools toward kids with disabilities, and by extension, to society in general regarding people with disabilities. Filled with facts, figures, stories, and solid evidence as to how we should strive to be a more inclusive society, the book struck a chord deep within me. The actual epiphany was the self-knowledge about being ready to enter a doctoral program. I knew because I had read the book over a few days on the beach while traveling to the far-flung Comoros Islands in the Indian Ocean, proving that if the content was right for me, I could appreciate reading an academic book even on vacation. The point I'm attempting to make (albeit in a longwinded way) is that part of me had hoped to work in an inclusive department, or at least in a special education department that wasn't so distinctly categorical in disability programs, along with a fair amount of resistance to inclusive education.

Hunter's special education department had formed some time ago because special education faculty believed their programs needed their own governance structure, claiming general education did not quite understand the nuances involved in specialized programs. Ironically, the situation made for divisions among educators that I had always sought to undo. Now, the School of Education consisted of three departments: Curriculum and Teaching, Educational Foundations, and Special Education. This organization made for sectionalism and rivalry, as a sizable majority of faculty strongly felt they owed primary allegiance to their department rather than the School of Education. Each department had a chairperson, and each one advocated—and sometimes competed for—limited resources.

Interestingly, although Hunter is a public university and one of the cheapest institutions, attracting working-class and first generation college students from all over the city, it happens to be located in one of the wealthiest neighborhoods in the world. While the main entrance is on Lexington Avenue, Hunter lists its primary address as being on Park Avenue often confusing first time visitors, as it's technically the back of the building. The neighborhood on the opposite side of Park Avenue is *very* swanky, composed of beautiful stately terraced townhouses from the Golden Age of New York, mansions, art galleries, exclusive residences, and designer label stores. Hunter's jewel in the crown is nearby Roosevelt House, bequeathed to the college by president Franklin Delano Roosevelt and his wife Eleanor, now a renovated center for the study of public policy. All that said, as Hunter is a public institution, it is manifest in its daily interactions. For example, a new colleague arrived and asked for pushpins to be used in her office: "How many do you need?" asked the secretary. "Err . . . six I guess," replied my colleague taken aback by the specificity. Then six were counted and dutifully placed into her palm.

Classrooms, too, were pretty much bare paces with 30 seats, and if you needed technology in the form of a projector for power point lecture notes or a TV/video/DVD player you had to book it, pick it up, and wheel it to your class through winding hallways and up full elevators. Having been used to work with so little at the Department of Education, the new digs did not phase me much (although I did feel equipment-envy when guest speaking at NYU or Teachers College with state of the art resources permanently installed in each room along with a telephone number for technical support). Many of the education classes were scheduled to be at the Hunter College High School located at 94th and Park Avenue, a three-stop subway hike for students and professors alike. In other words, in terms of environment, teaching college was very similar to teaching in a high school classroom. On the up side, space at the high school was bigger than many classrooms at Hunter campus. On the down side, security personnel did not let instructors in until 10 minutes before classes started, and janitors sometimes forgot to unlock classroom doors, impacting "set up" time—something I have always been particular about. It was all "doable" but hardly the glamorous gig that the general public envisioned it to be.

The new dean of the School of Education, Dr. David Steiner, arrived the same time as me. I had not known anything about him before, and everything I heard about him sounded a bit intimidating—educated at Eton, Oxford, and Harvard, reputedly a speaker of 10 languages, son of an eminent intellectual George Steiner, and unfettered critic of teacher education programs. The associate dean, Dr. Carla Asher, efficiently managed much of the daily bureaucratic business of the school. With over 3,000 students, over 70 full-time professors, and hundreds of adjuncts, she watched over organization and finances like a hawk, possessing a manner that was direct and business-like. What struck me immediately were feelings of being micromanaged by most colleagues who complained openly about the SoE administration at every opportunity. My modus operandi was to focus on teaching classes and keep a low profile. At the required monthly department meetings, I observed inevitable institutional politics in play, usually with a buttoned lip, as new faculty members do. There's always the real possibility of being voted off the island by the department's personnel and budgeting committee—a group of five tenured elected representatives—if they didn't like your views.

I tended to like most of my colleagues, although I rarely saw them. Only once a month everyone sat in the same room for a two-hour meeting. Hunter is considered "a commuter" university, meaning students come for the day and go home at night, unlike institutions with dormitories. As such, many faculty members only came in on days they taught, programming themselves for two days a week. It was hard to get to know several colleagues, with one person—whose office was next door to mine—taking a semester to say hello. Soon after, she experienced mice in her room and got it into her head that it was my fault because I always kept a bowl of fruit in my office. Matters came to a head when she openly blamed me, but in doing so let slip she had been into my locked office. When inquiring her how she gained access, my colleague lied and claimed the janitor was emptying my trashcan. I'd always kept my trashcan in the hallway outside of my door. Given that (1) our floor was directly above the faculty kitchen and cafeteria, (2) there were mice running around regularly in the hallways, (3) all students were on the move and brought food to classes, and (4) left trash in receptacles that were not always collected when classes ended at 9:40 p.m. . . . I was baffled that none of these factored into her thinking. On the contrary, although keeping fruit on hand so I could snack healthily when having long, unpredictable hours, I never once saw any evidence of mice droppings. The fact that she was snooping in my room indicated an unhealthy and unjustified obsession in pinning the mice on me, metaphorically speaking. When my colleague approached me for the umpteenth time, I clearly repeated in a measured tone, "I-am-not-your-rodent-problem," in manner that signified "stop this nonsense." Thankfully, she finally backed off. I figured I'd rather state my case and take my tenure chances alienating a colleague than work in an intolerable environment of pettiness.

I also wondered about philosophical differences with faculty members in the department as my paradigm for thinking about disability and education was now firmly within disability studies. Most were not curious about DS although the discipline was known to some colleagues. Simi Linton had actually taught in the educational foundations department at Hunter before I came. I recall one faculty member openly mocking me for claiming DS as my grounding as if I were betraying the special education cause, aspiring to be trendy, or both. I found the world of special education—and the department no exception, as evidenced in the mocking member—to be quite staid, static in thinking, without sufficient professional growth or innovation. It would be a strange tenure tightrope to walk, so I decided to be strategic and publish within both fields of special education and DS. This way, I'd be able to follow my passion and instincts in DS as well as provide evidence of research and engagement within special education journals.

ADJUSTING TO THE TRANSITION

The best part of being a professor, just like the best part of being a teacher, is the students. During the first full semester, I was given four courses to teach: Inclusive Instruction in General Education Classrooms for Students with Learning and Behavior Disorders; Methods of Teaching Reading to Students with LD; Practicum (job embedded student teaching); and Research Seminar. Each one took a fair bit of weekly preparation and grading time, and for

Practicum, I visited all 12 students at least twice in their classrooms. Once, going into a first grade class in Harlem to observe the teacher, I went to sit down on a spare seat at a table of kids. One of them became very excited and stammered, "Are you the-the-the—" I waited in anticipation, "—President?" Apparently, a middle-aged white man in a suit made me appear like G. W. Bush. Equal parts amused and mortified that I was interchangeable with Dubya, I quickly asked the kids to explain what they were working on.

The methods course was jam-packed with strategies for teaching broad domains within reading: phonemic awareness; phonics; vocabulary; fluency; and comprehension. It gave students a good handle on the intricacies and complications of why some kids struggled with reading, and involved opportunities to practice in class to explore, reflect upon, and critique each reading method. The National Institute for Literacy's Reading Panel's then recent findings and suggestions (2001) were already mirrored in the longstanding course, verifying my belief that the content was solid.

The research seminar was "the capstone" course of the degree in which students researched an area of interest, made a power point presentation to peers that synthesized the research, and wrote a grant proposal related to their findings. The course was interesting because students from all special education programs were mixed together—so everyone heard about issues in early childhood (including autism), deaf/hard of hearing, behavior disorders, learning disabilities, blind and visual impairment, severe and multiple disabilities, and so on. Alternatively, what lessened interest for me was the unquestioned emphasis on students using only quantitative methods that they would think to be the "gold standard" of research. It seemed a case of the Emperor's New Clothes, with students reciting the results of research but not really cognizant of the methodology or process. It was not long before I encouraged them to equally engage with qualitative and mixed methods.

During my first year, I worked with a group of teaching fellows (TFs), NYC locals who aspired to be teachers and signed up for a two-year program sponsored by the Department of Education. It was almost a trial-by-fire approach in which students immediately began as teachers after a summer training and a couple of introductory graduate courses, often being placed in high needs schools. The first few weeks were traumatic for TFs, and I empathized with them deeply, keenly aware of the culture shock being experienced. Some quit within the first week or two, and when this happened I would always wonder what we could have said or done differently to support them in the all-important first three weeks of the profession. Most rolled up their sleeves and got on with what they signed up to do. A small number felt angry, betrayed by the Department of Education's glossy subway advertisements about changing lives in comparison to how they actually experienced the job.

I recall a variety of students from my first year including Kristen, a feisty TF who challenged the program at every turn (but would, in a wonderful twist of irony, later come back and oversee it); Kerrianne, whose work was always "above and beyond," submitting beautifully assembled binders the size of telephone directories; Laura, a part-time actress who found a niche in teaching kids labeled BD in District 75; Jody, a thoughtful and creative educator who planned in great detail; Irene, who sought a return to work after raising three kids; and Greg, a carpenter who wanted to make a career change. In addition to those in classes I taught, I had other students to advise, keeping weekly office hours to help with registration, planning, and an assortment of general issues.

The main challenge for me during this time was working in a certification program spanning grades one through six. Since I graduated with a K-12 state certificate in special education, requirements had changed, resulting in more specialized areas. As each university had limited resources yet were required to reregister programs with the state, most had opted for offering early childhood and childhood programs. This meant I had to quickly learn the childhood (one to six) program, even though my expertise was in teaching adolescents. We had been taught as professional developers to "Fake it 'til you make it" and I embraced this saying so hard that it hurt. I was very anxious when learning elementary school materials and strategies, as my modus operandi for any methods class had been demonstrate method, do it together (several times), have students try it with moderate then minimum support, have them do it solo. This approach I came to find out was referred to as "to," "with," and "by." Although John and I had booked a trip to Hawai'i during Easter of my first year, I was so paranoid about messing up teaching elementary math to students with LD that I rose every day at 5:00 a.m. to read the copious manuals of a particular mathematical system (Stern, 1988) in our "escape" hotel.

TENURE

As the year progressed, an official tenure-track line opened up and I was encouraged by colleagues in the department to apply. Given that I sought a more progressive and less traditional special education (even inclusive!) department, I was still not 100 percent certain if this was the right place for me. However, I submitted an application and was scheduled for a complete day that consisted of an interview with the chairperson, and then another with the search committee; a presentation to students; a one-on-one with the dean; and, to top it all off, a group dinner in the evening. Despite "fitting in" for a year there, I was now in anxious competition for a full-time position.

Nothing was a sure thing. It didn't help that the date for my interview had been changed twice already, and, to be frank, I found the process to be less organized than anticipated. By that time, I just wanted it over and done with, and the chips fall where they may.

The day eventually came and I swallowed hard all morning and took the plunge. When talking with the dean, I could not quite tell how it was going. In some respects, it was with great irony that I sat in an office with another Brit, social worlds apart. He was upper class and privileged, with a clipped, ever-so-proper "posh" accent that I associated with vintage British movies. If I closed my eyes I could be talking to Trevor Howard in *Brief Encounter* (Coward & Lean, 1945). Without wanting to romanticize my roots, I was from the other side of the tracks, working class in origin, lucky to get into a redbrick university after state school. The culture of my formative years had taught me to feel inferior to people like the dean, to accept they were smarter, and it was natural for them to be in charge. I was therefore wary, somewhat intimidated, as I knew he was better educated than I from birth. However, I also wondered how much he knew of state schools in the United Kingdom, of public schools in the United States, of real teachers' lives? I took some comfort in knowing I likely knew more than he in this respect.

The group interview went fairly well, but the research presentation did not. The dean sat on the sidelines while my colleagues sat in front as I shared my dissertation work on the intersectional experiences of black and Latino/a working-class urban youth with LD—focusing on what they observed about life, both in schools and society (Connor, 2005). The projector was on a cart the size of Dr. Who's Tardis and, without a laser pointer, I had to stand behind it to change the slides. Talking about race and special education went down like a ton of bricks. It didn't help that I was anxious and likely showed signs. After all, it was high stakes. The dean circled both hands in a disco dance gesture signaling me to wrap up although I was barely half way through. Subsequently, I rushed through the balance of slides in an over-prepared presentation and felt the onset of that sinking feeling . . . having not hit the desired mark. I answered post-presentation questions perfunctorily, and when the room cleared I *knew* I had not done well. There was a sort of unspoken conspiratorial silence among colleagues as I passed them in the hallway. "You should have came out from behind that thing—the equipment," said Professor Garnett, my staunchest advocate, "to let them see you in action." But it was too late.

Presenting to students that evening was not easy either, although they were all familiar as I was allowed to have search committee and department members come into one of my classes. My voice shook a bit as I willed myself through it, hating being scrutinized on the spot. Despite a career of consistently strong student evaluations, I never liked to consciously "perform" an evaluation. At the required dinner that evening, I tried to listen more than speak, and declined wine in case I put a foot in my mouth. Finally, done. However, a day later, I was called into the chairperson's office and told there was a hitch. The department had nominated me for the position, but the dean had reservations, and had subsequently delayed the process. As a result, he required a second one-on-one interview. Allegedly, he held great distain for Teachers College, thinking the university's education programs emphasized ideology over good practice. Although Professor Garnett had assured him I was well versed in the practice of teaching methods to teachers that would help kids learn, he remained skeptical.

At this juncture, I was exhausted. I felt I'd worked for years as a teacher, then a professional development specialist, and a college adjunct who specialized in methods courses. I had spent most of my life savings on getting a doctorate, before a year giving everything I had to give at this institution—and now my abilities to teach were being doubted. "You MUST only talk about practice," warned the chairperson, visibly worried that I may not work there. "He needs to see you know your stuff."

When I arrived at his office for the second interview, there were quotations from philosophers printed on letter size paper spread across his table. We were to engage in a discussion about them:

"I'd really prefer to talk about practice," I ventured.

"Ahhh . . . Kate has told you to say that," he responded.

After a back-and-forthing, I agreed to engage about the quotations only if we could end our meeting talking about practice. He agreed. What followed was an enlightening and somewhat unexpectedly amicable conversation about the work of Michel Foucault. I had used some of Foucault's ideas in my analysis of special education structures (1972, 1977, 1994, 1995). The dean shared that his father had debated Foucault in Paris. Across our differences in social class, dispositions, and experiences—we wrestled with some of the problems in contemporary education. Unlike my research presentation and search committee interview, I felt extraordinarily relaxed. This was because I had decided to lay my cards on the table, just as the dean had laid philosophers' quotations on his.

"I think this is a good conversation," I said, "because I am equally interested in seeing whether Hunter is a good fit for me." It was true. I didn't want to be where my own thinking and experiences weren't understood or valued and I knew I could make a contribution somewhere else. By saying this, I felt parity in terms of power within the situation. If the first-year dean vetoed the department's wish to have me on faculty, it would likely have unfavorable consequences for him, too, in terms of confidence and popularity. As we wound down the meeting, it felt a peaceful situation. We had sparred about educational philosophy, and I'd managed to squeeze in some obligatory thoughts about practice. As educators, we were markedly different in politics, yet somewhat respectful of each other's perspectives.

I got the job. At the same time, an unforeseen occurrence happened in my favor. My only "ask" was for parity of salary when I left the Department of Education. It seemed fair not to take a drop in salary when entering higher education. But the only way this could be done was to immediately make me an associate professor, thereby skipping the rank of assistant professor. While uncommon, this could be done with president and provost approval if experience and publications were commensurate with expectations for an associate professor. Thankfully, Teachers College had prepared me well and I had sufficient publications to date—including a coauthored book published that year (Ferri & Connor, 2006). I was fortunate to enter academia at this level, and it was a huge relief to secure an academic job in my adopted city.

As my Hunter experience was the main measure for universities in the United States, at first I was unaware of how large it was in comparison to other places. With over 22,000 students in a vertical campus connected by Fritz Lang's *Metropolis*-like walkways between three city blocks, it buzzed with business. The Department of Special Education then had about 400 students, the largest programs being Childhood Education (grades first–sixth, with a focus on LD) and Early Childhood (birth–second grade). Teaching Fellows and other sponsored programs were increasing numbers of students served, and would come to grow more over the years to the point of arguably dominating the department. Faculty members were contractually bound to teach a workload of 21 credits that usually translated into 7 x 3 credit courses over fall and spring semesters. In reality, most professors had three credits of reassigned time to coordinate programs or do some form of administrative work to help the organization keep well oiled. Unlike many other colleges, CUNY has semesters all year around, so winter session began on January 2 and was three weeks long, summer session 1 was in June, and summer session 2 was in July (with options of stretching into August). The academic year commenced at the end of August, so Hunter is never really closed. Many of the sponsored programs needed to be mapped over these five semesters, generating a need for faculty to teach them. I was concerned about the quality of the content and skills learned in condensed winter and summer sessions, especially courses on teaching methodologies. Having taught in all five sessions, one cannot teach the same content in three weeks what one can do over four months. Yet the pressure to have students finish as fast as they can (whether it be from sponsored programs or the students themselves) is very real. The education of educators can be viewed in many ways, and that includes being a business. Coordinating, scheduling, teaching, and advising across the whole year involved a lot of organization.

LEARNING LAB

One task that was given to me during my first year being appointment to a tenure-track line was to coordinate the learning lab (LL), the heart of the LD program. In brief, LL was a yearlong intensive two-part course of study in which each graduate student tutored a child with learning disability twice a week. Students were taught how to assess reading, writing, and math skills, and spent the first three weeks bonding with their tutee while finding out their areas of strengths and needs. After that, there was meticulous twice-a-week lesson planning, along with reflective logs that were handed weekly. This arrangement allowed course instructors and graduate students to have an ongoing interactive dialogue about the practice of teaching and learning in relation to one student, thereby developing skills to individualize instruction, one of the cornerstones on which special education is built. In many ways, the course is somewhat like analyzing the learning process is slow motion. On Thursdays, much of the 12th floor in the East Building was taken over by LL and all course instructors walked around with a notepad or laptop in hand, observing student and tutee dyads, taking notes and pulling up a seat to join in when needed. Following every Thursday's tutorial session was a seminar in which students and instructor debrief and discus what was occurring within each dyad, problem solve around existing issues, share materials, discuss common interests, collectively respond to challenges, and so on.

Being placed in charge of this award-winning program felt daunting, yet my two other colleagues working in LD had spent years doing it, so it was only fair that it was my turn. There were nine course sections, with two placed off-campus in public schools. I was to teach my own section while coordinating and overseeing all others. In addition, the assignment involved coordinating scheduling with all parents of participating kids, responding to all inquiries of interest, and ensuring the provision of resources and materials to students. I received one course of reassigned time for this responsibility.

My first opening night proved to be unexpectedly tumultuous as I had not been alerted to some necessary logistics. Having 90 parents with 90 kids arrive at once, asking where their tutor was, resulted in an impatient crowd around me. Thankfully, I had made a list of matched graduate student-kid pairs. There were some inevitable crossed wires, no shows (who then showed the following week) and extras (who'd friend told them to come and see if something could be worked out for their kid). I soon realized I'd inherited a system that needed an organizational upgrade.

Despite its flaws, LL was a wonderful part of the LD program. Kids came from all socioeconomic backgrounds spanning different neighborhoods across the entire city. They varied in terms of race, ethnicity, nationality, and gender. There was also great diversity in their areas of need. Some kids struggled with the most basic skills of reading, writing, math, and organization. Others were, in my opinion, pretty much "average" but their "bright" parents feared their child had a learning disability in comparison to themselves and other "gifted" kids at school. There were kids from public and private schools, as well as some being home schooled. For parents, one-on-one supervised tutoring twice a week was a godsend. Most would never be able to afford a private tutor as NYC rates were high, then easily ranging from $60–100 an hour. Its "free" tutoring and overall success had made the program quite sought after. I preferred to, whenever possible, ensure that public school kids were given sufficient access, relying on key counselors at several schools who helped coordinate parents' applications. A downside of being a highly sought after program was the forcefulness of a small number of parents that occasionally transformed into aggression, to ensure they'd get what they want.

To make sure LL was successful meant maintaining certain expectations of parents, kids, and students. For parents, they had to make sure their children were brought on time to tutoring twice a week. This was non-negotiable, otherwise graduate students would not be able to accrue the required number of tutorial sessions to pass the course. As coordinator, I had to maintain policies to ensure this expectation worked. It was not a pleasant task to frequently remind some parents that their kid was at risk for losing eligibility to be in the program. Sometimes there were protests and tears, sometimes anger and despair. However, if firm rules were not in place, students and their course instructors would complain, with both becoming increasingly stressed and annoyed at the situation, as we'd guaranteed them twice-weekly sessions with an assigned kid. I always tried to work with the family first, cut them a little slack and understand their temporary difficulty (e.g., change in kid's school program, sports team participation, transportation issues). But if the problem was pervasive, a simple and straightforward message would be shared with parents about my not allowing graduate students to fail the course through lack of access to a child. One time, I had to stop a wonderful kid called Marco from attending, as his grandmother, a wheelchair user, was not getting him to the college on time. Several other mothers who had their kids in the program rallied around Marco's grandmother, and they all arrived at my office door one night, vociferously advocating for Marco who stood there, smiling at me and asking for a tutor. Although empathetic, I had to stand my ground and put the graduate student's needs student first. She no longer wanted to work with Marco and his family due to excessive absences and lateness. I was, however, willing to make a compromise. Whenever Marco was brought in on time, I'd find him a tutor for the night—even if it was me. This arrangement seemed to do the trick, at least temporarily, and I made sure he had a tutor every Thursday (as it was not that difficult to double up or reassign a tutor whose kid was absent). Once Marco came regularly over the next six or so weeks, I was willing to give him the next tutor available. I am pleased to share that Marco remained with us for many years.

Another kid and mom duo I recall was Jordan and Cheryl. The first time I met Jordan, he was in first grade, and lifted his woeful eyes to meet mine before saying, "I can't read." I assured him he was going to learn with us. Cheryl was always flustered and often late, but had a big heart, and always wanted a greeting hug. Over the years, Jordan was another kid who stayed with us and went from strength to strength, feeling proud of his accomplishments as he progressed through different reading levels.

When he arrived, Saul was a kid who looked at everyone with sullen eyes and did not want to work at all. Unlike Marco and Jordan from the projects in Spanish Harlem and the Upper West Side respectively, Jordan's mother was a lawyer who had a tendency to speak to everyone as if she was cross examining them in the witness stand. A pattern emerged of Saul consistently resisting being in the program, rejecting all work. Adopted at an early age from a Russian orphanage by his high power NY mother, a middle-aged single professional, he knew how to make a Type A personality flustered. Both the tutor and section instructor told me they'd tried engaging him but suggested his intense resistance was impeding any academic growth, exacerbated by poor attendance. I informed Saul's mother by voicemail that he simply did not want to be in the program, and his attendance issues seemed to verify this. She promptly returned the call and launched into a diatribe against the program and me, threatening to sue and report me to the college president. Appalled at such behavior, given how much we had tried to work with Saul, I found myself uttering words in a tone that matched hers, "Your sense of entitlement *galls* me." As I had to frequently point out that we were first a college course, not a free-tutoring service that guarantees placements.

I suggested speaking with Saul in a straightforward way, offering *him* the choice of whether he wanted to stay in the program. If he did, we would welcome his decision and discuss how he'd have to change his ways. So, soon after, his mother brought him into college presuming that we three would sit down together. If we did this, I figured, she would not be able to stop herself directing the child and the situation. On arrival, I therefore told her I wanted to chat with Saul alone, and I would do this in a public space within her vision. I then took him to the seventh floor glass walkway that spans Lexington Avenue, linking the East and West buildings. We sat in the middle and looked at the traffic passing beneath. His mother remained slightly agitated on the sidelines, sitting on a chair about 10 yards away, purposefully out of earshot. I took the opportunity to complement Saul on his always excellent artwork, sharing that my family "fostered" a kid called Dennis from Belarus who stayed with an aunt every summer for many years, how much I'd enjoyed visiting Russia, and told him I was going to let him choose about whether he stayed in or left the program. I asked him how he felt, and he shrugged.

Saul and I continued to chat and I informed him about student teachers, the commitments needed by families, and student participation—so he understood he'd have to change if he stayed. I shared how his mom wanted him to stay, but that wasn't enough, he had to want to. Finally, after opening up a bit more, Saul said he would like to stay and be willing to try harder and work with his tutor. I have no idea whether he'd been instructed to respond this way, but I gave him the choice. His reentry would be based on agreeing to participate and work. Saul, in fact, wanted to stay—and did for quite a few years afterwards. His mother was grateful, and thereafter shifted from being confrontational.

There were so many kids like this who I came to know. Most of them had an IEP stating they were classified as LD. However, we also worked with kids who were identified as intellectually impaired, behavior disordered, or those with a type of autism that was conducive to what we could offer. As an inclusionist, I didn't want to turn any kid away. There were a couple of times I did, though, albeit with a feeling of sadness. Both times involved a child with autism who had a "meltdown" and physically attacked others, including a tutor. Our resources were limited (curriculum, space, ratio of adult educators to graduate students and children, etc.) and students were primarily interested in teaching kids with LD. Based upon these experiences, we opened a "quiet room" in which we erected temporary cubicles and maintained a low noise level to help kids better focus more than in larger communal areas. It was times like this that I felt caught in the middle. I needed to provide graduate students with children who struggled in learning, and many of them did not want to work with children who were autistic and/or had violent tendencies. As we live in such a litigious country, I wondered about potential lawsuits if a graduate student became injured. At the same time, I felt for the mothers who were either at their wit's end or a staunch advocate for their child. In the former case, the firm-lipped mother collected her child and left, not to be heard from again. In the latter case, the mother wrote an angry letter to the college president denouncing me and the program.

LL really did feel like a school—with all its corresponding highs and lows of real life family dramas. I was interested in keeping as many kids with autism as we could in the program and so obtained a small grant one year to bring in specialists who helped us better serve and educate them. There were also kids who, like Saul, were either school phobic and/or resistant to learning. One such kid was Jose, a first grader whose parents were from the Dominican Republic. He and his twin Josefina came to LL because they were in first grade with IEPs. Whereas Josefina was smiling, willing, complaint with what was asked of her, Jose was the opposite—angry, unwilling, and non-compliant, upping and running around the hallways and refusing to come with us or seat at his desk. After a few times of chasing him around, we resigned ourselves to a temporary situation that was both exhausting and nonproductive. Jose's perplexed-looking mother answered him in Spanish, threatening his father's ire when they got home, making Jose's face show more fear than anger. I told his mother that he could continue on one condition; she must be at the table with the tutor to make sure Jose would sit and focus on the lesson that has been prepared for him. She did. It worked. So did moving her slightly every session to be further away, but always in the same room. Then, by the door. Then, outside of the door, in sight. Then out of sight. By then, Jose had bonded with his tutor, entering into a working routine. Josefina and her tutor had also been reassigned nearby so he'd always know she was there and doing a similar task. They are still in the program and are now poised to enter high school.

There are so many memories of students from this period, including Lulu, a young girl who had difficulty remembering anything; Stanley, a chronically shy boy whose father was a prominent TV newsreader; Rosa and Ernesto, siblings from Ecuador whose single mother pushed them as hard as she could; Timothy, who was unable to concentrate on his work when his parents divorced; Lawrence, lanky with cornrows and a swagger that disappeared every time when his mom came to pick him up; Loreli, who was being overtaken academically by her younger sisters and keenly felt the shame; Allan, a Hunter professor's child that puzzled us all with his erratic behaviors until his tutor figured out ways—by necessity—of engaging him. The list could continue for hundreds of kids over the years.

LL included developing an initial assessment of the child and then developing it throughout the year via periodic updates that culminated at the end of the semester. It also included interviewing parents in depth at the start of the year and writing them a letter at the end of the year summarizing their child's achievements while identifying areas needing continued attention. In addition, we held an annual Literacy Evening in which all kids were encouraged to share their work in one form or another—public readings, postings on a wall, recordings, in small group or pairs—and parents were welcome. A large portion of my time was also dedicated to interacting with interested and currently participating parents. One day, after someone at NYC's Department of Education made the program public, I found 92 voice mails on my phone from parents usually at the edge of despair, often in tears, about their child's academic and/or social struggles. It was at that time I decided to ask for a parent representative part-time worker in the department, as this community-based type of work, while an important contribution to the community, would not serve me at all when coming up for tenure.

Every Thursday I'd go to the ninth floor over an hour before LL was scheduled to start and set up five classrooms with furniture serving one-on-one tutoring. I loved the LL part of my time at Hunter because it kept me on my toes as a teacher and college instructor. It also emphasized teaching as problem-solving. Oftentimes there were no quick and easy answers and students had to make an informed choice to improve a situation. In contrast, what I found exasperating about LL was the lack of financial support by the institution. As the numbers of sections grew, LL posed the challenge of staffing and materials. I discovered the best way to have a solid instructor of this key course was to have a former student, now graduated, serve as an apprentice/assistant. However, financial assistance was not available for LL from department chair, dean, provost, or president's office (the latter, I am fairly sure would have provided support, but I was told my by dean not to ask). This, I found to be exasperating. After several years of asking up the chain, I solved the problem via a trusted colleague who knew my dilemma and kindly provided me with a philanthropist's name. Two letters and $40,000 in donations permitted me to set up a fund in CUNY for this program so it would always have money to compensate assistants in-training, instructional materials, and texts. CUNY struck me as a metaphor for life: If you need something, it's usually better to rely on yourself than anyone else.

As the numbers of graduate students increased sharply, so did the number of sections needed for LL. I became responsible for finding, opening, and maintaining new off-sites as there was no room on campus. All of this for three credits reassigned time, the equivalent of teaching a course, was an enormous amount of work. Additionally, my classes often had more than 25 students, the contractual maximum. One actually had 37 folks, all of whom were first semester teaching fellows. While I was willing to be flexible and accommodate the needs of the department, I began to feel taken advantage of. It's not uncommon phenomenon for untenured professors. I met with the associate dean and shared my frustrations about being expected to do so much with LL without corresponding support or compensation. Somehow, in the conversation, it became revealed that LL had been budgeted six credits of reassigned time by the School of Education, but I had only been given three. The three credits in question were being taken by the department programmer. This situation angered me. Early in my career, I had been told by a senior professor at the Graduate Center that "CUNY ran on exploitation of faculty." I didn't quite understand what she had meant at that juncture, but I began to reflect upon it now. It was times like this that I did feel ripped off as a new faculty member. There was always a lot of administrative and organizational work to be done, but at the end of the day—while programs could not run without such work—it counted for nothing when being considered for tenure. The irony of working administratively and pedagogically but not having it recognized in terms of tenure was lived every single day. I met with the chairperson and angrily stated feelings of being exploited by programming needs and administrative decisions. It was a risk to bite the hand that feeds, but I needed to state my dissatisfaction and advocate for change.

FORGING INCLUSIVE EDUCATION AND DISABILITY STUDIES

Being part of the department meant representing faculty on various committees and organizations too. One that piqued my interest was the impressive sounding New York City Task force on inclusive education. It was composed of faculty from schools of education around the city, and modestly funded by a grant received from the Federal Government to New York State, and then coordinated by Syracuse University. The local NYC task force met once a month on Friday mornings and once a year in Albany as part of the larger statewide network. If I look at the particular glass of this organization as half full, I met some wonderful people in the network, including parent-to-parent representatives who were great to work with (collaborators from a different New York State funded network supporting families who had children with disabilities). If I look at the glass half empty, I saw a loosely gathered group who had no clear vision, coordinated by Department of Education retirees working as adjunct faculty. So little of that grant money went into any real change. At meetings, I would be subject to nonsense such as one member inviting me to close my eyes and put my hand in a cardboard box to feel around because that's what a learning disability was like. Teachers College had all but pulled out of the group, and a NYU representative rarely came. It was part-time faculty from private colleges with reputations for providing fast-but-superficial programs who were in charge. They were nice people but did not have insights into the complexities involved, providing no direction to act upon making changes.

I was disappointed that this was "it" in terms of a higher education collective NYC advocacy for inclusive education. That said, I liked tangible products, especially placed in the hands of teachers, so advocated for a few small conferences in collaboration with the United Federation of Teachers for an educator audience (focusing on team teaching and flexible pedagogy) and parent-to-parent for a largely parent audience. In addition, I volunteered to create an edited book wherein all taskforce members were represented in sharing something that would help teachers and families. The physical volume was free for anyone interested and made available in pdf format covering a range of themes including the history of educating kids with disabilities, perspectives of all stakeholders, ways to effectively team teach, suggested strategies for mixed ability classrooms, and recommended readings. I figured at least we can try and "spread the word" in the often overwhelming world of teachers and administrators about how to include students responsibly. Bottom line: I was very disappointed that the higher education group on inclusive education had a low profile, little respect, and little (if any) impact in schools. At the same time, I knew everyone had a finite amount of things they could accomplish in a week and any taskforce work was additional to our official positions.

There was much greater satisfaction to be had in teaching inclusive education to students and helping them figure out their daily challenges, be it how to manage two or more differentiated working groups of children or best utilize the time in co-planning. Teaching the Inclusion class was always one of my favorites, as I could use Disability Studies in Education to frame the course (Connor, 2015b) and bypass the "should we do this?" conversation which had been given more than enough airplay in the department. By 2010, Jan Valle and I had cowritten a short text called *Rethinking Disability: A Disability Studies Guide to Inclusive Practices*. Our goal was to write the text we wished was already in existence, that is, grounded in our lived experiences as career special educators with a DSE disposition, culling from our work with kids, teachers, parents, administrators, and other stakeholders, as well as engaging with the literature around inclusive education. When New York State introduced a policy requiring all general educators to take one special education class, our department was divided as to which class: *Introduction to Special Education* or *Inclusion of Students with Disabilities in General Education*? I advocated for the latter class, as inclusion is what most general educators wanted to know about—the why and the how to of teaching a class of kids with diverse abilities, including students with disabilities (rather than a primary focus on history, laws, and classifications à la disability per week). By taking the opportunity of foregrounding inclusive education within the general education curriculum, I was able to introduce DSE to all graduate students. This was one of the most satisfying things to do when working within a big system, as it allowed a more progressive take on student diversity and how to respond to it.

Another opportunity I enjoyed being part of was the advocating for DS to become an official program within CUNY. Given its size, it seems an obvious thing to say that CUNY is a large network of people. While this is a definite plus, a downside is that it is so big we often do not know who else with similar research interests works within the system. I recall being at the national Society for Disability Studies conference in Seattle and noticing the number of CUNY people I previously had no idea about. In fact, we decided to have an impromptu meeting in the hotel lobby and discuss the irony that we came all the way across the country to find one another in NYC. As a result, there were several consequences, including the creation of an informal network of interdisciplinary DS scholars who are part of a listserv and a series of annual meetings and events. Another outcome was the strengthening of Mariette Bates's idea to develop a series of programs in DS (general certification, and bachelors and master's degrees) to be housed in CUNY's School of Professional Studies. What I liked about this development within CUNY was its emphasis on professionals already working within the disability-related fields, offering the chance to advance their studies while utilizing DS to focus upon rethinking disability and how "business as usual" should and can be changed. As part of a small group of scholars who testified to CUNY trustees to why DS programs should be established, I was happy that Mariette had the vision, drive, and skills to build this unique program that is currently thriving.

I was also happy to be part of the program, and sought to teach within the DS master's degree. The program was multidisciplinary and offered courses in disability and narrative, disability and health, disability and laws, disability and media, and so on. I taught a course in Disability Studies and Education and found it an interesting change to teach students who were not teachers but rather professionals who worked in disability-related contexts such as coordinated services, transition, group homes, work experience, and local institutions. We all engaged in issues around reconceptualizing traditional teachings about disability and related these to improving services in agencies for people with disabilities, along with reframing disability for professional development. I found the students committed to the idea of rethinking disability, and have remained in contact with several of them over the years. In one instance, a student called April was actually a former NYC teacher, and a wheelchair user. Based on her own life experiences both in and out of the classroom, coming to know DSE served as epiphany of sorts, galvanizing her ideas. April was so invested in attending class that when she reunited with her former longtime boyfriend John to rekindle their relationship, he assumed they'd be going out to dinner on their anniversary. However, April said she would not miss a class. Subsequently, John came to the college to pick her up so he could see for himself the man who took precedence over him that night (awkward). When April described the situation right before introducing me, I braced myself for either veiled or unveiled hostility. On the contrary, John's curiosity was satisfied, and he was an understanding guy who eventually invited me to their wedding. April went on to a doctoral program in DS at Syracuse University, cowrote a chapter with me on the influence of Martha Russell and her own experiences (Connor & Coughlin, 2016) and graduated with a wonderful dissertation about the highly limited access to schools for wheelchair using kids in NYC (Coughlin, 2016).

STUDENT (DIS)CONNECTIONS

While I have appreciated coming to know and attempt some version of a mentorship role to students who became successful tutors and teachers, school and district administrators, masters and doctoral students, and emerging scholars—I also think about those people who I did not reach or connect with in ways I would have liked. Many students are already teaching and can be fairly stressed when arriving to classes. Those who work as TF or TFAs can feel somewhat "trapped" within two-year contracts and run the gamut in how they deal with their situation. Some are not ready for what life in teaching is versus what they thought it was going to be. Regardless, as college instructors we have to teach them content and skills that we believe useful for the duration of their careers. What I found troubling about some TFA students was their dismissiveness about methods being taught. There were often complaints of "I'd never do that," or "This would never work for *my* kids," from first-year teachers. Part of the tension, from my perspective, lay in a lack of career-commitment. To learn teaching skills is time-consuming hard work that requires practice, flexibility, trial and error, and adaptations to contexts. If the university is teaching with view to preparing students for the next 30 years and students are focused on "getting through" 2 years, there's an inevitable cultural clash. That most TFAs came from ivy-league schools and were now in a public institution contributed to some of their dismissive attitude. This privileged self-positioning was reinforced by TFA institutional culture that would arrive every year with new programmatic and institutional demands that signaled the desire for a specialized, boutique-type program where they received the best instructors, preprogramming, schedules, and organization. An irony lay in that no full-time professors wanted to teach them, despite the prestige of our institution hosting them. Although undoubtedly smart, I was never convinced that TFA educators were best to serve the neediest kids in schools. I share these thoughts as a circular way to say, after several experiences with TFAs, while I made sure I served them fully in a professional capacity, I admit it was hard to invest in them personally the way I did with traditional students and those from other sponsored programs such as TFs.

Like many teachers and teacher educators, I have made mistakes, blunders, and missteps with students. I have also pondered right and wrong ways of handling situations, and know no one gets things right all of the time. Some situations I have shrugged off and chalked them up to experience, while others have lingered with me, as I try to make sense of them. In a relatively harmless situation, I recall one student badgering me to change her grade. I had, to date, held strong to my original assessment calculations, based on clear supporting evidence, as we live in a time where most students expect a grade of A and see anything less as a form of personal failure of professional indictment, rather than as an opportunity to reflect, review, and learn from the situation. To cut a long story short, the student called Sheelagh was relentless about her LL grade to the point where I was worn down ("never had a B+ before ever . . . . I went to NYU . . . my mother's a teacher . . . it will be on my transcript") and, although deep down against my better judgment, I changed her final grade from B+ to A–. However, in part two of the yearlong course, I assessed that she really was not pushing herself or the child she tutored, and was continuing doing her own thing rather than what all students were required to do. I therefore decided that she earned a grade of B+ (and wished I had not changed the original grade in part one of the course). This infuriated her so much that in student assessments from that class she submitted a no holds barred rant in identifiable handwriting that the course was "terrible" and I was "horrible," and "under no circumstances" was this information to be conveyed to me. It had been the only time I ever changed a final grade, and I regretted it. As fate would have it, Sheelagh had to take another class with me, but I never let her know I'd read the diatribe.

In another instance, when teaching an Inclusion class to urban teacher residency (UTR) students, one made a pronounced comment about kids, "That's if they *want* to learn." Her voice was snide and self-assured. I took issue immediately, and was surprised at my own reaction, finding myself saying forcefully, "You *cannot* say that. You're not experienced enough yet to be that cynical. It's actually part of your job to motivate and engage them in learning." This response immediately changed the tenor of the whole class, as I tend to be easygoing and flexible in "taking on" any student issues or questions. I'm not saying I was wrong about the content and manner of my response to the student's initial comment, but I was uncharacteristically "quick to jump," and in doing so had inadvertently shut down a potentially productive conversation with her. I was also aware that I am perceived, as are all professors, to have a lot of power in class, and had directed it to one person, strongly conveying the message "you're wrong." That night I went home feeling bad about unwittingly embarrassing a student. The force of my response came from a place of being pro-kid, yet I was also pro-teacher, and had failed to be empathetic to a first-year teacher. My actions weighed heavily on me all week, and I decided to face what happened when starting off the following week's class. To do this, I noted how we had ended abruptly in the previous class and I was perhaps too forceful in my response. At the same time, I wanted all students to understand the position of kids they teach, including why they may not be sufficiently engaged, forms of resistance to school, and the complexities of kids' (sometimes unsuccessful) learning histories, along with middle-class expectations of learning that are subconsciously projected. It made for an animated discussion, but I knew the student has switched off from the content and froze me out. A few weeks later, I entered the class early, and she happened to be the first and only student there. I took the opportunity to share my own discomfort and volunteered to apologize in front of the class for my forcefulness that day. "Drop it," she said curtly, so I did. In student evaluations, she wrote "useless class" and scored me in the lowest possible way.

Several discontented students have written me emails over the years. One disgruntled TFA who did little or no work in methods classes and broke his contract to leave after only one year's service sent a picture of himself standing in front of a Chinese University with a message telling me to go fuck myself. I responded by stating I was glad he had found the right area of study, as his email reaffirmed that he was not a good fit in terms of being a special education teacher. I also forwarded his email to TFA and suggested they contact him about professionalism, as I wanted them to be aware of who they recruited. In another example, I actually kept the email as I thought it would be worthy of inclusion in this book:

> *Hello, Dr. Connor,*
>
> *You might not remember me, but I was a student of yours not too long ago. I had always dreamed of becoming an educator and to help shape the minds of youth for a better tomorrow. I, like everyone I know, experienced some bumps on the long road to success, but it did not stop me from accomplishing my goal. In my darkest moment, I recall you had once stated to me that you "had my doubts about you," which made me fell less than nothing, especially because you were my role model. I rose up like the proverbial Phoenix from the ashes and decided that nothing would stop me from achieving my goal. Your doubts about me added more fuel to the fire that is burning brightly within me due to my unwavering passion for teaching. Your lack of support at a critical moment in my life inspired me to become my own hero. I want to thank you for opening my eyes because when you did not give me an opportunity, it motivated me to seek the impossible without any limits. Another professor mentioned my lessons were not sufficient and did nothing to aid me in improving them. My lessons did however, lack two things which were creatively* [creativity] *and myself. Now, all of my lessons are creative and have some part of me incorporated within, so that my students can relate to things such as my artistic talent. Many doors of opportunities were slammed closed in my face at Hunter College, but other doors of opportunities have been opened for me elsewhere. In December I graduated from ________ University with my master's degree in special education with dual certification in special education (grades 1-12) as well as general education (grades 1-6). I have made my dream into a reality and I now know that my self-worth is beyond measure, which has helped me become a highly effective and innovative educator.*
>
> *Thanks,*
> *Miguel Gonzalez*

I replied:

Dear Miguel

I appreciate your email. I am very happy that you have succeeded in your program at ________ University. I am sure that you will do well, now that you have your degree.

I agree that the difficult conversations we had at Hunter College have, in part, fueled your success. To your credit, you have believed in yourself, and made it a priority to become a special educator. I also think that your primary focus on becoming an educator in _____ was much easier than when you were at Hunter and working three jobs, and experiencing a significant level of anger and frustration when balancing your workload.

Contrary to how you may feel about your experience at Hunter, I am very happy for you at the beginning of what can be a long and fulfilling career.

Best wishes,
Dr. David J. Connor

What differentiates this email from the previous example is that Miguel's is a nicely written Fuck You. I admit I struggled with Miguel. He was in my Inclusion class and late almost every week, and when he arrived made a dramatic entrance rather than a discrete one. In class, he volunteered to read part of an interactive script and made countless mistakes. His written work was barely comprehensible and I spent a lot of time deciphering submissions and asking for clarifications. In brief, he was a student with high needs, and publicly shared that he'd received at least part of his schooling receiving special education services. Oftentimes, he'd talk inappropriately about his mother in class, miss the point about what we were talking about, and be unaware of his peers' body language that signaled his inappropriateness. I experienced a level of ambivalence with Miguel as I believe in supporting all students, particularly those with disabilities. So I worked with him until he demonstrated enough skills and knowledge to earn a grade of B. Coincidentally, I was also his academic adviser and when he met with me I made him aware of what was needed to earn the degree.

However, Miguel's struggles became even more apparent in LL where his instructor found him to be unprepared every week, unable to recall expected requirements, and unable to demonstrate the knowledge and skills expected. I know this instructor very well. She is deeply committed to, and highly respected by, her students. This particular year was far more pressurizing than the rest as it was the first time the department had to prepare students for the new and poorly New York State implemented Educational Teacher Performance Test (EdTPA). In brief, the bar for teacher certification had been raised swiftly and to much higher than it had previously been. What I became privy to was a series of emails from Miguel to his course instructor in which he viciously attacked her credibility, teaching skills, and ability to assess him. After almost one year of doing her best with Miguel, the instructor had contacted me, unsure of what to do. He had not earned a passing grade and would have to repeat the yearlong course. On reading the emails, I was angered by his anger and unprofessionalism, full of unfounded accusations and without merit. I instructed Miguel to no longer contact his instructor, and only directly interface with me about his dissatisfaction. When he continued to send emails to her, I required him to come meet with me. In his series of complaints about the instructor (one of the kindest and most effective we have), he took no responsibility for pervasive late and substandard work, and complained he had to work three jobs to pay his tuition and was perpetually tired. It was at that moment, in the capacity of chairperson, that I shared I now had doubts about whether teaching was the best profession for him to enter IF he had to work three jobs simultaneously. I suggested that he save up the money and then come to college full time so he could learn without the stress, interruption, and distraction of other obligations. I proposed he get a job as a paraprofessional or teacher's aide to make sure it was a good fit for him, if he really wanted to become a teacher. I also told him about his behaviors and substandard work, and the concept of professionalism being integral to being a teacher. To me, Miguel was in an artificial world where he thought his actions were right and his work performance was sufficient. I strove to put it into perspective, and even encouraged him to follow through with his inclination to consider another state and try their program that may not be the same format or nature as Hunter's.

The truth is that I was sad to receive his email. I am as certain as I can be that it was not crafted personally by Miguel, having a history of trying to make sense of all his written submissions. But I was primarily sad because he was still blaming other people. Miguel had changed place, program, and circumstance—and succeeded to graduate college with a teaching degree. I can't imagine him teaching, but sincerely hope I am wrong. Counseling students out, or at least planting the seed as to whether teaching is a right fit for them is never easy but is expected of institutions of higher education.

Although I have foregrounded difficulties in working with some students, overall, I have found teaching to be an incredibly rewarding profession, and the gas in my tank for the duration of an educational career. Advising a large body of students takes up time, so between required office hours and email access, the week can feel eaten up. That said, student advising allows professors to keep close to the program, courses within it, and provides access to knowing students. What students and the general public don't see is the balancing act needed for tenure between teaching (and advising), service, and scholarship. The service part can be at program, department, school, college, CUNY, city, state, national, and international levels. Each one may be considered in evaluating for tenure. Between 2005 and 2013, my service included but was not limited to department representative to the Faculty Delegate Assembly; department representative to the NYC Taskforce on Inclusion, the city and statewide network; developing program and departmental curriculum; observing and evaluating course instructors; coordinating the LD program for a year; coordinating Teaching Fellows & Teach for America's Adolescent Focus; liaison to Hunter College Campus School & School of Science; Faculty member at large in the Graduate Center's doctoral program; a member of their Admissions Committee; a member of their Advisory Committee; many search committees for tenure-track and non-tenure-track positions; the Curriculum Committee, Hunter College, CUNY (2012–present); School of Education Redesign Committee; Senate Representative at Hunter College; Video Analysis Committee; Middle School Program Design Committee; Fieldwork Redesign Committee: Learning Disabilities Program; Institutional Review Board, Hunter College; Admissions Committee, Disability Studies Master's Program, School of Professional Studies, Graduate Center, City University of New York; Admissions Committee at Hunter College; Faculty Committee, Urban Education Doctoral Program; member of the Faculty Delegate Assembly; member of the Executive Committee, Faculty Delegate Assembly; Future of Disability Studies: Think Tank, NY Metro Area, Barnard College; Professional Advisory Committee, The Gateway School, a private institution for children. Additionally, there were AERA committees too, including co-chairing the Specialty Interest Group/Disability Studies in Education and sitting as a member at large on the Social Justice Committee. As can be seen, it's easy for committee work to get out of control, particularly if you have difficulty saying no and/or largely enjoy what you do.

SECURING TENURE

The tenure process is an unusual phenomenon that varies enormously among universities. At Hunter, there was not a lot of guidance given within the department, and I was always a little worried that things could turn south at any given moment. Of course the hardest part is balancing teaching, scholarship, and community service. At an institution whose focus is primarily on producing certified teachers, faculty have to provide evidence of being good teachers. This is usually through student evaluations of each course taught since starting at the institution in quantitative and qualitative data, along with satisfactory peer observations. So, while teaching skills have to be excellent, publications are imperative. There's a reason for the oft-cited self-explanatory phrase, "Publish or perish." But it's not only being in print that counts, it's establishing a body of work that has a specific focus. Being a DSE grounded special educator meant I had to show I published in Special Education journals (to verify my location in the field) while I also sought to publish in DS journals (to establish myself in that as my field of choice). In addition, service was considered important, showing the ability to be a "good citizen," contributing to the community writ large.

The process of preparing for tenure can feel quite harrowing. I wanted it over as soon as possible, so I wrote like a fiend. At the time, CUNY was transferring from a five to seven-year tenure clock, and I was allowed to choose which I wanted. I chose five years, and the dean suggested I go up early, so I applied after four years, based on the number of publications. Tenure does seem like an all-or-nothing game, and during the years of being untenured, there is a palpable sense of vulnerability as tenured colleagues have the right to deny you a full time, secured position if they believe you're not a good fit for the department in terms of work ethic, philosophy, and collegiality. It was with great relief when letters went out to my external evaluators and I dropped off my three meticulously organized binders demonstrating accomplishments in publishing, teaching, and service. The formal interview with Dean Steiner and three departmental chairs was surprisingly relaxed for me, as I figured: I could not have tried harder. At the end of the day, that's what we must live with as individuals.

And so, tenure was granted and a huge weight was lifted from my shoulders as I joined the ranks of those professors recognized by their institutions and valued by their peers. At Hunter, we could suggest up to five examiners and the chairperson would also contact unknown others of their choice. Ellen Brantlinger happened to be one of my external evaluators and sent me a copy of her letter. I felt enormously honored and deeply humbled by her willingness to go to bat for me. Others let me know over time that they had written letters on my behalf, including Janette Klingner, Beth Ferri, Beth Harry, Deborah Gallagher, and Scot Danforth. I'd finally "made it"—tenured, as associate professor.

I once saw a feature on *Kelly and Michael's* morning TV show that one of the best jobs to have was a college professor. In describing the job, they painted a picture of living on a beautiful campus with manicured lawns and shady trees, teaching two classes of poetry a semester to small groups of students who hung onto ever word uttered, publishing occasionally, and having four months off per year at full salary. I found myself talking to the TV asking, "Are you out of your minds? You don't know what you're talking about!" To me, being a professor meant there were no boundaries to *limit* the work. Teaching three classes of 25 (or more) students a semester, often with weekly assignments, was a treadmill—worthwhile of course—but a treadmill nonetheless. Administrative work, student advising, community service at all levels, and conducting original research, as well as presenting at national and international conferences took up a lot of time. The trouble was, responsibilities kept growing. And as the school of education numbers in general were declining, special education seemed to be the cash cow. Sponsored programs in our department expanded exponentially, bringing sizable numbers of more students in programs such as Teaching Fellows, Teach for America, and Urban Teacher Residency. Our numbers grew in the hundreds but the infrastructure to support them in the form of personnel did not. Special education was carrying the heaviest load among three departments, and even within that, the ratios of faculty to students varied in extreme ways. I recall running the LL, advising students, being the faculty point person for all sponsored LD programs, and teaching three classes. This translated to me being responsible for about 600 graduate students when other professors had as little as 15.

Given the numbers, I wanted to quit. Instead, with a trusted colleague, I wrote a letter to the dean with a detailed analysis of numbers, including faculty-student ratios in departments and programs, illustrating gross inequities and asking him to stop admitting such vast numbers or provide the department with new faculty members. While not intended as such, it felt like a new wave of exploitation all over again. As a result, I was again toe-to-toe with David Steiner. To his credit, he saw the very real strains placed upon our department and made us a priority in allocating new faculty lines over the next few years. We were now educating over 1,000 students in the special education department in a school of education with 3,000 students. Our certification programs had expanded too, making programing even more complex. I came to regularly discuss all of these concerns with the dean when the current chairperson, battling illness and being overwhelmed with the position, had simply stopped coming to work.

Exasperation and loyalty were felt in equal measure, and I debated whether to leave for another institution. After being asked to be chairperson several times by the dean, I finally relented and agreed. With anti-aspirations to become an administrator, I felt a pervasive sense of general unease. I grappled with a sense of foreboding, not quite sure of its origins, and shared my deep reservations across the kitchen table with John.

"It's the next step for you," he said with certainty.

"I am not so sure," I replied. "But I am so fed up, I have to either get in the driver's seat or get off the bus."

Against my better judgment, I climbed into the seat, and became chairperson of the Department of Special Education. The irony was not lost on me. I'd been trying to get out of special education for the duration of my career, yet had now transitioned to a leadership position at the university. I rolled up my sleeves, ready to begin.

COMMENTARY

Teaching and Learning in Schools and Universities

When people ask what I like about my job, it is easy to answer, and revealed in this chapter: "The best part of being a professor, just like the best part of being a teacher, is the students." There's nothing quite like the satisfaction of teaching a good class. Both professor and students are animated, discussions lively, the atmosphere dense with questions and responses that deepen collective conversations, providing palpable evidence of students' engagement. A good class also paves the way to assessing student knowledge and skills. However, although teaching is often formally measured via various assessments, it is also a form of faith, as we simply cannot predict the impact of teaching and the myriad of ways in which it cannot be measured.

Tenure-track university positions have diminished drastically over the past few decades (Blumenstyk, 2014). I know in my department, approximately 85 percent of courses are taught by adjuncts, and feasibly a student can pass through the program without being taught by an appointed professor. The paucity of positions means they are highly sought after, with a surplus of applicants. In brief, without adjuncts, our teaching certification programs would implode. And, adjuncts tend to work more for loving what they do, than the money earned. Many are career educators who have largely worked in public, some private, settings—and enjoy teaching people entering into our profession. It can be quite a challenge for full-time faculty to develop and change syllabi when all sections of courses are taught by adjuncts who have day jobs. We monitor this situation as best we can, yet program coordinators are often stretched thin between teaching, advising, departmental work, and publishing, before they can orchestrate adjuncts for updates and changes—a phenomenon that is felt around the globe as the common good is increasingly subsumed within corporate efficiency (Brown & Scase, 2005).

Teaching teachers is a layered endeavor because we aim to incorporate good pedagogical practices, model them, and make them explicit via debriefing the experience of students as learners, similar to other fields of study (Fanning & Gaba, 2007). In various classes, professors demonstrate methods, provide opportunities for guided practice together, and then expect independent demonstration of targeted skills in the scaffolded "I do/we do/you do" approach (Campbell, 2009). In methods classes where a professor teaches reading, writing, and mathematics, multiple demonstrations are provided (Bley & Thornton, 2001; Stern, 1988; Traub, 1977/2000; Wilson, 1996) along with student deconstructions and reconstructions of procedures, and discussions of when and where to use specific methods along with their customization. Likewise, in the Inclusion class, instructors model ways students can create opportunities for using Bloom's Taxonomy for tasks and question types (Gershon, 2015), exploring the benefits of Universal Design (Meyer, Gordon, & Rose, 2014), and its compatibility with multiple intelligences (Gardner, 1983/2011). Teaching methodologies to teachers who need to demonstrate them themselves keeps them on their toes. Some professors find it works best for them to have one foot in teaching kids and the other in teaching teachers. Two of my colleagues—Jody Polleck and Billy Longsworth—did this for years, dedicating part of their week to teaching high school through the day, and teacher candidates in the evenings. It is a rare model, but synchronizes university and school in being intensely practitioner-focused, as can be evidenced in the professor/teacher-writings of Laura Robb who documents many effective literacy strategies by sharing multiple examples of student work (2003, 2004, 2008).

Class sizes in public universities can be similar to class sizes in public schools, such as 25 students as the official cap, with over-tallied extras as needed. Having large classes in small rooms, and using whatever equipment available also echoes life in public schools. And as much as they may reject the idea, as a whole, some graduate students are not so different from high school students in terms of lateness, absences, using private technology in class, handing in work late, and expecting high grades. Behaviors are not due to immaturity, but are rather general human reactions to our structures and expectations, I believe, that constitute the discourse of teaching and learning.

The LL, an idea Professor Garnett imported from her original experiences at Teachers College, namely a clinically rich year long experience as the core of the LD program, started off with one or two sections. When it grew into almost 20 sections with over 200 students, it evolved into being like a small school. As the coordinator of the LL for six years, I witnessed some students dreaded beginning the year as they thought the intensity of fifty 75-minute highly customized tutorials with one kid, chronicling all aspects of planning, teaching, and assessment, was excessive. However, by the end of the experience, invariably the same students would usually admit that it was one of the most meaningful and satisfying experiences in the program.

Educational Laws and their Impact

It was strange to be immersed in the widely respected special education program at Hunter, known to both the New York State Education Department and the New York City Department of Education, along with many other institutions around New York City (including the local Council for Exceptional Children) and its surrounding areas. On one hand, I knew the content of the LD program was very strong, providing teachers with the pedagogical tools they needed to help them to ultimately help kids. On the other hand,

I viewed much of what we did in the name of "special" was good, thorough teaching, and would be of benefit to all teachers. What I did not like was the reification of "special" into a distinct professionalization that, by extension, reified the kids it served—making them sufficiently different than their nondisabled peers that their school experiences were primarily driven by a disability label (Skrtic, 1991).

The passing of P.L. 94-142 created a need for specialist certifications and a whole sub-industry within the field of special education evolved with separate content, methods, laws, and history to be learned. And yet, the certifications issued by New York State Education Department have fluctuated according to its needs. For example, when I graduated with my master's degree in special education, it was in K-12 grades. This fulfilled the criteria for New York City licensure in high school, but I would have been as bad as Arnold Schwarzenegger in *Kindergarten Cop* (Reitman, 1990) had I been placed in that level of instruction. In the late 1990s, state certification was changed to reflect a narrower age group, so birth through 2nd grade, 1–6th grade, 5–9th grade, and 7–12th grade became options. However, as the emphasis on more inclusive practices influenced placements of students with disabilities, special education as a discrete license was no longer permitted because all teachers were expected to be familiar with the general education curriculum and common core standards. Thus, dual certification was expected of anyone who sought to be a special educator. That said, as the 7–12th dual certification failed to attract sufficient numbers of high school special education teachers, it became the exception to the rule and single certification in special education became allowed again. Teachers with this certification are expected to have a healthy working knowledge of 7–12th grade English language arts, mathematics, social studies, and science. Aspiring special education generalists (7–12) must therefore take the Content Specialty Test, required by New York, that involves being assessed in all content areas. Many teacher candidates struggle to pass the math portion, given the shifts to advanced algebra and geometry.

The structure and content of teacher certification programs shift in accordance to various influences, such as the passage of laws, and the number of certified teachers needed to serve students with IEPs. Programs such as Hunters' continue to morph in order to meet shifting requirements of the state, as well as the needs of sponsoring organizations such as Teach for America and Teaching Fellows. Once again, there exists a discrepancy of what is defined by federal law, the state organization of implementing laws, and the local actuality of what is needed to make it work "on the ground" (Foote, 2008). And, despite *No Child Left Behind*'s (2002) demands of having highly qualified teachers at the front of every classroom, a shortage of teachers continues to exist, particularly special educators and teachers of English Language Learners

(Brownell, Sindelar, Bishop, Langley, & Seo, 2002; Pierce, 2017), along with a high percentage of teacher burnout in special education (Brunsting, Srekovic, & Lane, 2014).

Models of Disability and their Influence on Educators and Researchers

Working within a traditional special education department was a strange phenomenon, and at times felt like a dilemma of sorts. I envisioned myself foremost as an inclusive educator, interested in supporting all children to do their best. I also wanted to make sure I did not neglect kids with learning profiles like the ones I used to teach, so learning disabilities (however defined) remained a high interest. Yet, our department was not particularly inclusive in outlook, although various programs seemed to value it somewhat over others. In analyzing the single course on Inclusion, I found it skewered toward a cautionary critique as reflected in readings, and knew those teaching it did not quite share an inclusive disposition.

As a whole, the faculty seemed wary of inclusion, at least those in my program, mirroring special education leadership in the field (Fuchs & Fuchs, 1994; Kauffman & Hallahan, 1995). The politics of how disability was understood arose occasionally, yet few faculty members seemed to challenge the party line of positivism, experimental controls, measured deficits, and interventions. Perhaps it was unsurprising, then, that my colleagues were not familiar with DS, but it was surprising to find DS was being featured within a course taken by our students in the Department of Educational Foundations. When I participated in a panel—one that focused on the educational experiences of actual students with disabilities' experiences, a point central to DS—no one from the special education department came. Perhaps because I brought that fact to my peers' attention at a department meeting, my chairperson Professor Garnett came to the next session, dedicated the interdisciplinary nature of DS. Still, it was easy to feel like the black sheep of disability beliefs in the department.

It did not help that efforts to shift to more inclusive models of education by New York City's Department of Education had limited success (Hehir et al. 2005; O'Day et al., 2011). In addition, and sadly, the New York City Task Force on Inclusive Education was a sham. Although the laws that sought change toward more inclusive practices seemed as if they had teeth, they were never quite sank into the school system. Still, I did not lose heart in seeking a more significant shift to inclusive education, grounded in DS. I knew colleagues in different parts of the country who worked in institutions that did this to varying degrees in: Miami University, Ohio; Syracuse University, New York; National Louis University, Chicago; and Chapman University,

California, among others. In addition, scholars who had critiqued how special education was conceptualized and operationalized came to find a full or partial home, in DS, such as Tom Skrtic (Skrtic & McCall, 2010), University of Kansas, Deborah Gallagher (2010), University of Northern Iowa; and Curt Dudley-Marling (2010), University of Boston, MA. In addition, high-profile scholar Tom Hehir, who served as Director of the US Department of Education's Office of Special Education Programs from 1993 to 1999, published a book *New Directions in Special Education: Eliminating Ableism in Policy and Practice* (2005). Tellingly, this was one of the first times I'd publicly seen "ableism" paired with special education by a special education scholar, a term that had not even been defined in dictionaries a short time ago.

Given my somewhat limited locus of control, I realized I could not infuse DSE throughout all programs, but I could do so in any class I taught, particularly the *Inclusion* class. In this course, I foregrounded DSE as the lens through which I wanted inclusion understood, spending several classes on alternative histories of disability (2015), defining and identifying ableism (Hehir, 2005), individual narratives (Raymond & Raymond, 2011), contrasting impairment and disability (Davis, 1997), critiques of special education by disabled scholars including Linton's (1998a, 1998b) charge that special education *is* the problem, and activist perspectives about navigating life in a society that disabled them (Golfus, 1995), analyzing media representation of disability (2010), and actively undoing stereotypes (Connor & Bejoian, 2017). I felt professional satisfaction in that this version of the course is required by all certification programs and is a small, but significant, step in the right direction for a more pluralistic teaching of disability as a diversity and related to issues of equity and social justice (Connor, 2013c; Connor & Baglieri, 2009; Connor & Gabel, 2010).

Educational Structures and Systems in Relation to People with Disabilities

In my initial years teaching full time in the Department of Special Education I mostly taught classes for students in sponsored programs such as Teaching Fellows and Teach for America. I recalled that "most rolled up their sleeves and got on with what they signed up to do." However, in contrast, "A small number felt angry, betrayed by the Department of Education's glossy subway advertisements about changing lives in comparison to how they actually experienced the job." As I had discovered myself at the start of my own teaching journey, public schools can be a rude awakening for the uninitiated. Schools are institutions that function within—and give rise to their own—complex structures. The "place" of special education within schools—literally and symbolically—causes some students to be immediately concern about what's best for kids, while others take to the regulations, nomenclature, and newfound specialized knowledge like a fish to water, and in a manner of weeks are ventriloquizing the discourse to student peers how IEPs are most effectively completed. As mentioned, I feared the two-year sponsored teacher programs were a short-term response to teacher shortages, and could not guarantee a people committed for the longer run. The mixture of the most vulnerable kids with the most inexperienced teachers was, and still is, a stopgap approach to keep the ship of public education afloat, rather than overhauling the existing vessel, or better yet, developing a new one.

Just as school cultures are not necessarily conducive to supporting teachers with disabilities (Pope, Bowman, & Barr, 2001), neither is the culture of higher education always constructive in supporting professors with disabilities (Linton, 2006), although this group has been identified a source of valuable knowledge (Anderson, 2006). This topic became of interest to me as I attended national conferences and listened to colleagues with disabilities describe some of the challenges they faced (Price, 2011; Titchkosky, 2011). Closer to my own experiences, I also grew interested in the support systems available at the college level for students. Hunter's Office of AccessAbility struck me as doing a good job of being the "go to" place for reassurance and support, usually resulting in accommodations being granted when documentation was presented. The system therefore requires students to be assertive in seeking their needs, and proactive in securing all documentation. Again, while well intended, the onus is on students to self-advocate—a skill that is not sufficiently taught in relation to disability within high schools transitioning into college (Gregg, 2009). Many undergraduate and graduate students seek to shed their disability label given their K-12 schooling experiences, and do not self-advocate until they're floundering in their management of coursework.

This trend of not registering as disabled was something I discussed with Sudi Shayesteh, director of the Office of AccessAbility, and later led to a research project in which I looked at ways in which students with LD negotiated their way through self-initiated and self-developed strategies (Connor, 2013d). In terms of my own graduate students with disabilities, a small number required accommodations such as the use of a laptop on written exams, large print handouts, and extended time. At the start of every class taught, I'd suggest a good idea would be for that students with disabilities self-identify to me in private if they're comfortable in doing so, and let me know how best I can support them.

In the case of Miguel, I received no documentation that he may have benefited from accommodations. Coupled with his overextended work schedule at three locations, and his difficulties in managing time and balancing energy, the existing program structures were not welcoming of him. While Miguel was assertive, it was in ways that did not serve him. People and programs need to be a "good fit," and while this may sound obvious, both the program and the person have to work together in order to make the situation successful. It is hard counseling anyone out, and personally harder to counsel out students with disabilities, documented or not. I have discussed this with a Latino principal friend who has similar feelings about letting go teachers of all kinds, but especially—for him—Latinos. It makes it easy to be targeted as a hypocrite, sell-out, or traitor. However, I agree with him in that the most important thing is making sure kids have teachers who are knowledgeable and skillful. That is our primary charge. At the end of the day, that thought must supersede the perceived loss, anger, pain, and retaliatory lashings-out by people who—for one reason or another—have not provided sufficient evidence of their abilities to teach. Not everyone can.

Social, Political, and Cultural Experiences of People with Disabilities

One of the pleasures of having taught the Inclusion class over the years has been to explicitly raise the social, political, and cultural experiences of people with disabilities—and show how they are intimately connected with inclusive education. I use a DS perspective to frame the course, including asking students to view "special education with a critical eye" (Connor, 2005, p. 127). By using powerful statements by DS scholars and allies, I question the sources traditional special education teacher programs use to enculturate graduates. For example, using the statement "nondisabled Americans do not understand disabled ones" (Shapiro, 1993, p. 1) provides a springboard for deeper conversations about where does the source(s) of our knowledge of disability come from? How much of it comes from able-bodied researchers versus the people with disabilities they seek to define? Who benefits from different types of conceptualizations? Who loses? Where should we look for our information as educators?

Sometimes I play devil's advocate and simulate disabilities for part of a class. This can take forms such as taping a student's fingers and thumb together and telling them to go to the restroom; asking students to write with their nondominant hand, and providing an exercise to "speed it up"; writing while looking at the page and pen in a mirror; asking students to tell a story orally, round robin style, but without using the letter "t." The exercises variously invoke fear, laughter, and discomfort. However, in a debriefing where students share their thoughts about feeling tense, frustrated, nervous, judged, and so on, they also suggest "experiencing" being disabled. At this juncture, I share how these types of activities have been popular in special education classes for years but they are trivial and misleading, because "trying on" an identity in a simulation-friendly environment can never approximate the reality of disabled people. Just as a white person being made up to appear as a black person, or a male dressing as a female for half an hour and walking down a street would never provide an authentic experience of a person's formative identity, one they can't put on and take off at will. In some ways, while a little disingenuous on my part, the exercise serves as metaphor about what we may think is a realistic understanding is in actuality, artificial and erroneous. I then finish with recommendations from DS scholar Blaser (2003) who writes if people really want to experience being disabled, try only using the accessible subway stations around New York (about 20 percent, when functioning); not entering bars and restaurants that have steps into the only entrance; only sit in a designated area when at the movies; not entering into a bathroom if it's not wide enough for a wheelchair user, and so on. It makes for an interesting session as students begin to notice all kinds of ways—small and large—that society is inaccessible to a group of people it has identified as disabled. The notion that *society disables people* becomes clear, and the need for disabled people to "call society out" about differences in opportunities for disabled and nondisabled citizens. In turn, this can be related to examples within schools and educational systems.

Finally, in having worked part time in the School of Professional Studies and their program for professionals in the disability services field, I came to see possibilities in working with "in service" professionals who largely understood disability studies. Students in this program seemed to become more politicized as they dug deep into a disability-centric view of the world that was crafted by disabled people, and applied it to the context of their current jobs. Many had to "unlearn" their original trainings from degrees taken years ago. However, as they came back for their master's degree with a lot of practical and/or administrative and/or advocacy experience in their field, students understood how doing business differently potentially benefits both themselves and the people they serve.

Chapter 6

Scholar

As a kid, I liked writing. My high school English teacher read aloud my stories to the class, and submitted one to a national competition called children as Writers where I won second prize within my age group for a story called *The Lives and Deaths of Edgar Lyle* (W. H. Smith, 1978). It was the tale of a man who was murdered by his wife and her lover, only to be reincarnated as a spider in his own house—in the same room as his wife who suffered from arachnophobia. In my undergraduate degree I dabbled in writing prose and poetry, taking a class with Malcolm Bradbury, a well-respected British novelist and another with the accomplished Rose Tremaine who told me I'd read too much Sylvia Plath (but then again, which university student of literature didn't in those days?). Fast forward to New York in the mid-1980s and an only partially fulfilling life in retail, I'd rise early each morning to write a novel based on a group of friends working and partying in Greenwich Village. Later, in my Creative Writing Master's Degree at City College I wrote a semi-fictional memoir that I shared with approximately two people. At the same time, as a high school educator, I enjoyed teaching kids to write. There's something both magical and powerful about putting thoughts into print, allowing other people to access those thoughts, and possibly stimulate an intra-active conversation within readers.

Deep down I always knew I was a writer. Never in a million years did I think I'd become an academic writer. As a genre, I have found academic writing to be quite exclusionary in nature. It uses language and concepts that tend to baffle most people, as if asserting membership to an elite club of knowledge is pending based upon degree of a reader's comprehension. This phenomenon seems worse in education wherein teachers, generally speaking, elect not to read academic writing. I know because I was one, and never encountered one colleague reading an academic book on education either.

In my doctoral degree it struck me that academics write for other academics, leaving them open to critiques of conversations within rarified air, high in the atmosphere. Yet I realized academic writing was a genre I needed to learn if I were to succeed in a doctoral degree. I viewed it as a challenge, but a welcome one. In many ways, it was like learning a new language (or, perhaps more accurately, a loftier version of the native tongue). Furthermore, a person's writing is usually viewed as a reflection of their intelligence and general abilities, an idea with which I do not concur, having worked with many smart people who struggle in the process of writing.

Thinking of myself as a "scholar" seemed pretentious as the word seemed grandiose. Yet I recognized this is the language of academia. Conventional wisdom in academia says that focusing on an area of interest and "making it yours" is the way to receive recognition and become established. While this is useful information, it can potentially be limiting, as many areas of interest that appear discrete and diverse can potentially be interrelated. If scholars can make connections among topics, generate original thoughts, suggest innovate solutions to problems, then their knowledge can make a contribution to society. I have always viewed academic writing in education as making a contribution to knowledge, with view to changing "things" in order to improve society. At the school level, "things" can be teacher dispositions, pedagogical practices, classroom configurations, collaborative teaching, educational leadership, and so on. At the society level, "things" can include challenging historical and contemporary racism, pervasive ableism, and disparities among various social classes, which impact everyone—including kids and teachers in schools.

There's a curious form of liberation in writing, even academic writing. A writer can share his or her own thoughts, yet there's always a specific target audience, and a degree of social responsibility, given that the topic is education. The content of my own work has consistently focused upon several themes: racial inequalities in special education, learning disabilities, effective teaching practices, and inclusive education. As a result, I have always thought of myself as a critical special educator, grounded in disability studies, who seeks engagement with issues of inequality. Disability studies scholar Simi Linton indicated, special education *is* the problem (1998b). I tend to agree that it is a *huge part* of maintaining inequities, and rife with contradictions and paradoxes, despite its good intentions (Connor & Ferri, 2007). Being critical and working "from the inside" of an institution to challenge conceptualizations of disability and the neat and tidy narrative of special education's growth as a field has been a fascinating and often frustrating journey. In moments of doubt, I tell myself that writing allows me to reach more people—and influence more minds—than I would have if I'd remained a classroom teacher. But I know that is an assumption.

In the remainder of this chapter I describe what motivated me to commit to book projects (along with articles and book chapters), all of which relate to the twin topics of disability and education. I do this in the hope that seeing "behind the scenes" of conceptualizing and constructing a book illuminates these twin concepts that have fascinated me throughout my career.

DEVELOPING BOOKS

During doctoral studies, my adviser Beth Ferri invited me to work together on a project she had recently begun. It was broadly conceived of as an exploration of connections between two marginalized groups within US education, African-Americans, and students with disabilities. The topic was timely as the 50th anniversary of Brown v. Board of Education (1954) was approaching, along with the 30th anniversary of PL 94-142 (1975) that became renamed as the Individuals with Disabilities Education Act (2004). The former was a ruling mandating the integration of African-Americans into public schools, and the latter was a law guaranteeing access to all children with disabilities for a public education. Given the lack of progress in terms of racially integrated schools, and the strong opposition toward inclusive education by a significant number of school districts and special education scholars, Beth's idea was to explore ways in which the full integration of black and disabled citizens had been resisted, even thwarted, despite being legally mandated. As we wanted to explore forms of resistance in public forums, we analyzed the public discourse around desegregation and integration found in mainstream (white) newspapers the *New York Times*, *Washington Post*, and the *Atlantic Journal and Constitution.* Likewise, we searched the independent African-American newspapers such as the *Chicago Defender*, *Philadelphia Tribune*, *Atlanta Daily World*, and *Richmond Afro-American.* Focusing on op-ed pieces, letters to the editor, political cartoons, and feature stories, we amassed over 1,000 pieces of data and stored them in a software program called HyperQual that helped us determine and organize themes.

One of my favorite chapters to develop was the analysis of political cartoons. Drawing from the cultural work of Roland Barthes (1972, 1977), we created an analytical tool that helped determine the symbols within cartoons, their meaning, and their possible interpretations. Out of over a hundred political cartoons about desegregation/integration in the mainstream press, not one featured a school or a classroom. The huff and puff of rhetoric was all about states' rights versus the federal government, deflecting the issue of race, racial inequalities, and power imbalances among citizens. In contrast, there was only one political cartoon to be found on inclusive education, and it explicitly degraded people with disabilities. This chapter whetted my appetite to the possibilities of visual analysis of data, something that I'd been intrigued by since reading John Berger's classic *Ways of Seeing* (1972), and arts-based approaches to research that did not seem widespread then but have recently flourished in educational literature (Barone & Eisner, 2012; Leavy, 2015; Rolling, 2013).

The book was named *Reading Resistance: Discourses of Exclusion in Desegregation and Inclusion Debates* (Ferri & Connor, 2006). In our findings we charted subtle and blatant methods in which school systems slowed down, and even blocked, integration and inclusion in a wide variety of ways. What came to the fore in this study was the connection between race and disability in schools and the public imagination. The creation of different disability labels, growth of a rigid tracking system, increased use of psychometric testing, white flight to the suburbs, closing of functional schools for African-American children, and decimated number of black teachers in integrated settings all contributed to reifying racial hierarchies within public schooling, including the disproportionate number of kids of color labeled disabled and in placed in restrictive special education settings. It struck us as a brute fact: school systems could not exclude African-Americans from mainstream classes by race, but they could by disability due to the interpretation of IDEA's Least Restrictive Environment clause. In many ways, the book sowed seeds for what would be our continued interest in this area, and the data gathered was so rich we were able to write in a variety of venues that allowed us to focus on specific aspects such as the subversion of *Brown* (Ferri & Connor, 2004), special education's complicity in racial segregation (Ferri & Connor, 2005a), the historical nexus of race and disability (Connor & Ferri, 2005), and how patterns of segregation are continuing (Ferri & Connor, 2005b). Because the topic was of interest to various constituents within the academic community, we strategized for submission to journals focused upon social justice, special education, the African-American historical experience, and the general community, respectively.

The second book project was transforming my dissertation. In conceptualizing the original study, I purposefully structured writing as much like a book as possible within the parameters of the dissertation genre, as I wanted it to end up as one. After reading the "go to" classic *From Dissertation to Book* (Germano, 2005), I transformed the text so it would have a wider appeal than the four readers of my committee, and revised the title to be *Urban Narratives: Portraits-in-Progress—Life at the Intersections of Learning Disability, Race, and Social Class* (Connor, 2008b). In doing so, I foregrounded the eight young people I had worked with, documenting and making sense of their lived experiences in and out of school. For me, it was important to bring their voices into the arena of educational research, and I included as many of their words as possible.

I began the book by describing my own positionality in terms of race, class, nationality, and educational experience, aware I was a white, middle-class male of working-class origins writing about young people of color who were working-class or poor. This "locating" of myself felt important to do, along with explaining why I was interested in the topic and particular methods of research used. Although the title was a bit of a mouthful, it reflected the elements I wanted to foreground. These were urban stories, renderings of "typical" adolescents in special education, who shared their perceptions of disability, race, and social class, describing what it meant to be simultaneously at the interstices of all three. I'd always conceived of the participants as co-researchers of their own lives, and was humbled by how much they had shared with me, and oftentimes, with each other.

The book was broadly divided into two sections. The first consisted of "portraits-in-progress" in narrative form, composed of fragments of writings, responses, and conversations, each playing a part in forming a picture. The words allowed students to speak for themselves; I had arranged them with their input and approval. Sometimes stark, sometimes complex, their thoughts were laid bare as they spoke of moments of pride, instances of struggle, self-knowledge, self-worth, and how they had come to make meaning of who they were, the schools in which they were taught, the society in which we lived, and their place in the world. The second section consisted of my analysis of their narrative portraits, individually and collectively. To do this I had used Patricia Hill Collins's (1990) "Matrix of Domination" developed within the framework of black feminist thought, contemplating their stories within four different realms that looked at the different types of domination and the forms of resistance toward that domination. As Collins notes:

> Whether viewed through the lens of a single system of power, or through that of intersecting oppressions, any particular matrix of domination is organized via four interrelated domains of power, namely, the structural, disciplinary, hegemonic, and interpersonal domains. Each domain serves a particular purpose. The structural domain organizes oppression, whereas the disciplinary domain manages it. The hegemonic domain justifies oppression, and the interpersonal domain influences everyday lived experience and the individual consciousness that ensues. (Collins, 1990, p. 276)

By using this matrix I sought to illustrate the "everyday" lives of working-class or poor Black and Latino students identified as disabled. In doing so, I wanted to convey differences and discrepancies portrayed of learning disabilities in professional literature. I had originally been influenced by a collection of narratives called *Learning Disabilities & Life Stories* (Rodis, Garrod, & Boscardin, 2001), a collection of moving tales by college students with LD.

However, most were middle-class and white. I wanted to create something similar for urban Black and Latino students, to show the complexities of their situation and convey their own perspectives.

Both books were published by Peter Lang, an international house based in Switzerland. The company had taken a leap of faith and began a book series of Disability Studies in Education (DSE) co-edited by Susan Gabel and Scot Danforth. I was thrilled to be a part of it as it signaled a growing recognition of, and interest in, DSE. The next venture into print would be with my longtime professional "twin," Jan Valle. She had been asked if she'd like to contribute a short book on inclusive education to a small series on various educational trends to be published by McGraw-Hill, and asked if I'd like to collaborate. We both saw this as a great opportunity to write a book on inclusive education that we had wished existed, allowing us to introduce DSE to a larger audience of practicing teachers and show how *useful* it is for creating and maintaining inclusive classrooms.

The book would be comprised of 10 chapters in which we endeavored to answer a direct question through discussions of topics and samples of units, lessons plans, activities, and various ways to engage a diverse body of students. Featured questions were based upon the types we'd be asked in our graduate classes, for example, "How do I figure out what to teach in an inclusive classroom?" "How can I be sure that I reach everybody?" "How do I know that they *all* got it [content and skills]?" and "What will happen if I am assigned a co-teacher?" The pleasure of doing this book lay in its primary focus on instruction, the bread and butter of teachers' lives. Our task was to, as came to be reflected in the title of the book, "rethink" disability by providing social, cultural, and historical lenses advocated within DSE. This approach was stark contrast to scientific, medical, and psychological framings of disability that pervade traditional special education texts, all deficit-based framings of disability with negative connotations. More than anything, we wanted to show the practicality of having a DSE headset/disposition/grounding as opponents portrayed it as ideologically based and therefore of limited use.

The result was a short text called *Rethinking Disability: A Disability Studies Guide to Inclusive Practices* written in accessible prose, designed to engage pre-service and in-service teachers. In Introduction we described our own journeys in education, from earliest memories of peers with disabilities in school to our careers as special educators, to our discovery of disability studies being compatible with our own understandings of human differences and how we respond to those differences. Throughout the text we shared approaches to planning, teaching, and assessing all students—from our own teaching experiences, as well as inviting other educators to contribute samples of their curriculum and lessons. We were thrilled it was originally priced around $30, reasonably low for a text book, as it meant more educators would buy it, and there was sufficient interest for it to be published in Brazil as *Resignificando a Deficiencia*.

The next book project came via Susan Gabel as, some time ago, she had been invited to contribute to a series on *Reflective Teaching and the Social Conditions of Schooling* edited by Daniel Liston and Kenneth Zeichner that highlighted pertinent issues within education. The initial volume in the series, written by the editors, *Reflective Teaching: An Introduction* (Zeichner & Liston, 2013), strongly encourages teachers to be thoughtful practitioners who evaluate multiple and complex situations on a daily basis by exploring options and weighing them against each other to ultimately make informed choices as professionals. In brief, the practice of reflective teaching encourages educators to trust themselves in decision-making about teaching children in their own context, and is often seen in stark contrast to scripted curricula and specific approaches for instruction. Titles in the book series address important issues that are always paired with the word teaching in the title, such as *Culture and Teaching* (Liston & Zeichner, 2013), *Gender and Teaching* (Maher & Ward, 2002), and *Linguistic Diversity and Teaching* (Commins & Miramontes, 2006). The series editors wanted to have a volume on *Disability and Teaching* and had asked Susan Gabel, who began to write the book and midway through decided she'd prefer to co-author—and asked me. As a result of joining forces, I drafted the remainder of the book, and we jointly revised and honed the text to our mutual satisfaction.

What was unusual this time around was that the series all adhered to a set formula. In sum, after a broad background of the issue was discussed, the reader was asked to consider the issue with three different perspectives: (i) a traditional, arguably conservative stance, (ii) a centrist stance, and (iii) a more radical, innovative stance. Our work in DSE leant itself to this challenge as we were able to write of special education, its knowledge base and assumptions as "traditional," and contrast it with the knowledge base and assumptions within DSE as an alternative. In the middle, we could cull from both "worlds." With many commonplace disability-related issues presented in context, such as a principal's resistance toward inclusive education, all three perspectives were explored and a series of thought-provoking questions were crafted to probe readers about where they located themselves in terms of beliefs, and the actions those beliefs would result in—traditional, middle-of-the-road, or desiring significant change.

I was pleased that the editors had the vision to include disability in their series and the end result fit well with the existing volumes on other important topics (Gabel & Connor, 2014). At the same time, I had found it to be somewhat of a challenge to write within prescribed areas, giving each perspective equal space and fair play. On the other hand, equal space also meant we had introduced ideas within DSE to a larger audience, and balanced the scales with arguments for its utility in the daily business of teaching and learning in schools. The desire to focus on having a DSE disposition with a practical application remained with me, and led me to proposing the next book.

As a result of guest co-editing a special edition of *Review of Disability Studies* dedicated to DSE (Connor, Vale, & Hale, 2012), Jan Valle, Chris Hale, and myself decided to expand our focus on the practical application of DSE in the four interrelated realms of theory, research, practice, and policy. We sought to do this with view to providing evidence of scholars who had used DSE in their own ways with view to advocating change. In Introduction we wrote a deliberately brief account of how DSE began, as the information already existed in several other venues (Connor, 2014; Danforth & Gabel, 2005). After that, the book was structured in four targeted sections wherein we invited both established and upcoming scholars to share their work. The more I thought about education in the broadest sense, the more I tried to think of it simultaneously in terms of theory, research, practice, and policy. To me, each one is the leg of the same table that supports education as a whole, and while it is useful to foreground one at times to consider aspects of education with nuance and in depth, it cannot stand alone in terms of meaning—it can only work if connected to the others.

Starting with theory, we recognized that all actions are rooted in belief systems, and beliefs exit because ideas inform them. Deborah Gallagher's introductory chapter on exploring some *moral* dimensions of the social model of disability set the stage for all contributions that followed. Both Beth Ferri and Phil Smith's chapters in this section continued to engage the reader in provocative ways about making sense of each individual's different forms of embodiment and their relationship to what can appear as a frenetic and fragmented society, filled with contradictions and inequities. The section on research featured creative ways in which scholars Jan Valle, Subini Annamma, and Joe Valente respectively used performative inquiry, intersectionality, and autoethnography to investigate aspects of disability, education, and society. In the section dedicated to practice, I wrote a chapter on using DSE to frame the course on inclusive education that I taught, detailing several relevant assignments, Geert Van Hove and Elisabeth De Schauwer described the creating of a campus coalition in Ghent, and, Nirmala Erevelles wrote about using DSE-based pedagogy in addressing issues of madness and higher education administration. In the final section on policy, Julie Allen shared experiences in the possibilities and limitations of using DSE to critique educational policy in Europe; Missy Morton described how DSE was instrumental in recognizing, resisting, and reshaping policies in New Zealand; and Kathleen Collins used DSE to provide a sobering look at how corporate based educational reform took advantage of New Orleans' decimated school system post Hurricane Katrina. In brief, we purposefully assembled a diverse group of international scholars whose writing provided strong examples of DSE "at work" within the four related realms of theory, research, practice, and policy. For our concluding chapter, we used the metaphor of jazz to convey how DSE is similarly about breaking with traditional form, reinterpreting, reshaping, and reforming notions of human differences that have come to be called disabilities.

While admittedly eclectic, these chapters come together in conveying ways in which we conceive of disability, investigate disability, teach about disability, and implement educational guidelines about disability as a socially just imperative, not something relegated to the separate realm of special education. We titled the book *Practicing Disability Studies in Education, Acting toward Social Change* (Connor, Valle, & Hale, 2015) with the hope that DSE could be introduced to a larger audience. About a year after its release we received an invitation from the *European Journal of Special Needs Education* to feature it in section wherein three international scholars review the work, and we editors write a response to the reviews. This request was satisfying because one of goals within scholarship has been to engage with the special education academic community about DSE, and advocate for a plurality of perspectives when considering issues of disability and education. It struck me that Europe seemed more amenable to DSE ideas than the United States of America where requests for special editions of publications to focus on DSE such as *Intervention in School and Clinic* have been rejected, along with requests to respond to distorted criticisms of DSE that have been published in *Exceptional Children* (Anastasiou & Kauffman, 2011). The three peer reviews of our book by Margaret McLaughlin (USA), Solveig M. Reindal (Norway), and Anastai Liasidou (Greece) provided an opportunity for scholars interested in disability and education an open door to engage in constructive criticism of both DSE and contemporary special education, which is what academia is truly about, rather than slamming that door shut (Connor, Valle, & Hale, 2017).

The next book project arose from originally co-writing an article on the intersection of disability and race. These concepts had been at the center of work Beth Ferri and I had done together. Having seen the benefit of contemplating disability and race in my dissertation, I had even gone so far as to write a chapter called *Not So Strange Bedfellows: The Promise of Disability Studies and Critical Race Theory* (Connor, 2008b) published *in Disability and the Politics of Education: An International Reader* (Gabel & Danforth, 2008). Beth, too, had written a chapter about the need to push the proverbial envelope about race and disability (Ferri, 2010). We felt an impasse has been reached and were not quite sure about how to advance this line of thought. Then Subini Annamma came along. The first time I met her was when presenting at a session sponsored by the Special Education Special Interest Group at AERA. Subini was in the audience and introduced herself to me as the session was disbanding. Janette Klingner, her doctoral adviser who noticed that we had overlapping interests, had presented Subini with a copy of my *Urban Narratives* book. In later years Subini would joke that she "stalked" me, but that initial meeting served to begin an academic alliance of sorts. Given that the focus of her dissertation was on young women of color with the label of Emotional Disturbance in the School-to-Prison Pipeline, I accepted an invitation to be a member of her committee. Subini studied at the University of Colorado at Boulder, and was part of an activist group of students who focused on issues of social justice. We began to work on several projects together, and in continuing the focus on race and disability, she proposed working on developing a theoretical framework she called DisCrit.

DisCrit drew heavily from two sources—Disability Studies and Critical Race Studies. From our shared vantage point, Disability Studies did not sufficiently engage with issues of race, and likewise, Critical Race Theory did not sufficiently engage with disability. We wanted to explore *why* and challenge both fields to recognize that their limitations allowed some of the most vulnerable citizens—both disabled and people of color—to be omitted from the dialogue, and by doing so, inadvertently reinforcing racist and ableist ideologies and practices. By naming DisCrit as a separate entity, Subini had claimed a theoretical disposition that had to date never been legitimately acknowledged in research literature, let alone explored as such. What was being claimed about life at the interstices is quite complex with many implications. So, together with Beth Ferri, we spent a year developing a theoretical framework, justifying its need, and illustrating ways in which it could potentially be used. The result was an article called "Dis/ability Critical Race Studies (DisCrit): Theorizing at the Intersections of Race and Disability" (Annamma, Connor, & Ferri, 2013), published in the UK-based *Journal of Race, Ethnicity, & Education.*

The piece generated some interest among some scholars who worked in either DS or CRT, and was later included in the second edition of *Foundations of Critical Race Theory* (Taylor, Gillborn, & Ladson-Billings, 2016). The next step seemed to be an edited book in which we could bring together DS scholars and CRT scholars who have shared areas of interest. At the same time, we wanted to invite these scholars to engage with our own original article and zoom in on a particular aspect—to critique it, to build upon it, to extend it—in sum, to help cultivate its possibilities as a useful theoretical framework. So, we identified six broad areas: (1) the intersection of race, class, and ability; (2) the achievement/opportunity gap; (3) overrepresentation of students of color in special education; (4) the school-to-prison-pipeline; (5) school reform; (6) race, disability, and the law. We invited a scholar from DS and CRT to contribute to each section, encouraging them to share aspects of their own research and thinking, as well as collaborating with other scholars of their choice. Each submission was peer-reviewed to ensure high quality, and after three rounds of feedback, I hand submitted the manuscript in hard copy to Teachers College Press, where it would be in a series called Disability, Culture, and Equity.

That afternoon I received an email stating that the book had to be cut by one-third, recommending four chapters to be axed. I realized we had gone over the length specified in our original contract, but I had checked in all along the way, requesting permission—and had been granted it. Ethically, I could not see cutting four chapters after people had spent close to two years in this process, so appealed to the series editors in justifying why the book was slightly longer than originally planned, and providing them emails that verified permission to extend. Going around the acquisitions editor to do this was a last resort, as we wanted to maintain the original format of what we thought to be a well-balanced book. The result was a compromise involving a 20 percent rather than 35 percent cut that could be implemented across all chapters, thereby allowing all contributors to remain in the volume. The turnaround was supertight and I decided, rather than send back chapters for a fourth time (during the inconvenient time of summer holidays), to trim all articles and send to the authors for immediate approval. I was visiting my folks in the UK during that summertime, en route to Sri Lanka, where I took the manuscript and worked on it for the first four days of my trip at a desk in my hotel room, looking out over the Indian Ocean. These are the breaks. When publishers say "jump," we usually do. The book came out as *DisCrit: Disability Studies and Critical Race Theory in Education* (Connor, Ferri, & Annamma, 2016), building upon our initial theorizing of using an intersectional approach in research with the intention that it would better help understand the long-standing inequalities based upon disability and race.

I wanted a change of pace for the next book and it came in the form of a collaboration with a person I'd originally met when coordinating activities for the New York City Task Force on Quality Inclusive Education. Her name was Diane Linder Berman, and she was a teacher, mother of Benny, a child who did not fit the mold of "typical," self-advocate, and a proponent of inclusive education. At a conference sponsored by the taskforce, Diane had donated copies of her book *Beyond Words: Reflections on our Journey to Inclusion* (Berman, 2009) for interested parents. I read the work and made contact to thank Diane for her generosity. Our shared interests led me to invite her to teach a course in inclusive education at Hunter College and, much to my delight, she agreed to do so. I became genuinely interested in her experiences as a mother of a child who had been given multiple disability categories by kindergarten, and who sought inclusion for her son within the public schools of New York City. Diane had fought placements offered in separate school settings, yet also became increasingly disheartened by the lack of choices. Subsequently, she searched around the state for a school that would include Benny, eventually finding a supportive principal in suburban Long Island.

Over the years, Diane had shared anecdotes and tidbits about Benny's story, his brother Adam, her husband David, and how the Boulder School in Long Island had welcomed them with open arms, and figured out—through teacher-parental collaboration and thoughtful trial and error—how to include and educate her son. What impressed me the most was the dedication of faculty at Boulder, evidenced every semester when half-a-dozen members travelled from Long Island to Hunter and talked to graduate students in back-to-back sections of Diane's inclusion class. As an observer I was impressed by their matter-of-factness and moved by their dedication and willingness to share what they knew with pre-service and neophyte teachers. Diane recognized what they had done for Benny, essentially saving him from a life of exclusion, and at the same time—learning from him how to be flexible, accommodating, and inclusive. She kept commenting how much she wanted to document what the school does, so other educators could learn from their practices. I became intrigued at the prospect of documenting these practices of a successful inclusive environment. What a labor of love, I thought, to write a book about a solid inclusive school, making transparent its practices. Everything she had ever told me about the place struck me as simpatico with the tenets of DSE. Was the school actually demonstrating a DSE philosophy without necessarily knowing? Might I be able to point out the instances where this occurred, providing further evidence of how a DSE disposition (whether consciously termed that or not) facilitated greater success with inclusion?

Diane and I agreed to collaborate upon a book designed to promote conversation between practice and theory. In brief, she would write chapters describing, in chronological order, Benny's transition into the school and his progression through each grade, focusing upon issues such as classroom management, academic achievement, teaching methodologies, assessment, socialization, and community integration. After each chapter I would write an analysis of the issues raised, bringing a DSE theoretical framework through which to consider all of her and Benny's experiences. This structure was deliberately dialogic, opening up a space to consider how practice can inform theory, as well as vice versa. The result is an accessible book called *A Child, a Family, a School, a Community: A Tale of Inclusive Education* (Berman & Connor, 2017) that can be read by parents and teachers who are interested in creating and maintaining authentic inclusive schools.

CONTRASTING CONFERENCES

I began writing about scholarship by focusing on books as each one is a large project taking two to three years from conception to publication. During this timeframe they remain in my head, sometimes on the front burner, sometimes on the back, but they're always there until completion. Sharing recently completed research or work in progress at professional conferences is also expected of an academic. By and large, I usually like conferences, although they took some getting used to. The there's-been-some-mistake-here feeling often descends upon me as I walk to the podium or have the microphone passed to me on a panel. I managed my anxieties by thinking: do your best; make sure to include interesting information; say something original; try to create connections that are new to people in the audience; if appropriate, and possible, make them smile or laugh.

It's at conferences where alliances form, opportunities arise, and projects are hatched. Audience members may be editors of journals who can ask you to submit your finished work to them. They can be like-minded scholars who seek a chapter from you, or guest editors of a special edition of a journal and seek a contribution, or hosts of a conference who invite you to speak. Networking can be strategic in the form of people specifically seeking other people out, or organic in that being in an audience or participating in a meeting enables public conversations in which academic allies are revealed. Two conferences I attended yearly from 2001 to 2015 are the American Educational Research Association (AERA) and Disability Studies in Education (DSE). A third I often attended was the Society for Disability Studies (SDS). All three are very distinct, yet I was able to share work and meet people who continued stimulating my interest in education and disability at these, and other, venues.

The American Education Research Association is simply enormous. With well over 15,000 people attending, it stretches over a cluster of jumbo hotel chains and spans five days. The program is as thick as a telephone directory and a "who's who" of educational research. The first time attending as a doctoral student I was star struck to see and hear scholars studied in seminars. They were rock stars of educational thinkers, and while I once was entranced by Deborah Harry, Siouxsie Sioux, David Bowie, Morrrisey, and Peter Gabriel, I now was mesmerized by the likes of Christine Sleeter, Gloria Ladson-Billings, Pedro Noguera, Sonia Nieto, and Michelle Fine. How does one be part of such a huge event? There's an irony in that anyone, and more accurately their research, can fit in at AERA. The trick is finding other members of your research tribe. This is done by looking at the Special Interest Groups (SIGs), with almost two hundred in existence. Although I was a member of several, it was the DSE-SIG that kept me connected to a community of scholars who became a kind of academic family that I saw once or twice a year, but could always reach out to them any time in between. We knew we were in the process of developing DSE as we went along, and sought to be mindful about not being exclusionary in our thinking, while actively challenging much of what we had experienced—and continued to experience—in special education.

I preferred presenting on roundtables and as part of thematic panels. Roundtables were far less stress as they simply involved sitting at a table and presenting your work as if in a coffee shop. However, looking out over a hundred round tables in a large space meant sometimes seeing a popular theme symbolized by three rings of people straining to hear, while a less popular theme could translate to the presenter sitting solitary like a wallflower waiting to be asked for a dance. On one occasion I was the latter, sitting alone and feeling forlorn when I saw Ellen Branlinger's smiling face come toward me from across the room. She'd came to see me! The paper happened to be a profile of a participant in my dissertation with the data about his life in and out of school represented in poetry, titled: *Michael's Story: "I get into so much trouble just by walking": Narrative Knowing and Life at the Intersections of Learning Disability, Race, and Class* (Connor, 2006). It was times like this, having a one-on-one quality conversation with an accomplished scholar whom I admired that I loved being at AERA.

As time went by I built up confidence to collaborate with colleagues and propose panels that would reach a wider audience. These were ideal when developing a special edition of a journal or an edited book, and I felt privileged to be on panels with eminent scholars such as Alfred Artiles, Wanda Blanchett, David Gillborn, Zeus Leonardo, Daniel Losen, Pedro Noguera, Tom Skrtic, Christine Sleeter, and Sally Tomlinson. Part of my interest in developing DSE has been to argue for disability to be "at the table" of diversity writ large, sitting alongside race, ethnicity, gender, sexual orientation, social class, and so on. This has meant actively contributing to compilations on social justice (Connor & Baglieri, 2009; Connor & Gabel, 2010; Gabel & Connor, 2009) and assessing educational volumes on diversity in regard to disability (Connor, 2012b).

As a DSE-SIG our own consciousness was raised at AERA when we were assigned rooms that were inaccessible for wheelchair users who had to stay by the door due to stairs leading down to the main floor. This sparked a conversation in our SIG about how accessible is AERA in general? For example, we rarely noted blind or deaf people attending. Once we started questioning, all kinds of issues were raised. How accessible were all bathrooms for wheelchair users? How far apart were the hotel venues for people with mobility impairments and could they get from one session to another in the 20 minutes of allotted time? Why were round table sessions packed so close together that those people hard of hearing (and *not* hard of hearing for that matter) could not understand the presenter in a sea of noise? It became apparent that it was incumbent upon us to engage with AERA's administration about accessibility issues as a legitimate concern. Subsequently, half-a-dozen of us crafted a White Paper (Allan, Connor, Ferri, Gabel, Gallagher, & Ware, 2007) outlining what we perceived to be the general problem, providing specific examples and corresponding suggestions. The paper struck a chord with AERA management. At that time Deb Gallagher and I were co-chairs of the DSE-SIG and responsible for discussing the whitepaper with AERA's Executive Director Felice Levine and Diversity Officer George Wimberly. First conversations felt somewhat strained, perhaps understandably so, asking AERA to rethink accessibility for all members. However, the administration soon acknowledged the need for some changes, what could be done, and how the DSE-SIG could help provide guidance. To illustrate issues of accessibility Robin Smith and I rolled/walked with central AERA staff when inspecting all hotels in New York City where the next conference was to be held. It was an eye-opener in terms of getting from A to B and, in some hotels, even getting into a room or a toilet. AERA took our white paper seriously and ultimately, we formed a partnership to establish changes at the AREA conference. Some of these included scheduling DSE sessions near accessible bathrooms, suggesting alternative formats for presentation handouts, the provision of a quiet room for those who needed to rest from the overwhelming constant (over) stimulation of the conference, more streamlined notification of sign language interpreters, wider spaces between round tables, the request for universal use of ASL silent applause at round tables, a mini-bus circulating in a loop between conference hotels for attendees with mobility impairments, use of microphones for questions and answers to include hard of hearing members, and so on. While more can still be done—as complete accessibility by nature is an ideal and always a work in progress—I believe AERA made good faith attempts to promote a more inclusive culture, although by its very nature, it should always be ongoing.

Another interesting experience I had was due to the DSE-SIG's insistence that disability be represented on the Social Justice Action Committee (SJAC). However, governance structures in AERA can be a little rigid and a place was not created for disability per se, as was the case with race, gender, and other markers of identity. Nevertheless, I was allowed to join as one of the two members-at-large for a two-year term. The committee's chairperson was Kris Gutierrez, a very thoughtful, hardworking, and highly principled scholar. She later went on to be president of AERA and as an adviser to President Obama's Education Team. Being on a central AERA committee allowed me to see behind the scenes of how, to a degree, the organization worked, and being on the Social Justice Committee meant collaborating with representatives from many active working groups. What I came to learn, in listening to many notable scholars, and working in various groups and subgroups, was AERA tends to be relatively apolitical in a country that is deeply divided on educational priorities. Many scholars sought AERA to take up their cause, but the organization only publicly responds to federal cases involving education. They do so by usually by filing an amicus brief, such as in the case of protesting the US Supreme Court cases of *Parents Involved in Community Schools v. Seattle School District* (2007) focusing on district policies encouraging integration that positioned race as a "tiebreaker" for public choice of high schools, and *Fisher v. University of Texas at Austin* (2013), that challenges the university's use of race in admission policies.

In addition to the serious work of conferences, there's a fun side in the form of opportunities to socialize and AERA is no exception. Should a starving doctoral student strategize, he or she can make timely appearances to schmooze at university-sponsored parties night after night with complementary food and drink. Members have their favorite sponsors, and mine is Syracuse University as I have found them to be the most progressive in their inclusive education programs led by a cadre of DSE-identified scholars throughout the years, including Douglas Biklen, Steve Taylor, Beth Ferri, Mara Sapon-Shevin, Julia White, Christy Ashby and Alan Foley, along with alumni such as Nirmala Erevelles, Chris Kleiwer, and Alicia Broderick, to name a few. People are happy to see each other, swap updates, projects, personal and professional tidbits. The event is usually in a restaurant so it's not as crowded as the bigger university evening soirees, and you can hear conversations without trying to drown out the noise. Party-hopping has been a pastime over the years and it's safe to say that unleashed academics en masse with unlimited alcohol are quite . . . um, human. I recall being invited by a Harvard alumna to their sponsored party, and bumped into a snobby colleague, also an alumna, who asked, "What are *you* doing here?" "Slumming," I replied, before heading over—as an invited ally—to the People of Color Dance Party where professors got down on the dance floor and, filled to the gills on free wine that enhanced the senses, I reflected on how wonderful and surreal life could feel at times. All at the expense of a slight hangover the next day.

In comparison with AERA, the annual Disability Studies in Education conference has been much smaller, and in many ways, far more personal. I have felt very loyal to this conference. It was initiated by a few scholars from Chicago's National Louis University taking a risk—and it grew to be an annual and an international event having been held in Belgium, New Zealand, and Australia. I have appreciated the informal nature of this venue, where nametags state only name and affiliation in an attempt to downplay hierarchies, both real and imagined. It was here we thought through how to assert a DSE identity, and develop the tenets of what we believed in (Connor, Gabel, Gallagher, & Morton, 2008). I have described the DSE conference at length in a special education of *Disability Studies Quarterly* (Connor, 2014) dedicated to highlighting how Disability Studies has grown in a myriad of ways, as it engages with other disciplines throughout the academy and beyond.

Invariably, in conversations comparing and contrasting DSE and Special Education, we can never let go of the somewhat artificiality of the differences. By this I mean ideologically it's easy to highlight how the belief systems and knowledge base on which each academic field rests are quite distinct, the comparison is asymmetrical as special education is a titanic cultural phenomenon composed of official histories, certification programs, professional institutions, laws and regulations, and so on. In contrast, DSE is a disposition, a way of thinking, and when applied to research, has yielded a body of knowledge that has asserted itself in engaging with areas of understanding human difference and education, challenging the monopoly and orthodoxy of special education, providing a critique of many taken for granted practices.

It is no exaggeration when I say that DSE has provided many critical special educators with sustenance and hope. We came, shared, and discussed our research and thinking, with a collective desire to seek new ways of "doing business" in schools around disability and education, greater inclusion, and recognition of disabilities as normal within the range of human diversity. I was involved in planning and hosting three DSE conferences, two at Teachers College and one at Hunter College. Each time the demands were worth it because each year built upon the efforts of the last, and helped continue provide a sense of continuity.

Another conference I have frequented regularly is that of the SDS. What I appreciate about this event is the sheer diversity of topics on which people present. As DS is interdisciplinary, disability is researched and theorized in potentially every subject area including fine arts, literature, sciences, gender studies, dance, history, queer studies, sociology, anthropology, medicine, rehabilitation, religion, law, media, and of course, education. Attending panels and presentations of people working within so many fields is incredibly stimulating as it influences the (re)view of one's own field. Listening to high profile scholars such as Lennard Davis, Simi Linton, and Rosemarie Garland Thomson, I still can't quite shake off their rock star status, and enjoy hearing their current thoughts.

My favorite part of the conference, without a doubt, is "The Dance." Toward the end of every SDS conference there's a dance held, usually in the ballroom of a hotel. As an aficionado of all kinds of dance clubs stretching over four decades, this has to be the most unique. Everyone just gets up and moves to great music—usually a nice mix of 70s and 80s, lots of soul and funk, with some modern classics featured throughout. The overwhelming majority of the dance floor is populated by people with disabilities. Atypical bodies take any shape or form, and to see them all together, mixed with a minority of typical bodies all letting go to the music is pure magic. It feels strangely liberating to lose oneself in music by dancing with professional acquaintances who are smiling and having a good time. Wheelchair users spin round and create audacious moves, sometimes moving out of their chairs and onto the floor, moving in any direction they wish. Bubble-wrap is sometimes taped to the dance floor to pop under foot and wheel-over. Some people with back injuries and cerebral palsy position themselves on the floor and dance horizontally. Feelings of joy, happiness, and liberation are palpable, a shared moment among disabled people and their allies who just want to dance. The last SDS dance I attended culminated the evening's festivities with Lady Gaga's "Born this Way," giving the song a whole new meaning, everyone joining in the chorus with pride.

In contrast, the special education conferences I have presented at over the years such as Council for Exceptional Children (CEC) have always felt somewhat staid, repetitive, and predictable in comparison. I value the approaches and methods used to engage kids who struggle in school, but know that if school practices were rethought and based more upon Universal Design for Learning (UDL) then the emphasis on interventions, accommodations, and modifications could be very different. Likewise, the National Council for Learning Disabilities (NCLD) seems lackluster, as if it is an organization chugging along without much stimulation from the outside. Of course this has been one of my critiques of special education as a whole. As a field it is very inward looking, wary of, and resistant to, other fields of study and the progress they have made, including innovative directions in which they have moved. For example, there are so many ways to contemplate what a learning disability is, and according to whom.

DOCUMENTING DYSLEXIA

The topic of what is a learning disability, specifically dyslexia, presented itself in an unexpected way. I was contacted by filmmakers Susan and Allan Raymond who were in the middle of making a documentary on dyslexia. Author and activist Jonathan Mooney (Mooney, 2006; Mooney & Cole, 2000) had given them my contact information. I'd become friendly with Jonathan after the publication of his first book and he agreed to speak at a DSE conference. He knew I'd done work on LD and race. The Raymonds wanted to racially diversify their interviewees, hence the call. I was able to put them in touch with some folks, including one of my former high school students, Angel. They loved interviewing Angel and visited his New Jersey art studio.

In helping them set up arrangements to do these interviews we spontaneously developed conversations about dyslexia, race, social class, and the social construct of disability. Subsequently, they also asked to interview me about some of the topics we chatted about, and arrived with a surprising amount of equipment. Time passed and one day, Angel and I received an invitation to see a screening of the film *Journey into Dyslexia* (Raymond & Raymond, 2011) at HBOs executive offices on 42nd Street.

The documentary provided multiple perspectives on what dyslexia is and how it is experienced. It opens with Jonathan Mooney, charming and loquacious, speaking to an auditorium of high school students, intriguing them with notions of rejecting "normal" and suggesting some of their learning problems are probably due to "dysteachia" (to put it mildly, he'd had some bad experiences in his own education). Susan then provides facts and figures on dyslexia, before we see a montage of students of all ages describing their experiences, what they knew, and how they felt. I found this section to be most moving—and I have used in teaching classes, as it has great impact upon teachers to hear what students know and think about dyslexia. Not long after, the Yale Center on Dyslexia and Giftedness headed by Sally Shaywitz is featured with detailed explanations of brain imaging of the typical brain versus the dyslexic brain. Then it cuts to me pretty much questioning claims made about brain imaging and the reification of two types of brain, shifting the focus onto the civil rights of dyslexic learners to be included in general education. The reminder of the movie features profiles of various people with dyslexia, many of them artistically talented and/or having business acumen. There is a very poignant section in which a highly accomplished entrepreneur breaks down when describing his life experiences. Angel, alas, had been left on the cutting room floor, along with Michael (from *Michael's Story*). The Raymonds later explained to me their process of creating a documentary, and the difficulties of distilling over 200 hours of footage into one hour.

It wasn't until after I spent a little time with them that I realized how accomplished they were, widely respected as some of America's most distinguished documentary filmmakers. The Raymonds had pioneered so many ideas, including reality TV, in the form of *American Family* (1971–1972). They also filmed *The Police Tapes* (1977) documenting crime and the life of cops in urban America, the inspiration for the popular TV series *Hill Street Blues* (Botchco & Kozoll, 1981–1987). In addition to cabinet full of Emmys, they won an Oscar for *I Am a Promise: The Children of Stanton Elementary School* (Raymond & Raymond, 1994). This documentary features Cornelius, a child with behavioral problems who defies his teachers and even the principal, and in many ways typifies the struggles of those born into what Derek Bell describes as "the bottom of the well" (1992, p. 1). I have used this film in classes, along with *Hard Times at Douglas High* (Raymond & Raymond,

2008), to reveal the realities and complexities of teaching and learning within inequitable school systems. After my request to see more of their work, they mailed me a box of CDs and I viewed them eagerly. Their body of work is largely socially conscious, focusing on education, the prison system, the effect of war on children, illiteracy, religion, among other topics. They kindly consented to screen and discuss *Journey into Dyslexia* at the DSE conference in 2012. The more I thought about it, the more I saw so many parallels between conducting research and making a documentary—being driven by a question, probing through an investigation, interviewing people, gathering data, reviewing it all, selecting the most pertinent parts and staging it so it will accessible to an audience who will engage with the chosen story to tell. I have to say that these two unassuming people are likely the best researchers I have ever met.

STRATEGIZING: SELECTED PROJECTS

As there are space limitations to this book, I will endeavor to go into the home stretch of this chapter by providing a commentary on selected projects and articles. Of the special editions of journals I have guest co-edited, two important ones come to mind. The first is a double special edition of *Learning Disability Quarterly*. As it happened, I had been a reviewer of manuscripts for them since 2003 but had not luck in being accepted myself when my work was being accepted regularly in other venues. In submitting an article that was, in essence, a highly distilled version of my dissertation called *Breaking Containment: The Power of Narrative Knowing--Countering Silences within Traditional Special Education Research* (Connor, 2009), I had received a conditional acceptance pending major revisions. I labored over revising so much of the content yet methodically integrated every suggestion from all three reviewers. Despite that, it was returned as rejected. This pissed me off. Why encourage a second submission if it was to be rejected after incorporating all feedback? I realize the content was challenging. I was critiquing special education as a form of containment that mirrored other imposed social and cultural parameters in the lives of young Black and Latino people. However, the compelling evidence was coming from young people themselves who were narrating very different versions of the realities of special education as perpetrated in glossy textbooks and CEC literature. It was a blatant example of special education choosing to censor ideas they found unpalatable, regardless of their authenticity.

So, I did two things. The first was to send it off to another publication. I chose the *International Journal of Inclusive Education*, a respected and wider circulating journal where it was accepted with minor revisions. The second thing I did, feeling my anger was justified, was to write a letter to the editor of LDQ, David Scanlon, in which I described how frustrating it was to be reviewer but not see any work like my own in the journal, knowing it would be interesting to others in the field of LD. Such an experience had verified my hunch that the journals in the field of special education, in this case represented by LDQ, were very narrow in scope and deliberately alienated those in the field who sought engagement about long-standing inequalities and a greater plurality of perspectives on LD, research topics, and methodology. I asked if he would consider a guest edited issue of LDQ that focused on what was lost or missed when the field adhered to one paradigm and its associated methods. To his credit, and to my surprise, David Scanlon said "Yes." In fact, as if standing at a bar, he asked, "Why not make it a double?" What ensued was a stimulating process in which my co-editors Deborah Gallagher and Beth Ferri and I invited a DSE oriented researchers to contribute either an empirical or conceptual piece. Each would be followed by a shorter response from a more traditional researcher in the field. This format would allow a dialogue to emerge about important issues. In addition to all three co-writing an introduction, we would also co-write a final synthesis, illuminating points that had arisen and asking more questions about what can be next steps in widening the self-imposed and quite restrictive parameters of our field? The result was a provocative double edition in which a group of us respectfully challenged the field of LD to rethink what we do, why we do it, and how we do it. Our opening article was titled "Broadening our Horizons: Toward a Plurality of Methodologies in Learning Disability Research" (Connor, Gallagher, & Ferri, 2011), and the closing article "Pluralizing Methodologies in the Field of LD: From 'What Works' to What Matters" (Ferri, Gallagher, & Connor, 2011). The title of the latter was an allusion to the gold standard of What Works Clearing House in which very few research-based teaching methods were actually listed as effective. As guest editors we presented this project at AERA and CLD conferences.

Another special edition of a journal I enjoyed working on was thanks to Scot Danforth, who was then co-editor of *Disability Studies Quarterly*. He made a direct suggestion of how interesting it would be to reflect upon the pioneering work of Christine Sleeter who questioned the invention and reification of the term "learning disability" (Sleeter, 1987). I agreed, and Beth Ferri and I contacted Christine to run this idea by her. She was delighted her work from decades ago still resonated with DS researchers. Subsequently, we invited a fair number of scholars—well established, middle career, and emerging—to share their work and thoughts in relation to the issues Sleeter originally raised. The result was a powerful array of articles that included contributions by Susan Baglieri, Wanda Blanchett, Bernadette Baker, Curt Dudley-Marling and Patricia Paugh, Faye Ginsberg and Rayna Rapp,

Tom Skrtic & Zac McCall, and an original culminating work by Sleeter—after reading all fourteen articles—titled *Building Counter Theory About Disability* (2010).

Over the years, my colleagues in DSE who alternatively often self-describe (myself included, depending on the context) as "critical special educators," have endeavored to build counter theory about disability. We have striven to publish in a variety of places that include disability studies journals, special education journals, discipline specific journals, and contributed chapters to a wide range of edited books. All of our work has been done with view to rethinking disability. Special education venues have been moderately receptive at times such as *Remedial and Special Education* who published "Disability Studies and Special Education: The Need for a Plurality of Perspectives on Disability" (Baglieri, Valle, Connor, & Gallagher, 2011). However, many have not and continue to publish position papers from long-established figures in the field such as James Kauffman who ring alarmist bells akin to Chicken-Licken that the sky is falling down (Ansastaiou & Kauffman, 2011a; Ansastaiou & Kauffman, 2011b; Ansastaiou & Kauffman, 2013). Occasionally, we critical special educators in DSE feel the need to "speak back" and do so, although it reinforces our beliefs about how limited research in special education remains when we cannot be published to refute inaccuracies and misconceptions about DSE and the social model of disability. While *Exceptionality* may reject our article such as "Beyond the Far Too Incessant Schism: Special Education and the Social Model of Disability," the *International Journal of Inclusive Education* publishes it (Gallagher, Connor, & Ferri, 2014). Yet a sense of déjà vu exists. Recent Kauffman iterations overwhelmingly cite his own former critiques of DSE scholars' work lest he mention the actual sources and readers take the initiative and read original works in his references. It is sad that his disengagement with ideas symbolize a relinquishing of intellectual responsibility and a preference for academic foot stomping that appears to go unchecked ad infinitum (Kauffman, Anastasiou, & Maag, 2017; Kauffman & Badar, 2017).

In this chapter I hope I have not presented special education and DSE in reductive ways. There have always been tensions and feelings of ambivalence working with our feet placed in special education teacher education programs yet researching with our heads and hearts in DSE ways of thinking and doing. For all scholars, there are serious implications for tenure and promotion in a world that may misunderstand or outright reject one's work. I tried to play it safe by publishing in multiple arenas so I had evidence of being a (critical) special educator, striving to engage the field, while also being more liberated when writing in non-special education venues about disability. Ideas I hold close that guide my work include striving to be responsible, clear, thoughtful, practical, and creative—along with making connections among research, theory, practice, and policy. After all, you never know where your words may end up. On the other hand, as one colleague noted, people have favorite movie stars and writers, even teachers, but do we know anyone with a favorite academic? (Other than academics? Even then, I wonder . . .)

COMMENTARY

Teaching and Learning in Schools and Universities

I often think of the reading sources we assign to courses. Text books that "fit the bill," or perhaps more accurately, "Fit the class," are few and far between. It is not uncommon for new textbooks to be around $150, and competition runs high among publishers about who gets their share of the market. I raise this point as selecting texts for teaching at the university level tells a lot about professors. Brantlinger's critique of what she called *The Big Glossies* (2006) struck a chord with me as she systematically took them to task for being voiceless, apolitical, and misleading for students going into teaching. Voiceless in that each one delivers the information in as neutral a way as possible, with all emotion flattened; apolitical in that they seek not to rock the boat of the field they're describing; misleading, as they are filled with attractive photos of idealized special education classrooms with a small group of eager-eyed children flanking a smiling teacher. There's no urgency, no passion, no outrage . . . and no reality. To counter this, I once assigned any book by Jonathan Kozol to contrast the reality of many urban kids. Most students got the point, but a few were angry, and their comments revealed to me how poor communities are blamed for being poor, without fully contemplating the complexities of poverty.

That special education is taught without the social context of social class, race, and gender, along with other markers of identity is troubling to me as an educator. These considerations help create the three-dimensional world in which we all inhabit, not a two-dimensional one flattened between the pages of yet another uninspiring educational textbook. In some ways, the traditional books are the interpreters and synthesizers of existing research, but authors do so without declaring their own positionality. However, the findings of research are stated almost as facts, without any explicit interpretation. I'd venture to say that teachers don't typically read research fist-hand, not because they're uninterested or lazy, but because it's largely inaccessible and divorced from how they know and understand teaching and learning. In attending conferences over the years I have seen multiple times how prominent special education researchers such as Doug and Lynn Fuchs have presented findings on, say, an intervention in reading at the Annual Learning Differences Conference hosted at Harvard. That the research took place in a reading laboratory, and not a classroom, seems not to influence the suggestions for teachers to implement what is simply impractical and therefore undoable in a classroom. It's one thing to view a possible method be successful and advocate it's use in a lab-type setting such as Sylvan Learning Centers where one-on-one is the norm, but to urge "teachers should do this" while willfully ignoring the lived realities of teachers misses the mark. Such comments infer teachers are to blame, rather than advocating for more appropriate resources, in this case reading clinics.

What is put in teachers' hands must work for them whether it be methods for teaching, strategies for learning, ideas to contemplate/adapt/experiment with, or frameworks for thinking about different types of learners. While the major laws are crucial for understanding the structures of special education and test cases in the Supreme Court are worthy of note, it is the stories of real teachers, real children, and real parents that I have noticed interest students most. That was one of the reasons I sought to develop several practitioner-based books that are not big glossy texts (Gabel & Connor, 2014; Valle & Connor, 2010), mindful of how works by scholar-educators such as Udvarni-Solner and Kluth (2008), Sapon-Shevin (2010), and C.A. Tomlinson (1999) have been understood and used by teachers. Likewise, real schools in their entirety and complexities are not sufficiently represented in scholarly literature that is accessible to teachers. This is one of the reasons Diane Berman and I sought to portray the Long Island school that accepted her son, Benny, after he was rejected from an inclusive placement within New York City's Department of Education. We wanted to describe what happened, to tell the story of Benny's successful inclusion in an elementary school. Folded into the main narrative were the stories of the principal, teachers, and school aides, how they viewed Benny and their actions. By describing the fears, anxieties, and mistakes of educators—along with their resourcefulness, creativity, and commitment—we show "real life" and disability in context (as represented by us) in one school.

In *Rethinking Disability* one of the chapters is called "Actively Challenging Normalcy," and is coupled with the question: "How can I talk about disability in my classroom?" Jan Valle and I thought it important to look at why disability should be explicitly taught, and ways that teachers could feel sufficiently comfortable and informed to do so. This is an integral part to a DSE approach to education about human differences, and designed to break the silence around disability and dispel discomfort. Looking at diversity as a basis for community, representations of disability diversity, language use, disability presence within the curriculum, and examples of teachers discussing topics, and listening to their students ("I think that people with disabilities should have the opportunity to do whatever they want to do") (Valle &

Connor, p. 188). I have not seen these topics addressed in the same way within traditional special education literature, and if they were, this approach would feel strained, given the dysfunction, disorder, and deficit conceptualizations that dominate the field.

Educational Laws and their Impact

Special education laws have served as a double edged sword. For some, IDEIA, and all of the components it guarantees, has enabled them to access a quality education with supports and services. For others, it has had deleterious effects. As Beth Ferri and I worked on *Reading Resistance*, we had confirmed what we'd seen with our own eyes, "It struck us as a brute fact: school systems could not exclude African-Americans from mainstream classes by race, but they could by disability due to the interpretation of IDEA's Least Restrictive Environment clause." The concept of disabilities has often been used against kids, under the guise of benevolence. On further reflection, and investigation, the law itself has been utilized to inhibit access of African-American students to general education. Rather than seeing each element of IDEIA in an enabling light, let's consider them with the possibility of being a disabling one, if contrasted with white, middle-class norms.

1. *A Free and Appropriate Public Education.* African-American and/or working-class or parents do not have the same cultural capital as upper- and middle-class white citizens. Those in the latter demographic are more likely to employ lawyers and advocate for specific labels, and specialized placements, often at public expense (Harry, 2002).
2. *In the Least Restrictive Environment.* African-American children are likely to be placed in more restrictive environments that their white counterparts with the same disability label (Losen & Orfield, 2002).
3. *Due Process.* Communication between schools and parents is less likely to be well-organized and within mandated timelines when in working-class or poor districts (Pasachoff, 2011).
4. *Parental Participation.* Parents are often intimidated by the process, and remain confused or uninformed (Lamorey, 2002). School personnel are more inclined to have made decisions before parents attend meetings, influenced by social class and race (Wolfe & Duran, 2013).
5. *Nondiscriminatory Identification and Evaluation.* Students of color continue to be overrepresented in disability categories requiring subjective interpretation, such a behavior disorders, learning disability, intellectual impairment, and speech and language (Harry & Klingner, 2006). In contrast, they are significantly underrepresented in the categories of Gifted

and Talented (Ford, Grantham, & Whiting, 2008), Autism/Asperger Syndrome (Mandell et al., 2009).

6. *IEP*. All of the above areas are reflected in the IEP document that encapsulates disability identification, placements, and goals of each student (Chun, 2008).

To clarify, I am not saying special education is evil incarnate. However, it has been misused—consciously or unconsciously—by many professionals within school systems who witness the inequitable distribution of opportunities perpetuate, without perhaps reflecting on the degree of their complicity.

The topic of overrepresentation is featured in special education courses, and students demonstrate interest in it, but are left troubled by what—if anything—they can do about it. This is one of the reasons I wrote, "Who is Responsible for The Racialized Practices within (Special) Education and What Can Be Done to Change Them?" (Connor, 2017a). The problem is much bigger than teachers, of course, but I do believe teachers do have a locus of control and can play an active role in redressing inequalities of opportunity. Issues they must grapple with include: recognizing overrepresentation as a historical legacy; committing to actively working against racism and ableism; considering unintended complicity; cultivating a disposition that is grounded in multiculturalism, student diversity, and culturally responsive pedagogy; rethinking behavior referrals in general; reconsidering teacher referrals to special education; supporting inclusive education; and, actively participating in school policies. This is a lot to work on. In addition, outside of a teacher's locus of control are federal policies that do not sufficiently acknowledge the impact of differences in wealth disparities on all aspects of special education, inadequate federal policies on overrepresentation, the shortcomings of educational research, the neglect within special education research, the underdeveloped notion of teacher disposition toward social justice, and the moral obligation of all citizens. Of course, teachers can exert some influence in these arenas through critique and contributions, but the phenomenon should be a public concern—not solely one of educators.

Models of Disability and their Influence on Educators and Researchers

The politics of research and researchers' disposition have long created what was called a "divide" in special education (Andrews, et al., 2000, p. 258), that evolved into an "incessant schism" (Gallagher, Connor, & Ferri, 2014, p. 1120). The more we try to get beyond it, the more it seems stalemate occurs. Having three decades in the field, I still see it as, "very inward looking, wary of, and resistant to, other fields of study and the progress they have made, including innovative directions in which they have moved." As DSE notes, there are many ways in which to contemplate what a disability is and according to whom. This has serious implications for all aspects of research and, of course, people with disabilities themselves. In many ways, as noted by Christine Sleeter, DSE has striven to develop counter theories about human differences we determine to be disabilities (2010). Special educators who critiqued the existing order within the field of special education research have been disparaged and maligned (particularly in the writings of Kauffman: see 1999, for example), as well as actively prevented from being published within special education journals. On one hand, it is difficult to receive critique, even when constructive. But, as a field within academia, it is necessary. Remember my high school student Evie who asked me why I didn't teach more like Mr. Schwartz? She made good points that I reflected upon and then incorporated into my teaching. In contrast, special education as a field seems to stick its head in the sand in terms of contemplating usefulness and relevance of critique.

I have found several leaders in the field to be either patronizing or passive-aggressive professional in interactions. In one example, when sitting at a conference table with Doug Fuchs, he asked where I taught and what I was working on? I told him I worked at Hunter College and had just published an article in *Teaching Exceptional Children* called "Pigs, Pirates, and Pills: Using Film to Teach the Social Context of Disability." "Oh . . . you must be from Syracuse," he said not without a hint of snideness, referring to Syracuse's nationally recognized programs that have pushed the boundaries of Disability Studies and education. In another, more recent example, Dan Hallahan emailed me having come across the "Who is Responsible for The Racialized Practices within (Special) Education and What Can Be Done to Change Them?" His email read:

> *Dear David*
>
> *You have missed a large body of literature that presents data documenting that students from ethnic minorities are actually under-represented in special education. I refer to the work of Paul Morgan and Frakas. A quick googling will take you to their articles.*
>
> *Dan*

I responded:

> *Dear Dan*
>
> *You have missed my co-authored article in Multiple Voices that responded to Morgan et al. It's further down my academic webpage: "Dangerous*

Assumptions and Unspoken Limitations: A Disability Studies in Education Response to Morgan, Farkas, Hillemeir, Mattison, Maczuga, Li and Cook (2015)." Happy to discuss after you've read it. DJC.

He did not respond.

What struck me about Hallahan's communication was his self-assuredness that I was uninformed (a quick googling), whereas he had obviously not read the special edition of *Multiple Voices*, (a publication *within* the field of special education), dedicated to challenging the results of Morgan et al.'s flawed research. Indeed, I am deeply troubled that—given data sets and methods—Morgan et al.'s work is being featured prominently in Special Education journals and even Educational Researcher, a prestigious publication of AERA (Morgan, Farkas, Hillemeier, & Maczuga, 2017). What Morgan et al. actually claim is that more children of color need special education services, despite forty years of research to the contrary providing evidence of how experiences in special education are significantly different for different racial groups (Losen & Orfeild, 2002), upheld by ongoing research from Think Tanks at Harvard University and New York University.

In a third example, when I submitted an article to the *Journal of Learning Disabilities* called "Actively Navigating the Transition into College: Narratives of Students with Learning Disabilities." Editor Lee Swanson did not send it out to be reviewed. Instead, he rejected it based up the following rationale:

> *The sample size is limited and the results do not directly extend the existing research base. In both qualititaive* [sic] *and quantative* [sic] *research we publish only studies that provide advancements in theory (Swanson, personal communication).*

I responded to his hastily written note:

> *Dear Dr. Swanson*
>
> *Thank you for your email notifying me that you had reviewed my manuscript "Actively Navigating the Transition into College: Narratives of Students with Learning Disabilities." I confess I was surprised at the two-day turn around time, and am writing to seek clarification of your comments, hoping you will guide me to better understand them. I would like to share that I am a longtime subscriber of JLD, and particularly appreciate its inclusion of qualitative research, noting strong examples that I use to guide my own work. It is important to note that I accept your decision and am not seeking another review. What I am concerned about is a far larger issue, that is, the quality and importance*

of the review process, including the reasonable expectation to be reviewed by one's peers.

I found your statement that "the sample size is limited" to be confusing because small sample size is integral to qualitative research. Unlike quantitative research, qualitative inquiry does not seek the goal of generalization leading to prediction and control. Rather, "qualitative research methods are used to understand some social phenomena from the perspectives of those involved, to contextualize issues in their particular socio-cultural-political milieu, and sometimes to transform or change social [or educational] conditions" (Glesne, 2006, p. 4). Thus, by its very nature, and in order to reveal these perspectives and contextualized issues, qualitative research designs necessitate a small (or smaller) number of participants. My point is that to say (a large) sample size is not "required" implies that it is still desirable . . . just not necessary. And that, in turn, sounds like qualitative research holds lower standards, is a weaker form of research, and so on. JLD's awareness of this fundamental difference between the quantitative and qualitative frameworks is evidenced by its publication of exemplary articles such as: "Anna's Story: Narratives of Personal Experience About Being Learning Disabled" by Reid & Button, JLD 28 (10), 602–614; "Why Does My Stomach Hurt?" by Cohn, JLD 31 (5), 14–16; and "Teachers with Learning Disabilities: A View from Both Sides of the Desk" by Ferri, Keefe, & Gregg, JLD 34 (1), 22–32.

Similarly, your comment "and the results do not directly extend the existing research base," gave me pause to think about the outcome of qualitative research, more appropriately conceived as "findings." Knowing that there are several existing research bases, I was also left wondering which one that you referred to? For example, I am aware a small but fairly strong research base in narrative knowing and learning disabilities. I myself have published a book and several articles in this area, and have continued to work in further adding to findings of the field to date.

I appreciate and agree with your comment, "In both qualitative and quantitative research we publish only studies that provide advancements in theory." I would also appreciate further elaboration of your thoughts that would enable me to examine how I did not meet important and necessary criteria established by JLD.

As a researcher who has had the fortune to be previously published in JLD, and as a scholar who has never before had an article returned without the opportunity of peer review, I am asking for your help. I understand that there may be some conceptual confusion between us, and earnestly seek to better understand your thoughts. I look forward to your response in relation to questions I have asked.

Sincerely,
Dr. David Connor
Learning Disabilities Program

He did not respond.

In yet another example, when Kauffman and Anastasiou wrote an article titled "A Social Constructionist Approach to Disability: Implications for Special Education" (2011) in *Exceptional Children*, it was filled with egregious inaccuracies. Subsequently, Deborah Gallagher, Beth Ferri, and I wrote a letter to the editors Margo Mastropieri and Thomas Scruggs. We asked if they would be amenable to our response to Kauffman and Anastasiou's article, or better yet, perhaps a special edition of *Exceptional Children* focused upon the positive implications for special education of socially constructivism by special educators who work within this area.

They responded by stating it was the journal's policies not to publish commentaries, and declined a special guest edited edition.

We then wrote asking when their policy had changed regarding commentaries, and could they provide that to us in writing, along with providing them with citations of several editions of *Exceptional Children* that did include commentaries.

They did not respond.

There is a clear pattern here. The lead researchers and journal editors within the field of special education tend to balk at any criticism of the field, using measures to actively stifle expansive thinking, interdisciplinary alliances, and innovative re-framings of old problems. Perhaps, more troubling is allowing longtime leaders of the field an open microphone for what often reads as wandering rants against any philosophies, theories, methodologies, findings, or re-interpretations of existing knowledge that does not align with their own world view (Kauffman, 1999; Kaufman & Badar, 2017). While we DSE scholars/critical special educators have argued for a plurality of perspectives when provided limited access to traditional journals (Baglieri, Valle, et al., 2011; Connor et al., 2011; Ferri, et al., 2011), this suggestion is met with befuddlement, anger, and allegations of "extremism" (Kauffman & Badar, 2017) and the need for a purely "scientific reconstruction" to buttress the field from "chic" ideas (Kauffman, Anastasiou, & Maag, 2017, p. 139).

It does not help matters that previous critics of existing special education practices have been openly attacked in a manner unbecoming of professionals. That Kauffman (1999) referred to Ellen Brantlinger variously as "loathing," (p. 245) "scurrilous," (p. 245) "charlatan," (p. 250) and a "scam artist" (p. 249). Likewise, Deborah Gallagher's ideas were belittled by Kauffman and Sasso (2006), although they did not directly address her concerns with the field of special education (Gallagher, 2006).

I share these accounts because it is important to acknowledge how academic fields work, often "behind the scenes" to maintain their identity by censoring peers who are as equally interested in, and invested in, the same areas (in this case providing education to students who have been identified as disabled) but who think differently. It is also important to challenge those who exert significant power of the knowledge base about disability and education. In all instances shared above, silence seems to be the order of the day. It is not so surprising that special education appears to be perpetually wrestling with an "identity crisis" (Kauffman, 1999), articulating similar concerns with an increasingly outraged tone as years pass by (Kaufman & Sasso, 2006; Kauffman et al., 2017). This is where we seem to be again, right now. Déjà vu, with everyone growing older, and the notion of paradigms live as long as the people who uphold them do.

That special education cannot seem to be very flexible, I believe, is to its own detriment. My sentiments are echoed by others in the field, as evidenced in a recent edition of *Educational Leadership* dedicated to "Differences not Disabilities." In the opening article, Armstrong begins by stating, "If we want to use the most effective approaches within kids—and draw on the research about the brain—special education needs to change its approach" (2017, p. 11). He points out that "special education has too often remained insular, holding fast to its diagnostic categories" (p. 14), and "The field of special education needs to embrace a more progressive way of educating students who learn differently" (p. 12). Armstrong goes on to compare different paradigms of how we conceptualize disability and, in turn, how that understanding grounds us in everything that we think and do.

If authors who are critical special educators are denied access to longstanding journals dedicated to education and disability within the field of special education, they simply take their work elsewhere. The article rejected by Lee Swanson was published in *The International Journal of Qualitative Studies in Education* (Connor, 2013d), and the response to Anastasiou and Kauffman's string of simultaneous critiques of disability studies (that basically said similar points in three different journals, to ensure making a point in a multipronged way) was published as "Beyond the Far Too Incessant Schism: Special Education and the Social Model of Disability," in the *International Journal of Inclusive Education* (Gallagher, Connor, & Ferri, 2014). Both of these international journals have wider audiences than US-based special education journals. It strikes me as unnecessarily feudal, and purely self-serving, that special education mobilizes to keep out the work DSE/critical educators. Surely there's room for more than one belief system in the world of education and disability?

Educational Structures and Systems in Relation to People with Disabilities

My entry into academia, the first research completed alone, was with similar students I used to teach. These *were* my experience with LD, how I came to study LD formally and informally, and inspired me to want to know more. I was also aware of limitations they experienced in their lives, and this phenomenon was eloquently described by Patricia Collins's in her articulation of a matrix of domination (1990). Her framework incorporated ways in which past history informed and shaped current society, the multiple and simultaneous discourses around markers of identity that individuals and groups negotiated, along with daily interactions between local and extended communities. I could now better see where the profile of kids I once taught were located within this matrix—having been subjected to ostensibly protective laws that could be manipulated in prejudicial ways, zoning regulations that impacted housing and schooling, labeling/sorting/placing within the education system, and vulnerability to self-fulfilling prophecies and the school-to-prison-pipeline.

In this chapter I wrote, "These were urban stories, renderings of 'typical' adolescents in special education, who shared their perceptions of disability, race, and social class, describing what it meant to be simultaneously at the interstices of all three." Furthermore, "I'd always conceived of the participants as co-researchers of their own lives, and was humbled by how much they had shared with me, and oftentimes, with each other." In their lives I viewed multiple forms of *containment.* It was a word that circulated repeatedly in my thoughts when conducting the research and it still lingers there. Containment. Speaking personally and professionally, it is a word that I associate with special education, yet it also symbolizes the lack of access to all aspects of society that people with disabilities experience in general.

The school system played a similar refrain when my co-author Diane sought an inclusive setting for her son. District 75, the citywide system for children and youth deemed severely and multiply disabled, offered her a classroom filled with a small number of first graders flapping and rocking. It is a sobering thought that his peers in that class may still be there doing the same thing today, while her son attends general education in high school, having benefited from years of inclusive experiences in elementary and middle school. Diane shares that Benny's academic performance is uneven, and he sometimes puts in five times the work and get half the results of his peers, but also recognizes the opportunity for Benny to grapple with who he is, claim how far he has come, and learn to self-advocate. It's also an opportunity for a school system and the educators within it to reconsider how to best work with kids who don't fit the rigid mold of "typical" kids. If Diane and her family were not teachers, unfamiliar with laws, and were working-class or poor and/or a family of color, it would be far more likely that Benny would still be where the Department of Education originally placed him.

In some ways, her situation can be seen as a metaphor of the current field of special education and the alternative of adopting a DSE disposition.

To accept the placements within a current special education structure in the country's largest school system—without question—trusting what was offered, would have simply reproduced the status quo. However, to pick up a whole family, to go into the future with hope, and acceptance of the unknown, and to try something new, be open to new ways of thinking about disability, or knowing and doing . . . this aligns far more with a critical special educator/DSE position. The field of education needs to understand disability in more expansive and authentic ways. That's why in *Practicing Disability Studies in Education: Acting toward Social Change* (Connor, Valle, & Hale, 2015), my colleagues and I document ways in which a body of critical special educators are working to "co-create new visions for what can be, instead of settling for what is" (p. ix).

The Social, Political, and Cultural Experiences of People with Disabilities

In elaborating upon the interrelated realms within the matrix of oppression, Collins (1990) explains, "The structural domain organizes oppression, whereas the disciplinary domain manages it. The hegemonic domain justifies oppression, and the interpersonal domain influences everyday lived experience and the individual consciousness that ensues" (p. 276). Although she developed this concept with view to race and gender, it is useful to contemplate disability as it intersects with other markers of identity. In doing so, the social, political, and cultural experiences of all people with disabilities merge to provide rich information about lived realities. At the same time, there is much variation among those realities.

My original interests lay in the experiences of kids with disability labels in schools. The more I read, the more I became interested in their holistic experience of schooling as most accounts were of struggles, perceived inferiority, frustration, and generally diminished status as human beings. The entire experience for many kids in schools was to feel "less than [others]" described by Pelkey (2000) as, "You hate yourself for being LD. . . . I expected to fail, so I set no goals, believing my ability was set (I had none)" (p. 25). In his recollection of elementary school reading procedures, Jonathan Mooney recalled of his dyslexia, "During reading I was so angry and ashamed I could taste my stomach acid come into my throat and seep behind my nostrils any time I burped. I used to imagine killing the teacher" (Mooney & Cole, 2000a, p. 31). Here we see the physical and psychological stress manifest as repressed rage while, from the outside, his teacher may only see a small child sitting in front of her. In a visual representation of his educational experiences as a labyrinth, Michael, a student in *Urban Narratives*, writes,

"Will this system ever end? . . . This system will never end. . . . Maybe one day they would let me out" (Connor, 2008a, p. 174). These three glimpses into how kids think about schools are important to listen to, and learn from because children's perspectives about schooling practices can—and should—inform us about how we create learning environments and engage with students who do not fit normed expectations of meet grade level academic performances.

For kids with disabilities who make it to college, their schooling experiences steeped in anxiety may (or may not) continue. The number of students with disabilities has continued to rise steadily since the passage of PL.94-142 (Stodden, Conway, & Chang, 2003), yet numbers who graduate are significantly lower than non-disabled peers (Gregg, 2009). Furthermore, research findings can be misleading when an intersectional framework is used for analysis. For example, although students in the category of LD now attend colleges in significantly greater numbers than they did 20 or 30 years ago, the demographics indicate a majority are white and middle-class (Reid & Knight, 2006). Likewise, professors with disabilities have grown in numbers, a desirable trend, although like Reid and Knight's observations, findings again reflect "norms" of who is more likely to succeed despite disability impacting all racial and ethnic groups (Anderson, 2006). And while "Disability as Diversity" is partially on the agenda of universities, and rights-based groundings acknowledged (Gabel, Reid, & Pearson, 2017), with innovative practices suggested (Kroeger & Kraus, 2017; O'Neil Green, Willis, Green, & Beckman, 2017), at the same time, many institutional barriers continue to exist and need negotiated (Albanesi & Nusbaum, 2017).

The politicization of people with disabilities within their educational experiences, while not explicitly stated as such, begins in K-12 schooling. For example, Mooney's personal experiences led him on a quest to seek other "outsiders" across the country, their formal and informal educational experiences, and how those impacted their lives mostly people with various disabilities, as documented in *The Short Bus: A Journey Beyond Normal* (Mooney, 2008). In another example, found in the essay titled "Revolution," a 22-year-old man writes with hindsight of his struggles:

> Learning disabilities exist, but they may be nothing more than an accumulation of variously culturally determined blocks and flows—*flows* being the states in which educational production is in tune/touch with the individual and *blocks* being the crisis points in which the individual is unable to produce what the educational world requires. Thus, whenever some teacher or parental frustration becomes the mirror of who you think you are, you're in danger of being blocked. (Piziali, p. 31)

Similarly, reflecting on her life experience to date, a young woman shares:

> Although most people look at ADHD as a negative condition, I disagree. I would believe that if you were to ask anyone that had a friend with ADHD, they would say that all of these crazy symptoms are what they love about that person. . . . The problem is that most of the literature about ADHD is written by people who do not have ADHD. They generalize and say that the symptoms are concrete. This is extremely offensive to me. I understand my symptoms, and I know how my ADHD affects me, but it's all personal. My situation can be totally different from another person with ADHD. (Connor, p. 71)

In these accounts, we see self-understanding that emerges in response to such negative conceptualizations of framing disability that pervade educational discourse. That's why answering questions such as "How can I talk about disability in my classroom?" is important for pre-service and in-service teachers to think about. If kids with disabilities feel powerless in classrooms, how can we restructure classrooms to provide access to learning for them all, and discuss their abilities as a way of helping them move forward in acquiring new knowledge and skills?

The cultural experiences of people are also fused with the political and social. For example, at AREA—America's biggest conference for educational researchers—in our whitepaper we called attention to making the conference as inclusive as possible, symbolizing any public or professional space (Allen et al., 2017). As part of our efforts, we culled from DS scholar Lennard Davis who points out the reticence of even progressive individuals and organizations:

> We have created a firewall between them and us. While many white people have embraced the cause of people of color, and while many straight people have taken up the cause of gay, lesbian, bisexual, and transgendered people, few "normal" have resonated with people with disabilities. The reasons for this are telling. No whites will become black; few straights will become gay; but every normal person can become disabled. All it takes is the swerve of a car, the impact of a football tackle, or the tick of the clock to make this transformation . . . what people fear is that disability is the identity one may become part of but didn't want. This is the silent threat that makes folks avoid the subject, act awkwardly around people with disability, and consequently avoid paying attention to the current backlash against disability rights. (pp. 3–4)

We believed it was necessary to write a whitepaper as we sought our own professional organization to be cognizant of, and work toward the removal of, physical and social restrictions.

In contrast, at the Society for Disability Studies Conference, attempts are made to welcome and accommodate all. There is a beauty about this concept—and this conference—that is symbolized in the annual dance, where "Atypical bodies take any shape or form, and to see them all together, mixed with a minority of typical bodies all letting go to the music is pure magic." That said, like the Queerness and Disability Conference, all folks cannot be accommodated all of the time. It is an ideal to which we all must strive toward. Lennard Davis once described how after delivering a keynote address, a new attendee showered him with expletives because she could not understand what he was talking about due to the academic language used (Davis, 2017). Yet we must humbly acknowledge that efforts are always ongoing, a work in progress, and the lessons we learn can, and must, be acted upon.

Chapter 7

Doctoral Faculty

Not all institutes of education have doctoral programs, and for those that do, faculty that work within them are often thought of by others, and sometimes by themselves, as—to steal a phrase from Miss Jean Brodie—the *crème de la crème* of educators (Spark, 1961). This idea partially makes sense as faculty have worked long and hard to get to the position of teaching doctoral level material and participating in dissertation committees that, in effect, determine who gets to be a member of academia. On the other hand, luck and the somewhat arbitrary nature of being at the right place at the right time also factors into success within academia. In my case, it was by accident rather than design. It began when I was asked to be a reader on a dissertation committee at CUNY's Graduate Center (GC).

The GC is arguably seen as CUNY's "jewel in the crown." It is an entity unto itself residing in a beautiful building on the corner of 34th Street and 5th Avenue, originally one of America's first department stores, diagonally opposite the Empire State Building. There are glorious views of this towering world landmark through windows of the GC's penthouse atrium. The GC is the primary institution that grants CUNY doctoral degrees and located within its many diverse programs is Urban Education. One of Urban Eductaion's historical challenges was that it did not have any full time faculty members with a background in special education. So, when a doctoral student needed an adviser with a special education background, someone from CUNY's sizable network could be called upon and in serving in such a capacity, become what's termed a "faculty member at large." With approximately six full time faculty members and approximately 75 more members at large, the Urban Education Program supports its hundred or so students.

Chris Hale invited me to be on his dissertation committee, and I was approved. His focus was on how privileged parents of children with dyslexia understand and negotiate their situation, namely, the dilemma of having financial resources without full community acceptance, even in private schools. It was a fascinating, in-depth look at one family, particularly sensitive about—and accurate in portraying—white, upper middle class parental perspectives of having a child with dyslexia that was later revised and published in book form (Hale, 2012). As the defense went well, I was subsequently asked to assist with other people's dissertations when their interest lay in special education. The power of a Chief Executive Officer (CEO) decides who gets invited to teach a course, and therefore influences the politics of curriculum. In other words, she or he oversees what information gets in and what information is left out of a doctoral program. As there was a small but critical mass of students who were interested in the topic of disability, I was asked by Tony Picciano, CEO, if I would be interested in teaching a course in special education.

My first reaction by default was the I-am-not-worthy, yet I quickly switched to "why not?" Although I had doubts that I was ready, it was also a case of "if not now, then when?" After all, many peers from my doctoral cohort graduated and took jobs in which they were expected to teach doctoral level courses and participate in dissertations. The satisfying things about teaching a doctoral course is that you can literally teach what you want. Of course it has to be approved, but if it's coherent, interesting, and relevant, it's a go. Given that the course had to be about special education and I really wanted to teach disability studies in education, I named it *A Critical Look at Special Education: History, Policy, Theory, Research, & Practice* as it allowed me to juxtapose paradigms, readings, and scholars in a way that would engage participants in questioning what we know, what we think we know, and how we know about disability and its relationship to education, including teacher education. The abstract was as follows:

> The institution of special education evolved as society's response to children and youth with disabilities. In 1975, with the passage of P. L. 94-142, *The Education of All Handicapped Children Act*, children and youth with disabilities came to enjoy the same civil rights as children without disabilities and, like their non-disabled peers, were guaranteed a "free and appropriate" public education. However, the institution of special education has always inspired disagreement among various constituents in society, including parents, policy makers, theoreticians, researchers, educators, and people with disabilities. Undeniably, it has offered hope to countless families whose disabled children, prior to 1975, had remained at home or were placed in institutions. Proponents of special education highlight how it guarantees an education to all citizens, reduces the number of students with disabilities dropping out of school, increases the number attending college, and develops many forms of innovative pedagogy. In contrast, critics have pointed out special education's role in: maintaining racial segregation in

schools; stigmatizing difference; diluting the curriculum; segregating, assimilating, and educationally impoverishing many migrant and indigenous children; and contributing to the "school-to-prison pipeline" in which three-quarters of those incarcerated have significant struggles in literacy. For decades, scholars critical of special education have questioned its foundations and the practices they undergird, including: labeling, structuring, segregation, pedagogy, professionalization, and institutionalization.

The work of groundbreaking scholars who sought to challenge traditional responses to disability paved the way for critical special educators who came to find the discipline of Disability Studies (DS) as more compatible with their beliefs and values. Subsequently, DS critiques of special education have focused on: its basis in positivism; its professionalization of school failure; its overreliance on interventions aimed at deficits; its reliance on intelligence testing, segregation, and the medicalization of disabled people. Taken together, these critiques reveal the limiting, oppressive conceptualizations of disability within special education. Instead, critical special educators situate disability within a sociological context—implicating society as actively disabling people through social practices, beliefs, attitudes, and expectations. In taking a critical look at all interconnected aspects of special education (history, policy, theory, research, and practice) this course will illustrate what it means to view disability within a social context, why this reframing radically shifts ways in which disability comes to be understood, and ultimately why this is an issue of social justice.

By selecting readings from traditional scholars such as Fuchs and Fuchs (1994), Kauffman and Sasso (2006), and Kauffman and Hallahan (1995) we would examine the foundational knowledge of special education, its anti-inclusion sentiment, while also looking at why and how disability studies in education evolved. Seminars were small with approximately six students and, as such, allowed for in-depth dialogues and earnest debates requiring everyone to participate. To state the obvious, it's also a different experience between teaching 6 and 26 (or more) students. As a result of this experience I became connected to people whose interest in special education and/or disability studies and we maintained contact until their dissertations, where some invited me to be on their committee.

At the GC I came to know some of the full time faculty. One of them was Ken Tobin, who took an active interest in dis/ability and DS, inviting my colleague Jan Valle and I to present our work frequently at doctoral student events he coordinated, and asked us to consider documenting our thoughts in a special edition of *The Journal of Cultural Studies of Science Education* of which he was editor, resulting in the article "A Socio-cultural Reframing of Science and Dis/Ability in Education: Past Problems, Current Concerns, and Future Possibilities" (Connor & Valle, 2015). I always thought it was important to share a disability studies perspective in as many venues as possible, and never wanted to pass up an opportunity when it presented itself. Earlier I had submitted work to a social studies journal, problematizing the notion that disability and education was often relegated automatically to special education, thereby absolving all educators to contemplate dis/ability in ongoing ways (Connor, 2013a). The Urban Education Program seemed to welcome disability studies, as long as students found it meaningful and useful.

I also had the pleasure of briefly coming to know Jean Anyon before she passed away. I had studied her works in my own doctoral degree (Anyon, 1997) and was a little intimidated by her reputation. However, doctoral students we had in common loved her, and I always got the impression that she was unequivocally dedicated to the job. Indeed, Jean was still working when her final illness overtook her. In going to the Urban Education Office for a meeting around that time, I heard heartfelt moans of her colleagues from their offices as they saw each other for the first time since the sad news. Earlier that year she had asked to meet me, to know more about my background and work. I had gone to her office and we'd had a good conversation about what motivated us, past works, and current students we shared, resulting in an offer to have a follow up dinner that, sadly, did not materialize due to Jean's ill health. In fact, I almost did not go to her office because my name had become a bit of a political football through no fault of my own. It was to do with Urban Education Program's internal policy. One permanent faculty member wanted me to be a faculty member at large and have the ability to teach courses and participate in dissertations, while Jean wanted all people serving in those roles to be tenured. I happened to be untenured at the time, although I was an associate professor. Although I had published sufficiently, the untenured part did not sit well with all GC faculty. Interestingly, emails among fulltime faculty were shared with me when, arguably—ethically speaking—they probably should not have been. While my name was the football being kicked around, it was the general point of only allowing tenured people to participate in Urban Education that was the actual game. Although I could see the point about faculty at large not being distracted from getting their tenure via GC duties, I was taken aback by the hostility of these senior faculty interchanges. I also thought it was up to untenured faculty with a proven track record in publishing to at least have a voice in the choice. Regardless, the intensity of professional vehemence reminded me of the clichéd phrase, "Academic politics are so vicious because the stakes are so small."

Over the years I have enjoyed working with Ofelia Garcia and Wendy Luttrell. Ofelia's work on translanguaging, her theory of how multilingual speakers utilize their unique communication system to mediate social and cognitive demands across various contexts, is fascinating (Garcia & Klein, 2016). Wendy's work also struck a chord with me as she is so accomplished in understanding and teaching qualitative methodology (Luttrell, 2010), and her research is some of the most detailed and sensitive that I have ever read, particularly her work with pregnant teens of color (Luttrell, 2003). Likewise, Michelle Fine's experience in social justice issues and marginalized youth had stayed with me since my doctoral studies, particularly her concept of "working the hyphens" (Fine, 1994). I recall seeing her at a high profile panel at AERA and being pleasantly surprised at her general irreverence, yet not for the gratuitous sake of it, but rather as part of critiquing values she thought hypocritical. To serve on dissertation committees with Michelle and come to know her as a peer has been a professional highlight. In addition, I have appreciated being on committees with Nick Michelli, educational historian Steve Brier, and psychologist Ana Stetsenko—as each experience have also been so informative. This is part of the beauty, value, and pleasure of working at the doctoral level.

Over the course of time, I was asked to develop other doctoral special education courses, and saw this as the opportunity to shift out of the default sped box and into looking at disability and education in a much more open, interdisciplinary way. So, the following courses titles and descriptions were developed:

Unpacking the (Ab)Normal Child

The word "normal" gives rise to a series of questions: What constitutes normalcy within current education systems and who decides? Where did the concept of normalcy originate? How has it shifted and morphed over time, and why? In what ways does normalcy serve as an ideology reinforced by synonymous concepts of "average," "typical," "standard," "regular" students? Conversely, how do unexamined notions of normalcy create "abnormal," "atypical," "below standard," and "special" students? Using an interdisciplinary frame and drawing theoretical insights from Disability Studies, Critical Race Theory, Queer Theory, and Feminist Theory, this class will explore these and other questions. Students will also examine the structure of schools and the composition of classrooms in relation to a variety of interconnected contemporary issues, such as inclusive education versus special education, the widespread enforcement of standardized curricula, policies such as Response to Intervention and No Child Left Behind. Implications for theory, research, practice, and policy will be explored in relation to how we understand the "mold" of normalcy into which all children are expected to fit.

Reframing Dis/ability Across Contexts

Throughout history, people deemed "disabled" have been portrayed from a deficit-based perspective as being lacking, incomplete, less than fully human. At worst, disabled humans were banished, hidden, segregated, even killed; at best, they were expected to be cured, fixed, remediated, or restored to an approximation of culturally determined "normalcy." Educational practices have mirrored these cultural mores. Traditional special education research has been predominantly founded upon scientific, medicalized, psychological, understandings of human difference—all contributing to the pathologization of human differences. However, a critical turn in educational theory has emerged to question what constitutes difference as dis/ability and subsequent implications for research, practice, and policy. This course will utilize critical writings about dis/ability from an interdisciplinary perspective, primarily culling from Disability Studies and Critical Race Theory to explore counter-stories to master narratives of dis/ability found in all aspects of society, including educational research and schools. Participants will study both research and "life writings" of/by people with disabilities *in context* using an intersectional lens composed of—race, social class, and gender (among others)—to explore alternative epistemologies, ontologies, and methodologies to those found in traditional special education research. Through this exploration of dis/ability in context, we will analyze long-standing educational problems such as: overrepresentation of children of color in special education; resistance to inclusive education; standardization; the achievement gap; the school to prison pipeline; and the "color-blind" stance of decontextualized educational research—with view to developing new ways to understand—and research—these pervasive problems.

Promises, Paradoxes, and Problematics of Inclusive Education: A Historical Look at Theory, Policy, Research & Practice

The year 1975 signaled a historical landmark in education with the passage of P. L. 94-142, *The Education of All Handicapped Children Act* in which children and youth with disabilities were guaranteed a "free and appropriate" public education. However, initial trends in the subsequent decade revealed students with disabilities tended to be placed in segregated facilities—leading special education to be initially understood as a place, rather than a service. In response to this trend, inclusive education appeared on the national radar in the late 1980s when the federal government instituted programs to support students with "mild" disabilities such as Learning Disabilities (LD), Behavioral Disorders (BD), and Intellectual Disabilities (ID, formerly known as mental retardation) in general education classrooms. Inclusion quickly grew into an international movement, encompassing the radical concept of "full inclusion" of *all* children. To many educators, the inclusive movement provided a welcome challenge to how buildings were configured, classrooms arranged, curriculum adapted, services provided, professional collaborations forged, responsibilities shared, and so on. At the same time, it divided the field of special education between progressive educators who sought fundamental change and traditionalists who feared a loss of power, influence, and services. As one scholar pointedly asked, "Included into *what*?" Nonetheless, the inclusion movement has forged a fascinating lens through which to view and potentially rethink all aspects of education, including the expansion of "who belongs" in "mainstream" classrooms to other groups of historically marginalized students such as the LGBTQ population and English Language Learners. This seminar will chart the history/ies of inclusive education from pre-PL 94-142 to the present day from multiple international perspectives and within the overlapping domains of theory, policy, research, and practice. Some selected elements of the course that participants will study include: the disability civil rights movement (history); international, federal, state, and local implementation of inclusion (policy); the development of disability studies in education as an alternative framework to special education (theory); a review of inclusive education literature (research), and; what has worked and what has failed in the name of inclusive education, in which contexts (practice). In sum, this course seeks to explore a wide variety of interconnected issues with view to developing a deep understanding of what is paradoxically both a simple idea and a complex phenomenon.

DOCTORAL SYSTEMS AND STUDENTS

Introducing doctoral students to disability studies has been satisfying, and they largely fall into two broad groups. The first group is those who entered the program as special educators, already aware that the academic field of special education to date has not reflected their own reality, and upon investigation, see it as quite a narrow and closed. The second group is students interested in social justice issues and come to see disability alongside race, gender, sexuality, social class, and so on, as a concept to be problematized and rethought with view to improving the lives of students and teacher in schools, and by extension, in society.

CUNY has been described by a high ranking colleague of mine as "exploitative" of its employees, a sentiment sometimes echoed by untenured professors. I am of two minds about this comment as CUNY has been good to me in many ways. As employees we recognize it is a public institution and simply does not have the same resources as private universities. I bring this point up now as the GC tends to rely a lot on faculty members at large to do much of its work. I cannot fault full time faculty about this because I feel I experience a parallel position as chairperson of the special education department. In our department, at least 80 percent of courses are taught by adjunct instructors. Once upon a time there was a ruling from New York State that required 50 percent of all courses to be taught by full time faculty members, but that seems to have gone by the wayside. Overwhelmingly, adjuncts do an excellent job. So much work for so little pay. I myself recall teaching a very detailed course for several years and spending about eight hours every Sunday grading, planning, and organizing, along with the two and a half hours of teaching class. Yet, the formula for pay is only two and a half hours of classroom contact time per week. I am sharing this information to make the point that faculty members at large in CUNY's doctoral programs serve in a similar function as adjuncts in terms of doing institutional work that needs to be done. So, coming to serve on the Admissions Committee or Executive Committee or Faculty members at Large Committee or even Committee on Committees

(I kid you not) is part of informal expectations of "pitching in" to make sure the machinery of the GC works. My intention here is not to sound ungrateful for the opportunities afforded in CUNY, but rather to call attention to what can feel like the limitlessness of working in academia. It's true we can say "no," to many things, yet the unofficial curriculum in professional life suggests I-will-scratch your-back-if-you-will-scratch-mine. The whole system at times, exemplified in this example, reminds me of a penguin colony in that each one has to construct a nest in the form of a circle of stones, yet they all wander off to steal stones from another penguin's nest, leaving their own vulnerable to pilfering. In sum, the "borrowing" is always at the expense of someone else in a world of finite resources.

At the same time, experience at the GC translated into more confidence when asked to be a member of committees at national universities and international universities. Each one of these experiences, I believe, stretches all committee members (or outside evaluator, as certain countries have different criteria). In an earlier chapter I mentioned Subini Annamma who tracked me down at AERA. One of the things that rose out of the relationship was being invited to participate as members of dissertations (and visit) the University of Colorado at Boulder. Being on the same committee as scholars such as Kris Gutierrez and Janette Klingner, both of whose work I deeply admired, was simultaneously an odd combination of feeling humbled and excited. Likewise, I have enjoyed working with professional colleagues at Teachers College, Boston University, Arcadia University, Arizona State, University of Rochester, University of Christchurch (New Zealand), University of Johannesburg (South Africa), York University (Canada), University of Ghent (Belgium), and LaTrobe University (Australia), all of which stretched me as a researcher, educator, and human being.

Sometimes, I must confess, I have had doubts about the value of the dissertation process. It is quite a strange phenomenon that has been passed on through the centuries, and varies so much among institutions. Nowhere did this become more apparent than when we at Hunter decided to develop a doctoral program. From our initial conversations with the entire faculty to our current level of progress (the first cohort of students are just about to complete their first year as I write this), each faculty member involved in planning defaults to the program in which she or he studied. But before I describe that program, I feel compelled to mention some of the challenges I have observed in working with the dissertation process.

Occasionally a doctoral student takes too long on their dissertation. Reasons are multifold, as life gets in the way (babies, weddings, deaths, new jobs, relocation, identity crisis, etc.). The longer a student waits, the less likely the dissertation will be completed. Full time doctoral faculty sometimes lose interest (and/or faith) in the student. It then means students have to knock on different professors' doors and this can be painful for both parties. If a student is ill prepared, I wonder how much of it is the responsibility of the institution. In other words, is a student appearing "weak" in terms of preparation because of him or herself, or because of the program? The answer is rarely clear and usually lies somewhere along a continuum. I have felt under pressure in a couple of these situations, as the clock is ticking and there is a lot of work to be done by adviser, committee members, and student, including dedicating time and energy during summer. In one such instance, a colleague and I were second and third committee members and the person defending *just* made it over the finish line. It was clear in the defense discussion that so much more could have been said, and dare I say should have been said. But these are the politics of dissertation committees too, and we felt we could not block or deny the student, given a highly complex context. That said, when he received the degree, we were asked to write letters of recommendation for college positions. Instead, we two wrote a joint letter explaining why we could not, citing the need for more experience, deeper engagement with important issues, and being patient in acquiring more skills and knowledge. It was the right thing to do, "tough love" as he was not ready to teach graduate school in terms of content. While we did not want to take away his dream, we did want him to have a realistic perspective.

Working with doctoral students can be intense—usually in a good way. They rely upon you to "show them the way," invoking a sense of responsibility for their well-being as scholars-in-development. It really does feel like a mentorship, although it is different with every one of them. I have seen them "try on" the language of academia, grapple with concepts and philosophers, struggle in synthesizing disparate knowledge, and sometimes experience a lengthy search for what they'll investigate. In my own classes, I enjoy working with them through the issues and oftentimes contradictions of special education and disability studies, almost hearing their brains stretching in unforeseeable directions as they develop. If a short cut to understanding how to navigate a doctoral program can be shared, I will provide it as I remember it being quite a solitary experience, despite having several great supportive peers.

The dissertation phase in particular is difficult for students and my advice is always to create a manageable study. It's not so much about changing the world, even though we want to (that's definitely a part of it). It's more a case of understanding a long and complex obstacle course and then tackling it. "Shopping" for the right committee is key as each member should contribute in ways based upon their area(s) of expertise, and agree to support students through the process in general. Things go south when the triumvirate of committee members (the minimum amount) don't quite see eye to eye, or feel adamant in requiring certain things be done or said in the research. For the most part, the committee members work together as nobody wants the student to fail. Yet, until it's completed, the process feels like an ongoing challenge for doctoral candidates. During this phase, there's nothing worse than being asked, "Are you done yet?" by family members and acquaintances alike, as if a dissertation was like writing a long shopping list.

In reflecting on doctoral degrees in general, and especially when a student contemplating application to a program comes for a chat, I say, "You really have to want to do it, because it takes over your life." At least it feels like that way during the process of taking difficult courses and then embarking on a dissertation. It's a huge commitment. So, when Dean David Steiner asked Hunter faculty to think about developing a doctoral program, we were both excited and a little wary as there would be much work involved building up something from the ground. Meetings were held for all faculty across three departments to share ideas, perspectives, and concerns. Conversations were often heated—even borderline divisive—yet we persisted in formulating a plan for an Ed.D. program in *Instructional Leadership*. It's a bit of a misnomer for me personally as it can easily be confused with educational leadership. However, as we are first and foremost an institution of teachers, the words are meant to convey educators who assume both formal and informal leadership positions in their places of work. This could be lead grade level teacher, staff developer, teacher coach, administrator, program coordinator, superintendent, and so on. Faculty co-wrote all doctoral level courses that were developed, and mine included the *Introduction to Research in Education*, *Special Education*, and *Qualitative Research* courses. Again, I think it important to have voice in the content of curriculum, and so was able to make sure multiple perspectives about disability were present in the special education course, along with a core of disability studies literature that would engage and challenge students in doctoral programs.

After several years of planning, we admitted our first cohort of sixteen doctoral students in fall 2016. I was privileged to co-teach the first course, *Introduction to Research in Education* with my colleague Marshall George. As a supporter of team teaching it was good to be in the co-driver's seat again as we planned a semester that encompassed the *whys* and *hows* of research in education. During the course we invited many of our colleagues to present their research and in doing so students saw a variety of ways educators come to this work, including portrayals of scientific and "objective" quantitative studies to very creative qualitative research in which the researcher-educator is the methodological tool. Over the course of the semester we variously saw light bulbs going off, cynicism rise, humility manifest, and struggles to reconcile new knowledge with old (when the purpose of introducing the new is often to challenge the old). Paradigms change. Shifts happen. To some degree, every student should experience disequilibrium, because the world they knew can no longer be seen so neat and tidy, safe and secure, and as easily defensible as it once was. The doctoral program is in its early days, and I am quietly confident that it will grow into a well-respected program as each year will provide the opportunity to build and refine.

In thinking about what satisfies me the most at this juncture of my career, I have to say that it is helping doctoral students and supporting new faculty members. I see both groups as the next wave, the carriers of the work in all forms—practical, theoretical, political. Evaluating the scholarship of disability studies/critical special educators for tenure and promotion packages, book proposals submitted, article reviews within traditional and progressive journals, along with letters of recommendation for doctoral students who seek scholarships and grants, and colleagues who wish to find a better fit for their teaching and research by changing universities—all of these I think are an effort to "play forward" what I believe in.

COMMENTARY

Teaching and Learning in Schools and Universities

In my own experience, teaching at the doctoral level permits more autonomy than in graduate level education programs. Professors can develop courses to teach from their own perspectives, interests, and areas of expertise—uncommon in the university-level instruction where almost all master's degrees leading to teacher certification are constructed of required courses, without electives. Being affiliated with the GC piqued my interest, and my mind percolated with questions such as: Who gets admitted to the programs? Who gets to teach students the courses they need? Who makes those choices? What is the content of core/required courses, and the content of electives or special topics? It turns out that the CEO wields considerable influence in making these choices either unilaterally or in conjunction with other faculty members.

Having served on the Admissions Committee, I witnessed how for each seat there were ten or twelve applicants, making it fairly competitive. Faculty were mindful of balancing experience, academic strengths, race, gender—and, importantly, compatibility with their own areas of interest. This made sense as it's easier to support and mentor like-minded nascent scholars, as well as provide opportunities for them to gain research experiences within existing projects. Likewise, savvy applicants would know this unspoken guideline and reveal areas of mutual interest with specific professors who taught there.

Small seminars really do allow close professional relationships with doctoral students as they find their way through the forest of educational and interdisciplinary research. The interchange of thinking and developing knowledge between doctoral faculty member and student serves to galvanize mentor-mentee roles (Jackson, 2017) that can result in shared publications and life-long professional relationships should the latter move into academia.

Educational Laws and their Impact

It was strange, I thought, for an urban program not have representation of special education as reflected in the core content or area of faculty expertise. Rightly or wrongly, perhaps given that all of my experiences had been in urban settings, I viewed special education as an integral part of urban education. This assumption felt justified when I recalled how in the Office of the Superintendent of Manhattan high schools one-third of all staff supported the subsystems within the larger special education system, and the Special Education Department at Hunter contained one-third of all graduate students in the School of Education. Although I had been asked to teach a course in special education for doctoral students in the Urban Education Program who self-identified as special educators or had an interest in special education, I wanted to teach a DS-oriented class, so to answer to both sides of the schism, I crafted the outline to foreground the law, namely P. L. 94-142, or *The Education of All Handicapped Children Act* (EAHCA) (1975). The class was designed to look at the "disagreement among various constituents in society, including parents, policy makers, theoreticians, researchers, educators, and people with disabilities." Of course, it was important to recognize the benefits of special education such as "how it guarantees an education to all citizens, reduces the number of students with disabilities dropping out of school, increases the number attending college, and develops many forms of innovative pedagogy." On the other hand, it is also important to explore special education's role in "maintaining racial segregation in schools; stigmatizing difference; diluting the curriculum; segregating, assimilating, and educationally impoverishing many migrant and indigenous children; and contributing to the 'school-to-prison pipeline' in which three-quarters of those incarcerated have significant struggles in literacy" (Winn & Behizadeh, 2011). One of the themes that runs through this book—implicitly and explicitly—is encapsulated in the divergent impact of EAHCA (1975) and its later incarnations IDEA (1997) and its reauthorization (2004); that is, contrasting the law's desired outcomes versus actual outcomes.

What can be discussed in a doctoral seminar are the knowledge(s) from which the field of special education is built and, given some of the outcomes, the need to consider other ways of conceptualizing and operationalizing disability. Criticism of the field has resulted in: "its basis in positivism; its professionalization of school failure; its overreliance on interventions aimed at deficits; its reliance on intelligence testing, segregation, and the medicalization of disabled people." The focus of the course, therefore, was "to illustrate what it means to view disability within a social context, why this reframing radically shifts ways in which disability comes to be understood, and ultimately why this is an issue of social justice." Thus, I was able to change what was expected as something pro forma, that is, special education issues of content, with a more complex, contrasting lens that challenges the research-base of the field to be more expansive. What I found, generally speaking, was that doctoral students, especially those who had experiences in public school systems, made sense of the ideas introduced within DSE, finding them akin to civil-rights issues, imbalances of power, and dominant discourses that silenced experiential knowledge (Wappet & Arndt, 2013).

Models of Disability and their Influence on Educators and Researchers

Of course introducing DSE is not just a case of switching teams/paradigms/orthodoxies, but more of a labored process in which previous knowledge becomes questioned and "pushback" is encouraged, specifically when talking about issues of best ways to educate kids identified as disabled. Academics themselves have grappled with this process, evidenced in vivid accounts of doubt, despair, and reframing beliefs, similar to people who have left one religion to find another, as evidenced in the edited text *From Positivism to Interpretivism and Beyond: Tales of Transformation in Educational and Social Research* (Heshusius & Ballard, 1996). In the section called Stories of Inner Change, Ballard (1996) shared his epiphany after struggling to reconcile a positivist-scientific approach to research on inclusive education, and the actual lived experiences of the people he was researching:

> It was this realization that struck me with physical force that day. There was the problem. I had been trying to live in two incompatible worlds . . . I was clinging to my training and the idea that science was detached and value-free, and so became anxious when challenged from that position. Yet I knew I was learning far more from involvement with people and with issues I was committed to than I ever had as a distant recorder of events that happened to others. . . . I would no longer break the world down into discrete bits for study, nor pretend I could separate who I am from what I do. As a result, I have continued to seek involvement with others as a participant learner, open to a range of interpretations, constructions, and reconstructions, and confronting problems of ideology, power and purpose in research and researchers. (p. 30)

In another account of realization about being present within—not detached—from research, Dudley-Marling wrote, "Hiding the "I" is a pretense, a fraud that forces me to hide my passion, to deny who I am, and to pretend that my words are separate from me" (1996, p. 36). Deborah Gallagher (1996), too, described how she grew to question—and ultimately reject—the assumed validity of quantitative research, writing

> I found it very hard to take seriously the notion that we could predict (much less control) human behavior by accounting for all of the variables that ostensibly influence people. And even if we could do so in an experimental setting, as it was thought could be done, what would that mean for the complexity of real life? . . . The superimposition of these models and methods [quantitative, statistical] on educational phenomenon is no more, and no less, than insisting it is our privilege to have control over others and over life. (p. 41)

Gallagher also noted that how the field of (special) education was complicit in propagating exclusivity in its dominant research practices noting, "The classroom teacher was on the bottom of the hierarchy, the university researcher was at the top" (p. 41). Herein lies much of the problem with the research-practice disconnect, as researchers claim forms of knowledge that are usually dismissed by teachers as impractical (Ferri, Gallagher, & Connor, 2011). In sum, the worlds of researchers largely fail to resonate with teachers and, ironically, actually serve to disenfranchise them, while researchers remain in comfortable careers often supported by large federal grants.

For instance, I recall a major special education researcher appealing in person to faculty at Hunter (once his connections at New York University failed to come through) for help securing access to public schools to try an experimental intervention for kids with intellectual disabilities. The intent and methodology did not resonate with faculty members, and what reaffirmed our mistrust was the fact that teachers were seen as unquestioning executors of an intervention. The researcher did not know the school, the classroom, the teacher, the kids, yet wanted to import his view of the world, first developed in a clinical setting, and impose it upon teachers and kids to achieve his own ends—to fulfill his grant obligations and be published. It would have been a lot of work for teachers to help facilitate this procedure without anything in it for them or the kids except experience. Ultimately, as a faculty, we did not facilitate access for the researcher, believing the request to be primarily self-serving.

In stark contrast, an oft-cited mantra of Disability Studies is "Nothing about us without us" (Charlton, 2000, p. 1). Disability Studies' scholars also see special education as a constellation of laws, professional practices, knowledge bases that have reified human differences. As such, special education and all of its connotations is a creation, a discourse deeply embedded within society, made "real" through how it has been organized. Yet, as I mentioned, a significant number of doctoral students arrive knowing "the academic field of special education to date has not reflected their own reality, and upon investigation see it as narrowed and closed." Of great interest to me are career educators who have not specialized in special education, yet recognize people with disabilities rightfully belonging under the larger umbrellas of Diversity, Civil Rights, and Social Justice. These students "see disability alongside race, gender, sexuality, social class, and so on, as a concept to be problematized and rethought with view to improving the lives of students and teachers in schools, and by extension, in society." Both groups are aware of the field of special education's limitations, and how this lies in contrast to DSE's open-endedness, the desire to seek knowledge about disability/differences within humans in an exponential way, paying particular attention to those who experience it (Blaser, 2003; Charlton 2000; Linton, 1998).

I have pondered the irony that the GCs Urban Education doctoral program developed without a special education focus or component. I can only speculate that as it was developing, the small body of faculty there were unsure about where it "fit" in their own schema of what constituted urban education. Given the social justice groundings of the program, it would have been hard to imagine traditional special education research fitting into their paradigm. In a way, an opportunity presented itself and I took it, asking students to step back from all previous knowledge and imagine the twin concepts of disability and education without the parameters imposed by special education. Students became intrigued by DSE's priorities and foci, relating them to their own knowledge and experiences, understanding them to be more accessible and less hierarchical in the way Gallagher (1996) noted the field of special education to be. As part of doctoral work and DSE, unpacking the concept(s) of normalcy is crucial in unlearning previous knowledge and moving forward to more liberating understandings of human differences (Armstrong, 2017). There is also a parallel, too, of unpacking the norms about what knowledge gets taught about disability in doctoral programs. That there are shortages of doctorates in the field of special education Medina (2011) suggests to me at least in part, how teachers from the field who seek doctorates feel somewhat disenfranchised, unmotivated by the type of research it values that does not relate to them.

EDUCATIONAL STRUCTURES AND SYSTEMS IN RELATION TO PEOPLE WITH DISABILITIES

Continuing with the theme of "unlearning" previous knowledge, one of the most pressing things I seek to do in teaching doctoral level courses is to deconstruct the pathology inherent throughout special education. This is done by: (1) going to the sources of special education publications and commentaries, and, (2) juxtaposing them with (a) critiques by DS/DSE scholars and (b) providing examples of rethinking disability, usually by people with disabilities (Linton, 2006; Oliver, 1996; Mooney, 2008). For example, course titles such as *Reframing Dis/ability Across Contexts* or *Unpacking the (Ab) Normal Child* are designed, in part, to attract doctoral students who do not self-identify as special educators. (I am aware of how telling it is that even at the doctoral level educators have been inculcated into their own educational identities as either non-disability focused or only disability-focused, so much so that they unquestioning self-inscribe into these artificial roles.)

Seeing schools as places wherein kids with disabilities are "expected to be cured, fixed, remediated, or restored to an approximation of culturally determined 'normalcy,'" shifts our gaze to the structures and systems within education, and how educators' dispositions serve as glue that keeps these structures and systems in place (or serves to make them unhinged). That "a critical turn in educational theory has emerged to question what constitutes difference as dis/ability and subsequent implications for research, practice, and policy," has been an exciting development, in my opinion. And the "master narrative" of disability forged by special education no longer has a monopoly on knowledge about disability and education. That students "study both research and 'life writings' of/by people with disabilities *in context* using an intersectional lens composed of—race, social class, and gender (among others)—to explore alternative epistemologies, ontologies, and methodologies to those found in traditional special education research," is highly fertile ground for developing new knowledge that honors the experiences of real people in real situations, making it far more authentic, accessible, and relatable to other educators, than research published within the field of special education.

Similarly, in the course titled *Promises, Paradoxes, and Problematics of Inclusive Education: A Historical Look at Theory, Policy, Research & Practice,* I sought to engage with the messiness of inclusive education, an ideal to which we work toward. Given the significant resistance toward inclusive education within the field of special education (Kavale & Forness, 2000) and the historical ambivalence of general education to including kids with disabilities (Martin, 1995), inclusive education—what seems like a simple concept—can actually be quite complex, depending upon the context of the school and its classrooms (Hehir & Katzman, 2012). I wanted to acknowledge that DSE does not have all of the answers to the complexities of inclusion, but it can provide ways to reframe human differences and rethink how we organize classrooms, plan lessons, teach a diverse group of students, and create environments in which everyone belongs (Shapiro, 1999). Participants studied "the disability civil rights movement (history); international, federal, state, and local implementation of inclusion (policy); the development of disability studies in education as an alternative framework to special education (theory); a review of inclusive education literature (research), and; what has worked and what has failed in the name of inclusive education, in which contexts (practice)," so that they can see how knowledge is manifest in, and flows through, connections in society that are not usually studied together by educators. Yet, when they are, they reveal to what degree inclusive practices occur and why there are such discrepancies in its actualization. This affords the opportunity for asking educators to contemplate both their own positionality as nascent researchers and as well where they are physically positioned within this web-like structure.

THE SOCIAL, POLITICAL, AND CULTURAL EXPERIENCES OF PEOPLE WITH DISABILITIES

As DSE scholars and/or critical special educators, foregrounding the social, political, and cultural experiences of people with disabilities is central to our work as doctoral level instructors. Why? Schools are primarily social spaces, embedded in a culture(s), and subject to the politics—of how power operates—in society. Schools are not laboratories in which teaching is primarily seen as a scientific endeavor, regardless of special education as a field clinging to this notion (Kauffman, Anastasiou, & Maag, 2017). Additionally, the lack of understanding by governmental agencies to fund research to improve the lived educational experiences of kids with disabilities inhibits meaningful growth in investigating how the context of learning influences students' abilities to learn. As some critical special educators have called attention to emerging interdisciplinary work that "suggests a robust theory of learning must be found in the systematic integration of biological, cultural, individual, contextual, and social domains" (Artiles, King-Thorius, Bal, Neal, Waitoller, & Saca-Hernandez, 2011, p. 170). At the same time, these scholars document ways in which academic structures and systems exercise power in the form of censorship via correspondence with journal editors, mismatching expert reviews for manuscripts, specific requirements within job postings, and rejection of cultural considerations within research. Artiles et al. share that one scholar

> reported re-submitting a research grant proposal focused on LD after having carefully addressed the suggested revisions from the first review, only to learn

> that the proposal received an even lower score than the first time around. When an inquiry was made to the funding agency, the answer was, "We are not funding culture." (p. 175)

Such experiences, similar to my own in having the article on *Breaking Containment: The Power of Narrative Knowing--Countering Silences within Traditional Special Education Research* (Connor, 2009) rejected by Learning Disability Quarterly after extensive rewrites addressing all issues by reviewers, serve as evidence to special education's deliberate non-acknowledgment of cultural locations of disabled kids, the kids' knowledge, and ways they recognize their positionality within our culture, system, and schools. By centering what special education rejects, namely, the voices of people with disabilities, and ways in which the cultural contexts they inhabit that can either enable or disable them, Disability Studies provides an authentic way to address important areas that the field of traditional special education seeks to repress. It is therefore imperative that doctoral programs continue to incorporate multiple perspectives about what constitutes disability/human differences and ask who do these perspectives benefit? Funders of research (including the federal government), grant reviewers, Research universities, and professors who engage in research, all serve to benefit from "business as usual" in terms of keeping existing special education systems, structures, and knowledge bases in place (Brantlinger, 2007; Skrtic, 1991). This is another form of containment, only this time it's for DSE scholars and/or critical special educators—both teachers and researchers—who are held hostage to special education's knowledge monopoly pertaining to disability and education.

That's why it's important to teach the work of critical special educators and/or DSE scholars. They refuse to be gagged.

Chapter 8

Department Chairperson

Very few people want to be a department chairperson. In fact, the saying goes, watch out for people who *do* want to be in the role. Never in a million years did I think I'd ever accept the position. It seemed endless and thankless, filled with many "no win" situations moderating among staff, students, and administration, and answerable to all. So, why did I do it? In nutshell, it was either become department chairperson or leave Hunter. The Special Education Department had seemed to veer out of control on several fronts. First of all, our student numbers since I started had tripled but our infrastructure has stayed the same. The rise in numbers was due to successful partnerships with the Department of Education, including Teaching Fellows and Teach for America. The perpetual shortage of special education teachers meant investing in new teachers, and they arrived in droves, many not quite knowing what they'd signed up for. As mentioned earlier in this book, at one point as a faculty member I was responsible for 600 graduate students. This was 60 percent of the Special Education Department and 20 percent of the school of education. While the numbers of students in other programs and departments were going down, the growth of ours balanced the overall figures, keeping administration happy. But I was deeply unhappy, going home at the end of the day feeling stressed with perpetually unfinished business. Of course I wanted to do a good job and ensure a solid experience for all students, yet realizing something was terribly wrong and unbalanced in this picture.

"I want to leave," I'd say regularly to John over the dinner table that now, unfortunately served as place to unload my daily frustrations. I was serious, knowing I could look for another university job or return to the Department of Education as a teacher or coach.

"You can't leave," he'd say. "You've come this far."

But I knew something was not right. And when the numbers projected for next year were looking even bigger, my colleague Ellen Trief and I decided to write a letter to Dean Steiner. In the letter we analyzed all three departments to show overwhelming inequities in the distribution of responsibilities of full time faculty, listing the ratio of students to programs and professors. As a department we were doing the lion's share of School of Education work without receiving any benefits; we needed more resources in the form of additional professors to coordinate and run programs. Given that the faculty are supposed to self-govern, we asked who was making decisions about student numbers for our department and can we change that by having more say? I'd simply had it with the situation, and from my perspective, it was worsening with no end in sight. My chairperson struggled with health issues and did not come to work for long periods of time. This meant decisions were being made for the department without any representation or advocacy. There was only one administrator's assistant in the special education office and due to the volume of work (all of these classes needed scheduled, instructors to hire/process/pay/guide, on top of the usual duties) she was perpetually and *noticeably* stressed. This situation made for a very bad "norm" for the office.

After two years as New York State Commissioner of Education, Dean Steiner had come back to Hunter. It was an unexpected return. The letter we sent him was to call attention to the vast inequities across the School of Education, and it hit a nerve. He responded by meeting with Ellen and I, along with Associate Dean Asher, to systematically address the numerous points we raised. The situation was tense. I was angered by the unfettered growth of programs without adequate infrastructure and felt no fear in stating that the administration needed to provide better support. To his credit, Dean Steiner then made assisting our department a priority. Ellen and I had invited him to our next department meeting. When he arrived, he acknowledged the unfairness of the situation yet also took the department to task for "not taking care of business." By this he meant with a chairperson in absentia, no one was taking responsibility for the well-being of the department. It felt like air had left the room. His observation was true, we'd all known it, but did not want to take on any more work. Ellen and I had previously approached the chairperson, and offered to take on some responsibilities discretely and behind the scenes, but we'd been turned down.

It was at that point I reluctantly agreed to be chairperson for one year until the department could get itself together. Deep down, I had huge misgivings, fearing I'd make mistakes, would let people down, and may not be able to manage the wide range of personalities. During my time there the department had gone downhill. It was simply not in order, with the office being run by an administrative assistant who had been there a long time, had work piled upon her unfairly, and developed challenging habits. Being chairperson would pull me from teaching, which I always enjoyed, and would potentially impact the number and quality of my writing projects. I'd been operating on a high stress level for sometime, and feared taking on more responsibilities may have a detrimental effect on my personal relationship. At the end of the day it all boiled down to, "I either try being chairperson or I have to leave," because I could no longer to tolerate how the department had evolved.

The dean was happy I'd stepped up to the plate, and members of the department were relieved. I had decided to ask for consideration to be promoted to full professor, but the dean beat me to the punch, saying he would be willing to support me. There were never any clear guidelines as to when someone could go up to the highest rank, and it was in the interest of the institution to not push people too fast as while they could dangle this carrot in front of them for some time. I was whisked up to the Provost's Office, welcomed by her, and given some general advice on starting off as chairperson.

THE INHERITANCE

I also pondered the irony of being Chairperson of a Special Education Department. Again, it seemed the defining characteristic of my career had been the more I try to get out of special education, the deeper I seemed to go into it. What I also came to see is how programs were placed together because they serve kids who are deemed outside of the boundaries of normal. The department reflected one of those Introduction to Special Education "big glossy" textbooks with a disability-a-week focus upon (Brantlinger, 2006) with faculty who were still quite divided about the merits of inclusive education. Strangely, I was a chair of a department I wish did not exist. While that statement can be interpreted in many (and possibly erroneous ways), let me clarify: I wish the "special" was responsibly integrated into the "general," and by doing so, the general would have a much-needed makeover, too. What bothered me enormously is that general and special classes and programs were very separate. This had a historical precedent as there was not always a Special Education Department; rather, it once ceded from within the Department of Curriculum and Teaching, and then grew tenaciously independent.

The moment I became chairperson I knew my work was cut out because I was aware how dysfunctionality had passed for normalcy. Ironically, the special education office was so full of files, cabinets, books, and various personal belongings, so much "stuff" that it was inaccessible to wheelchair users. Faculty members stood in line at the door waiting their turn to visit the eight square feet of standing space inside of the office. In contrast, the adjacent office used by the chairperson was fairly spacious. So, the first thing I decided to do was to switch offices. I took the smaller corner room, removed wall-to-wall, floor-to-ceiling clutter, and shifted the special education office to the larger space. My one request on entering the job was to have a personal assistant, as I could see managing over 1,100 people in the form of students and faculty would need more than the one office assistant. The larger office would therefore accommodate the new person.

I made no secret that I wanted our office to look like that of the other two departments, particularly Curriculum and Teaching, where anyone could walk in, be greeted, and helped. There was both an air of tranquility and a level of cohesion that I craved. I'd decided who I wanted to be my assistant. She was a former student by the name of Cathy, a middle aged mother of two teenagers, who had helped me for several years as the parent liaison in Learning Lab. Cathy took a little persuading, but eventually came on board. Unfortunately, the dean could not secure a permanent established position, but could create one from various funding sources cobbled together for a reasonable salary. It wasn't an ideal situation but it managed to secure us a much-needed and dependable extra body. For a quite a while, we all made the office work, adopting a "Three's Company" approach. I cannot put my finger on when things began to disintegrate, but when they did, there was no return to pleasanter times. What started as a series of differences of opinion and preferred ways of doing business between two people morphed into a personality clash between both support staff. This gave rise to a level of toxicity in the office that made it unpleasant to work for everyone involved. No matter how I tried, with one-on-one pep talks, weekly joint meetings, clear directions and occasional lunches and flowers, it became extremely draining, with threats of quitting from both parties.

I include this vignette of office life because entering a work environment overseen by someone who had been there for almost three decades with insufficient supervision, who had an enormous amount of institutional knowledge, and an unfair work load, was foreboding. I recall the morning where I was scheduled to be interviewed by my dean and fellow chairpersons to be considered for promotion to full professor. My head was spinning as I walked into the interview because moments earlier I had separated the administrative assistant and a professor embroiled in a vicious argument with one another. When I sat down across the table from my colleagues I was still mentally extricating myself from the debacle, questioning, "This is what I have gotten myself into?" When it came time for me to share my accomplishments in a forum wherein I'd presented before with relative ease, I suddenly felt my focus pull away. Although I had started with a steady voice, it began to waiver, and I began to breathe irregularly. In fact, the only thing I could now focus on was breathing. And somewhere, deep down, although it might be hindsight or fanciful thinking, I was concerned about my relationship with

John and the potential of placing increasing stress upon it. After stumbling for a short while, I stopped and said:

"I'm sorry, but I am having an anxiety attack."

Everyone was deeply sympathetic, concern clearly reflected in their eyes, and began saying comforting things, including the dean's story of having had one while stuck mid-air in a Swiss chairlift. I wanted the ground to open up and swallow me. My face burned red with humiliation because I thought I'd made myself look weak. However, after a few minutes of small talk among us, I was able to resume, and get through it well enough. I did not fear a negative vote as I had accrued a sizable number of publications and had the dean's support. As I left my colleagues within the meeting to discuss my case for full professor, I apologized and recall trying to make light of it by saying, "Oh, to be human . . ."

Being chairperson meant I had to have the big picture in terms of all master's programs and certifications we offered. The program in Childhood Special Education was complex enough. It was subdivided into specialty areas of Learning Disabilities and Behavior Disorders. New York State no longer allowed "stand-alone" special education certification. Students who were already certified in general education took a "short" master's program, while students who were not had to complete a "long" dual certification program in general and special education. In addition, we had separate and different versions for the Trans B certification students. We also had an adolescent special education generalist certification that *was* actually one of the few special education only degrees, and contained general education courses in the four areas of math, ELA, science, and social studies. Furthermore, there were also general education students who sought to come to us for four courses and get certified in special education, a provision of the state that did not go over well with faculty who thought twelve credits was too little in terms of qualifications. (We eventually compromised and developed Post Masters Additional Certification Programs of 18–21 credits.) Having worked in the LD program since I began there, I was familiar with its permutations. However, other programs I had to oversee scheduling of included Early Childhood Special Ed (birth through 2nd grade), Behavior Disorders, Blind and Visually Impaired, Deaf and Hard of Hearing, Applied Behavioral Analysis, and Gifted and Talented. Each of these had similar options and complexities akin to the LD program.

Scheduling for these programs over five semesters a year was my biggest challenge. It involved working with program coordinators to provide accurate information in a timely manner—including days, time slots for classes, room requests, format of course (in person, online, hybrid), and hiring personnel for core courses. The numbers of students were not always predictable so sometimes classes had to be added and sometimes dropped, causing great anger with those who had registered (and all kinds of unforeseeable complications if course load was tied to their student loans). The departments' scheduling also had to interface with the two other departments, including our requests for courses required for certification. As the college was open all year long, these concerns were always ongoing. I have always been thankful for adjuncts who work mostly for the love of teaching rather than money, and yet they're positions are tenuous by nature—always subject to the college's need.

I valued the guidance and mentorship of my colleagues Jenny Tuten and Gess LeBlanc, chairpersons of the Department of Curriculum and Teaching and Educational Foundations respectively, both of whom had served in that capacity before I joined them. Jenny's department was the largest, with approximately 1,700 students. What made it run smoother than ours included having an office manager, someone whose responsibilities involved scheduling. I made it a priority to seek such a person for the Special Education Department, but it would be a few more years until I secured one. On the bright side, I was able to "merge" Inclusion courses, but before I explain why or how, I want to call attention to the New York State Education Department's policy on general educators receiving special education knowledge.

It came to pass that the state created a new policy requiring all general education programs to have one course in special education. This regulation had implications for our department as we got to decide which course they'd get and subsequently schedule quite a few sections every semester. The choice boiled down to two options—*Issues and Practices in Educating Students with Disabilities* (the intro course to special ed. programs) or *Inclusive Instruction in General Education Classrooms for Students with Disabilities*. Faculty were divided on the issue but I urged for the latter choice, as the course was about instruction for kids with disabilities in general education classes, rather on history and laws that formed the core knowledge of the former class. When updating the Inclusion class, I included some information on disability studies, including how familiar issues could be reframed in new ways. It gave me some satisfaction that I could introduce DS and related concepts such as ableism to general educators.

What then occurred, due to the limitations of our scheduling system, the Inclusion course was being programmed for general and special educators separately. I found myself teaching the content of this class (including a few weeks' worth of approaches and options in co-teaching) to one side of the special/general coin at a time. It was beyond irony that we were educating about inclusion in a segregated way. So, working with the chair of Curriculum and Teaching, we found a way of programming both groups could be educated together about kids with disabilities. Imagine that in 2013 A.D.

Scheduling classes and getting them into the system way ahead of time is one thing. It's another thing when the countdown to each semester begins. Inevitably, in such a big institution, students cannot always get the classes that they want and most of them end up at my door. We do our best to make sure anyone who is on partial or full financial aid gets two and four courses respectively, but what came to bother me the most was the random nature in which some courses were taken. Students (and sometimes professor) challenged pre-requisites and co-requisites in their desire to get in (or help students get in) to classes. The beginning of every semester sees a bottleneck of students outside my office waiting to plead why they should be let into a course, some of them already having done the legwork of contacting the professor and wearing them down. I understand the desire to push through a program but sometimes the willy-nilly order of how some students took courses, yet their disregard for (1) faculty union contracts that specified a maximum of 25 people in a class, (2) room size availability, and (3) additional work for already underpaid adjuncts bothered me. The buck stopped with the chairperson for these decisions and I weighed them carefully as I could, keeping a large box of tissues on my windowsill for the inevitable tears of those students who did not get what they wanted.

PERSONNEL PROCEDURES

On a different note, in the role of chairperson I had to attend a fair number of meetings with my peers at the college level Personnel and Budgeting (P&B) committee, presided over by the college president and provost. These meetings were held in the president's conference room, and consisted of approximately 34 chairpersons who sat around a rectangular-shaped formation of tables with President Raab and Provost Rabinowitz (later, Provost Kaufman) sitting at the front. The president was a formidable figure, super-smart, well-connected, and an extremely hard worker. I could not imagine what it must be like to preside over 22,000 students, the faculty who taught them, and a host of administrative and custodial staff. Part of a chairperson's duties, I would come to find out, included presenting untenured colleagues for consideration of reappointment, tenure, and promotion. At these presentations, each chairperson would speak about colleague's publication record, teaching abilities, community service, and share the result of the confidential voting within the department's P&B. Once the presentation took place, questions could be asked about the professor. Most of these presentations went smoothly. They could be anywhere between fascinating and tedious, depending upon content, topic, and length. It is always interesting to hear about research, publication, and creative works of others in our big institution, as it includes art exhibitions, theater performances, classical compositions, cancer and HIV prevention treatments, animal communications, international architecture, histories, and so on, seemingly infinite in terms of specialized topics. It was also a little nerve wracking to present on behalf of a colleague, feeling like a lawyer making a case for a client, and knowing the person's fate was largely in my hands. Chairpersons were often questioned about any aspect of the person's professional performance. When presentations were long, I noticed, they chairpersons filled the space with stories of teaching accomplishments and community service, with shorter time spent on publications. Such a scenario was problematic, giving rise to sideways glances and seat-shifting, knowing that the case would likely be picked apart. Sometimes a dean challenged the recommendation of the chairperson and departmental P&B committee, making for a tense debate.

A sleepless night was experienced before I presented my colleagues in this arena, I'd take a Clonazepam pill to feel more at ease, and have notes ready to read from so I could systematically emphasize my colleague's research the most, then teaching, then service. As a peer once said, publications are a professor's capital and the only thing that can be taken to the next kingdom (referring to possibly changing universities, not dying). It was always the same formula: peer reviewed articles were the gold standard, preferably single or first author; chapters, if peer reviewed, also held sway; authored or coauthored books, too. Less important were edited books and book chapters without peer review, along with non-peer reviewed articles, commentaries, opinion pieces, and so on.

The politics of who gets recommended for renewal, tenure, and promotion were tricky, as there was always the possibility of letting people go. In one situation, Dean Steiner decided not to support an assistant professor in my department; faculty had voted marginally in his favor. Although I myself was somewhat on the fence, I decided to give the professor one last chance at becoming published and committing to more service. Subsequently, at the college wide P&B, I presented what was in essence a weak case and was obliged to share some misgivings of the department faculty. The dean then categorically opposed reappointment. A terse debate ensued among all in the room about "the right thing to do" regarding this person's career. It was at moments such as this that a chairperson is positioned between a rock and hard place. There is no "winning." My desire to be optimistic and provide a year for one more chance was, I knew deep down, almost certainly delaying the inevitable. Ultimately, he was not recommended for renewed appointment. I then had to carefully follow the college lawyer's instructions, and also sit down with him, a single parent, to tell the news about losing his job. Sometimes it takes this type of wake-up call for a person to get their act together. I am happy to say several years later, he is gainfully employed—and I had no reservation about writing a recommendation letter extolling his teaching abilities. Letting people go never sat easy.

As alluded to previously, in the School of Education level, the three chairpersons must also vote on professors in all departments who go up for tenure and/or promotion. The atmosphere in these meetings can be tense as chairs listen to the presenter and then ask questions. Presenters know its high stakes and in many ways their anxiety can sometimes be seen via awkward body language and speaking too fast. Most do well, but occasionally someone has not achieved the publishing record expected, and we are obliged to vote accordingly. Once, it was a case of a hardworking person who had published enough but department faculty did not deem a good "fit." These situations would make me go home at the end of the day feeling horrible, being part of losing someone's prestigious job. At the same time, the politics of academia mean a professor has to do their homework, (1) that is, publish original research and (2) get along with people in their department. These are the rules, written and unwritten.

BUILDING AND STRENGTHENING

What I did set about to accomplish was the rebuilding of the Special Education Department. Given that we had trebled in student size, I wanted the infrastructure to reflect that, applying polite yet relentless pressure on the dean to secure more positions. We discovered clinical professor lines were easier to obtain so began creating them to oversee different programs. Clinical professors have the same teaching responsibilities as tenure-track faculty, but are not required to conduct research and publish. The downside involves being on a nontenure track and a less developed automatic pay scale. Over the years we were able to add seven of these lines with wonderfully hardworking and vibrant faculty who injected a whole new dose of energy into the department. Additionally, we were able to get several new tenure track lines, ensuring the growth of new programs. Each one of these faculty searches consumed an enormous amount of time and effort as there are employment laws, university regulations, and protocols to adhere to, as well as an awkward but required CUNY-wide technology platform through which to navigate the entire process. Getting searches approved can take months and the actual interviewing of selected candidates usually occurs in spring semester, when many of the best candidates have already snapped up an offer elsewhere. Related paperwork includes justifying why every applicant was not selected. Navigating the bureaucracy to pay candidates expenses was mind-numbing at times. Hunter required candidates to pay for their own expenses and be reimbursed, which sometimes would take up to six months. In one instance, a candidate was taken for dinner by the search committee (as part of a day-long visit) to a kosher restaurant, as per her request. As the restaurant did not accept the company credit card from Hunter, the candidate paid with her own Amex. Alas, she was not offered the job, and had to wait some time for reimbursement from that meal. Instances like that made me cringe, and I am happy to say that they have since been vastly improved.

The bureaucratic systems in which we work often hampers our ability to execute our needs or be expeditious in those executions. Soon after becoming chairperson, the entire CUNY platform shifted from an outdated DOS to a citywide application called CUNY-First that cost hundreds of millions of dollars. Everyone had to transition into the system, and its ambition to be everything to everybody within CUNY. It was enormously unpopular with professors because it was not intuitive, user-friendly, or quick to use—yet we all made the shift, chairpersons first. These types of situations invariably induced anxiety as I function at an intermediate level in technology skills, and the new system had opened up all kinds of cans of worms that no one had predicted. All scheduling would now be within it, including new codes for all certification programs. This is all part and parcel of the tedious side of education that has often led me to reflect upon the structures of academia. Chairpersons usually have no qualifications or substantial experiences with administration. I believe this is because, at least in my case, our hearts lie in teaching. I do think, however, having an administrator of education at the helm may be a more productive scenario—as good administrators have certain skill sets and a disposition toward enjoying the particular day-today work.

AMONG ROCKS AND HARD PLACES

A part of the position that did translate to a welcome challenge was the need to constantly problem solve for many people and situations. Some of these situations have been tricky and several "no win." In these circumstances, it's a case of minimizing discontent by being fair as possible to everyone concerned. There are many instances of students coming to my office to complain about professors (both full-time faculty and adjuncts), grades earned, dismissal from the program, and so on. Other times, personal issues include bereavement of family members, domestic violence, problems with their own children, financial struggles, and so on. My goal has always been to have folks leave hopefully feeling better than when they entered, and if not possible, at least provided with a clear answer as to why what is being requested could not be granted. One of the most unpleasant tasks is to counsel a student out of the program. This usually happens if students fail student teaching placement(s), or have a series of poor grades, consistently falling below departmental standards, and have not rectified the situation during a time of granted probation. If someone has had their heart set on teaching, almost completed a program, spent their hard earned savings, envisioned their future, it is a tough call to share, "We think the profession may not be a good fit for you." No one wants to take away someone else's dream. At the same time, it is not fair for kids to have a teacher who has not demonstrated required knowledge and skills. The kids always trump graduate students. Still, there's a chance that a teacher candidate is not quite ready, and needs more time and experience. For those in this category, I often suggest becoming a teacher's assistant for a few years, to come to know the classroom from the inside and the day-to-day responsibilities of being a teacher, or to commit to volunteer work and spend more time with kids to get to know them better, their interests, how they think, act, and learn in general. That way, they can come to better know what being a teacher is really like, and cull from their own experiences. The nature and scope of a teacher's work is usually quite different than imagined, and the shifts in teacher preparation over the last decade or so have created a higher bar than in previous times. And some students struggle from the moment they enter.

One such student was Deborah. Of Irish decent, she was tall and imposing, yet a telltale sign of high anxiety could be seen in fingernails bitten down to the quick. She came to my office door at the end of a busy day and told me she had a problematic situation, and when invited to share it told me she had gone to class only to find that she'd dated the professor who she'd met on Irishsingles.com. Frankly, I was at a loss as she'd caught me at a busy moment, and told her it would probably be okay but let me think and get back to her. Because of the unusual situation, I was buying time. However, once I opened up my emails, I found one from the professor stating he did not want her in class, but under no circumstances to tell her that. I contacted Deborah, and told her we had assigned her to a different section of the class online with another professor because, in retrospect, the situation could raise some ethical dilemmas around grading. Deborah was not pleased with this resolution. In fact, she thought I was ignoring her rights as a student registered with the Office Support Services for Students with Disabilities. She stated this in an email to me that was copied to the provost and the president. I thus had to go to my colleague in another department and, as one chairperson to another, told her that Deborah was exercising her rights in front of the college president and the only way I could see the situation resolved was to replace the instructor. Given that classes had already began, and the person in question was a seasoned adjunct, this solution was not popular, although it was carried out. As a result, the professor was let go from the class, replaced by another, last minute, not quite prepared, about whom I heard many complaints from other students in the class. I knew it was Deborah's right, but felt she'd gone about business the wrong way—contacting the president before me, her adviser, about her discontent, to explain that she did not feel sufficiently confident with an online version.

It was one in a series of situations from which we did our best to untangle and support her. In another instance she exasperated a full time professor for additional time to process information, although this was not in her accommodations. Both of them came to see me separately. From my perspective the professor's offer of staying 20 minutes after class to help re-explain concepts and provide ongoing feedback on his lesson plans was very reasonable. But Deborah wanted 40 minutes. I arranged a meeting to mediate the situation, and explained to Deborah how 20 minutes of a professor's individualized time was a thoughtful and generous offer, as he was not obliged to do that. She shook her head and insisted "40 minutes." When the professor and I stood our ground, Deborah suddenly rose to her feet and abruptly closed the door when leaving the room. My colleague and I were taken aback and shared how difficult we thought Deborah was being. Several minutes later, I opened my office door to find her outside with her ear having been pressed against it, listening to our private conversation. Deborah was in a rage.

"Don't you dare talk about me to other people!" she ordered. "You're supposed to *advocate* for students with disabilities."

I was furious. I told Deborah I had every right to talk about her with her professors, while she had no right to spy, and this was another instance of mistakes in social judgment that would impact upon her suitability as a teacher. In sum, I told her she was her own worst enemy and I could not see how such levels of unprofessionalism would bode well as she moved forward to work in education because so much of education was built upon social relationships. It was as if I'd flicked a switch, making her anger turn to despair. "Please help me," she pleaded, collapsing into tears. I was torn how to best handle the situation. Tears can serve as a manipulative tool, providing leverage for a person to get what they want. On the other hand, an openly weeping person in my office seemed evidence of true despair. Either way, something had to be done.

I sat Deborah down and told her I was going to be brutally honest, and wanted her to see it as a form of tough love. I shared how her handling of situations was inappropriate and unprofessional, and that such actions alienated people who should be potential allies. Being intelligent was not enough; she had to stop and think about how best to handle problems, giving herself choices such as A, B, or C, weighing up the pros and cons, or more appropriately in her case, the risks and benefits, of each. She would receive the full support of our office, and at the same time, had to take responsibility for her actions, and strive to negotiate situations in a less combative, more compromising ways. This did help Deborah put some things into perspective, and I asked her to reflect on overreacting to small situations, and the habit of escalation, because schools are filled with a thousand of these situations a day that have to be dealt with effectively and efficiently. At the same time, I know it's hard to break dispositions and habits that have accrued over a lifetime, and Deborah would continue to come to me with a myriad of things. In her first placement of student teaching she wanted to report the entire school to child welfare services for not doing enough for the kids who were neglected at home. And yet when I asked her to provide details, she described what are some typical New York school scenarios such as kids arriving to school late, unkempt, and hungry. I emphasized the legal mandate to call child protection services if a child was suspected of being physically or sexually abused, or consistently neglected, and shared how difficult a teacher's job can be sometimes to support ordinary working class and poor kids, who were sometimes living in homeless shelters. I also asked her to work closely with his assigned teacher to talk about such perceptions and ask what the teacher thinks and does. Soon after, the school requested that Deborah not return, placing her into a tailspin as she had to repeat student teaching, a condition possible only if permitted by the chairperson.

It was make or break time, and that was the expression I used with her. I did not think Deborah was unfit to be a teacher, but I did feel she'd need a context that was understanding and supportive of her. So I sought out an experienced teacher who had an understanding disposition, and was also direct and honest. Deborah's placement with was not smooth sailing, and she just made it through in terms of being assessed in observations. But her collaborating teacher wanted Deborah to leave after the minimum number of days required. I surmised that Deborah's anxiety and intensity made for an uneasy time. I recall this student at length as she symbolizes those, thankfully few, who we simply don't know about until they have multiple opportunities and learn by doing. In cases such as this, being an assistant teacher in a private school for several years would do Deborah the world of good. I am always left with a question hanging, though: How much do we support and/or how much do we enable some students? I want them to succeed and thrive, yet I also want kids to have a solid teacher standing in front of them.

Like Deborah, students can and do exercise their rights to complain to the president. One instance in particular made me heavy hearted because the student, Janelle, charged racism as the reason she was dismissed from the program. Reasons for being dismissed were actually based upon multiple latenesses and absences to class, poor, and missing work, failed teaching observations by several people, and aggressive behavior toward professors. One professor was so unnerved that I had to send another professor to her class in the guise of an observation to make sure she was fine. Having brought

Janelle in for a consultation to steer her in the right direction, and clarify professional expectations and responsibilities, she glowered and called the conversation patronizing and condescending. The trouble was this: we have to give feedback to students who are not performing to expectations. If that feedback and offers of support are rejected openly and in a hostile manner, then this is not a good indicator for successful collegial relationships, problem solving, and receiving direction. And while the student was dismissed from the program for failing to achieve grades required, she fought tooth and nail at all levels up the chain, right up to college Senate. Charges of racism were registered with the president's office based on her having only had white professors. After a meticulous collection of all documents supporting our claim that she did not earn the grades needed to continue in the program, and a presentation of them to the college Senate, I was interviewed at length, as Janelle had been before me. The School of Education's decision to discharge Janelle was ultimately upheld. Having state and college standards has consequences; administering them is not pleasant.

There are also some events that cannot be expected and we have to respond to them as best we can. One such event was the death of a teacher who had recently graduated from Hunter. The circumstances were very sad. Her husband murdered the former student and then took off, although he was soon apprehended and made a full confession. In their grief, the teacher's parents sought to create a scholarship fund in memory of her name. In awarding the first recipient, I briefed the student on the sensitivity of the circumstance, as it was at a public event before graduation. The parents wanted to be in attendance, and we received them, offering condolences. As I presented the award I looked into the audience and saw the parents of the slain teacher. They were in pain beyond words, devastated by an unnecessary loss, faces crumpled and worn down by incessant tears, and all I could do was recall a phrase I'd heard spoken by a friend's mother as she prepared his remains, "No parent should ever have to bury a child." Faculty stayed after the ceremony and talked with the parents, reminiscing about what a good student their daughter was. In turn, they told us how dedicated she'd been to her work, and how much she had enjoyed being a student at Hunter. Graduation was bittersweet on that occasion.

Most times, graduation is usually a great day. I can never understand faculty who don't show up because they'd be bored. To be paid for sitting on stage smiling and dressed in finery while looking out onto hundreds of happy people who will remember this day for the rest of their lives . . . it's not hard, except to hold your bladder in if the speakers take three hours. I've seen a variety of invited speakers, many of whom I did not know, but did so by the time they finished and had great respect for them—be they entrepreneurs, war heroes, or entertainers. One I do recall is feminist Gloria Steinem who began by saying to a Radio City packed with graduating students, "You look faaaaaaan-fucking-tastic!" Another was jazz musician Winton Marsalis. When faculty filed on stage that day a human traffic jam occurred leaving me standing in front of him and President Raab, who kindly introduced us. I got to tell him, "I have quite a bit of your stuff" as I shook his hand. Senator Chuck Schumer invariably bounced on stage, looking dapper, full of energy and *always* told the same story about getting dumped at graduation time (so much so, that a newspaper article ran on this theme of one-story Chuck). However, the tale is always a crowd pleaser, and that's what counts. After all, it's a day for the students.

On a related note, education has always been a contentious topic, often foregrounded in the national dialogue through an angst-ridden desire to earn higher rankings in international league tables of achievement, and the passage of laws such as *No Child Left Behind* (NCLB) (2002) designed to facilitate this objective. Well intentioned in its assertion that every child should have a highly qualified teacher, NCLB also created a firestorm in how to make this happen. Dean Steiner had made his name on critiquing existing teacher education programs for being flabby, outdated, irrelevant, and in the service of institutions and professors more than the teacher candidates (Steiner & Rozen, 2004). As the state flexed its muscles in drastically changing teacher certification exams that are required in addition (or rather as a result of) a teacher education program, and numbers of applicants to be teachers declined throughout the state, including in CUNY, he wanted faculty to analyze their programs and come up with a more clinically rich experience for students. With that in mind, Dean Steiner created a Redesign Committee consisting of department chairpersons and two representatives from each department. Left in a room, we took baby steps in figuring out this task.

IMPROVING PROGRAMS

As we were usually ranked high within CUNY in terms of how its Schools of Education perform in national assessments, for what they are worth, we recognized the strengths of our existing programs. Yet, at the same time we observed that preparation for, and engagement in, clinical experiences occurred at somewhat random places, oftentimes quite fragmented in terms of coming to know knowledge and skills required. In other words, general cohesion of these knowledge and skills was assumed without being sufficiently checked for evidence. We were charged with bringing ideas to, and soliciting input from, faculty. As I'd come to know by now, educators—like many humans in many professions—are often set in their ways. On one hand there's the need to grow and move with the times, and on the other hand, many educators had tried many things that did not have an impact in the form of significant change. Our suggestion was fairly simple: to reorganize programs with view to (1) providing evidence where they were practitioner based, and (2) where and how students were being explicitly prepared for state examinations. If there was little or no evidence, then it would serve as an opportunity to revise existing courses, and possibly introduce new ones (as long as another was dropped, as the degree credit amount would have to be the same). Our suggestion was met with mixed enthusiasm, and I began to see how hard it was to make even modest or moderate changes in academia.

As a result of this initiative, four representatives from the committee were funded to go to a week-long seminar in Stanford, the number one ranking teacher education program in the country, to study its success. Stanford's campus is huge and beautiful, the center an impressive cluster of Spanish colonial style architecture. With most groups coming from South America and Europe, we were the only one from the United States. I found visiting Stanford to be one of the most fascinating experiences in my career because the institution had created a strong program through consciously crafting multiple connections. First, there were only one hundred students in the program, compared to Hunter's 3,000. Second, it was a concise fourteen-month course of study, with two summers serving as bookends and, most importantly, every semester included experience within actual classrooms. Third, the program's courses and requirements were all specifically tied to practice. Fourth, the adjunct mentors/field supervisors were well compensated financially and actually viewed as part of the faculty. Students were required to meet with a team of three faculty members who supported them in different ways, all invested in that student's growth. Even if a class was primarily theoretical, studying philosophers as diverse as Dewey (1997) or Freire (1970), student assignments required them to observe or reflect upon specific ideas manifest *in practice,* using the context of their current school placement. Each skill and knowledge set was articulated clearly without it seeming technocratic, and students knew what they should know and be able to do by when, and were well prepared for their required Californian state exams. We also visited a variety of local schools who had partnerships with Stanford, watching lessons and talking with student teachers, students, teacher mentors, field supervisors, and principals.

Fired up with great ideas, we returned to Hunter thinking about how to utilize what we'd learned, culling ideas yet customizing elements that would work for thirty times Stanford's number. We asked all faculty to review their programs and self-critique with an eye to aligning the overall student experience around cohesion and an explicit focus on student practice. In focusing on the Learning Disabilities program I was relentless in pushing for maps in which we could guarantee courses, structure the order of information about knowledge and skills, and help prepare for exams. It would mean limited options for part time and full time students in both single and dual certification programs. LD personnel met biweekly for over a year to create the patterns needed (including the logistics of numbers), which courses needed content changed and/or extended into more credits, which needed cut out, and which new ones could be inserted. To do this meant seeking approval from both other departments (that may be impacted, in their view, unfavorably by proposed changes), in addition to completing numerous documents that are rigidly formatted and submitted to the college Senate form approval, before they go to CUNY central for approval, before they go to the state for approval. After several years of doing the required foundational work and several more navigating various stalls, we are now ready to adhere to this new way of doing business. I share this story to convey how time consuming it is to initiate and manage much-needed changes. As of fall 2017, four and a half years after our Stanford trip to inspire changes, the LD program maps were implemented.

Part of reforms at the state level has included the generation of new and multiple examinations, the toughest being the practitioner-centered assessment called the Education Teacher Performance Assessment or EdTPA. This idea came from Stanford's Center for Assessment, Learning, & Equity (SCALE). However, so many people failed it during its first implementation. The Special Education Department at Hunter's pass rate was only 60 percent (the same as New York University) whereas we usually had achieved a 100 percent on the former exam. One local university first EdTPA attempt was as low as 13 percent. The state had to retread some steps and come up with a compromise of what constituted passing. In the meantime, faculty analyzed the Special EdTPA handbook, finding it fairly flawed and not user-friendly, particularly the language used. There also existed issues of accessibility such as whether inserted captions into video footage were permissible. These concerns were brought to my attention a colleague and clinical professor, Jennifer Klein, and I tended to agree with her, so I took them to the dean who was eager to see us rise above 60 percent. In turn, he sent Jen's comments to the State Education Department who, to their credit, took notice of them. The second edition of EdTPA incorporated Hunter's suggestions, and Jennifer was asked to be an ongoing reviewer of EdTPA materials and policy implementation as part of a statewide panel, which she still does. Numbers improved, and we were in the high 80 percentages, now in the 90 percentages. I recalled that Dean Steiner once commented that these new exams were deliberately intended to be too hard for 20 percent of teacher candidates to pass, thus ensuring "high quality teachers" demanded in No Child Left Behind, a necessity of reform.

Now several years into the position, and having finally struggled through the complexities of year-round programming, the department was finally provided an office manager due the expanded technological needs of almost any task within the university. Chris Leung was technologically savvy, gently assertive, polite, good with people, respectful, hardworking, collegial—and a problem solver. And while I kept an eye on all things programmaticaly, after the cycle of one year had rolled around, he "owned" it, alleviating me of the stress and providing opportunities to engage in other business. The administrative assistant simultaneously decided to retire, and the office became a pleasant place to go in the mornings. Cathy, was now trained in so many of the systems in which we must interact, including budgeting, personnel, and hiring, that the office atmosphere was finally professional, consistent, pleasant, and most importantly, functional. It had taken three years to get there.

MAKING THE MOST OF SABBATICAL TIME

Now that the place was in order, I wanted to file for sabbatical, and did so—being awarded two consecutive spring semesters. I needed to get away and regain some perspective on life. I had always known going into the job as chairperson that something would have to give, perhaps the focus on my teaching, or the steady obligations of scholarship, aspects of social life, perhaps the loss of some friendships. Never did I think it would be my personal relationship with John. I always considered it as the anchor of my life, making me happy, grounding me in reality, keeping me focused and relatively calm. Yet, without expecting it, the relationship did unfurl after 27 years together. While notoriously insular, John had given me the reason, "You've never stopped working since you started at Hunter." This was largely true. I'd thrown myself into the challenge of building programs and refining them, of cultivating students at both masters and doctoral levels to be the best practitioners and thinkers that they could be. In retrospect, I realized much of my weekends were spent sitting in the spare bedroom to write articles, chapters, and books. As mentioned, I'd always wanted to be a writer and once I began to publish, it became a priority. I could not seem to turn down many opportunities. The responsibilities for the dissolution of a wonderful experience we had together lay on both sides. I had never worked as hard while John, retired now for some years, had all his time free, coming to acquire different interests and develop new friendships. Nevertheless, this period was the most difficult time in my adult life, and I wanted to go far away, breathe, and relearn how to do many things again as a single person rather than thinking of myself as half of a whole. So I chose to be in Buenos Aires, the rambunctious capital of Argentina, for the first half of sabbatical, renting a loft in an old French-style building in San Telmo, one of the oldest parts of town. Here I buckled down to write a new book about Inclusive Education. I needed to put something optimistic into the world.

On return to Hunter that fall, I was pleased that Professor Jennifer Samson, the interim chairperson had initiated a departmental discussion about issues of race and multiculturalism. This had always been one of concerns with special education, and there were still so many people in the field who were noncommittal, disinterested, or even in denial that racial inequalities existed (Morgan et al., 2015). At the end of the first department meeting, handouts were given about the work of James Banks's multicultural curriculum (1993) and Peggy McIntosh's white privilege (1988). Several things struck me, including the fact that here we were 25 years later looking at the same Bank's handout I'd been given when I was a graduate student, and people were summarily shuffling it into their folders while making a beeline for the door. It was then I suggested to Jen that we make it a year-long project to look at race and special education. Subsequently, we enlisted a couple of other interested faculty members and dedicated between 60 and 90 minutes to placing race center stage. This did not go over well with some faculty, while other welcomed it. When asked why we should have this focus, I responded—calling to mind the powerful work of Kathleen Collins on racial and ability profiling (2003, 2015, 2016)—that we lived in a society in which a police officer can shoot a black man dead in the street without impunity (Weathersbee, 2015). How are we preparing our mostly white students, taught by mostly white professors to answer a kid if she or he poses the question, "How can cops do that?" It also opened a larger discussion that triggered many aspects of our field including overrepresentation of kids of color in "soft" disability categories, as well as more restrictive environments, less academic success, and a neglect of the special education field to face these issues—thereby being part of the problem. During the four sessions that semester we began to take some risks and, in a Department of Special Education without one African-American full time faculty member, asked: How can we do things better? How can we center race instead of thinking of it as additive, something layered upon a white, unquestioned norm (Leonardo, 2013)? I have written about this experience of talking about race at the department level (Connor, 2017c), sharing the tip of the iceberg about my thoughts, as I feel we need to be more proactive in any future faculty searches, so we grow beyond a department that is overwhelmingly white, with nominal representation of Asian-Americans and Latino/as.

In the second spring sabbatical I returned to Buenos Aires to enjoy being far from the madding crowd, and to write another book. This one. When I planned my return to New York in summer 2017, as no one had stepped up to the plate again, I agreed to be chairperson for one last fall semester, feeling the time is right to soon transition out of the position. I have found being chairperson simultaneously wonderfully rewarding at times and endlessly thankless at others, a strange combination that, to be frank, has given me pause to think about how we do much of our business in education.

COMMENTARY

Teaching and Learning in Schools and Universities

Looking through the lens of Department Chairperson, it is important to consider teaching and learning from an organizational perspective. As a publicly funded urban institution I have found we are always "bursting at the seams, like public schools," and it's best to adopt an attitude of "you must rely upon yourself" to get done what needs to be done. Space is a perpetual concern for programming more than 22,000 students for the college, 3,000 of those in the School of Education, and 1,000 of them in the Department of Special Education. A significant number of classes are now online, or hybrid, and potential students often "shop" with an eye to these options, some seeking fully online programs. Rapid shifts in technology and limited physical space have changed the landscape of our programs, like in most universities around the country.

All that said, it is the quality of content that is most important, once space has been secured and class format established. One of the most interesting challenges had been to respond to Dean Steiner's call to develop more clinically rich programs. By this he meant a more intensive focus on pedagogy and experiences for students to be in the field working with, and teaching, kids. As much as I disagreed with him in his educational politics, I saw the sense in re-thinking our programs because I had always wanted to arrange them in ways that were more structured and sequenced. As they stood, only a minority of courses were labeled as having pre or co-requisites, although several had multiple. The problem with this system of allowing students a lot of choice in what they took and when they took it meant students selected courses that best fit their work schedule and without essential background knowledge. Every one of the five semesters saw students rush and bottleneck the complex registration process, sometimes crashing the system. There were endless pleadings of what was needed in order to graduate, to "be on [self-determined] track," to secure financial aid, or to "make the program work," and so on. Deals were made between advisers and students and rules were bent and stretched, including bean-counting the minimum contact hours required for student teaching. All the while, the desired connections among knowledge and skills taught among courses were assumed to occur. Sometimes, a student would take student teaching in the very last semester of their degree and fail, feeling ill-prepared, and therefore (if a second chance was not granted) did not complete their master's degree. At department meetings faculty complained about these cyclical dilemmas. Meanwhile, the State Education Department had raised the minimum number of student teaching days from 40 to 60, insisting they be full days, prohibiting them being broken down into numbered hours of contact.

The experience of Stanford and their focus on teaching and learning as core values and expectations throughout every one of their courses impressed me. I returned with the desire to revise and reorganize all of our programs, and looked at the Learning Disabilities Childhood Program (grades 1–6) as the guinea pig. Our department had learned over a number of years to successfully developed curriculum maps in non-traditional, that is, alternative certification programs, sponsored by the likes of TF and TFA. It was my desire that we do the same for traditional programs. It was a simple enough idea that came to reveal how difficult it is to affect change within academic programs.

First, "buy in" by program faculty members was sought, each of 12 professional personalities having their own take on what was best for students (and professors). Second, having group consensus of how to proceed, we delineated "to do" lists, and met biweekly for over a year. Third, a systematic review of all courses and their content was made. Fourth, a discussion about the merits of each course—keep, modify, remove, add new ones?—was ongoing. Fifth, we had to then make these recommended changes. Sixth, we configured the courses in a map for the main semesters—fall and spring—for students in (1) single certification program in special education, (2) dual certification in special and general education, (3) part time schedule, and (4) full time schedule. Considerations were made for combining courses so students could receive the minimum number of credits for financial aid. Meetings for balancing eight maps in terms of programming, based on our own limited resources, were scheduled. Seventh, we coordinated these changes to present within a specified format as they had to be presented to—and approved by—Special Education Department, then the other two departments in SoE, the college Senate, then CUNY-wide, then New York State Education Department. To complicate matters further: other departments had traditionally voted "no" if they perceived the proposed changes were detrimental to their own department; the SoE had never asked for moderate changes to this effect during my experience there, and the infrastructure at that office level was initially not sufficiently prepared to help us.

I share this tale (knowing full well it may have incited sleep in some readers) because I want to share the realities of moderately re-arranging programs and developing improvements at the university level is very complex and very slow, fraught with potential misperceptions and opposition at every step of the way. Factors we had to consider included: not increasing the number of credits in programs as they were already high; how to "import" knowledge from a course in another department and fold it into an existing one, to make space for a brand new course of a second semester of student teaching; limiting choices of students in order to provide a more coherent program; and working with faculty feelings and concerns if their "old" courses were no longer taught. All in all, this took four and a half years to do.

The result is a much better program that focuses on clinical practice, integrates student diversity, and prepares students for the required New York State examinations. It also had a built-in first 12-credit "check" to make sure students are doing well or need additional support, embedded technology competencies, and a guaranteed program of classes. This translates into more accurate programming of classes (fewer canceled or over-tallied), less advisement hours, less confusion about course sequencing and when to take examinations, and so on. The other aspect of change is that students admitted into the "old" program may take one to four years to graduate, so we must be mindful of programming classes in this way. I confess, if it was not for my colleague Jennifer Samson who stepped in to help make this happen, I may have walked away defeated. This example illustrates what I mean when referring to how I have been given "pause to think about how we do much of our business in education." I consider myself a realistic optimist, a person who commits to strive for worthwhile goals, yet see how the bureaucratic structures, politics at programmatic/departmental/school/college levels, constantly changing priorities (e.g., new certification examinations), and shifting alliances among professionals can serve to immobilize those who seek change.

Educational Laws and their Impact

One result of educational law, as mentioned previously, is its impact upon teacher certification structures. I agreed when the State Education Department shifted from K-12 Special Education Certification for two reasons: (1) it did not pay sufficient attention to general education structure, curriculum, and pedagogies; and (2) the grade and age span was too wide to understand educational implications for all disabilities experienced from age 5 through 21. The requirement for special educators to be dually certified was an important shift that signaled a primary focus toward general education. Still, the perpetual shortage of special educators is evidenced in the trebling of numbers since I began at Hunter, largely in part "to successful partnerships with the Department of Education, including Teaching Fellows and Teach for America." These sponsors represent Local Education Authorities and independent organizations, both committed to supplying certified (albeit temporarily) teachers into a profession that—after 30 years of observations—seems like a bottomless well. Reinforcing this impression are the daily requests I receive via email from school administrators to provide special educators for vacancies far and wide across the city. This always left me puzzling: Why doesn't a society value teaching, particularly some of its most vulnerable citizens?

When thinking about how we can best reconceptualize certification programs and move to a more inclusive education system and society, I think all teachers should be dual certified in special and general education. Should special education as the tenacious behemoth it is now ever cease to exist, then teacher certification programs could be conceptualized in terms of diversity—that includes what we call disabilities, along with cultural, racial, regional, sexual orientation, social class, and gender considerations (etc.). Perhaps only then will the de-centering of adhered to white middle-class norms be expanded and be inclusive of the actual population in the United States of America.

In the meantime, we work within existing systems in a difficult political climate that vilifies public education and the teachers within it (Katz & Rose, 2014), and the higher educational systems with teacher education programs (Steiner & Rozen, 2004). Simultaneously, there are efforts underfoot to diminish existing teacher education programs and provide alternative teacher certification methods by organizations who seek to create a direct pipeline into their privately run organizations such as Relay (https://www.relay.edu.). Even the State Education Departments provide quick fixes for general educators seeking additional certification in special education, usually in the form of 12 credits. As there are a lot of general educators who seek to make themselves more "marketable," our department was asked to accommodate, with some pressure, applicants who sought to take classes with us. After years of rejecting potential students in this category, the department compromised and put together programs of 18–21 credits in which students received a program map of courses that provided them with a solid foundation of knowledge and skills rather than a "drive by" education taking courses when convenient to fulfill minimum requirements. We called these programs Post Masters Additional Certifications, and are our institutional response to being pressured yet wishing to maintain quality and integrity. That rival colleges have shorter-fully online versions speaks to the competition among universities as they strive to meet the market without selling their soul.

Finally, while grateful that all general education students take the Inclusion class, one course is simply not enough as the only link between potential general and special educators. It is my hope that our large bodies of classes can be more integrated and have general and special educators study alongside of each other at every opportunity possible, for they are now required to work closely together in schools.

Models of Disability and their Influence on Educators and Researchers

Where are the lines between ability and disability drawn? Who draws them? For what purposes? How have these shifted and morphed over time to influence our current understandings? Hopefully, these questions have reverberated explicitly and implicitly throughout this book. My experience working in a Department of Special Education has affirmed my fears and former critiques, "What I also came to see is how programs were placed together because they serve kids who are deemed outside of the boundaries of normal." As I leave the position after five and a half years, I exit with the same thought that I had when entering, "Strangely, I was a chair of a department I wish did not exist."

In a recent conversation with DSE colleague Joe Valente, he asked me whether I think special education should be abolished (personal communication, September 20, 2017). This is a big question, and one I suggested we develop into a special edition of journal to ask our colleagues in the field of DSE and perhaps critical special educators of different stripes too. Given the history of special education and its institutionalization, I don't think it will be going away, but it can be re-thought with view to its eventual reduction in influence *as is*, and better still, have a metamorphosis. What I don't want is to throw away or disregard is innovative and creative practices, some of which have been developed within special education as we know it. What I do want is new ways of thinking about how we better conceptualize disability, organize teacher education so that the special-general divide is dissolved, while our educational systems provide kids what they need in order to succeed. I would like to see more movement away from special and general separation in thought, curriculum, perceived responsibilities, programs, and certifications, and believe a DSE disposition helps us think through these necessary challenges. I know using a DSE lens in the Inclusion course helps special educators come to know other ways of thinking, other ways of knowing, and the role they each educator can potentially play in moving things forward. One of my own-shortcomings has been that I would have liked to infuse DS and DSE into other courses and programs. Although I have brought these related fields into teaching whatever I do, and introduced some of my colleagues to my academic work in which they are foregrounded, I did not manage to create a DS-focused program. The size, scope, and complexities of doing that at a public university that serves, in part, as a teacher factory seems daunting, although I know it has been done on a smaller scale such as in Syracuse University. I do believe it is possible, though.

Educational Structures and Systems in Relation to People with Disabilities

The complexities involved in higher education bureaucracies, especially in large public institutions, have led it to become more about organizational and managerial concerns rather than being educationally innovative—or even keeping abreast of the times sometimes. For example, recognizing that the Inclusion course was "beyond irony," because "we were educating about inclusion in a segregated way." How did this simple principle of educating future co-educators together take so long? That it was not a priority? Part of it was "limitations of our scheduling system," as this simple act of co-listing classes was impacted by programming all existing programs of study as eligible to take the course. This was a small victory that reflected collaboration and sharing among departments. I fear the epic "moderate" changes that took over four years to actualize impacts faculty investment in much-needed change. That programs could blend and meld so all students can be educated in how to work with all kids would take an enormous amount of work by faculty who identify as special educators and general educators. Still, it's possible, if complex at times (Friend, Cook, Hurley-Chamberlain, & Shamberger, 2010) and if we don't try in the future, largely separate teacher education programs will continue that reify differences.

Social, Political, and Cultural Experiences of People with Disabilities

One of the students who has stood out most in academic career is Deborah. Her difficulties in interpreting social situations, awkward manner, inclination to jump to wrong conclusions, anger in feeling her rights were abused, and strained relationships with peers and professor alike were hard for Deborah to manage. In addition, her demanding presence (she visited three professors regularly to discuss what best to do in numerous situations and then say, "But Professor X said . . ."), and general need of assistance in interpreting, evaluating, and acting upon situations reflected Deborah's complexities as a person. I was angered when she raised her voice to me and chastised, "You're supposed to be an advocate!" when refusing significant accommodations that were not in her plan. I am aware that not all accommodations that are needed are on a plan, and professors can and should respond to student requests when considered reasonable, but to relentlessly push for 40-minutes post-class one-on-one attention speaks more to a sense of aggression and entitlement. My friend and colleague Matthew Joffe told me one of the most consistent messages he could provide to students he supported in LaGuardia

Community College's Office of Supports for Students with Disabilities was, "Special needs are not special deals." I may be wrong, but I also saw this as an example of unacknowledged white and middle-class privilege at play.

At the crossroads of being ally of, and advocate for, people with disabilities, including teachers with disabilities, there sometimes exist contradictory pulls of loyalty. For example, there are some teachers who acknowledge their own various learning disabilities, ADD/ADHD, perfectionist tendencies associated with "obsessive compulsive disorder," and so on. Those I personally know run the range from competent to outstanding teachers. There are others, too, who, also motivated in part by their own experiences of being misunderstood and marginalized, want to be a teacher. Yet not everyone can be a teacher. I believe in giving folks the opportunity to prove themselves a good fit or not. As part of this process they must be able to demonstrate the knowledge, skills, and professionalism required—whether they are disabled or not. Otherwise the kids that they teach will be impacted negatively.

The case of Janelle weighed heavy on me. Race permeates all aspects of life in the United States of America. I understood how the structures, systems, expectations of our educational systems can seem oppressive and limiting, having studied and written about it myself (Connor, 2008a). It is discomforting to be viewed as "the gatekeeper" to someone's professional ambitions, maintenance of temporary provisional certification, and current job. It can feel more discomforting as a white male enforcing the rules and expectations of our system on students of color who may struggle. Janelle had been given the same opportunities as everyone else and had consistently failed to meet expected standards, while blaming others for her lack of growth in pedagogical capabilities in particular and professionalism in general. It would be easy to become influenced by into feelings white guilt or shame (Harvey & Oswald, 2000) in evaluating this situation. However, in all of my years of meeting with students to try and steer them toward what's expected and how they can achieve meeting those expectations, Janelle's was the only one in which I felt I failed (on my terms) to connect and guide the student. That said, at times our job requires us to be judges and, based upon the number of people's concerns about Janelle's documented inability to plan, teach, and assess students with disabilities, coupled with her practice of turning the tables to blame those charged with guiding her, she was dismissed from the program. Taking this decision to the level of the college Senate showed spirit and energy that should have been better harnessed to professional studies and teaching. Given the history of race in the United States of America, I can understand mistrust of people, professions, and systems, and the complexities those bring. Regardless of what Janelle thought, I wanted her to succeed, but she rejected guidance. She may have genuinely thought what nixed her plans was racially motivated—and that is the part pains me. But I knew it wasn't race; it was performance. Still, that thought didn't make me feel any better, and I wondered about the different realities that we all have to navigate, and times like this when they clash.

Heading into the home stretch as chairperson, I recognized that there was a small but critical mass of educators in the department who wanted to center issues of race and disability. This has been part of my own thinking throughout my career and although it did not hamper me in teaching and writing, I was wary of trying to integrate issues of cultural diversity including whiteness (McIntosh, 1988), disability as diversity (Connor & Gabel, 2010), and intersectional understandings of disability (Annamma, 2014). At the heart of these issues are the cultural experiences of people with disabilities that can inform educators about better facing and navigating diverse classrooms. Their knowledge can contribute to helping new teachers to succeed in everyday situations that can be challenging. Recently, the Early Childhood Special Education Program (ECSE) sought to change its name to "Diverse Children and Families: Learning and Development in the Early Years." This sparked a healthy series on intra-departmental listserv in which some faculty protested about the lack of "education," and more specifically, "special education," in the title. I wrote:

> *My take: I think it reflects the direction that the Early Childhood Special Education faculty wish to conceptualize and grow their program. For prospective graduate students we know that want to work with kids identified as disabled, I don't think the actual title would confuse or deter them. Conceptualizing disability as diversity is important. Disability is normal, yet access to all aspects of society for people with disabilities is denied. Disability is also increasingly included in the umbrella of diversity (along with race, gender, ethnicity, sexual orientation etc.), and I have written several chapters in edited books dedicated to diversity that sought disability representation. These very issues are part of contemporary scholarship.*
>
> *My points do not negate those of my colleagues. I agree that we must be mindful of not throwing the baby out with the bathwater (perhaps an unfortunate phrase when talking about ECSE), and maintaining specific knowledge(s). It is the fact that students with IEPs ARE diverse learners is the most important point here, and I therefore see the value of the name. The name also is, I recognize of a more inclusive leaning, which—in full transparency—I tend to side with.*
>
> *Others feel free to weigh in.*

The departmental proposal, and faculty exchange, made me smile with a dash of renewed hope.

Epilogue

A Note for Hope

In this autoethnographic memoir I sought to blend the personal, professional, and political domains across a narrative arc that spans eight phases of my career. I did this because I wanted to share an educator's life, complete with key events and everyday details. There are few accounts, in memoirs or research studies, of teachers' and professors' experiences in engaging about the inextricable and mutually constitutive categories of dis/ability for three decades. It is my hope that in striving to make sense of my own story, and the influences that have shaped it, I have helped clarify some issues, offered some answers, and raised some new questions, for other educators. All of us seek to make sense of our own lives. Writing this book has given me the opportunity to share how I have tried to make sense of mine, the context of my life in classrooms, schools, and universities, and society at large. Rather than believing I "captured" a career in narrative (implying it was there already waiting to be caught), I constructed the architecture of my story in deliberate ways. Some details are highly personal, and others, decidedly mundane. Between the two lies "the stuff of life" for an educator. Teaching. Learning. Research. Theory. Policy. Change, both real and imagined. And, perhaps above all, Hope—tethered to our desire for change.

In closing this book, as an educator I confess to grappling with hope throughout my entire career including up until the present time. I know I am not alone. When recently reading preeminent Puerto Rican scholar Sonia Nieto's autobiography, *Brooklyn Dreams: My Life in Public Education* (2015), I was drawn into a life of a teacher and researcher who has advocated for issues of diversity, multiculturalism, plurality, and social justice throughout her career. In reflecting on the current landscape of education she writes, "The tremendous hope I have always had for education for social justice has faded, although it will never die" (p. 241). This sentence while tinged with melancholy, signaled an unwavering adherence to hope, still rising above all of the arguments and battles around public education and its relationship to equity. I have always self-defined as being a relentless optimist. This has fueled my drive in decisions I made as a teacher, researcher, and writer. Nonetheless, like Sonia, I accept that possibilities I could envision within education or could see "in progress" are constantly being undermined or dismantled by others. And yet, her ability to maintain hope still prevails. So does mine.

A lot has happened since last year when I began planning and writing this book. One highlight has been the leadership by Dean Michael Middleton who earnestly endeavors to respectfully engage all professors as community members, with full expectations of them contributing to shaping Hunter's School of Education. Another highlight was to be invited as the keynote speaker at Bank Street College's convocation, starting off their 2017–2018 academic year. As usual, I went through the recurring internal dynamics of anxiety and impostorship. While admittedly daunting, the challenge of the occasion somehow felt right. The topic I settled upon for an audience of largely brand new students entering the profession was *Educational Stories from a Life in Teaching and Learning*. In fact, I chose to read selected sections from the first chapter of this book, focusing upon the errors I made as a first year teacher and the lessons they taught me. Embedded throughout the stories of me falling flat on my face, I found I automatically emphasized hope in talking to the next generation of educators. Speaking as a seasoned educator to an audience of fresh-faced soon-to-be novices, it was a satisfying and enlightening moment. I'd come full circle from 30 years ago, and remembered the care and kindness of Jayson, John, Iris, and Tom, as they held me together in my first three weeks of the profession.

I have also rolled my sleeves up to write more this year, including renewed critiques of the field of special education. For example, the topic of overrepresentation of students of color has become a lightening rod once again, as the field of special education centers the work of Morgan et al. (2015) and Morgan et al. (2017) who claim *underrepresentation* is the actual reality. That special education can ignore five decades of research to the contrary (Deno, 1970; Dunn, 1968, Artiles & Trent, 1994; Losen & Orfield, 2002; Artiles, 2017) and claim the problem is to label more children of color is acceptable (D. Hallahan, pers. comm., August 27, 2017) is beyond disturbing. That Morgan and his colleagues claim are influencing federal policy to freeze their research to monitor and reduce overrepresentation reveals a level of moral bankruptcy pervading some leaders of the field of education and in the federal government (Youdin, 2018). To put it mildly, these are indeed troubling times.

Yet teachers continue to show up to work every day and focus upon the children and youth in their care. Likewise, professors engage with undergraduate, graduate, and doctoral students, with the potential of greatly influencing their thoughts. Efforts to change how we "do business" in education for the better occur when hope, along with other elements such as desire and our vulnerabilities, mix together with realism and pragmatism. I truly believe that each educator is a crucible from which new ways of thinking can be forged. In my own case, a large part has been the need to rethink, reinterpret, and redefine dis/ability outside of the field of special education and within the larger umbrella of human diversity (Gabel & Connor, 2009), all with view to helping teachers, researchers, policy makers, and theorists make use of this knowledge (Connor, Valle, & Hale, 2015). That alternative voices to dominant discourses within the field of education can rise and challenge them, and improve "how we do business," in classrooms, has been most gratifying to witness (Cosier & Ashby, 2016).

Finally, it is my desire that more career-long educators will write their stories, too, so our worlds at the intersections of personal, professional, and political ring true and can become better known in all of their wonderful and worrying complexities, hopefully always with view to making our society a better place for everyone to live and learn.

Appendix

PERSONAL NARRATIVES FOR BOOK REVIEWS

Students may choose from this list *or select another book* that fits the criteria of first-person narrative focus.

Arrowsmith-Young, B. (2013). *The Woman Who Changed Her Brain: How I Left My Learning Disability Behind and Other Stories of Cognitive Transformation.* New York: Simon & Schuster.

Bralee, Q. (2009). *A Different Life: Growing Up Learning Disabled and Other Adventures*. New York: Public Affairs.

Brown, C. (1955). *My Left Foot*. London: Pan.

Brueggemann, B. J. (1999). *Lend Me Your Ear: Rhetorical Constructions of Deafness.* Wahington, DC: Gallaudet University Press.

Callahan, J. (1990). *Don't Worry, He Won't Get Far on Foot.* New York: Vintage.

Cheney, T. (2011). *The Dark Side of Innocence: Growing Up Bipolar.* New York: Atria.

Claire, E. (1999). *Exile and Pride.* Durham, NC: Duke Press.

Fadiman, A. (1997). *The Spirit Catches You and You Fall Down.* New York: Farrar, Straus, & Giroux.

Finger, A. (1998). *Past Due: A Story of Disability, Pregnancy and Birth.* London: Women's Press.

Finger, A. *Elegy for a Disease: A Personal and Cultural History of Polio.* London: St. Martin's Press.

Fries, K. (1997). *Body Remember.* Madison, WI: University of Wisconsin Press.

Fries, K. (Ed.) (1997). *Staring Back: The Disability Experience from the Inside Out.* New York: Plume.

Grandin, T. (1995). *Thinking in Pictures and Other Reports from My Life with Autism.* London: Bloomsbury.

Grealy, L. *Autobiography of a Face.* New York: Mariner.

Groce, E. (1990). *Everyone Here Speaks Sign Language.* Cambridge, MA: Harvard University Press.

Handler, L. (1999). *Twitch and Shout: A Touretter's Tale.* Minneapolis, MN: University of Minnesota Press.

Hall, K. (1988). *Aspergers Syndrome, The Universe, and Everything.* London: Jessica Kingsley Publishers.

Hammerschmidt, E. (2004). *Born on the Wrong Planet.* London: Jessica Kinglsey Publishers.

Hockenberry, J. (1995). *Moving Violations: War Zones, Wheelchairs and Declarations of Independence.* New York: Hyperion.

Hornbacher, M. (1998). *Wasted: A Memoir of Anorexia and Bulimia.* Glasgow, Scotland: Flamingo.

Hornbacher, M. (2009). *A Bipolar Life.* New York: Harper Perennial.

Jacobson, D. S. (1999). *The Question of David: A Disabled Mother's Journey Through Adoption, Family, and Life.* Seattle, WA: CreateSpace Independent Publishing Platform.

Jamison, K. R. (1995). *An Unquiet Mind: A Memoir of Moods and Madness.* London: Picador.

Kleege, G. (1999). *Sight Unseen.* London: Yale University Press.

Klein, B. S. (1998). *Slow Dance: A Story of Stroke, Love and Disability.* Toronto, ON: Vintage Canada.

Knighton, R. (2006). *Cockeyed: An Unsentimental Take on Blindness.* New York: Public Affairs.

Knipfel, J. (1999). *Slackjaw: A Memoir.* New York: Berkley.

Krieger, S. *Things No Longer There: A Memoir of Losing Sight and Finding Vision.* Madison, WI: University of Wisconsin Press.

Kuusisto, S. (1998). *Planet of the Blind: A Memoir.* Penguin: New York.

Kuusisto, S. (2006). *Eavesdropping: A Memoir of Blindness and Listening.* London: W.W. Norton & Company.

Lee, C., & Jackson, R. (1992). *Faking It: A Look Into the Mind of a Creative Learner.* Portsmouth, NH: Boynton/Cook.

Linton, S. (2006). *My Body Politic.* Ann Arbor, MI: University of Michigan Press.

Little, J. (1996). *If It Weren't for The Honor I'd Rather Have Walked: Previously Untold Tales of the Journey to the ADA.* Northampton, MA: Brookline Books.

Lorde, A. (1980). *The Cancer Journals.* San Francisco, CA: Aunt Lute Books.

Mairs, N. (1996). *Waist-High in The World: A Life Among the Nondisabled.* Boston, MA: Beacon Press.

Mickle, S. (2009). *The Polio Hole.* Gainesville, FL: Wild Onion Press.

Mooney, J., & Cole, D. (2000). *Learning Outside the Lines: Two Ivy League Students with Learning Disabilities and ADHD Give You the Tools for Academic Success and Educational Revolution.* New York: Simon & Schuster.

Mooney, J. (2008). *The Short Bus: A Journey Beyond Normal.* NewYork: Henry Holt.

Mukhopadhyay, T. R. (2003). *The Mind Tree: A Miraculous Child Breaks the Silence of Autism.* New York: Arcade Publishing.

Osborn, C. (1998). *Over My Head: A Doctor's Account of Head Injury from the Inside Looking Out.* Kansas City, MO: Andrews McMeel.

Padden, C., & Humphries, T. (1990). *Deaf in America: Voices from a Culture.* Cambridge, MA: Harvard University Press.

Panzarino, C. (1994). *The Me in the Mirror.* Seattle, WA: Seal Press.

Park, C. C. (2001). *Exiting Nirvana: A Daughter's Life with Autism.* New York: Little, Brown, & Company.

Patterson, K. (2004). *ADD and Me: Forty Years in a Fog.* London: Jessica Kingley Publishers.

Redfield Jamison, K. (1995) *An Unquiet Mind: A Memoir of Moods and Madness.* London: Picador.

Robison, J. E. (2007). *Look Me in the Eye: My Life with Aspergers.* New York: Three Rivers.

Savarese, R. J. (2007). *Reasonable People.* New York: Other Press LLC.

Schiller, L. (1996). *The Quiet Room: A Journey Out of the Torment of Madness.* New York: Grand Central Publishing.

Schmitt, A. (1994). *Brilliant Idiot: An Autobiography of a Dyslexic.* Intercourse, PA: Good Books.

Simon, R. (2002). *Riding the Bus with My Sister.* Boston, MA: Houghton Mifflin.

Stewart, J. (1989). *The Body's Memory.* London: St. Martin's Press.

Wright, M. (1999). *Sounds Like Home: Growing Up Black and Deaf in the South.* Washington, DC: Gallaudet University Press.

References

Albanesi, H., & Nusbaum, E. A. (2017). Encountering institutional barriers and resistance: Disability discomfort on one campus. In E. Kim, & K. Aquino (Eds.) *Disability as Diversity in Higher Education* (pp. 185–299). New York: Routledge.

Allan, J., Connor, D. J., Ferri, B. A., Gabel, S. L., Gallagher, D. J., & Ware, L. (2007). *Toward Increased Accessibility and A Culture of Inclusion at the American Educational Research Associations' Annual Conference: A White Paper from the Disability Studies in Education Special Interest Group* [White Paper].

Alper, J. (2016). *Developing a National STEM Workforce Strategy: A Workshop Summary.* Washington, DC: National Academies Press.

Alvarez, C. (2011). New cost saving proposals strike at heart of special ed. *United Federation of Teachers.* http://www.uft.org/vperspective/new-cost-saving-proposals-strike-heart-special-ed

Anastasiou, D., & Kauffman, J. M. (2011a). A social constructionist approach to disability: Implications for special education. *Exceptional Children, 77*(3), 367–384.

———. (2011b). Disability as cultural difference: Implications for special education. *Remedial and Special Education, 33*(3), 139–149.

———. (2013). The social model of disability: Dichotomy between impairment and disability. *Journal of Medicine and Philosophy, 38*(4), 441–459.

Andaluza, G. (1987). *Borderlands/La Frontera: The New Mestiza.* San Francisco, CA: Aunt Lutes.

Anderson, R. C. (2006). Teaching (with) disability: Pedagogies of lived experience. *Review of Education, Pedagogy & Cultural Studies, 28*(3–4), 367–379.

Andrews, J. E., Carnine, D. W., Coutinho, M. J., Edgar, E. B., Forness, S. R., Fuchs, L. S., Jordan, D., Kauffman, J. M., Patton, J. M., Paul, J., Rosell, J., Rueda, R., Schiller, E., Skrtic, T. M., & Wong, J. (2000). Bridging the special education divide. *Remedial and Special Education, 21*(5), 258–267.

Annamma, S. A. (2014). Disabling juvenile justice: Engaging the stories of incarcerated young women of color with disabilities. *Remedial and Special Education, 35*(5), 313–324.

Annamma, S. A., Connor, D. J., & Ferri, B. A. (2013). Dis/ability critical race studies (DisCrit): Theorizing at the intersections of race and disability. *Journal of Race, Ethnicity, & Education, 16*(1), 1–31.

Anyon, J. (1997). *Ghetto Schooling: A Political Economy of Urban Educational Reform.* New York: Teachers College Press.

Artiles, A. J. (2015). Beyond responsiveness to identity badges: Future research in culture in disability and implications for Response to Intervention. *Educational Review, 67*(1), 1–22.

Artiles, A. J. (2017, October 19). *Re-envisioning Equity Research: Disability Identification Disparities as a Case in Point* [14th Annual Brown Lecture]. Washington, DC: American Educational Research Association.

Artiles, A., Thorius, K., Bal, A., Neal, R., Waitoller, F., & Hernandez-Saca, D. (2011). Beyond culture as group traits: Future learning disabilities ontology, epistemology, and inquiry on research knowledge use. *Learning Disability Quarterly, 34*(3), 167–179.

Artiles, A. J., & Trent, S. C. (1994). Overrepresentation of minority students in special education: A continuing debate. *The Journal of Special Education, 27*(4), 410–437.

Armstrong, T. (2017). Neurodiversity: The future of special education? *Educational Leadership, 74*(7), 10–16.

Arzubiaga, A. E., Artiles, A. J., King, K., & Harris-Murri, N. (2008). Beyond research on cultural minorities: Challenges and implications of research as situated cultural practice. *Exceptional Children, 74*(3), 309–327.

Ashton-Warner, S. (1986). *Teacher.* New York: Simon & Schuster.

Baglieri, S., Bejoian, L, Broderick, A., Connor, D. J., & Valle, J. (2011). [Re]claiming "Inclusive Education" toward cohesion in educational reform: Disability studies unravels the myth of the typical child. *Teachers College Record, 113*(10), 2122–2154.

Baglieri, S., Valle, J., Connor, D. J., & Gallagher, D. (2011). Disability studies and special education: The need for plurality of perspectives on disability. *Remedial and Special Education, 32*(4), 267–278.

Bakhtin, M. M. (1986). Toward a methodology for the human sciences. In C. Emerson, & M. Holquist (Eds.) *Speech Genres and Other Late Essays* (pp. 159–172). Austin, TX: University of Texas Press.

Bal, A., & Trainor, A. (2016). Culturally responsive experimental intervention studies: The development for a rubric of paradigm expansion. *Review of Educational Research, 86*(2), 319–359.

Ballard, K. (1996). Paradigm lost and regained. In L. Heshusius, & K. Ballard, K. (Eds.) *From Positivism to Interpretivism and Beyond: Tales of Transformation in Educational and Social Research* (pp. 26–31). New York: Teachers College Press.

Banks, J. (1993). Approaches to multicultural curriculum reform. In J. Banks & C. Banks (Eds.) *Multicultural Education: Issues and Perspectives*. Boston: Allyn & Bacon.

Barone, T., & Eisner, E. (2012). *Arts Based Research.* Los Angeles: SAGE.

Barthes, R. (1972). *Mythologies.* New York: Hill & Wang.

———. (1977). *Image, Music, Text.* New York: Hill & Wang.

Bell, D. (1992). *Faces at the Bottom of the Well: The Permanence of Racism.* New York: Basic Books.

Ben-Moshe, L. (2006). Infusing disability in the curriculum: The case of Saramago's "Blindness." *Disability Studies Quarterly, 26*(2). http://dsq-sds.org/article/view/688

Berger, J. (1972). *Ways of Seeing.* London: Penguin.

Berliner, D. (2000). A personal response to those who bash teacher education. *Journal of Teacher Education, 51*(5), 358–371.

Berman, D. L. (2009). *Beyond Words: Reflections on Our Journey to Inclusion.* Harrisburg, PA: White Hat Press.

Berman, D. L., & Connor, D. J. (2017). *A Child, a Family, a School, a Community: A Tale of Inclusive Education.* New York: Peter Lang.

Bickens, S., Bittman, F., & Connor, D. J. (2013). Developing academic skills through multigenre autobiography. *Journal of English, 102*(5), 43–50.

Biklen, D. (2010). Constructing inclusion: Lessons from critical, disability narratives. *International Journal of Inclusive Education, 4*(4), 337–353.

Bittman, F., Bickens, S., & Connor, D. J. (2014). Respecting and reaching all learners in ELA classes: A glimpse into a New York City high school. In S. Danforth (Ed.) *The Best Inclusive Education: Stories and Lessons of Struggle and Success* (pp. 269–284). New York: Peter Lang.

Botchco, S., & Kozoll, M. (1981–1987). *Hill Street Blues* [Television series]. USA: MTM Enterprises.

Blake, H. (Producer), & Zinnemann, F. (Director) (1959). *The Nun's Story* [Motion picture]. USA: Warner Brothers Studios.

Blanchett, W. J. (2006). Disproportionate representation of African Americans in special education: Acknowledging the role of white privilege and racism. *Remedial and Special Education, 35*(6), 24–28.

———. (2010). Telling it like it is: The role of race, class, and culture in the perpetuation of learning disability as a privileged category for the white middle class. *Disability Studies Quarterly, 30*(2), 1230–1277.

Blaser, A. (2003). *Awareness Days: Some Alternatives to Simulated Exercises.* http://www.raggededgemagazine.com/0903/0903ft1.html

Bley, N. S., & Thornton, C. A. (2001). *Teaching Mathematics to Students with Learning Disabilities* (4th edition). Austin, TX: Pro-Ed.

Blumenstyk, G. (2014). *American Higher Education in Crisis? What Everyone Needs to Know.* New York: Oxford University Press.

Blythe, T., Allen, D., & Powell, B. S. (2015). *Looking Together at Student Work.* New York: Teachers College Press.

Board of Education v. Rowley (1982). No. 80-1002, 458 U.S. 176.

Bochner, A. (1997). It's about time: Narrative and the divided self. *Qualitative Inquiry, 3*(4), 418–438.

Bochner, A., & Ellis, C. (1992). Personal narrative as a social approach to interpersonal communication. *Communication Theory, 2*(2), 165–172.

Bogden, R., & Biklen, D. (1977). *Handicapism.* Mimeographed paper, Social Policy Corporation, New York.

Brantlinger, E. (1997). Using ideologies: Cases of non-recognition of the politics of research and practice in special education. *Review of Educational Research, 67*(4), 425–459.

———. (2003). *Dividing Classes: How the Middle Class Negotiates and Rationalizes School Advantage*. New York: Routledge Falmer.

———. (2004). Confounding the needs and confronting the norms: An extension of Reid and Valle's essay. *Journal of Learning Disabilities, 37*(6), 490–499.

———. (2006). The big glossies: How textbooks structure (special) education. In E. Brantlinger (Ed.) *Who Benefits from Special Education? Remediating (Fixing) Other People's Children* (pp. 45–75). Mahwah, NJ: Lawrence Erlbaum.

Brookfield, S. D. (2005). Overcoming impostorship, cultural suicide, and lost innocence: Implications for teaching critical thinking in the community college. *New Directions for Community Colleges, 130,* 49–57.

———. (2009). The concept of critical reflection: Promises and contradictions. *European Journal of Social Work, 12*(3), 293–304.

Brown v. Board of Education (1954). 347 US 483.

Brown, P., & Scase, R. (2005). *Higher Education & Corporate Realities: Class, Culture, and the Decline of Graduate Careers*. New York: Routledge.

Brownell, N., Sindelar, P. T., Bishop, A. G., Langley, L. K., & Seo, S. (2002). Special education teacher supply and teacher quality: The problems, the solutions. *Focus on Exceptional Children, 35*(2), 1–16.

Brunsting, N. C., Sreckovic, M. A., & Lane, K. L. (2014). Special education teacher burnout: A synthesis of research from 1979 to 2013. *Education and Treatment of Children, 37*(4), 681–711.

Campanile, C. (2003, April 3). Special ed: $20 less to do more. *New York Post,* 27.

Campbell, B. (2009). To-With-By: A three-tiered model for differentiated instruction. *Journal of National English Reading Association, 44*(2), 7–10.

Chapman, B. (2017, July 28). City sued on ed services for the disabled. *Daily News,* 13.

Chawla, D., & Rodriguez, A. (2008). Narratives on longing, being, and knowing: Envisioning a writing epistemology. *International Journal of Progressive Education, 4*(1), 6–23.

Charlton, J. I. (2000). *Nothing About Us Without Us: Disability Oppression and Empowerment.* Berkeley, CA: University of California Press.

Clandinin, D. J., & Connelly, M. F. (2000). *Narrative Inquiry: Experience and Story in Qualitative Research.* San Francisco, CA: Jossey-Bass.

Cohen, E. A. (Producer), & Day, R. (Director). *Love, Mary* [Television movie]. USA: CBS Entertainment Productions.

Cohn, P. (1998). Why does my stomach hurt so much? How individuals with learning disabilities can use cognitive strategies to reduce anxiety and stress at the college level. *Journal of Learning Disabilities, 31*(5), 514–516.

Collins, K. M. (2003). *Ability Profiling and School Failure: One Child's Struggle to be Seen as Competent.* New York: Routledge.

———. (2015). A disability studies in education analysis of corporate-based educational reform: Lessons from New Orleans. In D. J. Connor, J. W, Valle, &

C, Hale (Eds.) *Practicing Disability Studies in Education: Acing Toward Social Change* (pp. 217–233). New York: Peter Lang.

———. (2016). A discrit perspective on The State of Florida v. George Zimmerman: Racism, ableism, and youth out of place in community and school. In D. Connor, B. A. Ferri, & S. A. Annamma (Eds.) *Discrit: Disability Studies and Critical Race Theory in Education* (pp. 183–201). New York: Teachers College Press.

Collins, P. H. (1990). *Black Feminist Thought: Knowledge, Consciousness, and the Politics of Empowerment.* New York: Routledge.

Commins, N. L., & Miramontes, O. B. (2006). *Linguistic Diversity and Teaching.* New York: Routledge.

Connor, D. J. (1978). The lives and deaths of Edgar Lisle. In W. H. Smith (Ed.) *Children as Writers* (pp. 41–11). London: Heinemann.

———. (2004). Infusing disability studies into "mainstream" educational thought: One person's story. *Review of Disability Studies, 1*(1), 100–119.

———. (2005). *Life In and Out of School for Urban Black and/or Latino(a) Youth from Working Class Backgrounds* [Dissertation]. ISBN: 9780542146176.

———. (2006). Michael's story: "I get into so much trouble just by walking": Narrative knowing and life at the intersections of learning disability, race, and class. *Equity & Excellence in Education, 39*(2), 154–165.

———. (2008a). *Urban Narratives: Portraits-In-Progress—Life at the Intersections of Learning Disability, Race, and Social Class.* New York: Peter Lang.

———. (2008b). Not so strange bedfellows: The promise of disability studies and critical race theory. In S. L. Gabel, & S. Danforth (Eds.) *Disability and the Politics of Education: An International Reader* (pp. 451–476). New York: Peter Lang.

———. (2009). Breaking containment: The power of narrative knowing—countering silences within traditional special education research. *International Journal of Inclusive Education, 13*(5), 1–21.

———. (2012a). Suspended in liminal space: Special education administrators and the decade of educational reform within the NYC school system. *Journal of Special Education Leadership, 25*(1), 25–37.

———. (2012b). Diversifying "diversity": Contemplating dis/ability at the table(s) of social justice and multicultural education. *Disability Studies Quarterly, 32*(3).

———. (2012c). Common confusions with inclusion. In B. Cooper, C. Strax, & M. Strax (Eds.) *The Politics of Special Education: Problems, Promises, and Progress* (pp. 101–122). Lanham, MD: Roman and Littlefield.

———. (2012d). Diversifying "diversity": Contemplating dis/ability at the table(s) of social justice and multicultural education. *Disability Studies Quarterly, 32*(3).

———. (2012e). 21 ways to help support students with LD and/or ADD prepare for transitioning into college. *TEACHING Exceptional Children, 44*(5), 16–25.

———. (2013a). Who "owns" dis/ability? The work of critical special educators as insider outsiders. *Theory and Research in Social Education, 41*(4), 494–513.

———. (2013b). Picture this: Snapshots of my (A)typical family. In P. Smith (Ed.) *Families and Disability* (pp. 167–184). New York: Peter Lang.

———. (2013c). Social justice for children with disabilities. In L. Gurian (Ed.) *The Handbook of Special Education* (pp. 111–128). Thousand Oaks, CA: SAGE.

———. (2013d). Actively navigating the transition into college: Narratives of students with learning disabilities. *International Journal of Qualitative Studies in Education, 25*(8), 1005–1036.

———. (2014). The Disability Studies in Education Annual Conference: Explorations of working within, and against, special education. *Disability Studies Quarterly, 34*(2).

———. (2015a). Assembling all the jigsaw pieces together: The critical work of Dorothy Lipsky and Alan Gartner's "Inclusion and School Reform". In P. Jones, & S. Danforth (Eds.) *Foundations of Inclusive Education Research* (pp. 169–185). Bingley, UK: Emerald.

———. (2015b). Practicing what we teach: The benefits of using disability studies in an inclusion course. In D. Connor, J. Valle, & C. Hale (Eds.) *Practicing Disability Studies in Education, Acting Toward Social Change* (pp. 123–139). New York: Peter Lang.

———. (2017a). Who is responsible for the racialized practices evident within (special) education and what can be done to change them? *Theory Into Practice, 56*(3), 226–233.

———. (2017b). Questioning "normal": Actively undoing dis/ability stereotypes through teaching a critical analysis of films. In J. Stoddard, A. Marcus, & D. Hicks (Eds.) *Teaching Difficult History Through Film* (pp. 199–218). New York: Taylor & Francis.

———. (2017c, April). Teaching at the intersection of race and disability: A special education department reflects and (re)acts. *Roosevelt House Faculty Journal.* http://www.roosevelthouse.hunter.cuny.edu/faculty-journal-issues-equity-justice-education-policy/

Connor, D. J., & Baglieri, S. (2009). Tipping the scales: Disability studies asks "How much diversity can you take?" In S. Steinberg (Ed.) *Diversity: A Reader* (pp. 341–361). New York: Peter Lang.

Connor, D. J., & Bejoian, L. (2006). Pigs, pirates, and pills: Using film to teach the social context of disability. *Teaching Exceptional Children, 39*(2), 52–60.

———. (2007). Cripping school curricula: 20 ways to re-teach disability. *Review of Disability Studies, 3*(3), 3–13.

Connor, D. J., Bickens, S., & Bittman, F. (2009). Combining classic literature with creative teaching for essay building in an inclusive urban high school classroom. *TEACHINGExceptional Children Plus, 5*(6), 2–25.

Connor, D. J., & Cavendish, W. (in revision). "Sit in my seat": Perspectives of students with learning disabilities about teacher effectiveness in high school inclusive classrooms. *Journal of Teacher Education and Special Education.*

Connor, D. J., & Coughlin, A. (2016). Ramping it up: Calling attention to dis/ability at the end of education's social contract. In R. Malhotra (Ed.) *Disability Politics in a Global Economy: Essays in Honor of Marta Russell* (pp. 118–134). New York: Routledge.

Connor, D. J., & Ferri, B. A. (2005). Integration and inclusion—a troubling nexus: Race, disability, and special education. *Journal of African-American History, 90*(1–2), 107–127.

———. (2007). The conflict within: Resistance to inclusion and other paradoxes within special education. *Disability & Society, 22*(1), 63–77.

Connor, D. J., Ferri, B. A., & Annamma, S. (Eds.) (2016). *DisCrit: Disability Studies and Critical Race Theory in Education.* New York: Teachers College Press.

Connor, D. J., & Gabel, S. L. (2010). Welcoming the unwelcome: Disability as diversity. In N. Hobbel & T. Chapman (Eds.) *Social Justice Pedagogy in the United States: The Practice of Freedom* (pp. 377–399). New York: Routledge.

Connor, D. J., Gabel, S. L., Gallagher, D., & Morton, M. (2008). Disability studies and inclusive education—implication for theory, research, and practice: Guest editor's introduction. *International Journal of Inclusive Education, 12*(5–6), 441–457.

Connor, D. J., Gallagher, D., & Ferri, B. (2011). Broadening our horizons: Toward a plurality of methodologies in learning disability research. *Learning Disability Quarterly, 32*(2), 107–121.

Connor, D. J., & Lagares, C. (2007). Facing high stakes in high school: 25 successful strategies from an inclusive social studies classroom. *Teaching Exceptional Children, 40*(2), 18–27.

Connor, D. J., Newton, R., Pennisi, A., & Quarshie, A. (2004). Tales of body/space invasions in school. *Qualitative Inquiry, 10*(4) 495–508.

Connor, D. J., & Valle, J. W. (2015). A socio-cultural reframing of science and dis/ability in education: Past problems, current concerns, and future possibilities. *Journal of Cultural Studies of Science Education, 10*(2), 1103–1112.

Connor, D. J., Valle, J., & Hale, C. (2012). Forum guest editors' introduction: Disability studies in education "At work." *Review of Disability Studies, 8*(3), 5–13.

———. (Eds.) (2015). *Practicing Disability Studies in Education, Acting Toward Social Change.* New York: Peter Lang.

———. (2017). Authors' reply [To special feature on 'Practicing Disability Studies in Education, Acting Toward Social Change']. *European Journal of Special Needs, 32*(2), 295–298.

Corsey, M., Werner, T., Kukoff, B., & Leahy, J. (1984–1992). *The Cosby Show* [Television series]. USA: National Broadcasting Company.

Cosier. M., & Ashby, C. (Eds.) (2016). *Enacting Change from Within; Disability Studies Meets Teaching and Teacher Education.* New York: Peter Lang.

Coughlin, A. B. (2016). *Equal Access DENIED. Empowered Voices of Students with Physical Disabilities in New York City Public Schools.* ISBN: 9781369199307.

Coward, N. (Producer), & Lean, D. (Director). (1945). *Brief Encounter* [Motion picture]. UK: Eagle-Lion Distributors.

Crawford, L. (1996). Personal ethnography. *Communication Monographs, 63*, 158–170.

Crenshaw, K. (1993). Mapping the margins: Intersectionality, identity politics, and violence against women of color. *Stanford Law Review, 43*, 1241–1299.

Danforth, S. (Ed.) (2014). *Becoming a Great Inclusive Educator.* New York: Peter Lang.

Danforth, S., & Gabel, S. L. (2006). *Vital Questions Facing Disability Studies in Education.* New York: Peter Lang.

Davies, B. (1994). *Poststructuralist Theory and Classroom Practice*. Geelong: Deakin University.

———. (2000a). *(In)scribing Body/Landscape Relations*. Lanham, MD: AltaMira.

———. (2000b). *A Body of Writing*. Lanham, MD: AltaMira.

Davis, L. J. (1997a). *The Disability Studies Reader*. New York: Routledge.

———. (1997b). Constructing normalcy. In L. J. Davis (Ed.) *The Disability Studies Reader* (pp. 3–16). New York: Routledge.

———. (2017, September 15). *Disability, Culture, and Society Seminar*. New York: Columbia University.

Deno, E. (1970). Special education as developmental capital. *Exceptional Children, 37*(3), 229–237.

Deschler, D. D., Schumaker, J., Harris, K., & Graham, S. (Eds.) (1999). *Teaching Every Adolescent Every Day: Learning in Diverse Middle and High School Classrooms*. Cambridge, MA: Brookline.

Dewey, J. (1997). *Experience and Education*. New York: Touchstone.

Dudley-Marling, C. (1996). On becoming. In L. Heshusius, & K. Ballard, K. (Eds.) *From Positivism to Interpretivism and Beyond: Tales of Transformation in Educational and Social Research* (pp. 32–27). New York: Teachers College Press.

Dudley-Marling, C., & Gurn, A. (2010a). Troubling the foundations of special education: Examining the myth of the normal curve. In C. Dudley-Marling, & A. Gurn (Eds.) *The Myth of the Normal Curve* (pp. 9–23). New York: Peter Lang.

———. (Eds.) (2010b). *The Myth of the Normal Curve*. New York: Peter Lang.

Dunn, L. M. (1968). Special education for the mildly retarded: Is much of it justifiable? *Exceptional Children, 35*(1), 5–22.

Education for All Handicapped Children Act of 1975, PL 94-142, 20 U.S.C. 1400 *et seq*.

Ellis, C. (2004). *The Ethnographic I: A Methodological Novel About Autoethnography*. Walnut Creek, CA: AltaMira Press.

———. (2009a). Telling tales on neighbors: Ethics in two voices. *International Review of Qualitative Research, 2*(1), 3–28.

———. (2009b). *Revision: Autoethnographic Reflections on Life and Work*. New York: Routledge.

Ellis, C., Adams, T. E., & Bochner, A. P. (2010). Autoethnography: An overview [40 paragraphs]. *Forum Qualitative Sozialforschung/Forum: Qualitative Social Research, 12*(1), Art. 10. http://nbn-resolving.de/urn:nbn:de:0114-fqs1101108

Ellis, C., & Bochner, A. P. (2000). Autoethnography, personal narrative, reflexivity. In N. K. Denzin, & Y. S. Lincoln (Eds.) *Handbook of Qualitative Research* (2nd edition, pp. 733–768). Thousand Oaks, CA: Sage.

Erevelles, N., & Minear, A. (2010). Unspeakable offenses: Untangling race and disability in discourses of intersectionality. *Journal of Literary & Cultural Disability Studies, 4*(2), 127–145.

Ferri, B. (2010). A dialogue we've yet to have: Race and disability studies. In C. Dudley-Marling, & A. Gurn (Eds.) *The Myth of the Normal Curve* (pp. 139–150). New York: Peter Lang.

Fanning, R. M., & Gaba, D. (2007). The role of debriefing in simulation-based learning. *Journal of the Society for Simulation in Healthcare, 2*(2), 115–125.
Ferri, B. A., & Connor, D. J. (2004). Special education and the subverting of Brown. *Journal of Gender, Race & Justice, 8*(1) 57–74.
———. (2005a). Tools of exclusion: Race, disability, and (re)segregated education. *Teachers College Record, 107*(3), 453–474.
———. (2005b). In the shadow of Brown: Special education and overrepresentation of students of color. *Remedial and Special Education, 26*(2), 107–127.
———. (2006). *Reading Resistance: Discourses of Exclusion in Desegregation and Inclusion Debates*. New York: Peter Lang.
Ferri, B. A., Connor, D. J., Solis, S., Valle, J., & Volpitta, D. (2005). Teachers with LD: Ongoing negotiations with discourses of disability. *Journal of Learning Disabilities, 38*(1), 62–78.
Ferri, B., Gallagher, D., & Connor, D. J. (2011). Pluralizing methodologies in the field of LD: From "what works" to what matters. *Learning Disability Quarterly, 34*(3), 222–231.
Ferri, B., Keefe, C., & Gregg, N. (2001). Teachers with learning disabilities: A view from both sides of the desk. *Journal of Learning Disabilities, 34*(1), 22–32.
Ferris, J. (2004). *Hospital Poems*. Charlotte, NC: Main Street Rag Publishers.
Fine, M. (1994). Working the hyphens: Reinventing self and other in qualitative research. In N. K. Denzin, & Y. S, Lincoln (Eds.) *The Handbook of Qualitative Research* (pp. 70–82). Thousand Oaks, CA: Sage.
Fisher v. University of Texas at Austin (2013). 11–345.
Fleischer, D. Z., & Zames, F. (2011). *The Disability Rights Movement: From Charity to Confrontation*. Philadelphia, PA: Temple University Press.
Foote, D. (2008). *Relentless Pursuit: A Year in the Trenches with Teach for America*. New York: Random House.
Forrest, K. A., Judd, K. R., & Davison, J. (2012). Coming to know within "healthy uncertainty": An autoethnographic engagement and transformation in undergraduate education. *Teaching in Higher Education, 17*(6), 710–721.
———. (1972). *The Archaeology of Knowledge and the Discourse on Language*. New York: Pantheon Books.
———. (1977). History of systems of thought. In D. F. Bouchard (Ed.) *Language, Counter-Memory, Practice* (pp. 199–204). Ithaca, NY: Cornell University Press.
———. (1994). *The Birth of the Clinic: An Archaeology of Medical Perception*. New York: Vintage Books.
———. (1995). *Discipline and Punish: The Birth of the Prison*. New York: Vintage Books.
Freire, P. (1970). *Pedagogy of the Oppressed*. New York: Herder & Herder.
Friend, M., & Cook, L. (1996). *The Power of 2: Making a Difference Through Co-Teaching* [Video]. USA: Elephant Rock Productions.
Friend, M., Cook, L., Hurley-Chamberlain, D., & Shamberger, C. (2010). Co-teaching: An illustration of the complexity of collaboration in special education. *Journal of Educational and Psychological Consultation, 20*(1), 9–27.

Friedman, S. A. (2014). *The Education and Deconstruction of Mr. Bloomberg*. New York: Xiblis.

Fries, K. (1997). *Staring Back: The Disability Experience from the Inside Out*. New York: Plume.

Fuchs, D., & Fuchs, L. S. (1994). Inclusive schools movements and the radicalization of special education reform. *Exceptional Children, 60*(4), 294–309.

Gabel, S., & Connor, D. J. (2009). Theorizing disability: Implications and applications for social justice in education. In W. Ayers, T. Quinn, & D. Stovall (Eds.) *Handbook of Social Justice* (pp. 377–399). New York: Lawrence Erlbaum.

———. (2014). *Teaching and Disability*. Mahwah, NJ: Lawrence Erlbaum.

Gabel, S. L., & Danforth, S. (Eds.) (2008). *Disability and the Politics of Education: An International Reader*. New York: Peter Lang.

Gabel, S. L., Reid, D. P., & Pearson, H. (2017). Disability, diversity, and higher education: A critical study of California state university's websites. In E. Kim, & K. Aquino (Eds.) *Disability as Diversity in Higher Education* (pp. 171–184). New York: Routledge.

Gal, E., Schreur, N., & Engel-Yeger, B. (2010). Inclusion and children with disabilities: Teachers' attitudes and requirements for environmental accommodations. *International Journal of Special Education, 25*(2), 89–99.

Gallagher, D. J. (1996). On becoming an interpretist: From knowing as a teacher to knowing as a researcher. In L. Heshusius, & K. Ballard, K. (Eds.) *From Positivism to Interpretivism and Beyond: Tales of Transformation in Educational and Social Research* (pp. 38–42). New York: Teachers College Press.

———. (1998). The scientific knowledge base of special education: Do we know what we think we know? *Exceptional Children, 64*(4), 493–502.

———. (2010). Educational researchers and the makers of normal people. In C. Dudley-Marling, & A. Gurn (Eds.) *The Myth of the Normal Curve* (pp. 25–38). New York: Peter Lang.

Gallagher, D., Connor, D. J., & Ferri, B. A. (2014). Beyond the far too incessant schism: Special education and the social model of disability. *International Journal of Inclusive Education*. http://www.tandfonline.com/loi/tied20

Gallagher, D.J., Heshusius, L., Iano, P., & Skrtic, T. M. (2003). *Challenging Orthodoxy in Special Education*. Denver, CO: Love Publishing.

Garcia, O., & Klein, T. (Eds.) (2016). *Translanguaging with Multilingual Students: Learning from Classroom Moments*. New York: Routledge.

Gardner, H. (1983/2011). *Frames of Mind: The Theory of Multiple Intelligences*. New York: Basic Books Inc.

Garland Thomson, R. (1997). *Extraordinary Bodies: Figuring Physical Disability in American Culture and Literature*. New York: Columbia University Press.

———. (2009). *Staring: How We Look*. New York: Oxford University Press.

Gee, J. P. (1999). *An Introduction to Discourse Analysis: Theory and Method*. New York: Routledge.

Geertz, C. (1988). *Works and Lives: The Anthropologist as Author*. Stanford, CT: Stanford University Press.

Germano, W. (2005). *From Dissertation to Book*. Chicago. IL: Chicago University Press.

Gershon, M. (2015). *How to Use Bloom's Taxonomy in the Classroom: The Complete Guide*. Charleston, SC: Create Space Independent Publishing.

Glossary of Education (2014). http://edglossary.org/

Goffman, E. (1963). *Stigma: Notes on the Management of Spoiled Identity*. New York: Simon & Schuster.

Golfus, B. (Producer and Director) (1995). *When Billy Broke His Head and Other Tales of Wonder* [DVD]. Available from http://www.amazon.com/Billy-Broke-Other-Tales-Wonder/dp/B00HBMPV22

Gould, S. J. (1996). *The Mismeasure of Man*. New York: Norton.

Gregg, N. (2009). *Adolescents and Adults with ADHD: Assessment and Accommodation*. New York: Guilford.

Gunderson, L., & Siegel, L. S. (2001). The evils of the use of IQ tests to define learning disabilities in first and second language learners. *The Reading Teacher, 55*(1), 48–55.

Guskey, T. (2002). Does it make a difference? Evaluating professional development. *Educational Leadership, 59*(6), 45–51.

Harry, B. (2008). *Melanie, Bird with a Broken Wing: A Mother's Story*. New York: Paul H. Brookes.

Harry, B., Allen, N., & McLaughlin, M. (1995). Communication versus compliance: African American parents' involvement in special education. *Exceptional Children, 61*, 364–377.

Hale, C. (2012). *From Exclusivity to Exclusion: The LD Experience of Privileged Parents*. Rotterdam, Netherlands: Sense Publishers.

———. Behind the shortage of special ed. teachers: Long hours, crushing paperwork. *NPREd*. Retrieved from http://www.npr.org/sections/ed/2015/11/09/436588372

Haley, A. (1974). *Roots*. Philadelphia, PA: Da Capo Press.

Haller, B. (2010). *Representing Disability in an Ableist World*. Louisville, KY: Advocado Press.

Haney López, I. (1996). *White by Law: The Legal Construction of Race*. New York: New York University Press.

Hankivsky, O. (2012). Women's health, mens' health, and gender and health: Implications of intersectionality. *Social Science & Medicine, 74*(11), 1712–1720.

Harry, B. (2002). Trends and issues serving culturally diverse families of children with disabilities. *Journal of Special Education, 36*(3), 132–140.

Harry, B., & Klingner, J. (2006). *Why Are So Many Minority Students in Special Education*? New York: Teachers College.

Harvey, R. D., & Oswald, D. L. (2000). Collective guilt and shame as motivation for white support of black programs. *Journal of Applied Social Psychology, 30*(9), 1790–1811.

Hawthorne, N. (1850/2009). *The Scarlet Letter*. Mineola, NY: Dover Publications.

Hehir, T. (2005). *New Directions in Special Education: Eliminating Ableism in Policy and Practice*. Cambridge, MA: Harvard Education Press.

Hehir, T., Figueroa, R., Gamm, S., Katzman, L. I., Gruner, A., Karger, J., & Hernandez, J. (2005). *Comprehension Management Review and Evaluation of Special Education Submitted to the New York City Department of Education.* Cambridge, MA: Harvard School of Education.

Hehir, T., & Katzman, L. I. (2012). *Effective Inclusive Schools: Designing Successful School-Wide Programs.* San Francisco, CA: Jossey Bass.

Heshusius, L. (1989). The Newtonian mechanistic paradigm, special education, and the contours of alternatives: An overview. *Journal of Learning Disabilities, 22*(7) 402–415.

———. (2004). From creative discontent toward epistemological freedom in special education: Reflections on a 25-year journey. In D. Gallagher, L. Heshusius, R. Iano, & T. Skirtic (Eds.) *Challenging Orthodoxy in Special Education* (pp. 169–230). Denver, CO: Love.

Heshusius, L., & Ballard, K. (Eds.) (2004). *From Positivism to Interpretivism and Beyond: Tales of Transformation in Educational and Social Research.* New York: Teachers College Press.

Hidden curriculum (2014, August 26). In S. Abbott (Ed.) *The Glossary of Education Reform.* Retrieved from http://edglossary.org/hidden-curriculum

Holman Jones, S. (2005). Autoethography: Making the personal political. In N. K. Denzin, & Y. S. Lincoln (Eds.) *Handbook of Qualitative Research* (pp. 763–791). Thousand Oaks, CA: Sage.

Hooks, b. (1994). *Teaching to Transgress: Education as the Practice of Freedom.* New York: Routledge.

Hurston, N., & Hughes, L. (1930). *Mule-Bone.* New York: Hard Press.

Idol, L. (2006). Toward inclusion of special education students in general education: A program evaluation of eight schools. *Remedial and Special Education, 27*(2), 77–94.

Individuals with Disabilities Education Act, 20 U.S.C. § 1400 (2004).

Ingersol, R. M., & Smith, T. M. (2003). The wrong solution to the teacher shortage. *Educational Leadership, 60*(8), 30–33.

Jackson, K. C. (2017). *Exploring Perceptions of Mentor Relationships in Doctoral Programs: A Qualitative, Exploratory, Multiple-Case Study.* Virginia Beach, VA: DBC Publishing.

Jacob, B. A. (2001). Getting tough? The impact of high school graduation exams. *Educational Evaluation and Policy Analysis, 23*(2), 99–121.

Jones, K. D. (2012). A critique of the DSM-5 field trials. *Journal of Nervous & Mental Disease, 200*(6), 517–519.

Karagiannis, A. (2000). Soft disability in schools: Assisting or confining at risk children and youth? *Journal of Educational Thought, 34*(2), 113–134.

Katz, M. B., & Rose, M. (Eds.) (2014). *Public Education Under Siege.* Philadelphia, PA: University of Philadelphia Press.

Kauffman, J. M. (1995). Commentary: Today's special education and its messages for tomorrow. *Journal of Special Education, 32*(4), 244–254.

Kauffman, J. M., & Anastasiou, D., & Maag, J. W. (2017). Special education as the crossroad: An identity crisis and the need for scientific reconstruction. *Exceptionality, 25*(2), 139–155.

Kauffman, J. M., & Badar, J. (2017). Extremism and disability chic. *Exceptionality*. http://www.tandfonline.com/doi/full/10.1080/09362835.2017.1283632

Kauffman, J. M., & Hallahan, D. P. (Eds.) (1995). *The Illusion of Full Inclusion*. Austin, TX: ProEd.

Kauffman, J. M, & Sasso, G. M. (2006). Toward ending cultural and cognitive relativism in special education. *Exceptionality, 14*(2), 65–90.

Kavale, K., & Forness, S. R. (2000). History, rhetoric, and reality: Analysis of the inclusion debate. *Remedial and Special Education, 21*(5), 279–296.

Keefe, E. B., Moore, V. M., & Duff, F. R. (2006). *Listening to the Experts: Students with Disabilities Speak Out*. Baltimore: Paul H. Brookes.

Kelly-Jackson, C. (2015). Teaching for social justice and equity: The journey of a teacher educator. *The New Educator, 11*(3), 167–185.

Keyes, M. W., & Owen-Johnson, L. (2003). Developing person-centered IEPs. *Intervention in School and Clinic 38*(3), 145–152.

Kohl, H. (1967/1988). *36 children*. New York: Plume.

Kowarsky, E. (Producer), & Rozen, S. (Director) (1999). *Liebe Perla* [Motion picture]. Israel/Germany: Eden Productions.

Kozol, J. (1991). *Savage Inequalities: Children in America's Schools*. New York: Crown.

———. (1995). *Amazing Grace: The Lives of Children and the Conscience of a Nation*. New York: Harper Perennial.

Kuhl, P. (2002). *The Nazi Connection: Eugenics, American Racism, and German National Socialism*. New York: Oxford University Press.

Laczko-Kerr, I., & Berliner, D. C. (2002). The effectiveness of "Teach for America" and other under-certified teachers on student academic achievement: A case of harmful public policy. *Education Policy Analysis Archives, 10*(37), 1–53.

Ladson-Billings, G., & Tate, W. (1995). Toward a critical race theory of education. *Teachers College Record, 97*(1), 47–68.

Lagares, C., & Connor, D. J. (2009). 20 Ways to help students prepare for high school examinations. *Intervention in School and Clinic, 45*(1), 68–71.

Lamorey, S. (2002). The effects of culture in special education services: Evil eyes, prayer meetings, and IEPs. *Teaching Exceptional Children, 34*(5), 67–71.

Leavy, P. (2015). *Method Meets Art: Arts-Based Research Practice* (2nd edition). New York: Guilford Press.

Lee. H. (1961). *To Kill a Mockingbird*. New York: Harper & Row.

Lehrer, R. (2004). *Circle Stories*. Chicago, IL: Geschiede.

Leonardo, Z. (2013). *Race Frameworks: A Multidimensional Theory of Racism and Education*. New York: Teachers College Press.

Levine, M. (1993). *All Kinds of Minds*. Cambridge, MA: Educators Publishing Service.

———. (2002). *A Mind at a Time*. New York: Simon & Schuster.

Lewis, D. L. (1994). *W. E. B. DuBois, 1868–1919: Biography of a Race*. New York: Henry Holt.

Lincoln, Y. S., & Denzin, N. K. (2000). The seventh movement: Out of the past. In N. K. Denzin, & Y. S. Lincoln (Eds.) *Handbook of Qualitative Research* (pp. 1047–1065).

Linton, S. (1998a). *Claiming Disability*. New York/Thousand Oaks, CA: New York University Press/Sage.

———. (1998b). Disability studies/not disability studies. *Disability & Society, 13*(4), 525–540.

———. (2006). *My Body Politic: A Memoir*. Ann Arbor, MI: University of Michigan Press.

Lipsky, D. K., & Gartner, A. (1997). Historical background of inclusive education. In D. K. Lipsky, & A. Gartner (Eds.) *Inclusion and School Reform: Transforming America's Classrooms* (pp. 73–83). Baltimore, MD: Paul H. Brookes.

Liston, D. P., & Zeichner, K. M. (2013). *Culture and Teaching*. Mahwah, NJ: Lawrence Erlbaum Associates.

Livingston, J. (Producer and Director) (1990). *Paris Is Burning* [Motion picture]. USA: Miramax Films.

Lombardo, P. A. (2010). *Three Generations, No Imbeciles: Eugenics, the Supreme Court, and Buck v. Bell*. Baltimore, MD: John Hopkins University Press.

Lorde, A. (1984). *Sister Outsider*. Freedom, CA: Crossing Press.

———. (1998). Age, race, class, and sex: Women redefining difference. In M. L. Andserson, & P. H. Collins (Eds.) *Race, Class, and Gender: An Anthology* (pp. 187–195). Belmont, CA: Wadsworth.

Losen, D. J., & Orfield, G. (Eds.) (2002). *Racial Inequality in Special Education*. Cambridge, MA: Harvard Education Press.

Luczak, R. (Ed.) (1993). *Eyes of Desire: A Deaf and Gay and Lesbian Reader*. New York: Alyson Books.

Luttrell, W. (2003). *Pregnant Bodies, Fertile Minds: Gender, Race, and the Schooling for Pregnant Teens*. New York: Routledge.

Lutrell, W. (Ed.) (2010). *Qualitative Educational Research: Readings in Reflexive Methodology and Transformative Practice*. New York: Routledge.

Maher, F. A., & Ward, J. V. (2002). *Gender and Education*. Mahwah, NJ: Lawrence Erlbaum Associates.

Manning, L. (2005). *Weights: One Blind Man's Journey* [CD-ROM]. New York: Bridge Multimedia.

Martin, E. W. (1995). Case studies on inclusion: Worst fears realized. *The Journal of Special Education, 29(*2), 192–199.

Martin, J. (2003). *The Education of John Dewey*. New York: Columbia University Press.

McCourt, F. (2006). *Teacher Man: A Memoir*. New York: Simon & Schuster.

McDonald, J. P., Mohr, N., Dichter, A., & McDonald, E. C. (2003). *The Power of Protocols: An Educator's Guide to Better Practice*. New York: Teachers College Press.

MicIntosh, P. (1988). White privilege: Unpacking the invisible backpack. Retrieved from https://www.deanza.edu/faculty/lewisjulie/White%20Priviledge%20Unpacking%20the%20Invisible%20Knapsack.pdf

McLeod, F. (2001). Toward inclusion—our shared responsibility for disaffected pupils. British. *Journal of Special Education, 28*(4), 191–194.

Medina, B. (2011, September 14). Shortage of Ph.D.'s in special education is expected in next 5 years. *The Chronicle of Higher Education*.

Meier, D. (2002). *The Power of Their Ideas: Lessons for America from a Small School in Harlem*. Boston, MA: Beacon Press.

Meyer, A., Gordon, D., & Rose, D. H. (2014). *Universal Design for Learning: Theory into Practice*. Wakefield, MA: CAST.

Miller, J. (1994). *The Passion of Michel Foucault*. New York: Anchor.

Mitchell, D. T., & Snyder, S. L. (Eds.) (2000). *Narrative Prosthesis: Disability and the Dependencies of Discourse*. Ann Arbor, MI: University of Michigan Press.

Monroe, L. (1999). *Nothing's Impossible: Leadership Lessons from Inside and Outside of the Classroom*. New York: Perseus Books.

Mooney, J. (2008). *The Short Bus: A Journey Beyond Normal*. New York: Henry Holt.

Mooney, J., & Cole, D. (2000). *Learning Outside the Lines*. New York: Simon & Schuster.

Morgan, P. L., Farkas, G., Hillemeier, M. M., & Maczuga, S. (2017). Replicated evidence of racial and ethnic disparities in disability identification in U.S. schools. *Educational Researcher* [online]. https://doi.org/10.3102/0013189X17726282

Morgan, P. L., Farkas, G., Hillemeier, M. M., & Maczuga, S., Li, H., & Cook, M. (2015). Are minority children disproportionately represented in early intervention and early childhood special education? *Educational Researcher, 41*, 339–351.

Morrison, T. (1982). *Sula*. New York: Plume.

National Center for Education Statistics (2016). *Reading assessment*. Retrieved from https://nces.ed.gov/nationsreportcard/reading/

National Institute for Literacy (2001). *Put Reading First: The Research Building Blocks for Teaching Children to Read, Kindergarten Through Grade 3*. Jessup, MD: ED Publishers. Download document at http://www.nifl.gov/nifl/publications.html

Nieto, S. (2015). *Brooklyn Dreams: My Life in Public Education*. Cambridge, MA: Harvard Education Press.

No Child Left Behind Act of 2001, P.L. 107-110, 20 U.S.C. § 6319 (2002).

Oberti V. Board of Education of the Borough of Clementon School District (1992). Civ A. No. 91-2818.

O'Connor, G. (2001). Bad. In P. Rodis, S. Garrod, & M. L. Boscardin (Eds.) *Learning Disabilities and Life Stories* (pp. 62–72). Needham Heights, MA: Allyn & Bacon.

O'Day, J., Bitter, C. S., & Gomez, L. (Eds.) (2011). *Education Reform in New York City: Ambitious Change in the Nation's Most Complex School System*. Cambridge, MA: Harvard Educational Press.

O'Neil Green, D., Willis, H., Green, M. D., & Beckman, S. (2017). Access Ryerson: Promoting disability as diversity. In E. Kim, & K. Aquino (Eds.) *Disability as Diversity in Higher Education* (pp. 200–215). New York: Routledge.

Offit, P. A. (2017). *Pandora's Lab: Seven Stories of Science Gone Wrong*. Washington, DC: National Geographic Partners, LLC.

Oliver, M. (1996). *Understanding Disability: From Theory to Practice*. London: Macmillan.

Olkin, R., & Pledger, C. (2003). Can disability studies and psychology join hands? *American Psychologist, 58*(4), 296–304.

Ong-Dean, C. (2009). *Distinguishing Disability: Parents, Privilege, and Special Education.* Chicago and London: The University of Chicago Press.

Paley, V. G. (1993). *You Can't Say You Can't Play*. Cambridge, MA: Harvard University Press.

Parents Involved in Community Schools V. Seattle School District (2007). 551 U.S. 701 (2007).

Pavri, S., & Luftig, R. (2010). The social face of inclusive education: Are students with learning disabilities really included in the classroom? *Preventing School Failure, 45*(1), 8–14.

Pelkey, L. (2001). In the LD bubble. In P. Rodis, S. Garrod, & M. L. Boscardin (Eds.) *Learning Disabilities and Life Stories* (pp. 17–28). Needham Heights: Allyn & Bacon.

Pierce, H. (2017, June 24). Teacher shortage leaves special education classrooms with inexperienced, first-time educators. *Bakersfield Californian.* www.bakersfield.com

Piziali, A. (2001). Revolution. In P. Rodis, S. Garrod, & M. L. Boscardin (Eds.) *Learning Disabilities and Life Stories* (pp. 29–38). Needham Heights, MA: Allyn & Bacon.

Pope, C. A., Bowman, C. A., & Barr, K. (2001). Conversations form the commissions: Negotiating the tensions in the preparation of teachers with disabilities. *English Education, 33*(3), 252–256.

Price, M. (2001). *Mad at School: Rhetorics of Mental Disability and Academic Life.* Ann Arbor, MI: University of Michigan Press.

Rhodes, W. (1995). Liberatory pedagogy and special education. *Journal of Learning Disabilities, 28*(8), 458–467.

Rice, N. (2006). "Reining in" special education: Constructions of "special education" in New York Times Editorials, 1975–2004. *Disability Studies Quarterly, 26*(2). http://dsq-sds.org/article/view/679

Richardson, C. (2001, July 16). Help from role model is academic: A pal to disabled students. *New York Daily News.* http://www.nydailynews.com/archives/boroughs/role-model-academic-pal-disabled-students-article-1.930184

Richardson, L. (2000). Writing: A method of inquiry. In N. K. Denzin, & Y. V. Lincoln (Eds.) *Handbook for Qualitative Research* (pp. 923–948). Thousand Oaks, CA: Sage.

———. (2001). Getting personal: Writing stories. *Qualitative Studies in Education, 14*(1), 33–38.

Rodis, P., Garrod, A., & Boscardin, M. L. (Eds.) (2001). *Learning Disabilities & Life Stories.* Needham Heights, MA: Allyn & Bacon.

Rosen, R. (2006). An unintended consequence of IDEA: American sign language, the Deaf community, and Deaf culture into mainstream education. *Disability Studies Quarterly, 26*(2). http://dsq-sds.org/article/view/685

Rosenber, R. S. (2013, April 12). Abnormal is the new normal: Why will half of the U.S. population have a diagnosable metal disorder? *Slate Magazine* [Medical Examiner]. www.slate.com

Raymond, A., & Raymond, S. (Producer and Director) (1971–1973). *An American Family* [Television series]. New York: PBS.

———. (Producer and Director) (1977). *The Police Tapes* [Television documentary series]. New York: PBS.

———. (Producer and Director) (1994). *I Am a Promise: The Children of Stanton Elementary School* [Television documentary]. New York: PBS.

———. (Producer and Director) (2008). *Hard Times at Douglas High* [Television documentary]. New York: PBS.

———. (Producer and Director) (2011). *Journey into Dyslexia* [Motion picture]. USA: HBO.

Reid, D. K., & Button, L. J. (1995). Anna's story: Narratives about personal experience about being labeled learning disabled. *Journal of Learning Disabilities, 28*(10), 602–614.

Reid, D. K., & Knight, M. G. (2006). Disability justifies exclusion of minority students: A critical history grounded in disability studies. *Educational Researcher, 35*(6), 18–23.

Reid, D. K., & Valle, J. W. (2004). The discursive practice of learning disability: Implications for instruction and parent–school relations. *Journal of Learning Disabilities, 37*(6), 466–481.

Reitman, I. (Producer and Director). *Kindergarten Cop* [Motion picture]. USA: Universal Studios.

Richards , J., & Renanya, W. A. (Eds.) (2002). *Methodology in Language Teaching: An Anthology of Current Practice.* New York: Cambridge University Press.

Robb, L. (2003). *Teaching Reading in Social Studies, Science, and Math: Practical Ways to Weave Comprehension Strategies into Your Content Area Teaching.* New York: Scholastic.

———. (2004). *Non-Fiction Writing from the Inside Out: Writing Lessons Inspired by Conversations with Leading Authors.* New York: Scholastic.

———. (2008). *Differentiating Reading Instruction: How to Teach Reading to Meet the Needs of Each Student.* New York: Scholastic.

Rodis, P., Garrod, A., & Boscardin, M. L. (Eds.) (2001). *Learning Disabilities & Life Stories.* Needham Heights, MA: Allyn & Bacon.

Rolling, J. H. (2013). *Arts Based Research: A Primer.* New York: Peter Lang.

Ruijs, N. M., & Peetsma, T. D. (2009). Effects of inclusion on students with and without special educational needs. *Educational Research Review, 4*(2), 67–79.

Sailor, W. (1991). Special education in the restructured school. *Remedial and Special Education, 12*(6), 8–22.

Sapon-Shevin, M. (1996). Full inclusion as a disclosing tablet: Revealing the flaws of our present system. *Theory Into Practice, 35*(1), 35–41.

———. (2007a). *Widening the Circle: The Power of Inclusive Classrooms.* Boston: Beacon Press.

———. (2007b, May). All for one: Ten lessons from inclusive classrooms. *Scholastic Administrator,* 50–57.

———. (2010). *Because We Can Change the World: A Practical Guide to Building Cooperative Inclusive Classroom Communities.* Thousand Oaks, CA: Corwin Press.

Sellers, A., Winitsky, A. (Producers), & Ritt, M. (Director). *Stanley & Iris* [Motion picture]. USA: MGM Pictures.

Shange, N. (1975). *For Colored Girls Who Have Considered Suicide/When the Rainbow Is Enuf.* New York: Scribner.

Shanker, A. (1994, January 14). *Where We Stand on the Rush to Inclusion.* American Federation of Teachers National Convention. Washington, DC.

Shakespeare, T., & Watson, N. (2001). The social model of disability: An outdated ideology? *Research in Social Science and Disability*, 2, 9–28.

Shakespeare, W. (1992). *Macbeth.* New York: Simon & Schuster.

Shapiro, J. P. (1993). *No Pity: People with Disabilities Forging a New Civil Rights Movement.* New York: Times Books.

Shapiro, A. (1999). *Everybody Belongs: Changing Negative Attitudes Toward Classmates with Disabilities.* New York: Routledge.

Sellers, A., Winitsky, A. (Producers), & Ritt, M. (Director) (1990). *Stanley and Iris* [Motion picture]. USA: Metro-Goldwyn-Mayer.

Silver, L. B. (1981). The relationship between learning disabilities, hyperactivity, distractibility, and behavior problems: A clinical analysis. *Journal of the American Academy of Child Psychiatry, 20*(2), 385–397.

Skrtic, T. M. (1991). *Behind Special Education: A Critical Analysis of Professional Culture and School Organization.* Denver, CO: Love.

———. (1995). Theory/ practice and objectivism: The modern view of the professions. In T. M. Skrtic (Ed.) *Disability and Democracy.* New York: Teachers College Press.

Skrtic, T., & McCall, Z. (2010). Ideology, institutions, and equity: Comments on Christine Sleeter's "Why is there learning disabilities?" *Disability Studies Quarterly, 30*(2). http://dsq-sds.org/article/view/1230

Skrtic, T., Sailor, W., & Gee, K. (1996). Voice, collaboration, and inclusion: Democratic themes in educational and social reform initiatives. *Remedial and Special Education, 17*(3), 142–157.

Skaalvik, E. M., & Skaalvik, S. (2007). Dimensions of teacher self-efficacy and relations with strain factors, perceived collective teacher efficacy, and teacher burnout. *Journal of Educational Psychology, 99*(3), 611–625.

Sleeter, C. E. (1987). Why is there learning disabilities? A critical analysis of the birth of the field in its social context. In T. S. Popkewitz (Ed.) *The Formation of the School Subjects: The Struggle for Creating an American Institution* (pp. 210–237). Philadelphia, PA: Falmer Press.

———. (2010). Building counter theory about disability. *Disability Studies Quarterly.* http://dsq-sds.org/article/view/1244/1288

Smaller, H. (2005). Teacher informal learning and teacher knowledge: Theory, practice and policy. In N. Basica, A. Cumming, A. Datnow, K. Leithwood, & D. Livingstone (Eds.) *International Handbook of Educational Policy.* London: Springer.

Smith, P. (Ed.) (2013). *Both Sides of the Table: Autoethnographies of Educators Learning and Teaching with/in (Dis)ability.* New York: Peter Lang.

Smith, R. W. (1986). Labeling theory as applied to learning disabilities: Survey findings and policy suggestion. *Journal of Learning Disabilities, 19*(4), 195–202.

———. (2006). Reframing special education: Reclaiming effective education. *Disability Studies in Education, 26*(2). http://dsq-sds.org/article/view/680

Spark, M. (1961). *The Prime of Miss Jean Brodie*. New York: Harper Collins.

Starger, M. (Producer), & Bogdanovich, P. (Director) (1985). *Mask* [Motion picture]. USA: Universal Studios.

Steinbeck, J. (1937). *Of Mice and Men*. New York: Penguin.

Steiner, D. M., & Rozen, S. D. (2004). Preparing tomorrow's teachers: An analysis of syllabi from a sample of America's schools of education. In F. M. Hess, A. J. Rotherham, & K. Walsh (Eds.) *A Qualified Teacher in Every Classroom* (pp. 119–148). Cambridge, MA: Harvard Education Press.

Stern, M. (1988). *Experimenting with Numbers: A Guide for Preschool, Kindergarten, and First Grade Teachers*. Cambridge, MA: Educators Publishing Service.

Stetsenko, A. (2002). Knowledge as activity. In D. Robbins, & A. Stetsenko (Eds.) *Voices Within Vygotsky's Non-Classical Psychology: Past, Present, Future* (pp. 174–179). Huappauge, NY: Nova.

Stiker, H. J. (1999). *A History of Disability*. Ann Arbor, MI: Love.

Sting (2014). *The Last Ship*. Musical.

Stodden, R. A., Conway, M. A., & Chang, K. B. T. (2003). Findings form the study of transition, technology and post-secondary supports for youth with disabilities: Implications for secondary school educators. *Journal of Special Education and Technology, 18*(4), 29–43.

Study made of child behavior in St. Louis mixed classes. (1956, March). *Southern School News*, 12.

Sweet, K. (2006, October). *Small Schools, Few Choices: How NYC's High School Reform Effort Left SWD Behind*. New York: Parents for Inclusive Education.

Tatum, B. (1993). *Why Are All the Black Kids Sitting Together in the Cafeteria?* (Revised edition). New York: Basic Books.

Taylor, E., Gillborn, D., & Ladson-Billings, G. (Eds.) (2015). *Foundations of Critical Race Theory in Education* (2nd edition). New York: Taylor & Francis.

Taylor, S. (2006). Before it had a name: Exploring the historical roots of disability studies in education. In S. Danforth, & S. Gabel (Eds.) *Vital Questions Facing Disability Studies in Education* (pp. xiii–xxiii). New York: Peter Lang.

Taylor, Y., Hines, S., & Casey, M. E. (Eds.) (2010). *Theorizing Intersectionality and Sexuality*. New York: Palgrave Macmillan.

Thomas, P. (1967). *Down These Mean Streets*. New York: Vintage.

Thomas, G., & Loxley, A. (2007). *Deconstructing Special Education and Constructing Inclusion*. New York: McGraw-Hill.

Thousand, J. S., Villa, R. A., & Nevin, A. I. (2006). The many faces of collaborative planning an teaching. *Theory Into Practice, 45*(3), 239–248.

Titchkosky, T. (2011). *The Question of Access: Disability, Space, Meaning*. Toronto, Canada: University of Toronto Press.

Traub, N. (1977/2000). *Recipe for Reading*. Cambridge, MA: Educators Publishing Service.

Tomlinson, C. A. (1999). *The Differentiated Classroom: Responding to the Needs of All Learners*. Alexandria, VA: ASCD.

Tomlinson, C. A., & McTighe, J. (2006). *Integrating Differentiated Instruction and Understanding by Design*. Alexandria, VA: ASCD.

Tomlinson, S. (1982). *A Sociology of Special Education.* Boston, MA: Routledge & Kegan Paul.

———. (2017). *A Sociology of Special and Inclusive Education: Exploring the Manufacture of Inability.* New York: Routledge.

Towne, L., & Shavelson, R. J. (2002). *Scientific Research in Education.* Washington, DC: National Academies Press.

Trainor, A., & Bal, A. (2014). Development and preliminary analysis of a rubric for culturally responsive research. *Journal of Special Education, 47*(4), 203–216.

Udvari-Solner, A., & Kluth, P. (2008). *Joyful Learning: Active and Collaborative Learning in Inclusive Classrooms.* Thousand Oaks, CA: Corwin Press.

Valente, J. M. (2011). *D/deaf and D/dumb: A Portrait of a Deaf Kid as a Young Superhero*. New York: Peter Lang.

Valle, J. (2009). *What Mothers Say about Special Education: From 1960s to the Present*. New York: Palgrave Macmillan.

Valle, J. W. (2016). Learning from and collaborating with families: The case for DSE in teacher education. In M. Cosier, & C. Ashby (Eds.) *Enacting Change from Within: Disability Studies Meets Teaching and Teacher Education* (pp. 243–264). New York: Peter Lang.

Valle, J., & Aponte, E. (2002). IDEA and collaboration: A Bakhtinian perspective on parent and professional discourse, *Journal of Learning Disabilities, 35*(5), 471–481.

Valle, J., & Connor, D. J. (2010). *Rethinking Disability: A Disability Studies Guide to Inclusive Practices.* New York: McGraw-Hill.

Valle, J. W., Connor, D. J., & Reid, D. K. (2006). 30th Anniversary of I.D.E.A.: The Impact on American Education and Society. *Disability Studies Quarterly, 26*(2).

Valle, J. W., Solis, S., Volpitta, D., & Connor, D. J. (2004). The disability closet: Teachers with LD evaluate the risks and benefits of "coming out." *Equity & Excellence in Education, 37*(1), 4–17.

Vaughn, S., & Klingner, J. K. (1998). Students' perceptions of inclusion and resource room settings. *The Journal of Special Education, 32*(2), 79–88.

Vaughn, S., & Schumm, J. S. (1996). Responsible inclusion for students with learning disabilities. *Journal of Learning Disabilities, 28*(5), 264–270.

Villa, R., Thousand, J., & Chappie, J. W. (1996). Preparing teachers to support inclusion: Preservice and inservice programs. *Theory into Practice, 35*(1), 42–50.

Vygotsky, L. S. (1987). *The Collected Works of L.S. Vygotsky: Problems of General Psychology*. New York: Plenum Press.

Walford, G. (2009). For ethnography. *Ethnography and Education, 4*(3), 271–282.

Walker, A. (1982). *You Can't Keep a Good Woman Down.* Orlando, FL: Harcourt Books.

Wappet, M., & Arndt, K. (2013). *Foundations of Disability Studies.* New York: Palgrave MacMillan.

Ware, L. (2001). Writing, identity, and the other: Dare we do disability studies? *Journal of Teacher Education, 52*(2), 107–123.

Waters, J. (Producer and Director) (1974). *Female Trouble* [Motion picture]. USA: Dreamland/Saliva Films.

Weathersbee (2015, December 18) Double standard with police shootings. *Florida Times-Union* (Jacksonville), A-9.

Wehmeyer, M. L. (2010). Universal design for learning, access to the general education curriculum and students with mild mental retardation. *Exceptionality, 14*(4), 225–235.

Wertsch, J. (1988). *Vygotsky and the Social Formation of Mind*. Boston, MA: Harvard University Press.

West, P. R. (2002). 21st century professional development: The job-embedded, continual learning model. *American Secondary Education, 30*(2), 72–81.

Wilder, T. (1938). *Our Town*. New York: Harper Collins.

Will, M. C. (1986). Educating children with learning problems: A shared responsibility. *Exceptional Children, 52*, 411–415.

Williams, J. (1987). *Eyes on the Prize: America's Civil Rights Years, 1954–1965*. New York: Viking Penguin.

Williams, T. (1947). *A Streetcar Named Desire*. New York: New Directions.

Wilson. A. (1986). *Fences*. New York: Penguin.

Wilson, B. (1996). *Instructor Manual: Wilson Reading System*. Oxford, MA: Wilson Language Training Corporation.

Winn, M. T., & Behizadeh, N. (2011). The right to be literate: Literacy, education, and the school-to-prison pipeline. *Review of Research in Education, 35*(1), 147–173.

X, Malcolm (1964, June). Speech at founding rally of the organization of Afro-American unity. Retrieved from http://www.panafricanperspective.com/mxoaau-founding.html

Youdin, W. (2018, February 27). DeVos wants to roll back protections for students of color in special education. *Talk Poverty*. https://talkpoverty.org/2018/02/27

Zeichner, K. M. (2013). *Reflective Teaching: An Introduction*. Mahwah, NJ: Lawrence Erlbaum Associates.

Zhang, D., Hsu, H. Y., Kowk, O., Benz, M., & Bowman-Perrott, L. (2011). The impact of basic-level parent engagements of student achievement: Patterns associated with race/ethnicity and socioeconomic status. *Journal of Disability Policy Studies, 22*(1), 28–39.

Index

About the Author

David J. Connor is professor and former chairperson of the Department of Special Education at Hunter College. He is a faculty member at large of the Graduate Center's Urban Education PhD program, and teaches in Hunter's EdD program in instructional leadership. Dr. Connor has worked in the field of education for thirty years as a classroom teacher, tutor, teacher coach, regional professional development specialist, adjunct instructor, and full-time professor. His research interests include social, cultural, and historical understandings of disability; learning disabilities; inclusive education; and kindergarten-through college classroom pedagogy. Dr. Connor self-defines as a critical special educator and much of his work is informed by disability studies in education. He has authored or coauthored over ninety publications in the form of peer-reviewed journals and book chapters, in addition to seven books. Dr. Connor's most recent books are *DisCrit: Critical Conversations Across Race, Class, & Dis/ability* (2016), coedited with Beth Ferri and Subini Annamma, and *A Child, a Family, a School, a Community: A Tale of Inclusive Education* (2017), coauthored with Diane Berman. For more information about publications, see: http://hunter-cuny.academia.edu/DavidJConnor.

CPSIA information can be obtained
at www.ICGtesting.com
Printed in the USA
BVHW03*0000190618
519201BV00001B/1/P